JEAN-JACQUES ROUSSEAU

Modern Critical Views

Continued at back of book

Modern Critical Views

JEAN-JACQUES ROUSSEAU

Edited and with an introduction by

Harold Bloom
Sterling Professor of the Humanities
Yale University

CHELSEA HOUSE PUBLISHERS ◊ 1988
New York ◊ New Haven ◊ Philadelphia

© 1988 by Chelsea House Publishers, a division
of Chelsea House Educational Communications, Inc.,
  95 Madison Avenue, New York, NY 10016
  345 Whitney Avenue, New Haven, CT 06511
  5068B West Chester Pike, Edgemont, PA 19028

Introduction © 1988 by Harold Bloom

Printed and bound in the United States of America

10 9 8 7 6 5 4 3 2 1

∞ The paper used in this publication meets the minimum
requirements of the American National Standard for
Permanence of Paper for Printed Library Materials,
Z39.48-1984.

Library of Congress Cataloging-in-Publication Data
Jean-Jacques Rousseau.
      (Modern critical views)
      Bibliography: p.
      Includes index.
      Summary: A selection of critical essays, arranged in
chronological order of publication, devoted to the works of the
eighteenth-century French author and philosopher.
      1. Rousseau, Jean-Jacques, 1712–1778—Criticism and
interpretation. [1. Rousseau, Jean-Jacques, 1712–1778—
Criticism and interpretation. 2. French literature—History and
criticism] I. Bloom, Harold. II. Series.
PQ2053.J38 1988   848'.509   87-11796
ISBN 1-55546-296-0

Contents

Editor's Note

This book brings together a representative selection of the best modern criticism available in English of the writings of Jean-Jacques Rousseau. The critical essays are reprinted here in the chronological order of their original publication. I am grateful to Jim Swenson for his assistance in editing this volume.

My introduction centers upon the *Confessions* and follows William Hazlitt in his estimate as to the originality and historical importance of Rousseau's sensibility. Ernst Cassirer, authority upon the philosophy of the Enlightenment, begins the chronological sequence with an overview of the "question of Rousseau," in which Rousseau is judged to be the true precursor of Kant and thus a supreme philosophic example of rational insight.

Jacques Derrida, philosopher of deconstruction, follows with his famous account of the concept of the supplement, "a sort of blind spot in Rousseau's text, the not-seen that opens and limits visibility." The lyric drama in one scene, *Pygmalion*, is analyzed by Shierry M. Weber as a critical aesthetics, linking Rousseau to German Romanticism.

A Marxist reading of *The Social Contract* by Louis Althusser examines the contradictions in the "admirable 'failure' of an unprecedented theory." *La Nouvelle Héloïse* is seen by Tony Tanner as an incestuous romance, with an "unspeakable solitude at the heart of all relationships." *Emile*, Rousseau's other major novel, is judged by Allan Bloom to be a true rival to Plato's *Republic*, "which it is meant to supersede."

Jean Starobinski, in a total vision of Rousseau, presents him as the prophetic accuser of his civilization, the intimate adversary of its inadequate arts and sciences. A very different vision of reading informs Paul de Man's superb deconstruction of metaphor in the *Second Discourse*, where conceptual language is expressed as the necessary interplay of figurative and referential modes.

The *Rêveries* are studied by Eric Gans as a system in which the self as

subject is seen as the consumer victimized by the society organized supposedly to maintain him. In the critical mode of Paul de Man, E. S. Burt
contrasts the processes of reading and interpretation in regard to the *Confessions*'s account of the origins of Rousseau's masochism. In this book's final
essay, David Marshall relates Rousseau's *Letter to M. d'Alembert on the Theatre*
to the theatrical element in all of his work, which balances spectacle and
sympathy so as to achieve a new kind of autobiography.

Introduction

William Hazlitt, in my judgment still Rousseau's best critic, insisted that the Genevan moralist's sensibility was far more vital than either his Enlightened reason or his Romantic imagination. Finding less Negative Capability in Rousseau than in any comparable figure, Hazlitt cheerfully praised him for the gusts of his Egotistical Sublime. Rousseau's intense passion for himself was seen by Hazlitt as the necessary prelude to the French Revolution, carried out by men and women who had learned from Rousseau to give their self-love primacy over the claims of society, history, and tradition. In Hazlitt's shrewd insight, the Jacobin sensibility, which transformed societal tyranny into personal insult, owed everything to the tormented sensibility of that unique individual, Rousseau.

Praising the *Confessions* as a veritable Bible of revolution, Hazlitt saw in Rousseau the Romantic Prometheus, kindler of revolt against the sky-gods of Europe. With an English Dissenter's irony, Hazlitt wrote in praise of Rousseau, yet with distaste for a temperament both heroic and "morbid." Hazlitt's ambivalence towards Rousseau is roughly akin to his attitude towards Wordsworth. Each seemed to Hazlitt a true Original and so a prophet of literary rebellion, but both were judged to be egomaniacs, though only Wordsworth had betrayed the Revolution.

Rousseau to this day reads very differently to Anglo-American critics than he does to Continental exegetes. Except for the *Confessions*, he is read neither widely nor deeply in the contemporary English-speaking world. Allan Bloom, attempting to revive *Emile*, compares it to Plato's *Republic* as a survey of the entire human condition. These, he says, are "books for philosophers," but since we live now in a literary culture, not a philosophic one, I surmise that *Emile* is not likely to be revived. The *Nouvelle Héloïse* is more available to our sensibility and I am surprised it receives so little attention these days. The *Confessions*, though, are a crucial element in our literary culture, and have established the mode for modern autobiography.

1

Rousseau's *Confessions* indeed seem to me the inevitable link between Montaigne and our Montaigne, Freud, who has systemized self-reflection for us.

J. H. Van den Berg, in his *The Changing Nature of Man*, says of Rousseau that "he was the first to view the child as a child, and to stop treating the child as an adult," but remarks of him also that he was culpable for "pushing the child away." Van den Berg locates in *Emile* the invention of the trope of psychic "maturation," and so ascribes to Rousseau the authorship of adolescence as such. That may be partly an ironic tribute on Van den Berg's part, yet to me it seems accurate. Before Rousseau, where are we to find representations of adolescence? If we combine Hazlitt and Van den Berg on Rousseau, then there is a close relation between the new sensibility of a rebellious self-love, and the new crossing or transition of adolescence, and it seems plausible that one consciousness should have invented both. Psychosexually, the Rousseau of the *Confessions* never does make it out of adolescence, while the universalizing of his Egotistical Sublime is necessarily at the center of his autobiography.

"Such were the errors and faults of my youth. I have related the story of them with a fidelity that brings pleasure to my heart." That beginning of the final paragraph of *The First Part* of the *Confessions* is not exactly Rousseau at his worst but it does indicate his splendidly outrageous tendency to forgive himself everything, once he has confessed his guilt. John Calvin's reaction to his fellow Genevan's Romanticized sense of election would have been strenuous, and I delight to imagine Calvin and Rousseau confronting one another at the tomb of Farinata in Dante's *Inferno*, where the earlier heretic stands upright and proud, "as if of Hell he had a great disdain." But not even Farinata or Calvin is as massively self-assured as Rousseau. Here is a grandly outrageous moment from Book Twelve of the *Confessions:*

> I must leave nothing unsaid. I have never concealed my poor Mamma's vices or my own, and I must show no greater favour to Thérèse. However warm a pleasure I take in honouring a person who is dear to me, I still do not wish to disguise her faults, if an involuntary change in the heart's affection is truly a fault. For a long while I had observed a cooling off on her part. I was aware that she no longer felt for me as she had done in our good days; and I was the more conscious of the fact because I was as fond of her as ever. I was once more in the predicament which I had found so uncomfortable with Mamma; and in Thérèse's case it was no less uncomfortable. Let us not look for supernatural perfection; the case would be the same with any woman upon

earth. The attitude I had taken with regard to my children, logical though it had seemed to me, had not always left me easy in my mind. While thinking out my *Treatise upon Education*, I felt that I had neglected some duties from which nothing could excuse me. So strong did my remorse finally grow that it almost drew from me a public confession of my fault at the beginning of *Emile*. The allusion, indeed, is so clear that after such a passage it is surprising that anyone had the courage to reproach me. My situation was, however, at that time still the same, or even worse, because of the animosity of my enemies, who wanted nothing better than to catch me at fault. I was afraid that I might repeat the offence and, not wishing to run the risk, preferred to condemn myself to abstinence rather than expose Thérèse to the risk of finding herself in the same condition once more. I had noticed besides that intercourse with women sensibly aggravated my complaint. The compensatory vice, of which I have never been able entirely to cure myself, seemed to me less deleterious. For this dual reason, therefore, I had formed resolutions which I had sometimes only imperfectly kept, but in which I had been persisting with more success during the last three or four years. It was from the beginning of that time that I had noticed a cooling in Thérèse. She persisted in her attachment to me, but it was out of duty, not out of love. This naturally diminished the pleasure in our relations, and I imagined that, relying as she could on my continuing to look after her, she might perhaps have preferred to stay in Paris rather than wander about the world with me. However she had shown such grief at our separation, had extracted such emphatic promises from me that we should come together again, and had expressed her desire so strongly since my departure both to the Prince de Conti and M. de Luxembourg, and far from daring to speak to her of separation I scarcely had the courage to think of it myself; and once my heart had told me how impossible it would be to do without her my only thought was to call her back at the earliest possible moment. I wrote to her to start, and she came. It was scarcely two months since I had left her, but this was our first separation for many years. We had felt it most cruelly, both of us. How violent was our first embrace! Oh, how sweet are the tears of joy and affection, and how my heart feasts on them! Why have I been permitted to shed them so seldom?

I hardly know which to prefer, Rousseau's "Let us not look for super-natural perfection," in regard to poor Thérèse, of whom he was "as fond . . . as ever," or his surprise "that anyone had the courage to reproach" him for abandoning his own children, once he had almost confessed his "fault." How intensely his heart feasted upon "the tears of joy and affection" we need not doubt. The great Rousseau was certainly no hypocrite; he was merely a sacred monster, peculiarly pernicious for his women. For literary power in self-representation, for originality in sensibility, for strength of influence upon what came after—for all of these, the *Confessions* are beyond comparison with any possible rival in eighteenth-century literature, whatever any of us may choose to think of Rousseau as an individual.

Shelley, who revered Rousseau above any other writer between Milton and Wordsworth, nevertheless rendered a Dantesque judgment upon the author of the *Confessions* in his great death-poem, "The Triumph of Life." Rousseau appears with the grand disdain for Hell of Farinata, but also with a pride wholly his own, the pride of a sensibility that knew itself to be absolutely original and inevitably epochal:

> Before thy memory
> I feared, loved, hated, suffered, did, & died,
> And if the spark with which Heaven lit my spirit
> Earth had with purer nutriment supplied
>
> Corruption would not now thus much inherit
> Of what was once Rousseau—nor this disguise
> Stained that within which still disdains to wear it.—
> If I have been extinguished, yet there rise
> A thousand beacons from the spark I bore.—

ERNST CASSIRER

The Question of Jean-Jacques Rousseau

I shall speak of the question of Jean-Jacques Rousseau. Yet the very formulation of this topic implies a certain assumption—the assumption that Rousseau's personality and world of ideas have not been reduced to a mere historical fact that leaves us no further task but to comprehend it and describe it in its simple actuality. Even today, we do not think of Rousseau's doctrine as of an established body of single propositions that can be easily recorded and fitted into histories of philosophy by means of textual reproduction and review. True, that is how innumerable monographs have described it; but compared with Rousseau's own work all these accounts seem peculiarly cold and lifeless.

Anyone who penetrates deeply into this work and who reconstructs from it a view of Rousseau the man, the thinker, the artist, will feel immediately how little the abstract scheme of thought that is customarily given out as "Rousseau's teaching" is capable of grasping the inner abundance that is revealed to us. What is disclosed to us here is not fixed and definite doctrine. It is, rather, a movement of thought that ever renews itself, a movement of such strength and passion that it seems hardly possible in its presence to take refuge in the quiet of "objective" historical contemplation. Again and again it forces itself upon us; again and again it carries us away with it. The incomparable power which Rousseau the thinker and writer exercised over his time was ultimately founded in the fact that in a century that had raised the cultivation of form to unprecedented heights, bringing it to perfection

From *The Question of Jean-Jacques Rousseau*, translated and edited by Peter Gay. © 1954 by Yale University Press.

and organic completion, he brought once more to the fore the inherent uncertainty of the very concept of form. In its literature as well as in its philosophy and science, the eighteenth century had come to rest in a fixed and definite world of forms. The reality of things was rooted in this world; their worth was determined and guaranteed by it. The century rejoiced in the unmistakable precision of things, in their clear and sharp outlines and firm boundaries, and it viewed the faculty of drawing such precise boundaries as the highest subjective strength of man and at the same time as the basic power of reason.

Rousseau was the first thinker who not only questioned this certainty but who shook its very foundations. He repudiated and destroyed the molds in which ethics and politics, religion as well as literature and philosophy were cast—at the risk of letting the world sink back once more into its primordial shapelessness, into the state of "nature," and thus of abandoning it, as it were, to chaos. But in the midst of this chaos which he himself had conjured up, his peculiar creative power was tested and proved. For now there commenced a movement animated by new impulses and determined by new forces. The aims of this movement remained, at first, in the dark; they could not be characterized in abstract isolation or anticipated as settled and given points of destination. When Rousseau attempted such anticipations he never got beyond vague and frequently contradictory formulations. What was settled for him, what he grasped at with the fullest strength of thought and feeling, was not the goal toward which he was steering but the impulse which he was following. And he dared to surrender to this impulse: he opposed the essentially static mode of thought of the century with his own completely personal dynamics of thought, feeling, and passion. His dynamics still holds us enthralled today. Even for us, Rousseau's doctrine is not the object of mere academic curiosity nor of purely philological or historical examination. As soon as we cease to be content with examining its results and, instead, concern ourselves with its fundamental assumptions, his doctrine appears rather as a thoroughly contemporary and living means of approaching problems. The questions which Rousseau put to his century have by no means become antiquated; they have not been simply "disposed of"— even for us. Their *formulation* may frequently be significant and comprehensible only in a historical sense: their *content* has lost nothing of its immediacy.

That this should be so is in a large measure the result of the ambiguous portrait that purely historical inquiry has painted. After the most thorough research into biographical detail, after the countless investigations into the historical background and sources of Rousseau's doctrine, after the penetrating analysis of his writings that has extended to every detail, we should expect that clarity would have been achieved at least in regard to the basic characteristics of his nature or that a consensus would prevail concerning the basic intention of his work. But even a glance at the Rousseau literature disappoints this expectation. Particularly in recent years this colossal literature has been increased by several important and voluminous works. But if we look at these works—if we compare, for example (to mention only the most important names), the most recent account of Rousseau in Albert Schinz's book, *La Pensée de Jean-Jacques Rousseau* (Paris, 1929), with the accounts by Hubert and Masson—the sharpest conflict in interpretation becomes obvious at once. This conflict is not confined to details and nonessentials; it concerns, rather, the fundamental conception of Rousseau's nature and outlook. At times, Rousseau is portrayed as the true pioneer of modern individualism, a man who championed the unfettered liberty of feeling and the "right of the heart" and who conceived of this right so loosely that he completely abandoned every ethical obligation, every objective precept of duty. Karl Rosenkranz, for example, holds that Rousseau's morality "is the morality of the natural man who has not raised himself to the objective truth of self-determination through obedience to the moral law. In its subjective capriciousness it does both good and, occasionally, evil; but it tends to represent the evil as a good because the evil supposedly has its origin in the feeling of the good heart." But it is precisely the opposite reproach which is usually leveled against Rousseau, certainly with no less justice. He is seen as the founder and champion of a state socialism which completely sacrifices the individual to the group and forces him into a fixed political order within which he finds neither freedom of activity nor even freedom of conscience.

Opinions concerning Rousseau's religious beliefs and orientation diverge as widely as those concerning his ethical and political beliefs. The "Profession de foi du vicaire savoyard" in *Emile* has been most variously interpreted. Some have seen in it a high point of eighteenth-century Deism. Others have called attention to its close ties to "positive" religion and have laid bare the threads which connect this "Profession" with the Calvinist faith in which Rousseau grew up. And the most recent comprehensive account of Rousseau's religion, in Masson's *La Religion de Jean-Jacques Rousseau*, does not flinch from the paradox of fitting Rousseau's religious feeling and outlook entirely into the sphere of Catholicism and of claiming him for it. According to Masson, there exists a real, deep, all-too-long neglected connection not only between Rousseau and religion but between Rousseau and the Catholic faith.

The attempt to measure Rousseau's world of ideas by the traditional antithesis of "rationalism" and "irrationalism" results in equally ambiguous and uncertain judgments. That Rousseau turned away from the glorification of reason that prevailed in the circle of the French Encyclopedists, that he appealed, instead, to the deeper forces of "feeling" and "conscience"—all this is undeniable. On the other hand, it was precisely this "irrationalist" who, at the height of his struggle against the *philosophes* and the spirit of the French Enlightenment, coined the phrase that the loftiest ideas that man could form of the Deity were purely and exclusively grounded in reason: "Les plus grandes idées de la divinité nous viennent par la raison seule." Furthermore, it was this "irrationalist" whom no less a man than Kant compared with Newton and called the Newton of the moral world.

If we consider these divergences of judgment, we will immediately recognize that a true elucidation of Rousseau's nature can neither be gained nor be expected from these categories. We can achieve it only if we turn once more, untouched by all prejudgments and prejudices, to Rousseau's work itself—if we let it come into being before our eyes in accord with its own inner law.

However, such a genesis of his work is not possible unless we trace that work back to its point of departure in Rousseau's life and to its roots in his personality. These two elements—the man and the work—are so closely interwoven that every attempt to disentangle them must do violence to both by cutting their common vital nerve. True, it is not my purpose to maintain that Rousseau's world of ideas lacks independent meaning apart from his individual form of existence and personal life. It is rather the opposite hypothesis I want to defend here. What I shall try to show is this: that Rousseau's fundamental thought, although it had its immediate origin in his nature and individuality, was neither circumscribed by nor bound to that individual personality; that in its maturity and perfection this thought puts before us an objective formulation of questions; and that this formulation is valid not for him or his era alone but contains, in full sharpness and definiteness, an inner, strictly objective necessity. But this necessity does not stand immediately before us in abstract generality and systematic isolation. It emerges very gradually from the individual first cause of Rousseau's nature, and it must first, as it were, be liberated from this first cause; it must be conquered step by step. Rousseau always resisted the notion that a thought could have objective value and validity only when it appeared from the outset in systematically articulated and armor-plated form; he angrily rejected the idea that he should submit to such systematic compulsion. Rousseau's objection holds in the theoretical as well as in the practical spheres; it holds for the development of thought as well as the conduct of life. With a thinker of this sort the content and meaning of the work cannot be separated from the foundation of personal life; each can be comprehended only with the other and in the other, in repeated reflection and mutual illumination.

Rousseau's independent spiritual development began only at the moment of his arrival in Paris when he was nearly thirty. Here, for the first time, he experienced the true awakening of his intellectual self-awareness. From that moment childhood and adolescence lay behind him, cloaked in blurred dimness. They remained for him only as objects of memory and of yearning—a yearning, it is true, which was to haunt Rousseau till his old age and never lost its power. What made Rousseau return again and again to the first impressions of his Swiss homeland was the feeling that there, and there alone, he had still possessed life as a true entity, as an unbroken whole. The break between the demands of the world and the demands of the self had not yet taken place; the power of feeling and imagination had not yet found a fixed and harsh boundary in the reality of things. Accordingly, both worlds, the world of the self and the world of things, were not yet sharply separated in Rousseau's consciousness. His boyhood and youth were a peculiarly fantastic tissue, strangely woven together from dream and reality, experience and imagination. His most complete, his richest and most "real" moments were not the moments of action and accomplishment but those hours in which he could forget and leave behind all reality, lost in the dream world of his fantasies, feelings, and desires. In week-long aimless wanderings, roaming about freely, he sought and found this happiness again and again.

But the moment he entered Paris, this world sank from sight as with a single blow. Here another order of things awaited and received him—an order that allowed no scope to subjective arbitrariness and imagination. The day belonged to a mass of activities, and they controlled it down to the last detail. It was a day of work and of conventional social duties, each of which had its proper time and hour. This fixity of time regulation, of objective time measurement, was the first thing to which Rousseau had to become accustomed. From now on he had to do constant battle with this requirement, so alien to his nature. The rigid framework of time, determining man's ordinary working day and dominating him completely, this externally imposed and externally enforced budgeting of life, always appeared to Rousseau as an unbearable restraint on living. He could accomplish the most varied things and he could adjust himself to much that was really unsuitable to him, so long as the *time* for his activity was not prescribed along with the *kind*.

In that keen examination of his own nature, the dialogues to which he gave the characteristic title *Rousseau juge de Jean-Jacques*, Rousseau dwells expressly on this trait. Jean-Jacques, as he describes himself here, "loves activity, but he detests constraint. Work is no strain on him provided he can do it at his own rather than at another's time. . . . Must he accomplish some business, pay a visit, or take a trip? He will go to it at once if he is not pressed. If he is compelled to act immediately he becomes refractory. It was one of the happiest moments of his life when, renouncing all plans for the future in order to live from day to day, he got rid of his watch. " 'Thank heavens!' he exclaimed in a transport of joy, 'I shall no longer need to know what time it is!' "

To this revulsion against any regimentation and stereotyping of external life, Rousseau now added another feeling, deeper and more heartfelt, which estranged him more and more from traditional forms of sociability and drove him into himself. Shortly after his arrival it appeared that he might be able to adjust himself to these forms. During this time he was by no means the misanthropic hermit. He sought acquaintances and—especially in his friendship with Diderot, who was, so to speak, the personification of all vigorous spiritual forces of contemporary France—he found the tie which bound him firmly to the sociable and literary life of the time. Then, too, the personal reception which Rousseau got in Paris seemed destined, indeed expressly designed, gradually to divert his obstinacy into other paths and to lead to a reconciliation between him and the *esprit public*. Everywhere people were eager to extend him a friendly welcome. The Paris of that time was the acme and the zenith of courtly culture, and the characteristic virtue of this culture consisted of that exquisite courtesy with which every stranger was treated.

But it was precisely this pervasive courtesy, taken as a matter of course, which hurt and repelled Rousseau. For he learned, ever more clearly, to see through it to the bottom; he felt ever more strongly that this sort of friendliness knew no personal friendship. Rousseau has given the most intense description of this feeling in the letter of the *Nouvelle Héloïse* in which Saint-Preux relates his entry into Paris society. Here nothing is "invented"; every word is drawn from his own immediate experience. "I have been very warmly welcomed," writes Saint-Preux;

> People meet me full of friendship; they show me a thousand civilities; they render me services of all sorts. But that is precisely what I am complaining of. How can you become immediately the friend of a man whom you have never seen before? The true human interest, the plain and noble effusion of an honest soul— these speak a language far different from the insincere demonstrations of politeness [and the false appearances] which the customs of the great world demand. I am very much afraid that the

man who treats me as a friend of twenty years' standing at the
first meeting could treat me in twenty years as a stranger if I had
to ask him for some important favor; and when I discover in these
[dissipated] people such a tender interest in so many persons I
would gladly believe that they are not interested in anybody.

Such was Rousseau's first impression of Paris society, and this impression continued to work in him and to deepen incessantly. We must seek the
real source of his misanthropy at this point—a misanthropy which grew out
of a genuine and deep feeling of love, out of the yearning for unconditional
devotion and an enthusiastic ideal of friendship. It is the misanthropy which
the most profound judge and painter of men in classical French literature
described in an incomparable character. In the midst of the amiable and
officious, the courtly and courteous world of Paris society, Rousseau was
seized by that feeling of complete isolation which Molière has his Alceste
express:

> Non, non, il n'est point d'âme un peu bien située
> Qui veuille d'une estime aussi prostituée.
>
> . . . .
>
> Sur quelque préférence une estime se fonde,
> Et c'est n'estimer rien qu'estimer tout le monde.
>
> . . . .
>
> Je refuse d'un coeur la vaste complaisance
> Que ne fait de mérite aucune différence.
>
> . . . .
>
> J'entre en une humeur noire, en un chagrin profond,
> Quand je vois entre eux les hommes commes ils font.
> Je ne trouve partout que lâche flatterie
> Qu'injustice, intérêt, trahison, fourberie;
> Je n'y puis plus tenir, j'enrage; et mon dessein
> Est de rompre en visière à tout le genre humain.
>
> (No, by esteem thus cheaply prostituted
> No well-bred soul could wish to be polluted.
>
> . . . .
>
> Esteem is based on preference of some kind:
> He values none who values all mankind.
>
> . . . .
>
> I spurn the easy friendship of a heart
> To whom all merit is of equal sort.
>
> . . . .

I am all melancholy, sad, and blue
When I behold men acting as they do.
Where'er I turn, base flattery I see,
Injustice, greed, deceit, and villainy.
It is too much, I rage, and my desire
Is to defy the human race entire.)
(*Le Misanthrope*, 1.1)

But it was a different, a stronger impulse that drove Rousseau to this break. The same fundamental defect which he had earlier recognized in society he now recognized in its intellectual spokesmen as well, in the representatives of its true and most refined spirituality. This spirituality was as far removed from the genuine spirit of truth as the agreeable morals of the time were removed from true morality. For philosophy had long since forgotten how to speak its native language, the language of the teaching of wisdom. Now it only spoke the language of the time, fitting itself into the thought and interests of the era. The worst and harshest constraint of society lies in this power which it wields not only over our external actions but also over all our inner urges, all our thoughts and judgments. This power thwarts all independence, all freedom and originality of judgment. It is no longer we who think and judge: society thinks in us and for us. We no longer need search for the truth: it is pressed into our hand, fresh from the mint.

Rousseau describes this spiritual condition in his first philosophical essay. "There prevails in our morals an abject and deceptive uniformity, and all minds seem to have been cast in the same mold. Endlessly, politeness makes demands, decorum gives orders; endlessly, we follow customs, never our own bent. We no longer dare seem what we are; and, in this perpetual constraint the men who form this herd which we call society will all do the same things under the same circumstances." Sociable man, constantly living outside himself, knows how to live only in the opinion of others, and can gather the awareness of his own existence solely through this derived and indirect method, by this roundabout path of the opinion of others.

But with these last sentences, which belong to Rousseau's second philosophical work, the *Discours sur l'origine de l'inégalité*, we have already anticipated a later stage of his development. Let us turn back from it, in order to focus our eyes on the moment which we can describe as the actual hour of birth of Rousseau's fundamental thought. He himself has given us an incomparable and unforgettable description of it. It was on that summer's day of the year 1749, when Rousseau started from Paris to visit his friend Diderot, who had been confined in the Tower of Vincennes on the strength of a *lettre de cachet*. Rousseau was carrying an issue of the *Mercure de France* and, as he glanced through it while walking, his eyes suddenly fell on a prize question set by the Academy of Dijon for the next year. "Has the restoration of the sciences and the arts," so ran the question, "helped to purify morals?"

"If anything ever resembled a sudden inspiration," thus Rousseau describes this moment in a letter to Malesherbes,

> it was the emotion that worked in me as I read that. Of a sudden I felt my spirit dazzled by a thousand lights; swarms of [lively] ideas presented themselves to me at once, with a force [and confusion] that threw me into an inexpressible turmoil; I felt my head seized with a dizziness like that of inebriation. A violent palpitation oppressed me and made my chest heave. Since I could no longer breathe [while walking,] I let myself drop under one of the trees [by the wayside], and there I spent half an hour in such excitement that as I rose I noticed that [the whole front of] my jacket was wet with my [own] tears which I had shed without noticing it. Oh, [Sir] if I could ever have written one fourth of what I had seen and felt under that tree, with which clarity I should have revealed all the contradictions of the social system! With what force I should have exposed all the abuses of our institutions! With what ease I should have shown that man is naturally good, and that it is through these institutions alone that men become bad. All I have been able to retain of those swarms of great truths that enlightened me [in a quarter of an hour] under that tree has been scattered quite feebly in my [three] main works, [namely, in that first *Discourse*, in the one on *Inequality*, and in the *Treatise on Education*].

The event which Rousseau describes in this letter had taken place more than a decade earlier, but we feel with every word how the memory still affects and shakes him with undiminished force. Indeed it was that moment which decided his personal fate as a thinker. The question that suddenly confronted him focused all doubts which had previously assailed him on one point. His suppressed indignation against all that his epoch loved and revered, against the eighteenth century's ideals of life and of culture, now broke out in him like a boiling stream of lava. For a long time Rousseau had felt estranged from these ideals; still, he had hardly dared to confess this to himself, much less give it visible expression. The splendor of the spiritual civilization in whose center he stood had still dazzled him; the friendship with the leaders of the spiritual movement, with Condillac and Diderot, had still held him back.

But now all these laboriously constructed dams collapsed. A new ethical passion had awakened in him; irresistibly it drew from him a flood of new ideas. Now the inner tension which he had hitherto felt but vaguely and dimly became a distinct and certain knowledge. At a stroke, his feeling became clear and clairvoyant. Rousseau now *saw* where he stood; he not only felt, but he judged and condemned. He was not yet able to clothe this judgment in the form of philosophical conception and argumentation. If we consider his answer to the prize question of the Academy of Dijon from the philosophic and systematic point of view, the weaknesses and gaps in the chain of proof emerge throughout. As he looked back upon his first philosophical work, Rousseau did not conceal these weaknesses from himself. In a prefatory remark to a later edition of the *Discours* he points to the tragic irony that a work which does not bear comparison in content with any of his later writings should have laid the foundations of his literary fame. Indeed, the first *Discours* appears as a rhetorical masterpiece unsurpassed in the whole of Rousseau's writings; but in many respects it has remained a mere rhetorical display piece. And this rhetoric has lost its hold on us; it no longer has the overwhelming power over us that it had on his contemporaries. But no matter how we feel about it and about the single steps of Rousseau's argumentation, the truthfulness of Rousseau's inner sentiment impresses itself upon us in every sentence of the *Discours*. In every word there lives the urge to be rid of all oppressive learning, to shake off all the burden and splendor of knowledge in order to find the way back to the natural and simple forms of existence. Rousseau's ethics resolves itself into this one fundamental idea and feeling.

> O Virtue! Sublime science of simple souls, are such labor and preparation necessary before we can know you? Are not your principles engraved on every heart? To learn your laws, is it not enough to return to ourselves and to listen to the voice of our conscience in the silence of the passions? This is the true philosophy; we must know enough to be content with it, without envying the fame of the celebrated men who have become immortals in the republic of letters.

When Rousseau demanded the "return to nature" in *this* sense—when he distinguished between what man is and what he has artificially made of himself, he derived the right to make this contrast neither from the knowledge of nature nor from the knowledge of history. For him both elements were of strictly subordinate significance. He was neither historian nor ethnologist, and it seemed to him a strange self-deception to hope that man might be changed and brought nearer to his "natural state" by historical or ethnological knowledge.

Rousseau was neither the only nor the first man in the eighteenth century to coin the motto, "Back to Nature!" Rather, its sound was to be heard everywhere, in inexhaustible variations. Descriptions of the customs of primitive peoples were eagerly snatched up; there was a mounting urge to acquire a wider view of primitive forms of life. Hand in hand with this new knowledge—mainly derived from travelers' reports—went a new feeling. Diderot made a report of Bougainville on his trip to the South Seas his starting point for celebrating with lyrical exaggeration the simplicity, the innocence, and the happiness of primitive peoples. In Raynal's *Histoire philosophique et politique des éstablissemens et du commerce des Européens dans les deux Indes* (1772) the eighteenth century found an inexhaustible mine of information about "exotic" conditions and an arsenal for their enthusiastic praise. When Rousseau wrote the *Discours sur l'origine de l'inégalité*, this movement was already fully under way; but he himself seems hardly touched by it. He made it unmistakably clear right at the beginning of that essay that he neither could nor wanted to describe a historically demonstrable original state of mankind. "Let us begin then by setting aside all the facts, since they do not affect the question. We must not take the researches which we may undertake concerning this subject as historical truths but only as hypothetical [and conditional] observations, more appropriate to throw light on the nature of things than to show their real origins." The "nature of things" is present to us everywhere—to understand it we need not retrace our steps through the millennia, to the sparse and undependable evidence of prehistoric times. As Rousseau puts it in the preface to the *Discours sur l'inégalité:* The man who speaks of the "state of nature" speaks of a state which no longer exists, *which may never have existed, and which probably will never exist.* It is a state of which we must, nevertheless, have an adequate idea in order to judge correctly our present condition.

The expansion of the spatial-geographic horizon can help us as little as the road back to prehistory. Whatever data we might gather in this area remain mute witnesses unless we find in ourselves the means of making them speak. The true knowledge of man cannot be found in ethnography or ethnology. There is only one living source for this knowledge—the source of self-knowledge and genuine self-examination. And it is to this alone that Rousseau appeals; from it he seeks to derive all proofs of his principles and hypotheses. In order to distinguish the *"homme naturel"* from the *"homme artificiel,"* we need neither go back to epochs of the distant and dead past nor take a trip around the world. Everyone carries the true archetype within himself; still, hardly anyone has been fortunate enough to discover it and to strip it of its artificial wrappings, its arbitrary and conventional trimmings.

It is *this* discovery on which Rousseau prided himself and which he proclaimed to his age as his true accomplishment. All he could set against the scholarship, learning, philosophy, and political and sociological theories of his time was the simple testimony of his self-awareness and self-experience. Whence could the originator of this doctrine, as Rousseau writes in his *Rousseau juge de Jean Jacques,*

> whence could the painter and apologist of human nature, [today so defamed and maligned,] have taken his model, if not from his own heart? He has described this nature just as he felt it within himself. The prejudices which had not subjugated him, the artificial passions which had not made him their victim—they did not hide from his eyes, as from those of all others, the basic traits of humanity, so generally forgotten and misunderstood. . . . In a word, it was necessary that one man should paint his own portrait to show us, in this manner, the natural man; and if the author had not been just as singular as his books, he would never have written them. But where is he, this natural man who lives a truly human life; who, caring nothing for the opinions of others, acts only in accord with his impulses and reason, without regard for the praise or blame of society? In vain do we seek him among us. Everywhere only a varnish of words; all men seek their happiness in appearance. No one cares for reality, everyone stakes his essence on illusion. Slaves and dupes of their self-love, men live not in order to live but to make others believe that they have lived!

With these words and the disposition they express, Rousseau seems to profess an unfettered individualism; angrily he seems to cast off the burden of society once and for all. Up to this point, however, we have comprehended only one pole of his nature and only one goal of his thought. Shortly after the composition of the *Discours sur l'origine de l'inégalité* an almost inconceivable reversal occurred in his thinking. We are now led to a dramatic turning point which still astonishes his interpreters. Rousseau becomes the author of the *Contrat social:* he writes the code for the very society which he has rejected and castigated as the cause of all the depravity and unhappiness of mankind.

And what does this code look like? We might expect that it would keep society within bounds as much as possible—that it would narrow and delimit its powers so carefully that any attack on individuality would be checked.

But such an "attempt to determine the limits of the state" was far from Rousseau's mind. The *Contrat social* proclaims and glorifies a completely unbounded absolutism of the state. Every particular and individual will is shattered by the power of the *volonté générale*. The very act of joining the state signifies the complete renunciation of all particular desires. Man does not give himself to the state and to society without giving himself completely to both. We may speak of a real "unity" of the state only if the individuals are merged in this unity and disappear in it. No reservation is possible here: "L'aliénation se faisant sans réserve, l'union est aussi parfaite qu'elle peut l'être, *et nul associé n'a plus rien à réclamer*. (Since the alienation is made unconditionally, the union is as perfect as it can be, and no associate has anything more to claim [italics added by Cassirer].)"

This omnipotence of the state in no way stops with the actions of men; it claims their beliefs as well and places them under the harshest constraint. Religion, too, is civilized and socialized. The concluding chapter of the *Contrat social* deals with the establishment of the *religion civile*, which is absolutely binding on all citizens. It permits the individual complete freedom with respect to those dogmas that are irrelevant to the form of communal life, but it establishes all the more relentlessly a list of articles of faith concerning which, on penalty of explusion from the state, no doubt is permitted. The articles of faith include belief in the existence of an omnipotent and infinitely beneficent Deity, Providence, life after death, and a Last Judgment. Is it too harsh a verdict when Taine in his *Origines de la France contemporaine*, calls the *Contrat social* a glorification of tyranny, and when he describes Rousseau's state as a prison and a monastery?

The solution of this fundamental contradiction seems impossible, and indeed the majority of interpreters have despaired of it. Well-known works in the Rousseau literature—I only mention the names of Morley, Faguet, Ducros, Mornet—declare candidly that the *Contrat social* explodes the unity of Rousseau's work, that it implies a complete break with the philosophical outlook from which this work had originally sprung. But even admitting that such a break is possible, how can we explain that it remained so completely concealed from Rousseau himself? For into his old age Rousseau never tired of affirming and upholding the unity of his work. He did not see the *Contrat social* as an apostasy from the fundamental ideas he had advocated in his two essays on the prize questions of the Academy of Dijon; it was, rather, their consistent extension, their fulfillment and perfection.

Never, as *Rousseau juge de Jean-Jacques* emphasizes, had the attack on the arts and sciences been designed to throw mankind back into its original barbarism. Never would he have been able to form such a strange and chimerical plan:

> In his first writings it was necessary to destroy the illusion which fills us with an absurd admiration for the instruments of our unhappiness and to correct those false sets of values which heap honors upon pernicious talents and despise benevolent virtues. Everywhere he shows us humanity as better, [wiser,] and happier in its original state, and as blind, unhappy, and evil to the degree that it has departed from that state. . . .
>
> But human nature does not turn back. Once man has left it, he can never return to the time of innocence and equality. It was on this principle that he particularly insisted. . . . He has been obstinately accused of wishing to destroy the sciences and the arts . . . and to plunge humanity back into its original barbarism. Quite the contrary: he always insisted on the preservation of existing institutions, maintaining that their destruction would leave the vices in existence and remove only the means to their cure, putting plunder in the place of corruption.

Given the present stage of human development—with which our work must begin if it is not to remain empty and illusory—how are we to resist *both* plunder and corruption? How can we build a genuine and truly human community without falling in the process into the evils and depravity of conventional society? This is the question to which the *Contrat social* addresses itself. The return to the simplicity and happiness of the state of nature is barred to us, but the path of *freedom* lies open; it can and must be taken.

At this point, however, the interpreter is compelled to enter difficult and slippery ground, for of all of Rousseau's conceptions, his conception of freedom has been interpreted in the most divergent and contradictory ways. In the controversy that has been raging for nearly two centuries, the conception has almost completely lost its precision. It has been pulled hither and yon by the hatred or favor of the parties; it has been reduced to a mere political slogan which, glittering today in all the colors of the spectrum, has been made to serve the most divergent political goals.

But one thing may be said: Rousseau cannot be held responsible for this ambiguity and confusion. He defined, clearly and firmly, the specific meaning and true basic significance of his idea of freedom. To him freedom did not mean arbitrariness but the overcoming and elimination of all arbitrariness, the submission to a strict and inviolable law which the individual erects over himself. Not renunciation of and release from this law but free consent to it determines the genuine and true character of freedom. And that character is realized in the *volonté générale*, the will of the state. The state claims the individual completely and without reservations. However, in doing so it does not act as a coercive institution but only puts the individual under an obligation which he himself recognizes as valid and necessary, and to which he therefore assents for its sake as well as for his own.

Here lies the heart of the whole political and social problem. It is not a question of emancipating and liberating the individual in the sense of releasing him from the form and order of the community; it is, rather, a question of finding the kind of community that will protect every individual with the whole concerted power of the political organization, so that the individual in uniting himself with all others nevertheless obeys only himself in this act of union. "Each man, by giving himself to all, gives himself to nobody; and since there is no associate over whom he does not acquire the same right that he has given the other over himself, he gains the equivalent of everything he has lost and more power to preserve what he has." "As long as the subjects have to submit only to such conventions, they obey no one but their own will." To be sure, with this they give up the independence of the state of nature, the *indépendance naturelle*, but they exchange it for real freedom, which consists in tying all men to the law. And only then will they have become individuals in the higher sense—autonomous personalities. Rousseau did not hesitate for an instant in elevating this ethical conception of personality far above the mere state of nature. On this point his words are of such unmistakable clarity and precision as we should hardly expect of a writer who is generally considered a blind worshiper of "primitive man." Although by entering the community man deprives himself of several ad-vantages which he has possessed in the state of nature, he gains by this step such a development of his faculties, such an awakening of his ideas and refinement of his feelings, that if the abuses of his new condition did not frequently degrade him below the state of nature, he would have to bless without cease the happy moment that wrested him from this state forever and made him a spiritual being and a man instead of a limited and stupid animal.

It is true that the thesis which the *Discours sur l'inégalité* seems to defend is here finally abandoned. In the earlier essay the entrance into the realm of spirituality still appears as a kind of defection from the happy state of nature, as a kind of biological depravity. Thinking man is a depraved animal: "L'homme qui médite est un animal dépravé." Similarly, the essay on the arts and sciences had maintained that nature desired to protect man from knowledge—like an anxious mother who snatches a dangerous weapon from the hands of her child. Was all this now lost and forgotten for Rousseau? Had he decided unconditionally for "spirit" and against nature, and had he exposed himself without misgivings to all its dangers, which he himself had seen so clearly and judged so ruthlessly? And what can explain and justify this new orientation? We can find this explanation only if we do not overlook the right link. Knowledge—that is the insight which Rousseau had now achieved—is without danger as long as it does not try to raise itself above life and to tear itself away from it, as long as it serves the order of life itself. Knowledge must claim no absolute primacy, for in the realm of spiritual values it is the ethical will that deserves primacy.

In the ordering of the human community, too, the firm and clear formation of the world of the will must precede the construction of the world of knowledge. Man must first find within himself the clear and established law before he can inquire into and search for the laws of the world, the laws of external things. Once this first and most urgent problem has been mastered, once the spirit has achieved true freedom in the order of the political and social world—then man may safely give himself up to the freedom of inquiry. Knowledge will no longer fall victim to mere *raffinement*; it will not soften or enervate man. It was only a false ethical order of things which had diverted knowledge into this direction and which had reduced it to a mere intellectual refinement, a kind of spiritual luxury. It will return to the right path by itself once this impediment has been removed. Spiritual liberty profits man nothing without ethical liberty, but ethical liberty cannot be achieved without a radical transformation of the social order, a transformation that will wipe out all arbitrariness and that alone can help the inner necessity of law to victory.

This hymn to the law and to its unconditional universal validity runs through all of Rousseau's political writings, although he has been most thoroughly and most frequently misunderstood precisely on this point. Only one man correctly understood the inner cohesion of Rousseau's world of ideas. Kant alone became Rousseau's admiring disciple on this very point. The traditional conception and interpretation of Rousseau, however, here took another, exactly opposite, direction. As early as the eighteenth century, conceptions and interpretations stood sharply opposed to each other: following Kant's example, the *Genieperiode* lifted Rousseau on its shield and made him the patron of *its* interpretation of freedom. In this interpretation, freedom was invoked *against* the law; the meaning and purpose of freedom were to release man from the pressure and constraint of the law. "I am asked to squeeze my body into stays," exclaims Karl Moor, "and straitlace my will in laws. Law has perverted to snail's pace what might have been an eagle's flight. Never yet has law formed a great man, but freedom breeds giants and extremes" (Friedrich Schiller, *The Robbers*, 1.2).

But this mood of the *Sturm und Drang* was not the fundamental intellectual and ethical disposition of Rousseau. For him, law is not an opponent and enemy of freedom; on the contrary, it alone can give and truly guarantee freedom. This fundamental conception was fixed for Rousseau from his first political writings on. The *Discours sur l'économie politique*, which Rousseau wrote for the *Encyclopédie*, expresses it unmistakably. "It is to law alone that men owe justice and freedom; it is this [beneficial] organ of the will of all which reestablishes natural equality among men in the legal order; it is this celestial voice which prescribes to each citizen the precepts of public reason and teaches him to act in accord with the maxims of his own judgment, and not to be in contradiction with himself.

On the other hand, this common dependence on the law is also the only legal ground for any social dependency whatever. A political community that demands any other kind of obedience is internally unsound. Freedom is destroyed when the community is asked to subject itself to the will of a single man or to a ruling group which can never be more than an association of individuals. The only "legitimate" authority is that authority which the principle of legitimacy, *the idea of law as such*, exercises over individual wills. At all times, this idea claims the individual only insofar as he is a member of the community, an actively participating organ of the general will, but not in his particular existence and individuality. No special privilege can be granted to an individual as individual or to a special class; no special effort can be demanded of him. In this sense the law must act "without respect of persons." A bond that does not bind absolutely everyone, but only this man or that, automatically nullifies itself. There can and must be no exceptions within the law nor by virtue of the law; rather, every exceptional decree to which single citizens or certain classes are subjected means by its very nature the destruction of the idea of law and of the state: the dissolution of the social contract and the relapse into the state of nature, which is characterized in this connection as a pure state of violence.

In this sense it is the true fundamental task of the state to replace physical inequality among men, which is irremovable, with legal and moral equality. Physical inequality is unavoidable, and it ought not to be deplored. In this category Rousseau includes the inequality of property, which in itself— merely as the unequal distribution of possessions—is of minor and subordinate importance in his thought. Truly communistic ideas are not developed anywhere in the *Contrat social*. For Rousseau, inequality of property is an *adiaphoron* [a matter of no moral significance], a fact which man can accept as much as he must put up with the unequal distribution of bodily strength, skills, and mental gifts. Here ends the realm of freedom, and the realm of fate begins.

Rousseau never conceived of the state as a mere welfare state. Unlike Diderot and the majority of the Encyclopedists, he did not regard it as merely the distributor of happiness. It does not guarantee to each individual an equal share of possessions; it is exclusively concerned with securing an equal measure of rights and duties. The state is therefore entitled and qualified to interfere with property insofar as the inequality of property endangers the moral equality of the subjects under the law—for instance, when such inequality condemns specific classes of citizens to complete economic dependence and threatens to make them a plaything in the hands of the wealthy and the powerful. In such a situation, the state may and must interfere. Through appropriate legislation, as for example through certain limitations on the right to inheritance, it must attempt to establish an equilibrium of economic forces. Rousseau's demands did not go beyond this.

It is true, however, that Rousseau regarded it as the proper characteristic of society—its original stigma, as it were—that it had always employed economic inequality to establish its rule of force and the harshest political tyranny. Rousseau fully appropriated Thomas More's pointed phrase that what had hitherto been called "state" had been nothing but a conspiracy of the rich against the poor. "You have need of me," says the rich man to the poor, "because I am rich and you are poor. Let us therefore make an agreement: I shall grant you the honor of serving me, on condition that you will give me the little you have left in return for the trouble I shall take to command you."

Rousseau did not rebel against poverty as such. Rather, he fought with mounting bitterness the political and moral disfranchisement which is its inescapable consequence in the contemporary social order.

> Are not all the advantages of society with the powerful and the rich? Are not all the lucrative posts filled with them alone? Are not all the favors, all the exemptions reserved for them? And is not the public authority in their favor? When an important man robs his creditors or commits other rascalities, is he not always sure of impunity? The beatings he deals out, the acts of violence he commits, even the killings and murders of which he becomes guilty—are these not matters that are hushed up and that are

forgotten after six months? But if this same man is robbed, the whole police is set in motion immediately, and woe to the innocent whom he suspects! If he passes through a dangerous place, the escorts are out in force; if the axle of his post chaise breaks, everyone flies to his assistance. . . . If a cart finds itself in his way, his men are ready to beat the driver to death, and it is better if fifty honest pedestrians going about their business are crushed than that an idle scoundrel should be delayed in his carriage. All these attentions cost him not a penny—they are the rich man's right, and not the price of wealth.

Rousseau himself had experienced all the bitterness of poverty, but he was always armed with stoic equanimity against all physical deprivations. On the other hand, he never learned to endure the dependence of the will on the orders and arbitrariness of others. This is the starting point both for his ideal of the state as well as for his ideal of education. The fundamental idea of *Emile* consists in this: that no physical obstacles must be removed from the path of the pupil who is to be educated to independence of will and character. He is to be spared no suffering, no effort, no privation, and he is to be anxiously protected only from violent coercion by an outside will, from a command whose necessity he does not understand. He is to become acquainted with the compulsion of things from his earliest childhood, and he is to learn to bow before it; but he is to be spared the tyranny of men.

The tendency of Rousseau's political and social theory can be fully understood only from the perspective of this fundamental idea: its essential purpose, it is true, is to place the individual under a law that is universally binding, but this law is to be shaped in such a manner that every shadow of caprice and arbitrariness disappears from it. We should learn to submit to the law of the community just as we submit to the law of nature; we are not to acquiesce in it as in an alien dictate but must follow it because we recognize its necessity. This is possible when—and only when—we understand that this law is of such a nature that we must assent to it freely when we assimilate its meaning and can absorb this meaning into our own will.

With this conception, the state is faced with a new demand and challenge which has rarely been sounded so sharply and firmly since the days of Plato. For its essential task, the point of departure and the basis of all government, is the task of education. The state does not simply address itself to already existing and given subjects of the will; rather its first aim is to *create* the sort of subjects to whom it can address its call. Unless the will is thus formed, mastery over the will must always be illusory and futile.

The objection has frequently been raised against the social-contract theory in general and against Rousseau's *Contrat social* in particular that it is an atomistic-mechanistic theory, that it views the state's universal will as a mere aggregate composed of the wills of all individuals. But this reproach mistakes the essence of Rousseau's fundamental intention. From the formal point of view, it is true, Rousseau had a good deal of difficulty in delimiting, clearly and firmly, the *volonté générale* against the *volonté de tous*, and in the *Contrat social* we can find not a few passages that would seem to indicate that the content of the general will could be determined purely quantitatively, by the simple counting of individual votes. No doubt, there are flaws of exposition, but these flaws do not touch the core of Rousseau's fundamental thought.

Indeed, Rousseau did not by any means regard the state as a mere "association," as a community of interests and an equilibrium of the interests of individual wills. According to him, it is not a mere empirical collection of certain dispositions, impulses, and vacillating appetites, but the form in which the will, as ethical will, really exists. In that state alone can willfulness develop into will. Law in its pure and strict sense is not a mere external bond that holds in individual wills and prevents their scattering; rather it is the constituent principle of these wills, the element that confirms and justifies them spiritually. It wishes to rule subjects only inasmuch as, in its every act, it also makes and educates them into citizens.

This ideal task, not the happiness and welfare of the individual, is the real purpose of the state. But to comprehend this task in its essence, men must raise themselves above all hitherto existing empirical-historical forms of political communities. Neither a comparison of these forms nor their conceptual articulation and classification—as was attempted by Montesquieu in his *Esprit des lois*—can yield the real justification of the state. Rousseau explicitly objected to such an empirical, abstract method. "At first glance all human institutions seem to be founded on heaps of quicksand. It is only when we examine them closely, only when we have cleared away the dust and sand that surround the edifice, that we begin to see the firm foundation on which it is erected and that we learn to respect its basis." Instead of shaping the state freely and building within it the order appropriate to men, mankind had, up to then, been the property of the state. Need had driven man to the state and had held him there—long before he was able to understand and inwardly to comprehend its necessity.

But now at last this hold had to be broken. The state created by mere necessity was to become the state created by reason. Just as Bacon had called for the *regnum hominis* over nature, so Rousseau now made the same demand for the proper spheres of man—state and society. So long as these were left to merely physical wants and to the rule of emotions and passions, so long as they were made into the proving grounds of the instinct of power and domination, ambition and self-love, any additional strengthening of the state only created a new scourge for man. Society up to then had burdened man with innumerable evils and had entangled him ever more deeply in error and vice. But man is not subject to this entanglement as to an inescapable fate. He can and he ought to free himself from it by taking the control of his destiny into his own hands, by substituting "I will" and "I should" for a mere "I must." It is the business of man, and it is within his power, to transform into a blessing the curse which had up to then lain over all political and social developments. But he can accomplish this task only after he has found and understood himself.

Rousseau's *Contrat social* wraps both demands into one. State and society are to find each other in mutual interaction; they are to grow and unfold together, so as to become inextricably joined in this common growth. What Rousseau now recognized was that man as such is neither good nor evil, neither happy nor unhappy; for his essence and his form are not rigid data but are malleable. And the most important, the essentially plastic power Rousseau saw contained in the community. He now realized that the new humanity for which he yearned must remain a dream so long as the state was not radically transformed.

In this manner the *Discours sur l'inégalité* and the *Contrat social*, in spite of all apparent contradictions, interlock and complement each other. They contradict each other so little that each can rather be explained only through and with the other. If we regard the *Contrat social* as a foreign body in Rousseau's writings, we have failed to understand the spiritual organism of his work. Throughout, Rousseau's entire interest and passion were given to the doctrine of man. But he had come to understand that the question, What is man? cannot be separated from the question, What ought he to be?

Once, in the *Confessions*, he unambiguously described his inner development in that sense:

> I had realized that everything was basically related to politics, and that, no matter how one approached it, no people would ever by anything but what the nature of its government made it. Therefore that great question of the best possible government seemed to me to reduce itself to this: which is the form of gov-

ernment fitted to shape the most virtuous, the most enlightened, the wisest, and, in short, the "best" people, taking that word in its noblest meaning?

And this question leads us back to the other and separate question: Which is the form of government that most completely realizes within itself, by virtue of its nature, the pure rule of law?

It was by assigning this ethical task to politics, by subordinating politics to this ethical imperative, that Rousseau accomplished his truly revolutionary act. With that act he stood alone in his century. He was by no means the first nor the only man to have felt the grave political and social ills of his time and to have expressed himself on them openly. In the midst of the splendid era of Louis XIV these ills had been recognized and characterized keenly by the noblest and profoundest minds of the age. Fénelon had taken the lead; others, such as Vauban, Boulainvilliers, and Boisguillebert, had followed him. In the eighteenth century Montesquieu, Turgot, D'Argenson, Voltaire, Diderot, and Holbach joined and continued this movement. Everywhere, a genuine and strong will to reform was at work; everywhere, the most unsparing criticism was exercised on the Old Regime. And yet this will to reform neither explicitly nor implicitly rose to revolutionary demands. The thinkers of the Encyclopedist circle wanted to ameliorate and to cure; but hardly one of them believed in the necessity for, or in the possibility of, a radical transformation and reformation of state and society. They were satisfied when they succeeded in eliminating the worst abuses and in leading mankind gradually into better political conditions.

All these thinkers were convinced eudaemonists; they sought the happiness of men, and they agreed that this happiness could be truly promoted and secured only through slow, stubborn labor, in single, groping experiments. They expected that the progress of insight and intellectual cultivation would lead to new forms of communal life, but they professed to see that this progress was always reserved to the few, and that the impulse for improvement could therefore come only from them. Thus, with all their demands for freedom, they became advocates of "enlightened despotism."

Voltaire was not content with the theoretical proclamation and justification of his political and social ideals. He himself lent a hand, and in the last decades of his life he had a most extensive and beneficent impact. He paved the way for a number of highly important reforms through his personal intercession and by taking advantage of his European reputation. He spoke up for freedom of the person, for the abolition of slavery and serfdom, for freedom of conscience and of the press, for the freedom of work, for fundamental reforms within the penal code, and for decisive improvements in the tax system. But he did not demand a radical political renewal and he did not believe in a radical ethical renewal. All such thoughts and desires he regarded as dreams and Utopias, which he brushed aside with sarcasm. He professed to know and to see that all such chimeras make men neither better nor wiser but merely entangle them ever more deeply in error and guilt:

> Nous tromper dans nos entreprises,
> C'est à quoi nous sommes sujets.
> Le matin je fais des projets,
> Et le long du jour des sottises.
>
> (To turn out wrong is, as a rule,
> The fate of human enterprise.
> I form great projects as I rise
> And all day long act like a fool.)

These are the words with which Voltaire introduces his philosophical satire, *Memnon, ou La Sagesse humaine* (1747). It describes the fate of a man who one day resolves to become completely wise—to surrender to no passion, to renounce all the pleasures of life, and to be guided entirely by reason. The outcome of this resolution is pitiful: Memnon ends up in misery and disgrace. A good spirit appears to him and promises him salvation, but only on condition that he will renounce once and for all his foolish intention to become completely wise. Such was the fundamental disposition to which Voltaire held fast in his literary and philosophical work. For him the wise man was not the one who liberates himself from all human weaknesses and shortcomings but the man who sees through them and uses them to guide humanity. " 'Tis folly to wait for fools to grow wise! Children of wisdom, make fools out of fools, as indeed they deserve" (Goethe).

The next generation, the younger Encyclopedists, went beyond Voltaire's political ideas and demands. Diderot did not remain within the horizon of ideas of enlightened despotism; he developed pronounced democratic ideas and ideals, and he was naive enough to submit them to his patroness, Catherine II of Russia, who brushed them aside as absurd. But he too was content with details; he too believed that the political and social world could not be saved by a drastic cure. This political opportunism marked the true spirit of the *Encyclopédie*. Holbach, who in respect to religion and metaphysics pursued radical logic to its extreme limits and who advanced to a consistent atheism, was no exception here. "No," he exclaims in the draft of his social system, "not through dangerous convulsions, not through struggle, through regicides and useless crime, can the wounds of the nations be healed. These violent remedies are always more cruel than the evils they are intended to cure. . . . The voice of reason is neither seditious nor bloodthirsty. The reforms which it proposes may be slow, but therefore planned all the better." It was this circumspection, this prudence, this shrewd and cautious weighing of all circumstances that the whole Encyclopedic circle felt lacking in Rousseau's political and social system. D'Alembert, who embodied all the ideals of this circle, a mathematician of genius and an independent philosophical thinker, made this very demand the center of his critique of Rousseau's *Emile:* It is futile to rave against evils; men must seek cures for them, and the cures that philosophy can suggest can be nothing but palliatives. "We can no longer conquer the enemy; he has advanced too far into the land for us to attempt to drive him out; our task is reduced to waging guerrilla warfare against him."

But Rousseau's personality and mentality did not dispose him to such guerrilla warfare, such a *guerre de chicane*, as D'Alembert called it, nor would he have been able to wage it. He was no more of an active revolutionary than the Encyclopedists were; direct intervention in politics was always far from his mind. Rousseau, the outcast and the eccentric, shied away from the turmoil of the market place and the noise of battle. And yet the truly revolutionary impetus emanated from him, not from the men who represented and dominated the public state of mind of contemporary France. He did not concern himself with single evils, nor did he seek single cures. For him there was no compromise with existing society, no attempt at alleviating mere superficial symptoms. He rejected all partial solutions; first and last, and with every word he wrote, it was all or nothing with him. For he saw in the state neither the creator and preserver of happiness nor the guardian and increaser of power. To the ideas of the welfare state and the power state he opposed the idea of the constitutional state (*Rechtsstaat*). For Rousseau this was not a matter of more or less, but of either/or.

Radicalism of this sort is possible only to a thinker who is more than a mere thinker, a man who is not exclusively dominated by celebration but who is driven onward by an ethical imperative. This is why the only absolute ethical thinker that the eighteenth century produced, the champion of the "primacy of the practical reason," was almost alone in understanding Rousseau completely on this point. When Kant writes that there is no value to human existence on this earth if justice is not brought to triumph, he expresses a genuinely Rousseauist thought and sentiment. Rousseau himself, it is true, was unable to break theoretically the hold of the eudaemonism which dominated all eighteenth-century ethics. From the outset, his whole thought was moved by the problem of happiness: its aim was to find a harmonious union of virtue and happiness.

Here Rousseau called upon religion for help; he clung to the belief in immortality, which to him seemed the only possible way of bringing about and guaranteeing the ultimate union of "being happy" (*Glückseligkeit*) and "deserving to be happy" (*Glückwürdigkeit*). "Toutes les subtilités de la Métaphysique," he wrote to Voltaire, "ne me feront pas douter un moment de l'immortalité de l'âme et d'une Providence bienfaisante. Je le sens, je le crois, je le veux, je l'espère, je le défendrai jusqu'à mon dernier soupir. (All the subtleties of metaphysics will not make me doubt for a moment the immortality of the soul or a beneficent Providence. I feel it, I believe it, I want it, I hope for it, and I shall defend it to my last breath.)" And yet we would be mistaken if—as has been done in the most recent comprehensive account of Rousseau's thought—we sought to make this point the center and core of his doctrine, and if we regarded this doctrine as the answer to the question, How can happiness and virtue be reconciled in human existence? For even when speaking the language of eudaemonism, Rousseau in his inner being transcended this formulation of the problem. His ethical and political ideal does not pursue, as does that of Voltaire and Diderot, purely utilitarian goals. He did not inquire into happiness or utility; he was concerned with the dignity of man and with the means of securing and realizing it.

Rousseau never paid special attention to the problem of physical evil; he faced it almost with indifference. The only way of meeting it—this is the fundamental thought which he makes the center of his educational plan in *Emile*—is to despise it and to learn to inure oneself to it. But this solution had no validity for social evil. This could not be borne because it ought not to be borne; because it robs man not of his happiness but of his essence and his destiny. At this point no retreat, no pliancy or submissiveness is permitted. What Voltaire, D'Alembert, Diderot, regarded as mere defects of society, as mere mistakes in organization which must be gradually eliminated, Rousseau saw rather as the guilt of society, and with flaming words, again and again, he reproached society with this guilt and called for atonement. He rejected the arguments of bare need and inescapable necessity; he denied all appeals to the experience of centuries. The verdict of the past had no validity for him because he had fixed his eyes imperturbably on the future and had assigned to society the task of bringing into being a new future for mankind.

And with this we stand before a new problem which will take us a step closer in our approach to the true center of Rousseau's world of ideas. Kant,

in a well-known pronouncement, credited Rousseau with no less an achievement than the solution of the theodicy problem and placed him, for this
reason, behind Newton. "Newton was the first to see order and regularity
combined with great simplicity, where disorder and ill-matched variety had
reigned before. Since then comets have been moving in geometric orbits.
Rousseau was the first to discover in the variety of shapes that men assume
the deeply concealed nature of man and to observe the hidden law that
justifies Providence. Before them, the objections of Alfonso and Manes still
had validity. After Newton and Rousseau, God is justified, and from now
on Pope's maxim is true."

These sentences are strange, and difficult to interpret. What are those
"observations" of Rousseau's which justify the ways of God? What new
principles concerning the problem of theodicy did Rousseau add to the
thought of Leibniz, of Shaftesbury, of Pope? Does not everything he said
on this problem move in familiar paths, known to the whole eighteenth
century? And in any event, is it not part of that dogmatic metaphysics whose
fundamental form Kant himself had done away with and which he later
exposed with all its defects in a special essay, "Über das Misslingen aller
philosophischen Versuche in de Theodizee"? And yet Kant, even as the
critic of pure and practical reason, never wavered in this estimate of Rousseau. He saw through the surface of the metaphysical chain of proof. He
comprehended the core of Rousseau's fundamental ethical and religious outlook, and in that outlook he recognized his own. Rousseau's *Emile*, which,
as we know, was among Kant's favorite books, begins with the statement,
"Tout est bien en sortant des mains de l'Auteur des choses; tout dégénère
entre les mains de l'homme. (All is good as it leaves the hands of the Author
of things, all degenerates in the hands of men.)" Thus God seems relieved
of responsibility, and blame for all evil is ascribed to man.

This, however, presents us with a difficult problem and an apparently
insoluble contradiction. For was it not precisely Rousseau who again and
again proclaimed the doctrine of the original goodness of human nature, and
who made this very doctrine the center and pivot of all his thought? How
can evil and guilt be attributed to human nature if it is free from both in its
original state, if it knows no radical depravity? This is the question around
which Rousseau's thought circled ever anew.

For us, theodicy is a historical problem. We no longer consider it a
current question that immediately concerns and presses us. But in the seventeenth and eighteenth centuries the preoccupation with this question was
by no means a mere conceptual and dialectical game. The profoundest spirits
of that epoch constantly wrestled with it and regarded it as the truly vital

question of ethics and religion. Rousseau, too, found himself inwardly bound to and rooted in religion because of this problem. He took up the old battle for the justification of God against the philosophy of the century, and as a result he quarreled with the Encyclopedist movement, with Holbach and his circle.

He was to find out, however, that he, who considered himself a genuine "defender of the faith" on this point, was to be most implacably opposed, persecuted, and even excommunicated by the official guardians of that faith. It was one of the tragic misunderstandings of Rousseau's life that he never understood the significance of this struggle, that he never saw anything but violence and arbitrariness in the persecution directed against him. Yet, from a purely historical point of view, this judgment was unjust to the Church and, in a certain sense, to himself. In fact, an inescapable decision, vital to the history of the world and to cultural history, was involved. What irrevocably separated Rousseau, despite all his genuine and deep religious emotion, from all traditional forms of faith was the decisiveness with which he rejected every thought of the *original* sin of man.

No understanding or reconciliation was possible here: in the seventeenth and eighteenth centuries the dogma of original sin stood in the center and focus of Catholic and Protestant theology. All great religious movements of the time were oriented toward and gathered up in this dogma. The struggles over Jansenism in France; the battles between Gomarists and Arminians in Holland; the development of Puritanism in England and of Pietism in Germany—they all stood under this sign. And now this fundamental conviction concerning the radical evil in human nature was to find in Rousseau a dangerous and uncompromising adversary.

The Church fully understood this situation: it stressed, at once, the decisive issue with full clarity and firmness. The mandate in which Christophe de Beaumont, archbishop of Paris, condemns *Emile*, laid the chief emphasis on Rousseau's denial of original sin. The claim that the first emotions of human nature are always innocent and good, he asserted, stands in sharpest contradiction to all the teachings of Holy Writ and of the Church concerning the essence of man.

Rousseau now seemed to have placed himself in a completely untenable position: on the one hand he upheld—against the Church—the original goodness of human nature and the right and independence of human reason; on the other hand, he repudiated the noblest achievements of this reason—art, science, and all spiritual cultivation. Could he still legitimately complain of his complete isolation, an isolation which he himself had created by estranging himself from the dominant forms of faith as well as by quarreling with the philosophical Enlightenment? In addition to this external isolation, he now seemed torn by an insoluble inner dilemma. The obscurity of the theodicy problem henceforth seemed completely impenetrable. For if we can neither trace evil back to God nor find its cause in the character of human nature, where are we to find its source and origin?

Rousseau's solution of this dilemma lies in his placing responsibility at a point where no one before him had looked for it. He created, as it were, a new subject of responsibility, of "imputability." This subject is not individual man, but human society. The individual as such, as he emerges from the hands of nature, is not yet involved in the antithesis of good and evil: he gives himself up to his natural instinct of self-preservation. He is governed by *amour de soi;* but this self-love never degenerates into "selfish love" (*amour propre*), whose only satisfying pleasure is the oppression of others. Selfish love, which contains the cause of all future depravity and fosters man's vanity and thirst for power, is exclusively to be charged to society. It is selfish love that makes man a tyrant over nature and himself; awakens in him needs and passions which the natural man had not known; and at the same time places into his hands ever new means for achieving the unfettered and ruthless gratification of these desires. Our eagerness to be talked about, our furious ambition to distinguish ourselves before others—all this keeps us constantly from ourselves and throws us, as it were, outside ourselves.

But is this alienation of the essence of *every* society? Can we not imagine a development toward a genuine and truly human community which will no longer require these springs of power, greed, and vanity but will be rooted wholly in common subjection to a law that is inwardly recognized as binding and necessary? Should such a community arise and endure, evil, as social evil (and this, as we have seen, alone counts in Rousseau's considerations), will be overcome and removed. The hour of salvation will strike when the present coercive form of society is destroyed and is replaced by the free form of political and ethical community—a community in which everyone obeys only the general will, which he recognizes and acknowledges as his own will, rather than be subjected to the willfulness of others. But it is futile to hope that this salvation will be accomplished through outside help. No God can grant it to us; man must become his own savior and, in the ethical sense, his own creator. In its present form society has inflicted the deepest wounds on humanity; but society alone can and should heal these wounds. The burden of responsibility rests upon it from now on.

That is Rousseau's solution of the problem of theodicy—and with it he had indeed placed the problem on completely new ground. He had carried it beyond the realm of metaphysics and placed in in the center of ethics and politics. With this act he gave it a stimulus which continues to work unabated even today. All contemporary social struggles are still moved and driven by this original stimulus. They are rooted in that consciousness of the *responsibility* of society which Rousseau was the first to possess and which he implanted in all posterity.

The seventeenth century had not yet known this idea. When that century was at its height, Bossuet once more proclaimed the old theocratic ideal and established it in its unconditionality and absoluteness. The state coincides with the ruler, and the ruler is subject to no human power or human control; he is responsible to God alone and can be called to account only by him. In opposition to this theocratic absolutism there arose the resolute resistance of the natural law of the seventeenth and eighteenth centuries. Natural law is not a divine but a specifically human law, and it is equally binding on all human wills, rulers as well as ruled. But even this declaration of original, inalienable "rights of man" did not immediately destroy the form of the coercive state, though it limited its powers. In the *Contrat social* Rousseau still carried on a running argument with Grotius, because the latter had admitted at least the possibility of the legality of slavery. Grotius had argued that slavery could possibly be justified by the original contract from which society had arisen. The conqueror of a country, for example, might have concluded a contract with the vanquished that would assure them their lives under the condition that they surrender themselves and their descendants to the victor as his property. Rousseau, in contrast, angrily pushed aside all these reservations as mere formal juristic constructions. Against them he insisted on the "right with which we are born"—and he believed that this right is violated by slavery in any form. If we say that the son of a slave is born a slave, that means no less than that he is not born a man. The true, legitimate society can never honor such a claim; for it is nothing if not the guardian of that *volonté générale*, to which there are no exceptions and from which no one can escape.

Rousseau's solution of the theodicy problem, then, consisted in his removing the burden of responsibility from God and putting it on human society. If society cannot shoulder this burden, if it fails to accomplish, in free responsibility, what its self-determination demands of it, it is guilty. It has been pointed out, and rightly so, that there are quite definite formal analogies between Rousseau's doctrine of the "state of nature" and the Christian doctrine of the state of innocence. Rousseau, too, knew an expulsion of men from the paradise of innocence; he, too, saw in man's development into

a rational animal a kind of "fall from grace" that excludes man forever from
the secure and well-protected happiness that he had enjoyed up to then. But
if, in this respect, Rousseau deplored the gift of "perfectibility" which differentiates man from all other living creatures, he also knew that it alone
can bring ultimate deliverance. It is only through this gift, not through divine
aid and salvation, that man will finally reap freedom and master his fate:
"Car l'impulsion du seul appétit est l'esclavage et l'obéissance à la loi qu'on
s'est prescrite est liberté. (For the impulse of mere appetite is slavery, and
the obedience to the law which we have prescribed to ourselves is liberty.)"

It is only in this context that the controversial problem of Rousseau's
"optimism" is placed in its proper light. At first glance it seems strange that
this brooding and melancholy hermit, this disappointed man whose life ended
in complete darkness and isolation, should cling to the thesis of optimism
to the end of his life and become one of its most zealous champions. In his
correspondence with Voltaire, Rousseau had not failed to point out the tragic
paradox that he, the stepchild of fortune, the hunted and the outcast of
society, should take up the defense of optimism against Voltaire, who was
living in the splendor of fame and in the enjoyment of all worldly goods.
But this paradox disappears when we observe that Rousseau and Voltaire
understood the problem of optimism in two completely different senses. For
Voltaire, this was fundamentally not a question of philosophy but purely a
question of temperament and mood. In the first decades of his life he did
not only indulge without restraint in all the enjoyments of life but made
himself their advocate and glorifier. In the midst of the deep decadence and
depravity of the age of the Regency he became the apologist of the era. His
philosophical poem *La Mondain* sings the praise of his age:

> Moi je rends grâce à la nature sage
> Qui, pour mon bien, m'a fait naître en cet âge
> Tant décrié par nos tristes frondeurs;
> Ce temps profane est tout fait pour mes moeurs.
> J'aime le luxe, et même la mollesse,
> Tous les plaisirs, les arts de toute espèce,
> La propreté, la goût, les ornements;
> Tout honnête homme a de tels sentiments.
>
> . . . .
>
> L'or de la terre et les trésors de l'onde
> Leurs habitants et les peuples de l'air
> Tout sert au luxe, aux plaisirs de ce monde,
> O le bon temps que ce siècle de fer!

(I say, let kindly nature e'er be praised,
Who in her wisdom caused me to be raised
In this our age which malcontents revile:
These worldly times exactly suit my style.
I'm fond of luxury and even of soft ease,
I love all pleasures, all the arts that please,
Cleanliness, taste, and ornaments refined:
On this, all decent men are of my mind.
. . . .
All the gold of the earth and all the ocean's treasures,
The creatures of the land, the air, the sea,
All serve to heighten luxury and pleasures—
Oh iron age, what bliss to live in thee!)

It would seem that Voltaire later regretted this glorification. The earthquake of Lisbon frightened him out of his calm and complacency and he nearly became a moral preacher against a generation that could skip lightheartedly over even such horrors:

Lisbonne, qui n'est plus, eut-elle plus de vices
Que Londres, que Paris plongés dans les délices?
Lisbonne est abîmée et l'on danse à Paris!

(Had Lisbon, now destroyed, more vices to repent
Than London or than Paris, still on pleasure bent?
Yet Lisbon's ruins smoke while Paris dances.)

Explicitly Voltaire now opposed the earlier hymn of praise with this ode of retraction:

Sur un ton moins lugubre on me vit autrefois
Chanter des doux plaisirs les séduisantes lois:
D'autres temps, d'autres moeurs: instruit par la vieillesse
Des humains égarés partageant la faiblesse
Sous une épaisse nuit cherchant à m'éclairer
Je ne sais que souffrir, et non pas murmurer.

(I praised you once, in less lugubrious measures,
Seductive laws that guide our gentle pleasures.
Time changes customs; age has taught my mind.
Weak like the rest of wayward humankind,
I seek the light of truth in darkest night
And without murmuring accept my plight.)

Unwilling to grumble against the sufferings of the world, he would rather exercise his wit at the expense of the "system" of optimism, over which he pours all the vials of his scorn in *Candide*. In this work his satirical mood found ever bitterer expression, but this bitterness was far removed from embitterment. Fundamentally, Voltaire's attitude toward life had remained almost unchanged since his youth. Now as before he combined the sharpest skepticism with a decisive affirmation of the world and of life.

These two moods emerge most clearly in the philosophical tale *Le Monde comme il va, Vision de Babouc* (1746). Ituriel, an angel of the highest rank, orders Babouc to go to the capital of the Persian Empire to observe the activities of men and the customs of the city. On his report and verdict depends the survival or destruction of Persepolis. He becomes thoroughly acquainted with the city. He observes its unbridled excesses; he learns of the abuse and insolence of office, the venality of judges, the fraudulent machinations of commerce. But at the same time he sees the city in its glory, in its magnificence, its spiritual and sociable civilization. And thus he makes up his mind. He has a small statue made by the most skillful goldsmith in the city—made up of all metals, the most precious and the basest—and brings it to Ituriel. "Would you break this pretty statue," he asks the angel, "because it does not consist wholly of gold and diamonds?" Ituriel understands: "Il résolut de ne pas même songer à corriger Persépolis, et de laisser aller *le monde comme il va*; car, dit-il, si tout n'est pas bien, tout est passable. (He decided not even to dream of correcting Persepolis, and to let the world go its own way; for, he said, if all is not well, at least all is passable.)"

This was Voltaire's last word on the world and on worldly life. Even his pessimism remained playful, while Rousseau's optimism was filled with and sustained by tragic seriousness. For even when Rousseau painted the bliss of the senses and the sensual passions in the most glowing colors, he was not satisifed with this picture alone, but placed it against a dark and gloomy background. He did not believe in the unrestrained surrender to passion but demanded of men the power of renunciation. The meaning and worth of life disclosed themselves to him only in that power. Rousseau's optimism is the heroic optimism of Plutarch, his favorite author, and of the great models of ancient history, to whom Rousseau liked to turn for inspiration. He demanded that men, instead of losing themselves in idle laments over the miseries of existence, should understand their destiny and master it themselves. All his political and social ideals grew out of this demand. Rousseau himself reports in his *Confessions* that while he was occupied in the composition of the *Discours sur l'inégalité* he was constantly driven by the urge to call out to men: "Fools, who endlessly complain about nature, learn that all your troubles come from yourselves!"

In this manner this supposed "irrationalist" ended up with the most resolute belief in reason. For Rousseau, the belief in the victory of reason coincided with his belief in the victory of the genuine "cosmopolitan constitution." This belief, too, he communicated to Kant. Kant displays a Rousseauist outlook and mentality when he describes as mankind's greatest problem the establishment of a society of citizens which administers law universally, and when he regards the history of mankind in general as the fulfillment of a hidden plan of nature, designed to achieve an internally and, for this purpose, externally perfect constitution. The theodicy problem can be solved only in and through the state. It is man's business and it is his loftiest task to accomplish the justification of God—not by means of metaphysical broodings over happiness and unhappiness and over good and evil but by freely creating and freely shaping the order in accordance with which he wants to live.

JACQUES DERRIDA

"... That Dangerous Supplement ..."

How people will cry out against me! I hear from afar the shouts of that false wisdom which is ever dragging us onwards, counting the present as nothing, and pursuing without a pause a future which flies as we pursue, that false wisdom which removes us from our place and never brings us to any other.

—Emile

All the papers which I have collected to fill the gaps in my memory and to guide me in my undertaking, have passed into other hands, and will never return to mine.

—Confessions

The praise of living speech, as it *preoccupies* Lévi-Strauss's discourse, is faithful to only one particular motif in Rousseau. This motif comes to terms with and is organized by its contrary: a perpetually reanimated mistrust with regard to the so-called full speech. In the spoken address, presence is at once promised and refused. The speech that Rousseau raised above writing is speech as it should be or rather as it *should have been*. And we must pay attention to that mode, to that tense which relates us to presence within living colloquy. *In fact*, Rousseau had tested the concealment within speech itself, in the mirage of its immediacy. He had recognized and analyzed it with incomparable acumen. We are dispossessed of the longed-for presence in the gesture of language by which we attempt to seize it. To the experience of the "robber robbed" that Starobinski admirably describes in *L'Oeil vivant*. Jean-Jacques is subjected not only in the play of the mirror image which "captures his reflection and exposes his presence." It lies in wait for us from

---

the first word. The speculary dispossession which at the same time institutes and deconstitutes me is also a law of language. It operates as a power of death in the heart of living speech: a power all the more redoubtable because it opens as much as it threatens the possibility of the spoken word.

Having in a certain way recognized this power which, inaugurating speech, dislocates the subject that it constructs, prevents it from being present to its signs, torments its language with a complete writing, Rousseau is nevertheless more pressed to exorcise it than to assume its necessity. That is why, straining toward the reconstruction of presence, he valorizes and disqualifies writing at the same time. At the same time; that is to say, in one divided but coherent movement. We must try not to lose sight of its strange unity. Rousseau condemns writing as destruction of presence and as disease of speech. He rehabilitates it to the extent that it promises the reap-propriation of that of which speech allowed itself to be dispossessed. But by what, if not already a writing older than speech and already installed in that place?

The first movement of this desire is formulated as a theory of language. The other governs the experience of the writer. In the *Confessions*, when Jean-Jacques tries to explain how he became a writer, he describes the passage to writing as the restoration, by a certain absence and by a sort of calculated effacement, of presence disappointed of itself in speech. To write is indeed the only way of keeping or recapturing speech since speech denies itself as it gives itself. Thus an *economy of signs* is organized. It will be equally dis-appointing, closer yet to the very essence and to the necessity of disappoint-ment. One cannot help wishing to master absence and yet we must always let go. Starobinski describes the profound law that commands the space within which Rousseau must move:

> How will he overcome the misunderstanding that prevents him
> from expressing himself according to his true value? How escape
> the risks of improvised speech? To what other mode of com-
> munication can he turn? By what other means manifest himself?
> Jean-Jacques chooses to be *absent* and to *write*. Paradoxically, he
> will hide himself to show himself better, and he will confide in
> written speech: "I would love society like others, if I were not
> sure of showing myself not only at a disadvantage, but as com-
> pletely different from what I am. The part that I have taken of
> *writing and hiding myself* is precisely the one that suits me. If I
> were present, one would never know what I was worth" (*Confes-
> sions*). The admission is singular and merits emphasis: Jean-

Jacques breaks with others, only to present himself to them in
written speech. Protected by solitude, he will turn and re-turn
his sentences at leisure.

(*La Transparence et l'obstacle*)

Let us note that the economy is perhaps indicated in the following: the
operation that substitutes writing for speech also replaces presence by value:
to the *I am* or to the *I am present* thus sacrificed, a *what* I am or a *what I am
worth* is *preferred*. "If I were present, one would never know what I was
worth." I renounce my present life, my present and concrete existence in
order to make myself known in the ideality of truth and value. A well-known
schema. The battle by which I wish to raise myself above my life even while
I retain it, in order to enjoy recognition, is in this case within myself, and
writing is indeed the phenomenon of this battle.

Such would be the writing lesson in Jean-Jacques's existence. The act
of writing would be essentially—and here in an exemplary fashion—the
greatest sacrifice aiming at the greatest symbolic reappropriation of presence.
From this point of view, Rousseau knew that death is not the simple outside
of life. Death by writing also inaugurates life. "I can certainly say that I
never began to live, until I looked upon myself as a dead man" (*Confessions*,
book 6). As soon as one determines it within the system of this economy,
is not the sacrifice—the "literary suicide"—dissipated in the *appearance?* Is
it anything but a symbolic reappropriation? Does it not renounce the *present*
and the *proper* in order to master them better in their meaning, in the ideal
form of truth, of the presence of the present and the proximity or property
of the proper? We would be obliged to decide that a ruse and an appearance
are necessary if in fact we were to abide by these concepts (sacrifice, expenditure, renunciation, symbol, appearance, truth, etc.) which determine
what we here call economy in terms of truth and appearance, starting from
the opposition presence/absence.

But the work of writing and the economy of differance will not be
dominated by this classical conceptuality, this ontology, or this epistemology.
On the contrary, these furnish its hidden premises. Differance does not *resist*
appropriation, it does not impose an exterior limit upon it. Differance began
by *broaching* alienation and it ends by leaving reappropriation *breached*. Until
death. Death is the movement of differance to the extent that that movement
is necessarily finite. This means that differance makes the opposition of
presence and absence possible. Without the possibility of differance, the
desire of presence as such would not find its breathing space. That means
by the same token that this desire carries in itself the destiny of its non-

satisfaction. Differance produces what it forbids, makes possible the very thing that it makes impossible.

If differance is recognized as the obliterated origin of absence and presence, major forms of the disappearing and the appearing of the entity, it would still remain to be known if being, before its determination into absence or presence, is already implicated in the thought of differance. And if differance as the project of the mastery of the entity should be understood with reference to the sense of being. Can one not think the converse? Since the sense of being is never produced as history outside of its determination as presence, has it not always already been caught within the history of metaphysics as the epoch of presence? This is perhaps what Nietzsche wanted to write and what resists the Heideggerian reading of Nietzsche; differance in its *active* movement—*what* is comprehended in the concept of differance without exhausting it—is what not only precedes metaphysics but also extends beyond the thought of being. The latter speaks *nothing other than* metaphysics, even if it exceeds it and thinks it as what it is within its closure.

FROM/OF BLINDNESS TO THE SUPPLEMENT

In terms of this problematical scheme, we must therefore think Rousseau's experience and his theory of writing together, the accord and the discord that, under the name of writing, relate Jean-Jacques to Rousseau, uniting and dividing his proper name. On the side of experience, a recourse to literature as reappropriation of presence, that is to say, as we shall see, of Nature; on the side of theory, an indictment against the negativity of the letter, in which must be read the degeneracy of culture and the disruption of the community.

If indeed one wishes to surround it with the entire constellation of concepts that shares its system, the word *supplement* seems to account for the strange unity of these two gestures.

In both cases, in fact, Rousseau considers writing as a dangerous means, a meanacing aid, the critical response to a situation of distress. When Nature, as self-proximity, comes to be forbidden or interrupted, when speech fails to protect presence, writing becomes necessary. It must *be added* to the word urgently. I have identified in advance one of the forms of this *addition*; speech being natural or at least the natural expression of thought, the most natural form of institution or convention for signifying thought, writing is added to it, is adjoined, as an image or representation. In that sense, it is not natural. It diverts the immediate presence of thought to speech into representation and the imagination. This recourse is not only "bizarre," but dangerous. It is the addition of a technique, a sort of artificial and artful ruse to make speech present when it is actually absent. It is a violence done to the natural destiny of the language:

> Languages are made to be spoken, writing serves only as a supplement to speech. . . . Speech represents thought by conventional signs, and writing represents the same with regard to speech. Thus the art of writing is nothing but a mediated representation of thought.

Writing is dangerous from the moment that representation there claims to be presence and the sign of the thing itself. And there is a fatal necessity, inscribed in the very functioning of the sign, that the substitute make one forget the vicariousness of its own function and make itself pass for the plenitude of a speech whose deficiency and infirmity it nevertheless only *supplements*. For the concept of the supplement—which here determines that of the representative image—harbors within itself two significations whose cohabitation is as strange as it is necessary. The supplement adds itself, it is a surplus, a plenitude enriching another plenitude, the *fullest measure* of presence. It cumulates and accumulates presence. It is thus that art, *technè*, image, representation, convention, etc., come as supplements to nature and are rich with this entire cumulating function. This kind of supplementarity determines in a certain way all of the conceptual oppositions within which Rousseau inscribes the notion of Nature to the extent that it *should* be self-sufficient.

But the supplement supplements. It adds only to replace. It intervenes or insinuates itself *in-the-place-of*; if it fills, it is as if one fills a void. If it represents and makes an image, it is by the anterior default of a presence. Compensatory (*suppléant*) and vicarious, the supplement is an adjunct, a subaltern instance which *takes-(the)-place* (*tient-lieu*). As substitute, it is not simply added to the positivity of a presence, it produces no relief, its place is assigned in the structure by the mark of an emptiness. Somewhere, something can be filled up *of itself*, can accomplish itself, only by allowing itself to be filled through sign and proxy. The sign is always the supplement of the thing itself.

This second signification of the supplement cannot be separated from the first. We shall constantly have to confirm that both operate within Rousseau's texts. But the inflexion varies from moment to moment. Each of the two significations is by turns effaced or becomes discreetly vague in the presence of the other. But their common function is shown in this: whether it adds or substitutes itself, the supplement is *exterior*, outside of the positivity to which it is super-added, alien to that which, in order to be replaced by it, must be other than it. Unlike the *complement*, dictionaries tell us, the supplement is an "*exterior addition*" (Robert's *French Dictionary*).

According to Rousseau, the negativity of evil will always have the form of supplementarity. Evil is exterior to nature, to what is by nature innocent and good. It supervenes upon nature. But always by way of compensation for (*sous l'espèce de la suppléance*) what *ought* to lack nothing at all in itself.

Thus presence, always natural, which for Rousseau more than for others means maternal, *ought to be* self-sufficient. Its *essence*, another name for presence, may be read through the grid of this ought to be (*ce conditionnel*). Like Nature's love, "there is no substitute for a mother's love," says *Emile*. It is in no way *supplemented*, that is to say it does not have to be supplemented, it suffices and is self-sufficient; but that also means that it is irreplacable; what one would substitute for it would not equal it, would be only a mediocre makeshift. Finally it means that Nature does not supplement *itself* at all; Nature's supplement does not proceed from Nature, it is not only inferior to be other than Nature.

Yet all education, the keystone of Rousseauist thought, will be described or presented as a system of substitution (*suppléance*) destined to reconstitute Nature's edifice in the most natural way possible. The first chapter of *Emile* announces the function of this pedagogy. Although there is no substitute for a mother's love, "it is better that the child should suck the breast of a healthy nurse rather than of a petted mother, if he has any further evil to fear from her who has given him birth." It is indeed culture or cultivation that must supplement a deficient nature, a deficiency that cannot by definition be anything but an accident and a deviation from Nature. Culture or cultivation is here called habit; it is necessary and insufficient from the moment when the substitution of mothers is no longer envisaged only "from the physiological point of view":

> Other women, or even other animals, may give him the milk she denies him, but there is no substitute for a mother's love. The woman who nurses another's child in place of her own is a bad mother; how can she be a good nurse? She may become one in time; use [habit] will overcome nature.

Here the problems of natural right, of the relationship between Nature and Society, the concepts of alienation, alterity, and corruption, are adapted most spontaneously to the pedagogic problem of the substitution of mothers and children:

And this affection when developed has its drawbacks, which should make every sensible woman afraid to put her child out to nurse. Is she prepared to divide her mother's rights, or rather to abdicate them in favor of a stranger; to see her child loving another as much as and more than herself.

If, premeditating the theme of writing, I began by speaking of the substitution of mothers, it is because, as Rousseau will himself say, "more depends on this than you realize."

How emphatically would I speak if it were not so hopeless to keep struggling in vain on behalf of a real reform. More depends on this than you realize. Would you restore all men to their primal duties, begin with the mothers; the results will surprise you. Every evil follows in the train of this first sin; the whole moral order is disturbed, nature is quenched in every breast.

Childhood is the first manifestation of the deficiency which, in Nature, calls for substitution (*suppléance*). Pedagogy illuminates perhaps more crudely the paradoxes of the supplement. How is a natural weakness possible? How can Nature ask for forces that it does not furnish? How is a child possible in general?

First Maxim.—Far from being too strong, children are not strong enough for all the claims of nature. Give them full use of such strength as they have and which they will not abuse. *Second Maxim.*—Help them and supply what they lack, in intelligence or in strength, whenever the need is of the body.

All the organization of, and all the time spent in, education will be regulated by this necessary evil: "supply (*suppléer*) . . . [what] . . . is lacking" and to replace Nature. It must be done as little and as late as possible. "One of the best rules of good farming [*culture*] is to *keep things back* as much as possible." "Give nature time to work before you *take over her business* (act in her place—*agir à sa place*)" (italics added).

Without childhood, no supplement would ever appear in Nature. The supplement is here both humanity's good fortune and the origin of its perversion. The health of the human race:

Plants are fashioned by cultivation, and men by education. If man were born big and strong, his size and strength would be useless to him until he had learned to use them; they would create a prejudice against him, by not allowing others to think of as-

sisting him; and let to himself, he would die miserably before
knowing his needs. We complain of the state of infancy; we do
not see that, if man had not begun by being a child, the human
race would have perished.

The threat of perversion:

While the Author of nature has given children the active principle,
He takes care that it shall do little harm by giving them small
power to use it. But as soon as they can think of people as tools
that they are responsible for activating, they use them to carry
out their wishes and to *supplement* their own weakness. This is
how they become tiresome, masterful, imperious, naughty, and
unmanageable; a development which does not spring from a natural love of power, but one which gives it to them, for it does
not need much experience to realize how pleasant it is to act
through the hands of others and to move the world by simply
moving the tongue.

(italics added)

The supplement will always be the moving of the tongue or acting
through the hands of others. In it everything is brought together: progress
as the possibility of perversion, regression toward an evil that is not natural
and that adheres to the power of substitution that permits us to absent
ourselves and act by proxy, through representation, through the hands of
others. Through the written (*par écrit*). This substitution always has the
form of the sign. The scandal is that the sign, the image, or the representer,
become forces and make "the world move."

This scandal is such, and its evil effects are sometimes so irreparable,
that the world seems to turn the wrong way (and we shall see later what
such a *catastrophe* can signify for Rousseau); then Nature becomes the supplement of art and society. It is the moment when evil seems incurable: "As
the child does not know how to be cured, let him know how to be ill. The
one art takes the place of (*supplée*) the other and is often more successful; it
is the art of nature." It is also the moment when maternal nature, ceasing
to be loved, as she ought to be, for herself and in an immediate proximity
("O Nature! O my mother! behold me under thy protection alone! Here
there is no cunning or knavish mortal to thrust himself between me and
thee" [*Confessions*, book 12]) becomes the substitute for another love and for
another attachment:

The contemplation of Nature always had a very great attraction
for his heart; he found there a supplement to the attachments that

he needed; but he would have left the supplement for the thing, if he had had the choice, and he was reduced to converse with the plants only after vain efforts to converse with human beings.

(*Dialogues*)

That botany becomes the supplement of society is more than a catastrophe. It is the catastrophe of the catastrophe. For in Nature, the plant is the most *natural* thing. It is natural *life*. The mineral is distinguished from the vegetable in that it is a dead and useful Nature, servile to man's industry. When man has lost the sense and the taste of true natural riches—plants— he rummages in the entrails of his mother and risks his health:

> The Mineral Kingdom has nothing in itself either amiable or attractive; its riches, enclosed in the breast [womb—*sein*] of the earth, seem to have been removed from the gaze of man in order not to tempt his cupidity; they are there like a reserve to serve one day as a *supplement* to the true wealth which is more within his grasp, and for which he loses taste according to the extent of his corruption. Then he is compelled to call in industry, to struggle, and to labor to alleviate his miseries; he searches the entrails of earth; he goes seeking to its center, at the risk of his life and at the expense of his health, for imaginary goods in place of the real good which the earth offers of herself if he knew how to enjoy it. He *flies from the sun and the day, which he is no longer worthy to see.*
>
> (*Rêveries*, Septième Promenade)

Man has thus put out his eyes, he blinds himself by the desire to rummage in these entrails. Here is the horrible spectacle of the punishment that follows the crime, in sum a simple substitution:

> He buries himself alive, and does well, not being worthy of living in the light of day. There quarries, pits, forges, furnaces, a battery of anvils, hammers, smoke and fire, succeed to the fair images of his rustic labors. The wan faces of the unhappy people who languish in the poisonous vapors of mines, of black forgemen, of hideous cyclops, are the spectacle which the working of the mine substitutes, in the heart [womb] of the earth for that of green fields and flowers, the azure sky, amorous shepherds and robust laborers upon its surface.

Such is the scandal, such the catastrophe. The supplement is what neither Nature nor Reason can tolerate. Neither Nature, our "common mother" (*Rêveries*), nor the reason which is reasonable, if not reasoning (*De l'état de nature*). And had they not done everything to avoid this catastrophe, to protect themselves from this violence and to guard and keep us from this fatal crime? "so that," says the second *Discourse* precisely of mines, "it looks as if nature had taken pains to keep the fatal secret from us." And let us not forget that the violence that takes us toward the entrails of the earth, the moment of mine-blindness, that is, of metallurgy, is the origin of society. For according to Rousseau, as we shall often confirm, agriculture, marking the organization of civil society, assumes the beginning of metallurgy. Blindness thus produces that which is born at the same time as society: the languages, the regulated substitution of signs for things, the order of the supplement. One goes *from blindness to the supplement*. But the blind person cannot see, in its origin, the very things he produces to supplement his sight. *Blindness to the supplement* is the law. And especially blindness to its concept. Moreover, it does not suffice to locate its functioning in order to *see* its meaning. The supplement has no sense and is given to no intuition. We do not therefore make it emerge out of its strange penumbra. We speak its reserve.

Reason is incapable of thinking this double infringement upon Nature: that there is *lack* of Nature and that *because of that very fact* something *is added* to it. Yet one should not say that Reason is *powerless to think this*; it is constituted by that lack of power. It is the principle of identity. It is the thought of the self-identity of the natural being. It cannot even determine the supplement as its other, as the irrational and the nonnatural, for the supplement comes *naturally* to put itself in Nature's place. The supplement is the image and the representation of Nature. The image is neither in nor out of Nature. The supplement is therefore equally dangerous for Reason, the natural health of Reason.

Dangerous supplement. These are the words that Rousseau uses in the *Confessions*. He uses them in a context which is only apparently different, and in order to explain, precisely, a "condition almost unintelligible and inconceivable [to reason]": "In a word, between myself and the most passionate lover there was only one, but that an essential, point of distinction, which makes my condition almost unintelligible and inconceivable."

If we lend to the text below a paradigmatic value, it is only provisional and does not prejudge what the discipline of a future reading might rigorously determine. No model of reading seems to me at the moment ready to measure up to this text—which I would like to read as a *text* and not as a document. Measure up to it fully and rigorously, that is, beyond what already makes the text most legible, and more legible than has been so far thought. My only ambition will be to draw out of it a signification which that presumed future reading will not be able to dispense with (*faire économie*); the economy of a written text, circulating through other texts, leading back to it constantly, conforming to the element of a language and to its regulated functioning. For example, what unites the word "supplement" to its concept was not invented by Rousseau and the originality of its functioning is neither fully mastered by Rousseau nor simply imposed by history and the language, by the history of the language. To speak of the writing of Rousseau is to try to recognize what escapes these categories of passivity and activity, blindness and responsibility. And one cannot abstract from the written text to rush to the signified it *would mean*, since the signified is here the text itself. It is so little a matter of looking for a *truth signified* by these writings (metaphysical or psychological truth: Jean-Jacques's life behind his work) that if the texts that interest us *mean* something, it is the engagement and the appurtenance that encompass existence and writing in the same *tissue*, the same *text*. The same is here called supplement, another name for differance.

Here is the irruption of the dangerous supplement in Nature, between nature and nature, between natural innocence as *virginity* and natural innocence as *pucelage* ("*Pucelage*" is the more earthy French word for the actual physical fact of sexual intactness, in the female the membrane itself. Rousseau applies the word to his own case with some derision, contrasting it to the spiritual innocence of true "virginity"): "In a word, between myself and the most passionate lover there was only one, but that an essential, point of distinction, which makes my condition almost unintelligible and inconceivable." Here, the lineation should not hide the fact that the following paragraph is destined to explain the "only one point of distinction" and the "almost unintelligible and inconceivable" "condition." Rousseau elaborates:

> I had returned from Italy not quite the same as I had entered it, but as, perhaps, no one of my age had ever returned from it. I had brought back, not my virginity by my *pucelage*. I had felt the progress of years; my restless temperament had at last made itself felt, and its first outbreak, quite involuntary, had caused me alarm about my health in a manner which shows better than anything else the innocence in which I had lived up to that time. Soon reassured, I learned that dangerous means of assisting it [*ce dangereux supplément*], which cheats Nature and saves up for young men of my temperament many forms of excess at the expense of their health, strength, and, sometimes, their life.

We read in *Emile* (book 4): "If once he acquires this dangerous habit [*supplément*] he is ruined." In the same book, it is also a question of "mak[ing] up . . . by trading on . . . inexperience" (*suppléer en gagnant de vitesse sur l'experience*; literally "supplementing by out-distancing experience"), and of the "mind, which reinforces (*supplée*) . . . the bodily strength."

The experience of auto-eroticism is lived in anguish. Masturbation reassures ("soon reassured") only through that culpability traditionally attached to the practice, obliging children to assume the fault and to interiorize the threat of castration that always accompanies it. Pleasure is thus lived as the irremediable loss of the vital substance, as exposure to madness and death. It is produced "at the expense of their health, strength, and, sometimes, their life." In the same way, the *Rêveries* will say, the man who "searches the entrails of earth . . . goes seeking to its center, at the risk of his life and at the expense of his health, for imaginary goods in place of the real good which the earth offers of herself if he knew how to enjoy it."

And indeed it is a question of the imaginary. The supplement that "cheats" maternal "nature" operates as writing, and as writing it is dangerous to life. This danger is that of the image. Just as writing opens the crisis of the living speech in terms of its "image," its painting or its representation, so onanism announces the ruin of vitality in terms of imaginary seductions:

> This vice, which shame and timidity find so convenient, possesses, besides a great attraction for lively imaginations—that of being able to dispose of the whole sex as they desire, and to make the beauty which tempts them minister to their pleasures, without being obliged to obtain its consent.
>
> *(Confessions)*

The dangerous supplement, which Rousseau also calls a "fatal advantage," is properly *seductive*; it leads desire away from the good path, makes it err far from natural ways, guides it toward its loss or fall and therefore it is a sort of lapse or scandal (*scandalon*). It thus destroys Nature. But the scandal of Reason is that nothing seems more natural than this destruction of Nature. It is myself who exerts myself to separate myself from the force that Nature has entrusted to me: "Seduced by this fatal advantage, I did my best to destroy the good constitution which Nature had restored to me, and [to] which I had allowed time to strengthen itself." We know what importance *Emile* gives to time, to the slow maturation of natural forces. The entire art of pedagogy is a calculated patience, allowing the work of Nature time to come to fruition, respecting its rhythm and the order of its stages. The dangerous supplement destroys very quickly the forces that Nature has slowly constituted and accumulated. In "out-distancing" natural experience, it runs nonstop (*brûle les étapes*—literally "burns the halting-points") and consumes energy without possibility of recovery. As I shall confirm, like the sign it bypasses the presence of the thing and the duration of being.

The dangerous supplement breaks with Nature. The entire description of this moving away from Nature has a *scene* (*théâtre*). The *Confessions* stage the evocation of the dangerous supplement at the moment when it is a question of making visible a distancing which is neither the same nor an other; Nature draws away at the same time as the Mother, or rather "Mamma," who already signified the disappearance of the true mother and has substituted herself in the well-known ambiguous manner. It is therefore now a question of the distance between Mamma and the person she called "Little one." As *Emile* says, all evil comes from the fact that "women have ceased to be mothers, they do not and will not return to their duty." A certain absence, then, of a certain sort of mother. And the experience of which we speak is such as to reduce that absence as much as to maintain it. A *furtive* experience, that of a thief who needs invisibility: that the mother be invisible and not see. These lines are often quoted:

> I should never have done, if I were to enter into the details of all the follies which the remembrance of this dear mamma caused me to commit when I was no longer in her presence. How often have I kissed my bed, since she had slept in it; my curtains, all the furniture in my room, since they belonged to her, and her beautiful hand had touched them; even the floor, on which I prostrated myself, since she had walked upon it! Sometimes, even in her presence, I was guilty of extravagances, which only the most violent love seemed capable of inspiring. At table one day, just when she had put a piece of food into her mouth, I exclaimed that I saw a hair in it; she put back the morsel on her plate, and I eagerly seized and swallowed it. In a word, between myself and the most passionate lover there was only one, but that an essential, point of distinction, which makes my condition almost unintelligible and inconceivable . . . [A little above, we read] I only felt the full strength of my attachment when I no longer saw her.

THE CHAIN OF SUPPLEMENTS

The discovery of the dangerous supplement will be next cited *among* these "follies," but it will still retain a privilege; Rousseau evokes it after the others and as a sort of explanation of the state inconceivable to reason. For it is not the question of diverting total enjoyment toward a particular substitute, but now of experiencing it or miming it *directly and in its totality*. It is no longer a question of kissing the bed, the floor, the curtains, the furniture, etc., not even of "swallowing" the "piece . . . [that] she had put into her mouth," but of "dispos[ing] of the whole sex as . . . [one] desire[s]."

I remarked that the stage of this theater was not only a setting in the generally understood sense: an ensemble of accessories. The topographic disposition of the experience is not unimportant. Jean-Jacques is in the house of Madame de Varens; close enough to *Mamma* to see her and to nourish his imagination upon her but with the possibility of a partition. It is at the moment when the mother disappears that substitution becomes possible and necessary. The play of maternal presence or absence, this alteration of perception and imagination must correspond to an organization of space; the text argues as follows:

> Add to this habit the circumstances of my position, living as I was with a beautiful woman, caressing her image in the bottom of my heart, seeing her continually throughout the day, surrounded in the evening by objects which reminded me of her, sleeping in the bed in which I knew she had slept! What causes for excitement! Many a reader, who reflects upon them, no doubt already considers me as half-dead! Quite the contrary; that which ought to have destroyed me was just the thing that saved me, at least for a time. Intoxicated with the charm of living with her, with the ardent desire of spending my life with her, I always saw in her, whether she were absent or present, a tender mother, a beloved sister, a delightful friend, and nothing more. . . . She was for me the only woman in the world; and the extreme sweetness of the feelings with which she inspired me did not allow my senses time to awake for others, and protected me against her and all her sex.

This experience was not an event marking an archaic or adolescent period. Not only did it construct or sustain a particular hidden foundation, an edifice of significations. It remained an active obsession whose "present" is constantly reactivated and constituted in its turn, until the end of Jean-Jacques Rousseau's "life" and "text." A little later, a little further on in the text of the *Confessions* (book 4), "a little incident, which I find some difficulty in relating," is related to us. The encounter with a man "addicted to the same vice." Terrified, Jean-Jacques runs away, "trembling as if" he had just "committed a crime." "The recollection of this incident cured me of it for a long time."

For a long time? Rousseau will never stop having recourse to, and accusing himself of, this onanism that permits one to be himself affected by providing himself with presences, by summoning absent beauties. In his eyes it will remain the model of vice and perversion. Affecting oneself by another presence, one *corrupts* oneself [makes oneself other] by oneself (*on s'altère soi-même*). Rousseau neither wishes to think nor can think that this alteration does not simply happen to the self, that it is the self's very origin. He must consider it a contingent evil coming from without to affect the integrity of the subject. But he cannot give up what immediately restores to him the other desired presence; no more than one can give up language. This is why, in this respect as well, as he says in the *Dialogues*, "to the end of his life he will remain an aged child."

The restitution of presence by language, restitution at the same time symbolic and immediate. This contradiction must be thought. Immediate experience of restitution because as experience, as consciousness or con-science, *it dispenses with passage through the world*. What is touching is touched, auto-affection gives itself as pure autarchy. If the presence that it then gives itself is the substitutive symbol of another presence, it has never been possible to desire that presence "in person" before this play of substitution and this symbolic experience of auto-affection. The thing itself does not appear out-side of the symbolic system that does not exist without the possibility of auto-affection. Experience of *immediate* restitution, also because it *does not wait*. It is satisfied then and there and in the moment. If it waits, it is not because the other makes it wait. Pleasure seems no longer to be deferred. "Why give oneself so much trouble in a hope remote from so poor and uncertain a success, when one can, from the very instant . . . " (*Dialogues*).

But what is no longer deferred is also absolutely deferred. The presence that is thus delivered to us in the present is a chimera. Auto-affection is a pure speculation. The sign, the image, the representation, which come to supplement the absent presence are the illusions that sidetrack us. To cul-pability, to the anguish of death and castration, is added or rather is assim-ilated the experience of frustration. *Donner le change* ("sidetracking" or, "giving money"): in whatever sense it is understood, this expression describes the recourse to the supplement admirably. In order to explain his "dislike" for "common prostitutes," Rousseau tells us that in Venice, at thirty-one, the "propensity which had modified all my passions" (*Confessions*) has not dis-appeared: "I had not lost the pernicious habit of satisfying my wants (*donner le change*)."

The enjoyment of the *thing itself* is thus undermined, in its act and in its essence, by frustration. One cannot therefore say that it has an essence or an act (*eidos, ousia, energeia*, etc.). Something promises itself as it escapes, gives itself as it moves away, and strictly speaking it cannot even be called presence. Such is the constraint of the supplement, such, exceeding all the language of metaphysics, is this structure "almost inconceivable to reason." *Almost* inconceivable: simple irrationality, the opposite of reason, are less irritating and waylaying for classical logic. The supplement is maddening because it is neither presence nor absence and because it consequently breaches both our pleasure and our virginity: " . . . abstinence and enjoyment, pleasure and wisdom, escaped me in equal measure" (*Confessions*).

Are things not complicated enough? The symbolic is the immediate, presence is absence, the nondeferred is deferred, pleasure is the menace of death. But one stroke must still be added to this system, to this strange economy of the supplement. In a certain way, it was already legible. A terrifying menace, the supplement is also the first and surest protection; against that very menace. This is why it cannot be given up. And sexual auto-affection, that is auto-affection in general, neither begins nor ends with what one thinks can be circumscribed by the name of masturbation. The supplement has not only the power of *procuring* an absent presence through its image; procuring it for us through the proxy (*procuration*) of the sign, it holds it at a distance and masters it. For this presence is at the same time desired and feared. The supplement transgresses and at the same time respects the interdict. This is what also permits writing as the supplement of speech; but already also the spoken word as writing in general. Its economy exposes and protects us at the same time according to the play of forces and of the differences of forces. Thus, the supplement is dangerous in that it threatens us with death, but Rousseau thinks that it is not at all as dangerous as "cohabitation with women." Pleasure *itself*, without symbol or suppletory, that which would accord us (to) pure presence itself, if such a thing were possible, would be only another name for death. Rousseau says it:

> Enjoyment! Is such a thing made for man? Ah! If I had ever in
> my life tasted the delights of love even once in their plenitude,
> I do not imagine that my frail existence would have been sufficient
> for them, I would have been dead in the act.
>
> (*Confessions*, book 8)

If one abides by the universal evidence, by the necessary and a priori value of this proposition in the form of a sigh, one must immediately recognize that "cohabitation with women," hetero-eroticism, can be lived (effectively, really, as one believes it can be said) only through the ability to reserve within itself its own supplementary protection. In other words, between auto-eroticism and hetero-eroticism, there is not a frontier but an economic distribution. It is within this general rule that the differences are mapped out. This is Rousseau's general rule. And before trying—what I do not pretend to be doing here—to encompass the pure singularity of Rousseau's economy or his writing, we must carefully raise and articulate between them all the structural or essential necessities on their different levels of generality.

It is from a certain determined representation of "cohabitation with women" that Rousseau had to have recourse throughout his life to that type of dangerous supplement that is called masturbation and that cannot be separated from his activity as a writer. To the end. Thérèse—the Thérèse of whom we can speak, Thérèse in the text, whose name and "life" belong to the writing we read—experienced it at her cost. In book 12 of the *Confessions*, at the moment when "I must speak without reserve," the "two reasons combined" of certain "resolutions" is confided to us:

> I must speak without reserve. I have never concealed either my poor mamma's faults or my own. I must not show greater favor to Thérèse either; and, pleased as I am to render honor to one who is so dear to me, neither do I wish to conceal her faults, if it be that an involuntary change in the heart's affections is really a fault. I had long since observed that her affection for me had cooled . . . I was conscious again of an unpleasantness, the effects of which I had formerly felt when with mamma; and the effect was the same with Thérèse. Let us not look for perfections which are not to be found in nature; it would be the same with any other woman whatsoever. . . . My situation, however, was at that time the same, and even aggravated by the animosity of my enemies, who only sought to find me at fault. I was afraid of a repetition; and, not desiring to run the risk of it, I preferred to condemn myself to strict continence, than to expose Thérèse to the risk of finding herself in the same condition again. Besides, I had observed that intercourse with women distinctly aggravated my ill-health. . . . These two reasons combined caused me to form resolutions which I had sometimes been very inconsistent in keeping, but in which I had persevered with greater firmness for the last three or four years.

In the *Manuscrit de Paris*, after "distinctly aggravated my ill-health!" we read: "the corresponding vice, of which I have never been able to cure myself completely, appeared to me to produce less injurious results. These two reasons combined. . . . "

This perversion consists of preferring the sign and protects me from

mortal expenditure. To be sure. But this apparently egotistical economy also
functions within an entire system of moral representation. Egotism is redeemed by a culpability, which determines auto-eroticism as a fatal waste
and a wounding of the self by the self. But as I thus harm only myself, this
perversion is not truly condemnable. Rousseau explains it in more than one
letter. Thus: "With that exception and [the exception of] vices that have
always done harm to me alone, I can expose to all eyes a life irreproachable
in all the secrets of my heart" (to M. de Saint-Germain, 2–26–70). "I have
great vices, but they have never harmed anyone but me" (to M. Le Noir,
1–15–72).

Jean-Jacques could thus look for a supplement to Thérèse only on one
condition: that the system of supplementarity in general be already open in
its possibility, that the play of substitutions be already operative for a long
time and that *in a certain way Thérèse herself be already a supplement.* As Mamma
was already the supplement of an unknown mother, and as the "true mother"
herself, at whom the known "psychoanalyses" of the case of Jean-Jacques
Rousseau stop, was also in a certain way a supplement, from the first trace,
and even if she had not "truly" died in giving birth. Here is the chain of
supplements. The name Mamma already designates one:

> Ah, my Thérèse! I am only too happy to possess you, modest
> and healthy, and not to find what I never looked for. [The ques-
> tion is of "maidenhood" (*pucelage*) which Thérèse has just con-
> fessed to have lost in innocence and by accident.] At first I had
> only sought amusement; I now saw that I had found more and
> gained a companion. A little intimacy with this excellent girl, a
> little reflection upon my situation, made me feel that, while think-
> ing only of my pleasures, I had done much to promote my hap-
> piness. *To supply the place of* my extinguished ambition, I needed
> a lively sentiment which should *take complete possession of* [literally
> "fill"—*remplit*] my heart. In a word, I needed a successor to
> mamma. As I should never live with her again, I wanted someone
> to live with her pupil, in whom I might find the simplicity and
> docility of heart which she had found in me. I felt it necessary
> that the gentle tranquility of private and domestic life *should make
> up* to me for the loss of the brilliant career which I was renouncing.
> When I was quite alone, I felt a void in my heart, which it only
> needed another heart to *fill.* Destiny had deprived me of, or, at
> least in part, alienated me from, that heart for which Nature had
> formed me. From that moment I was alone; for *with me it has*

always been everything or nothing. I found in Thérèse the substitute
[supplément] that I needed.

Through this sequence of supplements a necessity is announced: that
of an infinite chain, ineluctably multiplying the supplementary mediations
that produce the sense of the very thing they defer: the mirage of the thing
itself, of immediate presence, of originary perception. Immediacy is derived.
That all begins through the intermediary is what is indeed "inconceivable
[to reason]."

THE EXORBITANT. QUESTION OF METHOD

"For me there has never been an intermediary between everything or
nothing." The intermediary is the midpoint and the mediation, the middle
term between total absence and the absolute plenitude of presence. It is clear
that mediacy is the name of all that Rousseau wanted opinionatedly to efface.
This wish is expressed in a deliberate, sharp, thematic way. It does not have
to be deciphered. Jean-Jacques recalls it here at the very moment when he
is spelling out the supplements that are linked together to replace a mother
or a Nature. And here the supplement occupies the middle point between
total absence and total presence. The play of substitutions fills and marks a
determined lack. But Rousseau argues as if the recourse to the supplement—
here to Thérèse—was going to appease his impatience when confronted with
the intermediary: "From that moment I was alone; for me there has never
been an intermediary between everything and nothing. I found in Thérèse
the substitute that I needed." The virulence of this concept is thus appeased,
as if one were able to *arrest it*, domesticate it, tame it.

This brings up the question of the usage of the word "supplement": of
Rousseau's situation within the language and the logic that assures to this
word or this concept sufficiently *surprising* resources so that the presumed
subject of the sentence might always say, through using the "supplement,"
more, less, or something other than what he *would mean (voudrait dire)*. This
question is therefore not only of Rousseau's writing but also of our reading.
We should begin by taking rigorous account of this *being held within (prise)*
or this *surprise*: the writer writes *in* a language and *in* a logic whose proper
system, laws, and life his discourse by definition cannot dominate absolutely.
He uses them only by letting himself, after a fashion and up to a point, be
governed by the system. And the reading must always aim at a certain
relationship, unperceived by the writer, between what he commands and
what he does not command of the patterns of the language that he uses. This

relationship is not a certain quantitative distribution of shadow and light, of weakness or of force, but a signifying structure that critical reading should *produce*.

What does produce mean here? In my attempt to explain that, I would initiate a justification of my principles of reading. A justification, as we shall see, entirely negative, outlining by exclusion a space of reading that I shall not fill here: a task of reading.

To produce this signifying structure obviously cannot consist of reproducing, by the effaced and respectful doubling of commentary, the conscious, voluntary, intentional relationship that the writer institutes in his exchanges with the history to which he belongs thanks to the element of language. This moment of doubling commentary should no doubt have its place in a critical reading. To recognize and respect all its classical exigencies is not easy and requires all the instruments of traditional criticism. Without this recognition and this respect, critical production would risk developing in any direction at all and authorize itself to say almost anything. But this indispensable guardrail has always only *protected*, it has never *opened*, a reading.

Yet if reading must not be content with doubling the text, it cannot legitimately transgress the text toward something other than it, toward a referent (a reality that is metaphysical, historical, psychobiographical, etc.) or toward a signified outside the text whose content could take place, could have taken place outside of language, that is to say, in the sense that we give here to that word, outside of writing in general. That is why the methodological considerations that we risk applying here to an example are closely dependent on general propositions that we have elaborated above; as regards the absence of the referent or the transcendental signified. *There is nothing outside of the text* [there is no outside-text; *il n'y a pas de hors-texte*]. And that is neither because Jean-Jacques's life, or the existence of Mamma or Thérèse *themselves*, is not of prime interest to us, nor because we have access to their so-called "real" existence only in the text and we have neither any means of altering this, nor any right to neglect this limitation. All reasons of this type would already be sufficient, to be sure, but there are more radical reasons. What we have tried to show by following the guiding line of the "dangerous supplement," is that in what one calls the real life of these existences "of flesh and bone," beyond and behind what one believes can be circumscribed as Rousseau's text, there has never been anything but writing; there have never been anything but supplements, substitutive significations which could only come forth in a chain of differential references, the "real" supervening, and being added only while taking on meaning from a trace and from an invocation of the supplement, etc. And thus to infinity, for we have read, *in the text*, that the absolute present, Nature, that which words like "real mother" name, have always already escaped, have never existed; that what opens meaning and language is writing as the disappearance of natural presence.

Although it is not commentary, our reading must be intrinsic and remain within the text. That is why, in spite of certain appearances, the locating of the word *supplement* is here not at all psychoanalytical, if by that we understand an interpretation that takes us outside of the writing toward a psychobiographical signified, or even toward a general psychological structure that could rightly be separated from the signifier. This method has occasionally been opposed to the traditional doubling commentary; it could be shown that it actually comes to terms with it quite easily. *The security with which the commentary considers the self-identity of the text, the confidence with which it carves out its contour, goes hand in hand with the tranquil assurance that leaps over the text toward its presumed content, in the direction of the pure signified.* And in effect, in Rousseau's case, psychoanalytical studies like those of Dr. Laforgue transgress the text only after having read it according to the most current methods. The reading of the literary "symptom" is most banal, most academic, most naive. And once one has thus blinded oneself to the very tissue of the "symptom," to its proper texture, one cheerfully exceeds it toward a psychobiographical signified whose link with the literary signifier then becomes perfectly extrinsic and contingent. One recognizes the other aspect of the same gesture when, in general works on Rousseau, in a package of classical shape that gives itself out to be a synthesis that faithfully restores, through commentary and compilation of themes, the totality of the work and the thought, one encounters a chapter of biographical and psychoanalytical cast on the "problem of sexuality in Rousseau," with a reference in an Appendix to the author's medical case history.

If it seems to us in principle impossible to separate, through interpretation or commentary, the signified from the signifier, and thus to destroy writing by the writing that is yet reading, we nevertheless believe that this impossibility is historically articulated. It does not limit attempts at deciphering in the same way, to the same degree, and according to the same rules. Here we must take into account the history of the text in general. When we speak of the writer and of the encompassing power of the language to which he is subject, we are not only thinking of the writer in literature. The philosopher, the chronicler, the theoretician in general, and at the limit everyone writing, is thus taken by surprise. But, in each case, the person writing is inscribed in a determined textual system. Even if there is never a pure signified, there are different relationships as to that which, from the signifier, is *presented* as the irreducible stratum of the signified. For example, the philosophical text, although it is in fact always written, includes, precisely as its philosophical specificity, the project of effacing itself in the face of the signified content which it transports and in general teaches. Reading should be aware of this project, even if, in the last analysis, it intends to expose the project's failure. The entire history of texts, and within it the history of literary forms in the West, should be studied from this point of view. With the exception of a thrust or a point of resistance which has only been very lately recognized as such, literary writing has, almost always and almost everywhere, according to some fashions and across very diverse ages, lent itself to this *transcendent* reading, in that search for the signified which we here put in question, not to annul it but to understand it within a system to which such a reading is blind. Philosophical literature is only one example within this history but it is among the most significant. And it interests us particularly in Rousseau's case. Who at the same time and for profound reasons produced a philosophical literature to which belong *The Social Contract* and *La Nouvelle Héloïse*, and chose to live by literary writing; by a writing which would not be exhausted by the message—philosophical or otherwise— which it could, so to speak, deliver. And what Rousseau has said, as philosopher or as psychologist, of writing in general, cannot be separated from the system of his own writing. We should be aware of this.

This poses formidable problems. Problems of outlining in particular. Let me give three examples.

1. If the course I have followed in the reading of the "supplement" is not merely psychoanalytical, it is undoubtedly because the habitual psychoanalysis of literature begins by putting the literary signifier as such within parentheses. It is no doubt also because psychoanalytic theory itself is for me a collection of texts belonging to my history and my culture. To that extent, if it marks my reading and the writing of my interpretation, it does not do so as a principle or a truth that one could abstract from the textual system that I inhabit in order to illuminate it with complete neutrality. In a certain way, I am *within* the history of psychoanalysis as I am *within* Rousseau's text. Just as Rousseau drew upon a language that was already there—and which is found to be somewhat our own, thus assuring us a certain minimal readability of French literature—in the same way we operate today within a certain network of significations marked by psychoanalytic theory, even if we do not master it and even if we are assured of never being able to master it perfectly.

But it is for another reason that this is not even a somewhat inarticulate psychoanalysis of Jean-Jacques Rousseau. Such a psychoanalysis is already obliged to have located all the structures of appurtenance within Rousseau's text, all that is not unique to it—by reason of the encompassing power and that already-thereness of the language or of the culture—all that could be inhabited rather than produced by writing. Around the irreducible point of originality of this writing an immense series of structures, of historical totalities of all orders, are organized, enveloped, and blended. Supposing that psychoanalysis can by rights succeed in outlining them and their interpretations, supposing that it takes into account the entire history of metaphysics—the history of that Western metaphysics that entertains relationships of cohabitation with Rousseau's text, it would still be necessary for this psychoanalysis to elucidate the law of its own appurtenance to metaphysics and Western culture. Let us not pursue this any further. We have already measured the difficulty of the task and the element of frustration in our interpretation of the supplement. We are sure that something irreducibly Rousseauist is captured there but we have carried off, at the same time, a yet quite unformed mass of roots, soil, and sediments of all sorts.

2. Even supposing that Rousseau's text can be rigorously isolated and articulated within history in general, and then within the history of the sign "supplement," one must still take into consideration many other possibilities. Following the appearances of the word "supplement" and of the coresponding concept or concepts, we traverse a certain path within Rousseau's text. To be sure, this particular path will assure us the economy of a synopsis. But are other paths not possible? And as long as the totality of paths is not effectively exhausted, how shall we justify this one?

3. In Rousseau's text, after having indicated—by anticipation and as a prelude—the function of the sign "supplement," I now prepare myself to give special privilege, in a manner that some might consider exorbitant, to certain texts like the *Essay on the Origin of Languages* and other fragments on the theory of language and writing. By what right? And why these short texts, published for the most part after the author's death, difficult to classify, of uncertain date and inspiration?

To all these questions and within the logic of their system, there is no satisfying response. In a certain measure and in spite of the theoretical precautions that I formulate, my choice is in fact *exorbitant*.

But what is the exorbitant?

I wished to reach the point of a certain exteriority in relation to the totality of the age of logocentrism. Starting from this point of exteriority, a certain deconstruction of that totality which is also a traced path, of that orb (*orbis*) which is also orbitary (*orbita*), might be broached. The first gesture of this departure and this deconstruction, although subject to a certain his torical necessity, cannot be given methodological or logical intraorbitary assurances. Within the closure, one can only judge its style in terms of the accepted oppositions. It may be said that this style is empiricist and in a certain way that would be correct. The *departure* is radically empiricist. It proceeds like a wandering thought on the possibility of itinerary and of method. It is affected by nonknowledge as by its future and it *ventures out* deliberately. I have myself defined the form and the vulnerability of this empiricism. But here the very concept of empiricism destroys itself. To *exceed* the metaphysical orb is an attempt to get out of the orbit (*orbita*), to think the entirety of the classical conceptual oppositions, particularly the one within which the value of empiricism is held: the opposition of philosophy and nonphilosophy, another name for empiricism, for this incapability to sustain on one's own and to the limit the coherence of one's own discourse, for being produced as truth at the moment when the value of truth is shattered, for escaping the internal contradictions of skepticism, etc. *The thought of this historical opposition between philosophy and empiricism is not simply empirical and it cannot be thus qualified without abuse and misunderstanding.*

Let us make the diagram more specific. What is exorbitant in the reading of Rousseau? No doubt Rousseau, as I have already suggested, has only a very relative privilege in the history that interests us. If we merely wished to situate him within this history, the attention that we accord him would be clearly disproportionate. But that is not our intention. We wish to identify a decisive articulation of the logocentric epoch. For purposes of this identification Rousseau seems to us to be most revealing. That obviously supposes that we have already prepared the exit, determined the repression of writing as the fundamental operation of the epoch, read a certain number of texts but not all of them, a certain number of Rousseau's texts but not all of them. This avowal of empiricism can sustain itself only by the strength of the question. The opening of the question, the departure from the closure of a self-evidence, the putting into doubt of a system of oppositions, all these movements necessarily have the form of empiricism and of errancy. At any rate, they cannot be described, *as to past norms*, except in this form. No other trace is available, and as these errant questions are not absolute beginnings in every way, they allow themselves to be effectively reached, on one entire surface, by this description which is also a criticism. We must begin *wherever we are* and the thought of the trace, which cannot not take the scent into account, has already taught us that it was impossible to justify a point of departure absolutely. *Wherever we are*: in a text where we already believe ourselves to be.

Let us narrow the arguments down further. In certain respects, the theme of supplementarity is certainly no more than one theme among others. It is in a chain, carried by it. Perhaps one could substitute something else for it. *But it happens that this theme describes the chain itself, the being-chain of a textual chain, the structure of substitution, the articulation of desire and of language, the logic of all conceptual oppositions taken over by Rousseau,* and particularly the role and the function, in his system, of the concept of Nature. It tells us in a text what a text is, it tells us in writing what writing is, in Rousseau's writing it tells us Jean-Jacques's desire, etc. If we consider, according to the axial proposition of this essay, that there is nothing outside the text, our ultimate justification would be the following: the concept of the supplement and the theory of writing designate textuality itself in Rousseau's text in an indefinitely multiplied structure—*en abyme* [*in an abyss*]—to employ the current phrase. And we shall see that this abyss is not a happy or unhappy accident. An entire theory of the structural necessity of the abyss will be gradually constituted in our reading; the indefinite process of supplementarity has always already *infiltrated* presence, always already inscribed there the space of repetition and the splitting of the self. Representation *in the abyss* of presence is not an accident of presence; the desire of presence is, on the contrary, born from the abyss (the indefinite multiplication) of representation, from the representation of representation, etc. The supplement itself is quite exorbitant, in every sense of the word.

Thus Rousseau inscribes textuality in the text. But its operation is not simple. It tricks with a gesture of effacement, and strategic relations like the relationships of force among the two movements form a complex design. This design seems to us to be represented in the handling of the concept of the supplement. Rousseau cannot utilize it at the same time in all the virtualities of its meaning. The way in which he determines the concept and, in so doing, lets himself be determined by that very thing that he excludes from it, the direction in which he bends it, here as addition, there as substitute, now as the positivity and exteriority of evil, now as a happy auxiliary, all this conveys neither a passivity nor an activity, neither an unconsciousness nor a lucidity on the part of the author. Reading should not only abandon these categories—which are also, let us recall in passing, the founding categories of metaphysics—but should produce the law of this relationship to the concept of the supplement. It is certainly a production, because I do not simply duplicate what Rousseau thought of this relationship. The concept of the supplement is a sort of blind spot in Rousseau's text, the not-seen that opens and limits visibility. But the production, if it attempts to make the not-seen accessible to sight, does not leave the text. It has moreover only believed it was doing so by illusion. It is contained in the transformation of the language it designates, in the regulated exchanges between Rousseau and history. We know that these changes only take place by way of the language and the text, in the infrastructural sense that we now give to that word. And what we call production is necessarily a text, the system of a writing and of a reading which we know is ordered around its own blind spot. We know this a priori, but only now and with a knowledge that is not a knowledge at all.

SHIERRY M. WEBER

The Aesthetics of Rousseau's Pygmalion

Pygmalion, Rousseau's one-scene lyric drama, may be fruitfully considered as a meditation on the nature of the relationship between the artist and his work. The last lines of *Pygmalion* give us an indication as to Rousseau's implicit aesthetic theory. The sculptor Pygmalion is in love with a statue he has made, Galathée. Galathée comes to life. She touches herself, identifies herself as "moi," touches Pygmalion and says "Ah! encore moi." To this Pygmalion responds, "Oui, c'est toi, c'est toi seule: je t'ai donné tout mon être; je ne vivrai plus que par toi." Rousseau will define both artist and work in terms of consciousness or selfness—"moi" and "toi." It is clear already from these lines, however, that the relation of "moi" and "toi," of artist and work, will not be a simple one. On the one hand artist and work share a common self; Pygmalion has given his being to Galathée. The work might thus be said to be the externalized self of the artist. On the other hand the common self is now Galathée's rather than Pygmalion's—"c'est toi seule." The work is given priority over the artist. The sort of double perspective in effect here derives from Rousseau's notion of the reflective, discontinuous nature of the self. This conception, as we shall see, is implicit throughout in *Pygmalion*, and it is the basis for the aesthetic notions implied in these final lines.

Rousseau develops his notion of the self and works out his aesthetic conceptions through an exploration of Pygmalion's desire for Galathée, the dominant motif of *Pygmalion*. We can arrive at the aesthetic conceptions

From *Modern Language Notes* 83, no. 6 (December 1968). © 1968 by the Johns Hopkins University Press, Baltimore/London.

developed in *Pygmalion* only through an interpretation of this desire. An examination of two important characterizations of the work, however, reveals how difficult this task has proven to be. Writing of *Pygmalion* in *Dichtung und Wahrheit*, Goethe accuses Rousseau of degrading the work of art, a product of mind or spirit, to a mere sensuous object:

> Diese wunderliche Produktion schwankt . . . zwischen Natur und Kunst, mit dem falschen Bestreben, diese in jene aufzulösen. Wir sehen einen Künstler, der das Vollkommenste geleistet hat, und doch nicht Befriedigung darin findet, seine Idee ausser sich, kunstgemäss dargestellt und ihr ein höheres Leben verliehen zu haben; nein! sie soll auch in das irdische Leben zu ihm herabegezogen werden. Er will das Höchste, was Geist und Tat hervorgebracht, durch den gemeinsten Akt der Sinnlichkeit zerstören.
>
> *(Dichtung und Wahrheit*, 3, book 11)

As we have seen, Rousseau is actually in agreement with Goethe on the spirituality of the work of art, but Goethe considers Pygmalion's desire for Galathée to contradict that conception of the work. Jean Starobinski, on the other hand, in his *Jean-Jacques Rousseau, La Transparence et l'obstacle*, interprets Pygmalion's desire not as a sensuous but as a narcissistic one, with complete union of self and other as its object: "Pygmalion implore le miracle qui abolira l'extériorité de l'oeuvre et substituera l'intériorité de la passion narcissique." Accordingly, he accuses Rousseau of being unwilling to distinguish between artist and work. He describes the end of the play as follows:

> Le deux parts d'un même moi sont réunies. La séparation est abolie, qui divisait l'artiste de ce qu'il avait produit. Le travail créateur n'a eu lieu que pour être repris dans l'unité d'un moi aimant.

Starobinski sees that Rousseau conceives artist and work as sharing a common self, but he fails to see the distinction Rousseau maintains within that unity. Unlike Goethe, he insists on the importance of the work's "exteriority," its existence as sensuous object (which becomes united with spirit in some undefined manner); he offers no other characterization of what makes the work of art something other than the artist:

> /Pygmalion/ s'est dédoublé, une partie de son âme a passé dans cette chose sans vie; mais Pygmalion ne consent pas à se séparer de ce qu'il a créé. Il n'accepte pas que l'oeuvre d'art soit autre que lui-même, qu'elle lui reste étrangère.

Both Goethe's and Starobinski's interpretations err in being only partial descriptions of *Pygmalion*, but they do indicate crucial points in Rousseau's conception. They see one aspect of Rousseau's enterprise and imagine it to be necessarily incompatible with one of their aesthetic premises. Rousseau is engaged in relating things which to them seem mutually exclusive. He shows how artist and work can both be characterized in terms of selfness and yet be different, and he tries to relate that difference to the physical existence of the work of art, its presence within "earthly life." Focussing on Pygmalion's desire for Galathée permits Rousseau to raise both these questions.

With these aspects of Rousseau's aesthetics in mind we can situate him within the development of aesthetic thought in the eighteenth and nineteenth centuries. His starting point is the eighteenth-century question of the relation of the work of art to reality, the question which is the basis both of mimetic aesthetic notions and of speculations, like Baumgarten's, concerning a "sensuous rationality"—the possible general validity of judgments relating to the senses rather than to reason. Rousseau answers the question in terms of the self, the subject, as do all varieties of early nineteenth-century idealist aesthetics. Despite many common elements, however, Rousseau's position differs from an idealist one in several important respects. He does not present the work as the objectification or representation of an absolute subject but rather defines it in relation to the finite self of the artist, and he does so by means of a phenomenology of the consciousness of the finite aesthetic subject. Nor, as we shall see in more detail later, does he conceive objectification of the spirit to consist in a harmonizing or unification of matter and spirit in the aesthetic phenomenon. Rousseau's position is closest to Kant's critical enterprise, which occupies a similarly pivotal position in the development from eighteenth- to nineteenth-century thought. For Kant, critical philosophy means establishing the nature and limits of reason through an analysis of the a priori nature of the subject and its role in making experience possible. Rousseau's enterprise is akin to Kant's in taking the a priori structure of the representative individual, of finite consciousness, as its starting point and its horizon. Kant takes empiricism's insistence on experience and rationalism's interest in the a priori nature of reason and unites them in an analysis of reason and its limits. His successors go beyond him in insisting that something unlimited—absolute—must be the basis for the operations of the understanding and in particular for the ability of reason to construct its own critique. They also move beyond Kant in exploring the dynamic nature of reality, as, for example, in Schelling's notion of reality as the progressive unfolding of the absolute. They remain, however, decisively influenced by

Kant in that they retain the subject as the explicitly acknowledged basis of their systems. Kant's position, however, is unique in attempting to establish a sphere of validity while renouncing knowledge of the absolute.

In aesthetics, the influence of the "critical turn" in philosophy can be seen in the movement from a neoclassical conception of art as the imitation of real essences to the idealist-romantic conception of it as the objectification of the absolute subject through a dynamic process. Art is made subjective and dynamic but is still seen in relation to an absolute which transcends the finite subject. In this development as in the philosophical one Kant's conceptions are crucial turning points. Kant took up the empiricist notion of a subjective, nonconceptual faculty of aesthetic judgment, taste, and interpreted its subjectivity as consisting not in its irrationality but in its being reflective awareness of a subjective state of mind, the harmony of imagination and understanding. In his theory of artistic production and genius, Kant emphasized the negative or paradoxical presence of the absolute in the work of art. The aesthetic idea which genius externalizes or represents is itself a representation within the forms of intuition—i.e., in the sensuous realm— of an idea which can have no place in experience. The sensuous artistic representation thus points beyond itself to the infinitude of the supersensuous realm. The uniqueness of these notions, as of Rousseau's, lies in their joining of finite subjectivity with validity on the one hand and limitation or negativity insofar as the absolute is concerned on the other. While sharing Kant's standpoint and developing many aesthetic notions similar to his, Rousseau moves beyond Kant's aesthetic in certain respects. He unites the productivity and receptive aspects of the aesthetic subject (genius and taste) in the figure of the artist as spectator, and he moves beyond the artist-spectator to consider the nature of the work of art itself more fully than Kant will do. *Pygmalion* can thus be considered a further step in the development of a critical aesthetics.

Only a detailed examination of *Pygmalion* can reveal its full import. I shall proceed in this examination as Rousseau does, from the nature of consciousness as such to the specific characteristics of the aesthetic subject and then to the nature of the work of art. We may begin by returning to Pygmalion's last words—"je t'ai donné tout mon être; je ne vivrai plus que par toi," and asking what kind of self, what underlying conception of consciousness, is implied by the possibility of this transfer of being. It is important to note that Pygmalion does not give Galathée life as God did Adam, without it diminishing him, nor does he die on finishing his work, having passed his life on to it, as is the case in some legends concerning artists. In creating Galathée Pygmalion dies in some sense, as we shall see, but in another sense he survives to be the experiencing consciousness of the "scène lyrique." What we have is a self which experiences separation from itself as an event in time. This experience is not simply the positive one of giving; it also has a negative quality for Pygmalion, for it seems that the better part of himself has left him. "Je survis à mon talent," he complains near the beginning of the scene. "J'ai perdu mon génie." His genius has left him, one might say, to become Galathée's animating spirit. The loss which Pygmalion suffers is a radical one. The very source of being has moved from Pygmalion to Galathée: at first he created her, but at the end he lives only through her. Thus for Rousseau the self, as represented by Pygmalion, neither enjoys unbroken duration nor suffers final apocalyptic annihilation. Rather—and here we see what finiteness means for Rousseau—it contains within it, that is, it experiences, a moment of negation or radical discontinuity.

This negativity of the self, which means that the self is not identical with itself or that it is not substantial, determines two central aspects of *Pygmalion*. The first we may call its reflective structure, which is related to the role of time mentioned above. Its importance becomes evident if we ask *when* the central event of the scene, the animation of Galathée occurs. Obviously the animation of the statue is in some sense equivalent to the making of the statue by Pygmalion, which occurs before the beginning of the scene. The animation is a recapitulation of the creation. In both senses, Rousseau is saying, the artist gives life to the work. But why should Rousseau need to understand the event in these two ways, and what is the difference between them? The difference is that between action and reflection, and what Rousseau presents us with in *Pygmalion* is not action but reflection. When the play opens the transition between them has been made; this is one meaning of Pygmalion's saying, "Quelle étrange revolution s'est faite en moi?" As the designation "scène lyrique" indicates, *Pygmalion* is a phenomenon of reflective consciousness; in Kantian terms, it is ideal rather than real. The recapitulation of Galathée's creation is an internal reliving of it, and the scene is Pygmalion's mind. Rousseau shows us the aesthetic subject not as producer but as one now contemplator, having been artist. He shows us not Pygmalion making a statue but Pygmalion reflecting on the act of making it, Pygmalion interpreting creation as animation. Or, what is in fact the same thing, he shows us not physical but mental action—Pygmalion's feelings toward the statue he has made. Pygmalion's desire for Galathée, that is, is a reflective state. The "scène lyrique" is thus reflection both in the sense of interpretation after the fact and in the sense of a movement inward to become aware of subjective states of mind. These two aspects of reflection are closely related, for not only are Pygmalion's feelings reflective but his interpretation is subjective, or directed toward the nature of the self. In that what reflection examines is not only action but the transition from action to reflection—for the act of making the statue is itself the transition, the transfer of being—it is a movement inward toward the self, as reflective consciousness. The dichotomy of action and reflection, it should be emphasized, is not apocalyptic and absolute but is integrated into the temporal experience of finite consciousness. Action is experienced as past, reflection as present. Pygmalion made the statue before the beginning of the scene. Not only action but the acting self is experienced as past. This is one form of the division of self from self, and the movement inward bridges the discontinuity.

The fact that Rousseau conceives the self in terms of the discontinuity between action and reflection throws an interesting light on the primitivism with which he is frequently charged. Why should Rousseau turn back to an old Greek legend about an artist? Ernst Kris, in [an] article in *Psychoanalytic Explorations in Art, . . .* discusses the Pygmalion story as dealing with the separation of the realm of the aesthetic from that of nature. It turns, that is, on the distinction between the natural object and the artistic image or imitation of it. In calling *Pygmalion* an attempt to dissolve art in nature, Goethe is accusing Rousseau of aesthetic primitivism, of trying to return to the stage before the separation of art from nature. Kris's remarks on the Greek story suggests that Goethe's point is indeed relevant. But Goethe construes Rousseau's relation to the legend falsely. Both the Greek and the Rousseauian versions of the story are concerned not with a movement to reunite art and nature but with the separation of art from nature. Both are premised on a distinction between the work of art and the natural object (according to the Greek legend, Galathea could not have children). Rousseau's *Pygmalion,* however, is a reflection on the Greek story, a conscious reinterpretation of it, not a nostalgic one which seeks to return to an earlier stage but one which moves to a still further stage in aesthetic thought, a stage in which the work of art is still further distinguished from the natural object. In this sense also Rousseau's reflective *Pygmalion* is a *Reflexion in sich,* for it shows that the question of the distinction between the model and the image, the subject of the Greek story, leads to and has as its real content the nonmimetic notions Rousseau develops in *Pygmalion.* Thus Rousseau's primitivism, his interest in the early stages of a process, indicates not a desire to return literally— really—to those stages but the intention of considering the development ideally, in reflection. Furthermore, Rousseau's reflection is concerned not with an original stage but with the passage, made discontinuous by the nature of reflective consciousness, from one stage to another. The Greek story deals with the movement away from the identification of the work of art with natural objects, Rousseau's with the passage beyond the mimetic notions thus established. Rousseau's primitivism, in short, is characterized by the same reflective structure that governs *Pygmalion*.

Rousseau's conception of the negativity of the self is manifested not only in the reflective structure of the *scène* in its form, but also in Pygmalion's desire for Galathée, which governs the internal dynamic of *Pygmalion*. Desire implies a subject and an object, a desiring self and an other which is desired. Starobinski's criticism of *Pygmalion* asserts that Pygmalion wishes to obliterate this distinction. What Rousseau shows, however, is that the self encompasses the polarities subject and object, self and other. The ideal moment of desire, as opposed to its real or sensuous moment, is desire for something which is self and other at once. The reflective structure of *Pygmalion* means that it is this ideal moment that Rousseau is concerned with and that for the relation of the aesthetic subject to the work of art the ideal moment of desire is the relevant one. Pygmalion's final recognition that he and Galathée share the same self is not the successful exclusion of otherness but the recognition that his desire for her is ideal rather than real.

Pygmalion's own reflections on his desire lead to a crucial passage in the text. When the play opens, Pygmalion feels that his productive force, his genius, has been exhausted, but he is still tormented by an "ardeur interne" which, he finally admits, is desire for Galathée. This admission leads him to various attempts to formulate the nature of the work of art such that it would be possible to feel sexual desire for it. He finally justifies his desire as being aroused by beauty: "Ma seule folie est de discerner la beauté, mon seul crime est d'y être sensible." Thus he has characterized his desire as aesthetic rather than sensual. The passage with which we are concerned occurs at this point. Pygmalion turns his attention to the statue and says:

> Quel traits de feu semblent sortir de cet objet pour embraser mes sens, et retourner avec mon âme à leur source! Hélas! il reste immobile et froid, tandis que mon coeur embrasé par ses charmes, voudroit quitter mon corps pour aller échauffer le sein. Je crois, dans mon délire, pouvoir m'élancer hors de moi; je crois pouvoir lui donner ma vie, et l'animer de mon âme. Ah! que Pygmalion meure, pour vivre dans Galathée . . . Que dis-je, o Ciel! Si j'étois elle, je ne la verrois pas, je ne serois pas celui qui l'aime! Non, que ma Galathée vive, et que je ne sois pas elle. Ah! que je sois toujours un autre, pour vouloir toujours être elle, pour la voir, pour l'aimer, pour en être aimé.

This passage shows the paradoxical, self-contradictory structure of desire and provides the basis for the interpretation of Galathée's animation given by Pygmalion in his last speech. Desire as Pygmalion articulates it here has two moments. The first is a movement toward the object, with union with the object, dissolution in the object, as its goal: "Que Pygmalion meure, pour vivre dans Galathée!" The second is a movement back away from the object, because the love relationship is possible only when lover and beloved are separate. In order to love Galathée, Pygmalion must be other than she. What is important is that the result of these two moments is a movement of self-alienation. The self becomes one with the other and then retreats from the self it has become, having given up its selfhood to the other. The whole process is represented, in condensed form, in the words "que je sois toujours un autre." For the movement back from the other, the rebirth after death in union, is not simply a return to the original state of affairs. Rather, the self is now, in the second phase, conceived in terms of the other, as not the other. "Que je sois toujours un autre" means not "let Pygmalion become other than Pygmalion" so much as "let Pygmalion become other than Galathée, who he has become." Thus the state of desire encompasses the same moment of negativity that characterizes the reflective state. In that it represents a movement back to the self it is a reflective state and must be distinguished from desire conceived as appetite, an impulse which has its end outside itself. Rousseau's notion of desire does not have the assimilation or destruction of the object as its goal but rather preserves the object in negating, momentarily, the subject. The animation of Galathée follows from the conception of desire. When Pygmalion says at the end of the scene that he has given Galathée his being, he is affirming that he has become another.

The negative moment in desire, its effect of alienating the self from itself appears in *Pygmalion* in the form of irony. The paradoxical structure of desire is such that desire can never be fulfilled because union with the object is experienced as having already occurred. To Starobinski's assertion that Rousseau ends *Pygmalion* with the realization of the desired union between artist and work, one would have to respond that the union has in fact been achieved, in the transfer of self from Pygmalion to Galathée which is both creation and animation, but that when *Pygmalion* ends artist and work have once again become separate. At the moment when Galathée comes alive, Pygmalion's mood has already turned to "ironie amère," to an awareness of the negativity of his situation, and this mood persists through the conclusion of the scene.

Thus desire involves the other becoming self and the self becoming other. The "real," authentic self is separated from the experiencing self, and the experiencing self seems to be merely the negation of that other, real self. Rousseau represents this discontinuity temporally—the real self is the one which one has become but is no longer—just as he represents the structure of reflection in terms of time. But sexual difference is also, for Rousseau, a way of representing the discontinuity of self and other. This, and not the desire to equate the work of art with a sensuous natural object, is why Rousseau presents the relationship of artist to work as one of sexual desire. It is ideal rather than material or sensuous sexuality with which Rousseau is concerned. This assertion is crucial to the interpretation of *Pygmalion*; it is the basis for a refutation of Goethe's interpretation of it. It is borne out by the other contexts in which Rousseau treats the theme of love and sexuality as well as by the structure of Pygmalion's desire. In an important passage in the *Confessions*, for instance, Rousseau distinguishes between the "besoins du sexe" and those of the heart and comments:

> Le premier de mes besoins, le plus grand, le plus fort, le plus inextinguible, étoit tout entier dans mon coeur: c'étoit le besoin d'une société intime et aussi intime qu'elle pouvoit l'être: c'étoit surtout pour cela qu'il me fallait une femme plustot qu'un homme, une amie plustot qu'un ami. Ce besoin singulier étoit tel, que le plus étroite union des corps ne pouvoit encore y suffire: il m'auroit fallu deux âmes dans le meme corps: sans cela je sentois toujours du vide.

Rousseau is describing a relationship which is completely inward, nonmaterial. It is of the heart but not of the body. He calls it intimacy; I have called it ideal sexuality. Intimacy is more important, more urgent than physical sexuality—it is the first of Rousseau's needs—but, as the connotations of the word imply, it is related to sexuality in an important way. It demands representation in terms of sexual difference: "c'est surtout pour cela qu'il me fallait une femme plustot qu'un homme. . . ." What sexual difference corresponds to in this case is simply the difference between two selves, or between the self and the self as other. For intimacy is a relation within selfness. Rousseau characterizes it—though with an irony akin to that in *Pygmalion*—not as union but as closeness in which a difference is maintained: "il m'auroit fallu deux âmes dans le meme corps." This means not only that he requires more closeness than physical union can give but also that the structure of desire demands doubling of the self, lack of complete identity.

In his early drama *Narcisse* Rousseau is also concerned with establishing the relationship of the self to sexuality. He begins by showing a conflict between the vanity of the central character, Valère, and his love for his fiancée Angélique. The conflict is represented in Valère's falling in love with a portrait of himself which has been given feminine features. He looks for the original of the portrait in order, or so he thinks, to marry her. When

Valère recognizes himself in the portrait, the problem is resolved; vanity yields to love of another person. But it is not simply that the object of Valère's love has changed from the self (as the term *amour-propre* indicates) to the other. Were that the case, *Narcisse* would represent Rousseau's renunciation of the sort of narcissism Starobinski charges him with. But the simple polarity of narcissism and sexuality, self and other, can account for neither the conflict around *amour-propre* nor the details of the action in the play. Valère's *amour-propre* is not narcissism in the sense of unity with oneself, for he is still in search of the object of his desire. Nor does its resolution into love for Angélique exclude a type of love for himself: speaking of the portrait now recognized to be an image of himself, he tells Angélique, "Et moi je ne veux plus l'aimer que parcequ'il vous adore." There is no simple opposition of self and other; rather, here as in *Pygmalion*, the self is separated from itself. It is a question of the proper understanding of this separation and thus of self-knowledge. Angélique indicates this when she says to Valère of the image in the portrait, "Vous deviez autant moins méconnoitre cet objet que vous avez eu avec lui le commerce le plus intime, et qu'assurément on ne vous accusera pas de l'avoir négligé." Here as in the passage from the *Confessions* Rousseau is concerned with a relationship of intimacy, of ideal sexuality. Sexual otherness, the femininization of Valère's image in the portrait, is a representation of the otherness of the self, as in *Pygmalion*. Rousseau's undertaking is a critical one in the Kantian sense of the term; he is concerned with making distinctions on the basis of an examination of the nature of the self. Here too Rousseau works by presenting a process of reflection in the central character's consciousness. Valère's confused search for the original of the portrait leads to self-knowledge. "Il se cherche," says his valet of him. The reflection is, in another sense, the *Reflexion in sich* of his *amour-propre*, its resolution into ideal and material sexuality.

We have seen that reflection and desire are both shown by Rousseau to be manifestations of an ironic negativity of the self, a discontinuity within the self. This negativity means simply that the self is finite, or mortal. I have said that for Rousseau the moment of union with the object, the culminating moment in artistic production, is experienced as already past. What Pygmalion says is that the moment of union is the same as death: "que Pygmalion meure, pour vivre dans Galathée!" There is a discontinuity between action and reflection, past and present, self and other, because the moment of union transcends the limitations of experience inherent in the finite self and is thus equivalent to the death of the self. Rousseau emphasizes the negative aspect of this moment. He does not present death as harmonious union so much as he presents union as death, as the ultimate negation.

Rousseau's perception of discontinuity as basic to the self shows how much closer he is to Kant than to later idealist philosophy. His critical undertaking examines the finite self and finds its finiteness, its mortality, implicit in all its activities, in sexuality, in artistic production, and in reflection. Idealist philosophy, in contrast, takes the standpoint of the absolute subject in which contraditions are reconciled, and resolves the problem of mortality by presenting a process in which the finite is integrated into the absolute, the totality. Rousseau and Kant do not present the death of the finite subject, either positively as union with the absolute or negatively as apocalyptic annihilation, so much as its mortality, experienced negativity.

Rousseau's position on many aesthetic questions can be inferred from his conception of the self. Central to his conception as to Kant's, as we have seen, is the distinction between the ideal and the real, which reflects the negativity or the limitations of the finite self. This distinction is ironic for Rousseau; it is ironic that Pygmalion's desire for Galathée should be ideal rather than real. In the area of aesthetic thought where he moves beyond Kant, in his conception of the work of art as such, Rousseau still works from this ironic distinction between the ideal and the real. That the work is subject or self, that the self has a negative moment, and that the ideal is the negation of the real—these notions form the basis of his conception of the work of art. Just as he approaches the question of the nature of the self through Pygmalion's desire, which brings up the question of ideality and reality, Rousseau approaches that of the work through the question, in what does the sensuousness of the work of art consist? Pygmalion's desire for the statue forces this question on him; he assumes his desire to be material and its object to be some material quality in the statue. There is a basis for this assumption, for undeniably the statue does have physical reality; it exists as a thing in space. But the same process of reflection that reveals the ideality of Pygmalion's desire reveals an ideal moment in the statue to be its object. Furthermore, in *Pygmalion* the question of the sensuousness of the work of art is equivalent to the central question in aesthetic speculation, that of the nature of beauty. For in designating the statue's beauty as the cause of his desire, Pygmalion is forced to explore the ambiguous double nature of beauty, the fact that it characterizes both erotic and aesthetic objects, as he is forced to explore the relationship of material and ideal moments in desire.

In Pygmalion's attempts to locate the sensuousness of the work of art he thinks of the work in analogy to a number of polarities which are themselves attempts to formulate the nature of the sensuous—body and soul, matter and form, death and life, nature and spirit. He finds that the aesthetic phenomenon cannot be subsumed under the sensuous side of any of these polarities and that, indeed, these polarities cannot be correlated among themselves. Pygmalion tries at first to consider the statue as physical object the cause of his desire. He equates the statue with the marble, the inanimate matter, of which it is made, and considers this analogous to the body of a woman. "C'est donc pour cet objet inanimé que je n'ose sortir d'ici," he exclaims indignantly on first admitting that what is tormenting him is in fact sexual desire. But on reflecting on the statue as physical object Pygmalion is constantly led toward something nonmaterial. For the statue's beauty seems to imply soul as well as body. "Que l'âme faite pour animer un tel corps doit être belle!" he exclaims. The spiritual component, soul, which would seem to be absent until the statue is animated, seems to be necessary to the essence of the statue: "Il te manque une âme; ta figure ne peut s'en passer." Without realizing it, Pygmalion has designated an aesthetic category, figure, or form, as the locus of beauty. Reflection on matter thus brings Pygmalion beyond the polarity body-soul to the notion of form. But Pygmalion must still deal with the question of the distinction between the work of art and a living person:

> Ce n'est point de ce marbre mort que je suis épris, c'est d'un être vivant qui lui ressemble; c'est de la figure qu'il offre à mes yeux. En quelque lieu que soit cette figure adorable, quelque corps qui la porte . . . elle aura tous les voeux de mon coeur.

Here the material of the statue seems to be merely the occasion for the form, its background, as it were, necessary in order for the form to be perceived but not essential to it. Pygmalion speaks of "la figure qu'il [le marbre] offre à mes yeux." But he has implicitly moved to a second hypothesis concerning the material component of the statue, one in terms of nature: he has decided that it is not the statue itself but a living person which is the cause of his desire. Thus the life which the statue lacks is now seen as natural. But this means that Pygmalion is no longer thinking of the statue as matter rather than spirit, for nature is the material side of the polarity nature-spirit. Pygmalion is in fact now thinking of the work of art as purely formal and natural life as in contrast more real, more material than the work of art. Pygmalion imagines form to be too purely spiritual to arouse desire. Thus whereas at first he needed to show a spiritual component in his desire in order to justify it to himself, Pygmalion now feels the need to ground his desire in the natural, in life, lest it be an unnatural desire. It has been clear from the beginning, however, that the statue of Galathée surpasses in beauty the models which Pygmalion actually used in making it. Pygmalion refers to them as "chefs-d'oeuvre de la nature que mon art osoit imiter," but he then dismisses them with the words, "depuis que je vous ai surpassés, vous m'être tous indifférens." The real significance of his feeling that there must be somewhere a living original of his statue lies not so much in the idea that he must have been imitating something in making the statue—for, as he says, the imagined model would resemble the statue rather than the other way around—but in the idea that aesthetic phenomena must somehow be grounded in nature. At this stage, when Pygmalion has not yet understood the ideality of his desire—or accepted its irony—he accords priority to the natural and imagines that the aesthetic must somehow be derived from it.

Pygmalion has worked himself into a set of very paradoxical notions. It is the physically existing statue rather than any living person which in fact arouses his desire, but he concludes that it is the form rather than the matter of the statue which is beautiful. He decides that it must be a living person like the statue which he really desires, but the only model of which this could be true is an imaginary one, or at least an absent one. Neither actually existing material aspect of the statue, then, neither model nor material, is the locus of its beauty or its foundation. Pygmalion finally comes to the decisive formulation of this paradox in the prayer to Venus which is the turning point of the *scène*. This prayer is at once the culmination of Pygmalion's error and the transition to correct understanding. It effects the animation of Galathée, which, considered as real, is the fulfillment of a false desire, and, considered as ideal, is a correct representation of the nature of the work of art: "Déesse de la beauté, épargne cet affront à la nature, qu'un si parfait modèle soit l'image de ce qui n'est pas."

"L'image de ce qui n'est pas" is in fact what the work of art, considered as form or figure, is. This formulation, however, is as many-sided and ironic as the corresponding formulation of the nature of desire, "que je sois toujours un autre." On the simplest level, it means that Galathée is not the image of a natural object. She *is* an affront to nature, as *Pygmalion*'s aesthetics are a rejection of mimetic aesthetics. Her animation does not mean that she has become a living person. Were this the case, *Pygmalion* would indeed be no more than wish-fulfillment on Rousseau's part. But Pygmalion understands the animation not as the fulfillment of his sensuous desires but as the height of irony. "Il est trop hereux pour l'amant d'une pierre de devenir un homme à visions." Her animation demonstrates instead the correctness of the formulation "l'image de ce qui n'est pas." Pygmalion prayed for the original of the statue, and the result was the animation of the statue. The statue thus has no model other than itself; it is its own original. But it remains an image as well as its original; it is not real as a natural object or a living person is real. Thus the nonexistent thing of which the statue is an image is itself, and one important meaning of the formulation "l'image de ce qui n'est pas" is that the statue is the image of an image. The statue thus contains a moment of negativity within itself analogous to that which characterizes consciousness. It has an analogous reflective structure; it is a reflection of its own negativity. The reflective structure of the work of art is shown in Galathée's first movement: she points to herself and says, "Moi." In a second but closely related sense, "l'image de ce qui n'est pas" means that the work of art is selfness because it has been constituted by reflective consciousness. The statue derives not from nature but from Pygmalion's consciousness; it is "l'image de ce qui n'est pas" in that it is the image of his negativity. This implies a radical discontinuity between matter and consciousness. Consciousness constitutes itself through its negativity as negativity, as lacking the continuity of the organic.

Rousseau here locates the specifically aesthetic in the notion of image as he earlier located it in that of form or figure. The notions are closely related; in each case the aesthetic is ideality seen in the sensuous and is contrasted to life or nature. Rousseau's conception of the work of art in *Pygmalion* is in large measure equivalent to his development of the notion of image or figure. The animation of the statue, which signifies Pygmalion's full understanding of the nature of the work of art, is its realization as image. Rousseau's notion of image includes those of illusion and appearance: "Ravissante illusion qui passes jusqu'à mes oreilles, ah! n'abandonne jamais mes sens," Pygmalion addresses the animated statue. This linkage is simply another way of putting the question of the relation of art to nature. "Soll die Kunst täuschen oder bloss scheinen," was Friedrich Schlegel's formulation of the question. By differentiating appearance from illusion or deception, he asserted that art does not have to deceive by simulating nature. For idealist aesthetics art is rather the appearance or manifestation of the infinite in the finite, and thus the notion of aesthetic illusion (*ästhetischer Schein*) is a positive one. For Rousseau, however, the notion of illusion or image still has a negative aspect as well as that positive one. It is thus, like Rousseau's notion of desire, ironic. The image is negative for Rousseau in two senses. First, as has already been pointed out, it is negative in that as image of a reflective self, the work of art contains the negativity inherent in consciousness as such. The second sort of negativity has to do with the relation of the aesthetic image to the natural realm. The image as it is traditionally conceived refers to but is not a natural object. In developing a notion of image as referring not to something natural but to itself as a phenomenon of consciousness, Rousseau does not obliterate the reference to the natural but leaves it in the form of an illusion. Thus the aesthetic image for him is not something totally unrelated to nature but something which instead of referring *to* the natural refers *away* from it. The aesthetic image seems to refer to the natural but, having provoked this mistaken idea, leads away from it. To put this in slightly different terms, illusions are called illusions of the senses because although perceived by the senses they negate their own sensuousness in that they do not have natural existence. Art is sensuous in a similar way; it is perceived through but is not of the senses. Unlike a mere illusion of the senses such as a mirage, however, the aesthetic image does not stop with the negation of itself as natural but moves inward to become self-referential. Galathée is an image of that which does not exist not only in that she lacks or transcends a model but also in that what she does come from is the negativity of Pygmalion's consciousness.

We must still account for the priority of Galathée over Pygmalion which appears at the end of *Pygmalion*. This priority is important in that it emphatically differentiates Rousseau's aesthetics from an expressive aesthetics in the psychologistic sense, where the work is a mere reproduction of the artist's subjective state of mind. From Pygmalion's point of view, as has already been explained, Galathée is prior simply in that she is his externalized better or past self and thus seems free from the negativity of reflective consciousness. Although the image is in one sense less real than the original, it is more real than nothingness. One must only be careful not to confuse this priority with the objectness of the natural object. Going beyond what Rousseau actually touches on in *Pygmalion*, one might infer that the work of art has priority over consciousness in that it is more self-contained in its anti-natural reflective structure. Galathée can designate herself as "moi," but Pygmalion must move outside himself, to her, to find himself. Pygmalion, participating in both the ideal and the real, in experience and life, is less purely an end in himself, in the Kantian sense, than the work of art, which, as ideal but not mortal, has no continuity with the natural. It should be noted, however, that the priority of Galathée over Pygmalion means the priority of the work over the artist within the realm of the aesthetic but does not necessarily mean the priority of the aesthetic over other realms of experience. The latter question does not arise in *Pygmalion*.

Rousseau works out a similar conception of image in the second preface to the *Nouvelle Héloïse*, where the subject is also the relation of love to the aesthetic. Speaking of the language of the lovers' letters, the partner in the dialogue who represents Rousseau says:

Si les pensées sont communes, le style pourtant n'est pas familier, et ne doit pas l'être. L'amour n'est qu'illusion; il se fait, pour ainsi

> dire, un autre Univers; il s'entoure d'objets qui ne sont point, ou
> auxquels lui seul a donné l'être; et comme il rend tout ses sen-
> timents en images, son langage est toujours figuré.

When Rousseau speaks of love as illusion here he means not that one actually
feels something other than love but that love is ideal, that it is not an emotion
aroused by existent objects but that it is the constitution of inward or ideal
objects—"objets qui ne sont point, ou auxquels lui seul a donné l'être."
Though not so definitively as in *Pygmalion*, Rousseau associates the constitutive activity of love with aesthetic phenomena, images and figurative language. By implication we might conclude here that the figures of speech of
the language of love are the illusory objects love creates, and that for Rousseau
the defining characteristic of the figure of speech is not its reference to the
material object it names but the fact that it is an ideal constituted by consciousness. The femininized portrait of Valère in *Narcisse*, another example
of Rousseau's interest in the nature of the aesthetic image, is referred to as
"metaphorisé," which means that it refers not to an actual feminine person
but to the otherness within Valère himself.

In conclusion, it should be noted that the aesthetic conceptions which
Rousseau develops in *Pygmalion* are of importance in defining his relationship
to romanticism. Modern interpretations of romanticism tend to organize
romantic thought on aesthetic matters in one of two directions: either toward
an expressive theory of art in which the artist's feelings and personal experiences are central or toward a theory of art akin to that of German Idealism,
which stresses the relation of the aesthetic to the absolute and conceives
imagination as a faculty for higher knowledge or for union with Nature.
The first type of interpretation stresses Rousseau's importance in the development of romantic sensibility, viewing him as a proponent of the free
expression of feeling and as a primitivist advocating a return to natural ways
of being. The second type tends to ignore Rousseau, even where it traces
the genesis of romanticism in the development of eighteenth-century aesthetics which culminates in Kant. *Pygmalion* shows, however, that Rousseau
participated in the central aesthetic speculation of his age, in the development
which replaced realistic mimetic notions of art with an interest in the nature
and role of subjectivity. Furthermore, Rousseau unites in his aesthetics, as
does Kant, both the subjectivism and the idealism which modern interpreters
see as the chief characteristics of romanticism. Like Kant, he develops his
aesthetics from an analysis of the self into which feeling is integrated. But
in uniting and relating these two strains Rousseau comes to a position different from either. His thought is not merely personal or merely psychol-

ogistic, for, as I have tried to show, feeling and primitivism occur only in conjunction with a movement inward of reflection or interpretation. On the other hand, Rousseau stops short of idealism, as does Kant, in stressing neither union with the absolute nor union with Nature but rather the negativity which separates consciousness from both. One might call Rousseau's aesthetics a critical aesthetics and as such a variety of romantic aesthetics.

LOUIS ALTHUSSER

The Social Contract *(The Discrepancies)*

In interrogating the philosophy we have inherited, we can start from one simple observation: each great doctrine itself thinks itself in a specifically *philosophical* object and in its theoretical effects. For example: the Platonic Idea, Aristotelian Action, the Cartesian Cogito, the Kantian Transcendental Subject, etc. These objects have no theoretical existence outside the domain of philosophy proper. Within Rousseau's doctrine, the *Social Contract* is a theoretical object of the same kind: elaborated and constructed by a philosophical reflection which draws from it certain definite theoretical effects.

I should like to suggest vis-à-vis Rousseau's philosophical object, the "Social Contract," that an examination of the mode of theoretical functioning of the fundamental philosophical object of a theory may enlighten us as to the objective function of that philosophical theory: to be quite precise, as to the problems it eludes in the very "problems" it elects.

Indeed, a schematic analysis of the theoretical functioning of the object *Social Contract* confronts us with the following fact: this functioning is only possible because of the "play" of an internal theoretical discrepancy (Discrepancy I). The "solution" of the political "problem" by the "social contract" is only possible because of the theoretical "play" of this Discrepancy. However, the "Social Contract" has the immediate function of masking the play of the Discrepancy which alone enables it to function. To mask means to denegate and reject. In fact, the functioning of the Social Contract in Discrepancy I is only possible because this Discrepancy I is carried over and

From *Montesquieu, Rousseau, Marx: Politics and History,* translated by Ben Brewster. © 1972 by NLB. Verso Editions/NLB, 1982.

transposed in the form of a Discrepancy II, which alone enables the corresponding solution to function theoretically. Discrepancy II then leads by the same mechanism to a Discrepancy III, which, on the same principle still, leads to a Discrepancy IV. We thus find that we are confronted by the observation of a chain of theoretical discrepancies, each new discrepancy being charged to make the corresponding solution, itself an effect of an earlier solution, "function." In the chain of "solutions" (Social Contract, alienation-exchange, general will-particular will, etc.) we thus discern the presence of another chain, one which makes the first theoretically possible: the chain of pertinent Discrepancies which at each stage enable the corresponding solutions to "function" theoretically. A comparison of these two chains, of the "logic" peculiar to each, and of the very special logic of their relationship (the theoretical repression of the Discrepancy) direct us towards an understanding of the theoretical function of the philosophical system in which Rousseau proposed to think politics.

If this type of analysis proved well-founded, it would also have the following dual interest:

1. It would make intelligible Rousseau's problematic and the theoretical effects of that problematic (including the apparently technical arrangements for the organization of power, the distinction between its organs, its working procedures).

2. It would make intelligible the possibility of a number of "readings" of Rousseau's *Social Contract*, and the subsequent interpretations (Kantian, Hegelian, etc.). These interpretations will no longer seem to us to be merely arbitrary or tendentious, but as founded in their possibility in Rousseau's text itself: to be quite precise, in the "play" allowed by the "space" of the theoretical Discrepancies constitutive of Rousseau's theory. In their turn, the interpretations may provide us with an index and proof of the necessary existence of those Discrepancies.

My analysis will essentially concern book 1, chapter 6 of the *Social Contract*.

A. RESULT OF CHAPTERS 1–5

Book 1 chapter 4 sustains the whole of the *Social Contract*, since it poses and resolves the problem which constitutes the fundamental question (that "theoretical abyss") of political life.

This fundamental question is posed in the following terms:

> The problem is to find a form of association which will defend
> and protect with the whole common force the person and goods

of each associate, and in which each, while uniting himself with all, may still obey himself alone, and remain as free as before. This is the fundamental problem of which the Social Contract provides the solution.

But chapter 6, which formulates the question in this way, has five chapters preceding it.

Chapter 1 only promises the solution:

The social order is a sacred right which is the basis of all other rights. Nevertheless, this right does not come from nature, and must therefore be founded on conventions. Before coming to that, I have to prove what I have just asserted.

Rousseau proves it in chapters 2–5: a refusal to found society in nature, or in illegitimate conventions.

In chapter 2, Rousseau shows that society cannot have the family as its origin. In chapter 3, that it cannot be founded on the "right of the strongest." In chapter 4, that it cannot depend on "conventions" sanctioning the effects of violence (the submission of the slave to his master, of a nation to its conqueror).

In chapter 5, Rousseau draws the conclusion: "That we must always go back to a first convention," first in principle with respect to all possible conventions, in particular with respect to that convention called the "contract of subjugation" which, according to Grotius, a people might conclude with the king to whom it submits.

It would be better, before examining the act by which a people gives itself to a king, to examine that by which a people is a people; for this act, being necessarily prior to the other, is the true foundation of society.

And, in the final paragraph of this same chapter 5, Rousseau rejects one last objection concerning the majority principle:

The law of majority voting is itself something established by convention, and presupposes unanimity, on one occasion at least.

With this last thesis Rousseau is rejecting the Lockean theory of the "natural" character ("natural" in the physical sense of the word) of the law of the majority. The majority does not belong to the social body as weight does to the physical body. It presupposes an act of convention prior in principle to its stipulation: it therefore presupposes a unanimous act of convention which adopts it as a law.

Having set aside every hypothetical natural foundation for the social body and rejected the classical recourse to false contracts derived from force, chapter 5 thus leads to two results:

1. It is necessary to elucidate the question of the primordial contract, prior in principle to every contract: the contract concluded in *"the act by which a people is a people."*

2. Since the law of the majority can only act on the basis of a first unanimous convention which adopts and establishes it, the contract by which "a people is a people" implies *unanimity*.

B. POSING THE PROBLEM

Chapter 6 can then pose the problem in all its rigour. This posing contains three moments: (a) the conditions for posing the problem; (b) the absolute limits to posing the problem; and (c) the posing of the problem properly speaking.

a. The conditions for posing the problem

They are expressed in the first paragraph of chapter 6.

> I suppose men to have reached the point at which the obstacles in the way of their preservation in the state of nature show their power of resistance to be greater than the forces at the disposal of each individual for his maintenance in that state. That primitive condition can then subsist no longer; and the human race would perish unless it changed its manner of existence.

Let us examine the important terms in these two sentences, which define the objective conditions for posing the problem.

The first condition is that "men" have "reached" a "point" which is nothing but a limit-point, a critical point in their existence: the point dividing the life of the human race from its death. This fatal critical "point" for the human race takes us back to the *Discourse on Inequality*: it is the fully developed *state of war*.

This point is critical and fatal because it is the site of an insurmountable contradiction in that state between on the one hand the "obstacles" in the way of the life of the human race, and on the other the "forces" that individuals can oppose to them. What are these *"obstacles?"* What are these *"forces?"*

i. The "obstacles"

They are not external obstacles. They do not come from nature (catastrophes, cataclysms, "natural" difficulties—climate, resources—in the production of sustenance, etc.). We know that Nature has been tamed, she is no longer at war with herself, once men have cultivated her: the only catastrophes left are human ones. Nor do the "obstacles" come from other human groups.

They are purely internal to existing human relations. They have a name: they are the effects of the generalized state of war, of universal competition and, even in the breathing-space of a precarious "peace," the constant threat which everyone feels hanging over his goods, his liberty and his life. State of war must be understood in the strong sense, as Hobbes was the first to define it: this state is a constant and universal relation existing between men, i.e., it is independent of individuals, even if they are peaceful. This state defines their very condition: they are subject and condemned to it, unable either to find any shelter in the world to protect them from its implacable effects or to hope for any respite from the evils afflicting them.

These "obstacles" stand "in the way of" the "preservation" of men "in the state of nature." What the state of war threatens is what constitutes the ultimate essence of man: his free life, his life as such, the instinct that "preserves" him alive, what Rousseau calls "self-respect" (*amour de soi*) in the *Discourse on Inequality*.

I shall take the liberty of calling this state of perpetual and universal war the state of human *alienation*. This is a theoretical "anticipation." Although Rousseau does speak and make use of the concept of alienation, he does not do so to designate the effects of that state of war. I shall give reasons for the liberty I am thus taking.

ii. The "forces"

These "resistant" "obstacles" are opposed by the "forces" at the disposal of "each individual" for his maintenance in the state of nature.

These forces are constituted by the attributes of the natural man, having arrived at the state of war. Without this last specification, the problem of the Social Contract is incomprehensible.

When, in the *Social Contract*, Rousseau mentions these "forces" it is clear that he is not mentioning the "forces" of man in the "first state of nature" in which we find no more than a free animal, with zero "intellectual and moral faculties." We are concerned with an animal which the double impact of the Natural Catastrophes and the Great Discovery (metallurgy) has made a social being with developed and alienated faculties. The animal of the first state of nature has as its "forces": its body (life) + its liberty. The man of the generalized state of war has quite different forces. He still has his body (though his physical powers have declined), but he has intellectual forces and also "*goods*," too. "Each member of the community gives himself to it, at the moment of its foundation, just as he is, with all the forces at his command, including the goods he possesses." He has "acquired" these goods during the development of his social existence, which induced the development of his intellectual and "moral" faculties.

The "forces" of the individual in the state of war can thus be resumed as follows: physical forces (life) + intellectual and "moral" forces + goods + liberty. Liberty still features alongside "force": "The force and liberty of each man are the chief instruments of his self-preservation."

I have not made this comparison for the fun of noting distinctions, but because their registration is the index of a development—the *alienation* of man even within the state of nature, as a result of the historical process which culminates in the state of war.

We can grasp this transformation in the presence of "goods" among the "forces" of the individual, and in the appearance of a new category of human existence: the category of *interest*. "If the opposition of particular interests made the establishments of societies necessary. . . . It is enough to put this definition of the condition of the Contract (the opposition of particular interests) alongside the effects of the generalized state of war to see that while the process of the socialization of men transformed their faculties, it simultaneously transformed their "self-respect" into particular interest. When particular interest is reflected by the individual, it takes the abstract (and subjective) form of egoism (*amour propre*), the alienation of self-respect (*amour de soi*). But the objective content of particular interest links it directly with the nature of the state of war. The category of particular interest immediately betrays its universal basis. One particular interest can only exist as a function of the other particular interests in rivalry, in universal competition. This is revealed by the sentence of Rousseau's I have just quoted: "The opposition of particular interests . . . " means that particular interest is constituted by the universal opposition which is the essence of the state of war. There are not first individuals each with his own particular interest: opposition intervening subsequently as an accident. The opposition is primary: it is the opposition that constitutes the individual as a particular individual with a particular interest. Remembering the exclusive seizure of lands (taken away from the "supernumeraries") which induces the state of war in the universal sense of a state, and all its subsequent effects: rich and poor, strong and weak, masters and slaves, it is clear what meaning is concealed by the apparently anodyne inclusion of "goods" in the list of the elements constituting the "forces" of the individuals when they have reached the state of war.

It is important to mark the category of particular interest as specific to the state of social ties existing in the state of war. Literally speaking, the human animal of the first state of nature has no particular *interest* because nothing can oppose him to other men—the condition of all opposition, i.e., of necessary ties, being then still absent. Only developed-alienated man acquires little by little, as a result of the ties in which he is engaged by the dialectic of involuntary socialization, the advantage (if such it can be called) of the category of particular interest, the form taken by egoism in nascent society. Particular interest only ever truly becomes particular interest in its radicality in the state of war. Particular interest features in so many words in the conditions of the establishment of society: "If the opposition of particular interests made the establishment of societies necessary, the agreement of these very interests made it possible." Let us bear this text in mind.

iii. The fatal contradiction: obstacles / forces

If the obstacles are purely human and internal, if they are the effects of that state of war, it is clear that the forces of each individual cannot carry him through: for individuals would have to be stronger than the very forces to which they are subject and which make them what they are, each "stronger" on his own account than the implacable (universal and perpetual) relations in which they are trapped, those of the state of war.

Individuals are trapped in a very special way. These "obstacles" are not external ones. To specify: there is a close bond between the "forces" of the individuals and these obstacles, which justifies my speaking of the state of war as a universal state of *alienation*. What indeed are these universal relations constituting the state of war? These relations in which the individuals are trapped are nothing but the product of their own activities. Hence the relations are not external to the individuals and the individuals cannot change them from the outside. They are co-substantial with the individuals. Indeed, the whole development of human history has been produced by a dialectic such that the effects of the first, involuntary socialization developed but also simultaneously alienated the individual: such that in response this first alienation developed existing social relations while alienating them more and more. So long as "there was still some forest left," men could partially escape the tyranny of social relations and the alienating effects of their constraint. When the "end of the forest" came and the whole earth came under cultivation and was seized by its first occupiers or the strong men who supplanted them, then there was no longer any refuge for human liberty. Men were forced into the state of war, i.e., into alienation. That is how they were trapped in the very relations that their activity had produced: they became the *men of those relations, alienated like them*, dominated by their particular interests, powerless against those relations and their effects, exposed at every moment to the fatal contradiction of the state of war. Fatal in the threat it held over their lives and their liberty, henceforth inseparable from the particular interest in which that liberty no longer found anything but its alienated expression. A contradiction in the strict sense of the term, since the state of war is liberty and human activity turned against themselves, threatening and destroying themselves; in the form of their own effects. A contradiction not only between the individuals and their forces on the one hand, and the human "obstacles" of universal competition on the other, but also (as a function of the nature of this state of universal alienation) between each individual and himself, between self-respect and particular interest, between liberty and death.

Such is the ultimate argument for this critical "point" at which the "primitive condition" can "subsist no longer": "the human race would perish unless it changed its manner of existence."

b. The absolute limits to posing the problem

These are the conditions (the state of war on the one hand; the forces of each individual on the other) which define the absolute limits to posing the problem. They are gathered together in the second paragraph of chapter 6: "But, as men cannot engender new forces, but only unite and direct existing ones. . . ."

What is interesting about this text is that it defines in a rigorous manner the theoretical field of the problem and suggests the impossibility of any solution which introduces an element *external* to that field itself. There is thus no transcendental solution, no recourse to a third party, be it God or Chance. The solution cannot be found outside the existing givens, a ruthless enumeration of which has just been established. The only solution possible inside the theoretical field constituted by man and the alienated relations whose authors and victims they are is for them to change their "*manner of existence.*" Rousseau "takes men as they are." He takes their forces as they are. Men only have these forces at their disposal. No solution in the world can change either the nature of these forces or the nature of the "obstacles" they collide with. The only way out is to play on the "manner of existence" of men, or the arrangement of these forces. " . . . As men cannot engender new forces, but only unite and direct existing ones, they have *no other means* of preserving themselves than the formation, by aggregation, of a sum of forces great enough to overcome the resistance. These they have to bring into play by means of a single motive power, and cause to act in concert."

The whole of the *Social Contract* is defined by the absolute limits of the theoretical field in which the problem is posed. It is a question of creating a force capable of surmounting the "obstacles" which block the forces of each individual, of creating this force by inaugurating new relations between the existing forces (union instead of opposition): "changing the manner of existence" of men. This clearly means posing the problem of the contract as a function of the individuals and of their forces.

c. Posing the problem

What is the existing individual, considered as a subject of definite *forces?* We can summarize the set: life + physical forces + intellectual and moral forces + goods + liberty, in the form: forces + liberty.

And here is the problem definitively posed:

> As the force and liberty of each man are the chief instruments of his self-preservation, how can he pledge them without harming his own interests, and neglecting the care he owes to himself? This difficulty, in its bearing on my present subject, may be stated in the following terms:
>
> The problem is to find a form of association which will defend and protect with the whole common force the person and goods of each associate, and in which each, while uniting himself with all, may still obey himself alone, and remain as free as before.

The solution lies in a particular "form of association" which guarantees the "unity" of the "forces" of the individuals without harming the instruments of their self-preservation: their forces (including their goods) and their liberty.

Let us not lose sight of the fact that forces (including goods) + liberty = particular *interest.* Reread the second sentence of the *Social Contract*: "In this inquiry I shall endeavour always to unite what right sanctions with what is prescribed by interest, in order that justice and utility may in no case be divided."

The solution to the problem posed lies in the nature of the act by which a people is a people: this act is a *contract.*

Apparently Rousseau is here returning to the traditional solution of the school of Natural Law, which thinks the origin of civil society and of the State in the *juridical* concept of the contract.

What does a contract consist of? What are its constitutive elements? Reduced to a schematic expression, a contract is a convention agreed between two Recipient Parties (which I shall call Recipient Party number one or RP_1, and Recipient Party number two or RP_2) in order to proceed to an exchange: give and take. For example, in the classic contract of submission between the People and the Prince, the RP_1 is the People, the RP_2 the Prince. The exchange involves the following "terms": the People promises obedience to the Prince; the Prince promises to guarantee the good of the People (above all by his respect for the Fundamental Laws). With the sole exception of Hobbes, whose contract has a quite different and quite unprecedented structure, the jurisconsults and philosophers of Natural Law generally respected the juridical structure of the contract (give and take exchange between RPs) in the use made of the concept of the contract to "resolve" the problem of the "origin" of civil and political society.

Rousseau, too, adopts the juridical concept, but immediately warns that "the clauses of this contract are so determined by the nature of the act that the slightest modification would make them vain and ineffective." In *Emile* he is more explicit: "The nature of the social pact is private and peculiar to itself." In fact, the "nature of the act" of this contract is such that the structure of the Social Contract in Rousseau is profoundly modified in comparison with its strictly *juridical* model. Behind the juridical concept of the contract we are dealing with an exceptional contract with a paradoxical structure.

The paradox of this peculiar contract lies completely in its central clause.

Its "clauses, properly understood, may be reduced to one—the *total alienation* of each associate, together with all his rights, to the whole community."

The mystery of the Social Contract lies in these few words, to be precise, in the concept of total alienation. This time it is Rousseau himself who speaks of alienation.

What is alienation? Rousseau has already defined the term in book 1 chapter 4:

> If an individual, says Grotius, can alienate his liberty and make himself the slave of a master, why could not a whole people do the same and make itself subject to a king? There are in this passage plenty of ambiguous words which would need explaining; but let us confine ourselves to the word *alienate*. To alienate is to give or to sell. Now, a man who becomes the slave of another

does not give himself; he sells himself, at least for his sustenance: but for what does a people sell itself?

What emerges from this definition of alienation is the distinction between "give itself" (as a gratuitous act without exchange) and "*sell itself*" (as a nongratuitous act, containing the counterpart of an *exchange*). Hence:

> To say that a man gives himself gratuitously, is to say what is absurd and inconceivable; such an act is null and illegitimate, from the mere fact that he who does it is out of his mind [or mad. But] madness creates no right.

Strictly speaking the slave sells himself, since he negotiates his submission at least for his sustenance. Strictly speaking: for this concession of Rousseau's is no more than a demonstrative device, to bring out the fact that even accepting its underlying principle, the thesis of the contract of slavery cannot be extended to the contract of (political) submission. Indeed, a people cannot sell itself: it does not get in exchange for its submission, even from the king, the sustenance that the slave at least receives from his master. A people that thinks it is selling itself (i.e., in an advantageous contract of exchange) is really giving itself for nothing, completely for nothing, including its liberty.

Liberty: it is out, the great word that takes us past the fictions accepted up to this point for the purposes of refuting Grotius. Sell whatever you like (give and take), *you cannot sell your liberty.*

> To renounce liberty is to renounce being a man, to surrender the rights of humanity and even its duties. For him who renounces everything no indemnity is possible. Such a renunciation is incompatible with man's nature; to remove all liberty from his will is to remove all morality from his acts.

The formal conclusion of chapter 4 on alienation: total alienation is illegitimate and inconceivable because a contradiction in terms: "incompatible with man's nature."

And yet: it is this total alienation itself that constitutes the single clause of the Social Contract: "the total alienation of each associate, together with all his rights, to the whole community."

There can be no ambiguity: *liberty* is certainly included in "all the rights" of each associate.

Let us stop a moment at this paradox. I can say: the total alienation of the Social Contract is the solution to the problem posed by the state of universal alienation that defines the state of war, culminating in the crisis resolved by the Social Contract. *Total alienation is the solution to the state of total alienation.*

Obviously, as I have already noted, Rousseau does not use the term alienation to designate the mechanism and effects of the state of war. Nevertheless I have shown that I am justified in using this anachronistic term to designate what Rousseau thinks of the nature of the state of war. The advantage of this substitution of terms is to make this conversion of sense, this change in the "manner of existence," the sole solution offered to men, "play" on a single concept: alienation.

Before the Contract, we are in the "element" (in the Hegelian sense) of alienation without any external recourse. This alienation is the work of the very men who suffer it. The slavery of the state of war is a real alienation of man, forced to give his liberty for nothing in exchange for a pure illusion, that of believing himself to be free. We are certainly in the element of alienation: but it is unconscious and involuntary.

There is no solution to this total alienation except total alienation itself, but conscious and voluntary total alienation.

If this is indeed the case, we return in the solution itself to what I called the absolute limits to any possible solution. The solution cannot come from outside, and even within the world of alienation it cannot come from outside the single law governing that world. The solution is only possible on condition of "playing" on the "manner of existence" of this implacable law. It can only consist of returning in its origin to that law itself, total alienation, while "changing its manner of existence," its modality. This is what Rousseau very consciously states elsewhere when he says that the remedy of the evil must be sought in its very *excess*. In a word, a forced total alienation must be turned into a free total alienation.

But the scandalous thing is as follows: how can a *total alienation* really be *free*, since we know from chapter 4 that this association of terms (alienation, liberty) is incompatible, an absolute contradiction? Hardly has it been glimpsed than the solution retreats into impossibility. The solution itself needs a solution.

This solution of the solution is contained in the Discrepancy between the Recipient Parties to the contract (Discrepancy I).

THE TWO RECIPIENT PARTIES AND THEIR DISCREPANCY

Indeed, so far we have only examined one aspect of the Social Contract: what happens between the two Recipient Parties (RPs) in the form of total alienation. But who are these RPs?

On the one hand they are the individuals taken one by one, and on the other, the "community." Hence RP_1 = the individual and RP_2 = the "community."

The contract is an act of exchange between the RP_1 and the RP_2. We know what the RP_1 *gives* in this act of exchange: *everything* (total alienation). But we do not yet know what is given by the RP_2.

RP_1 (individual) RP_2 (community)

(total alienation)   ⟶ ⟵   (?   )

(exchange)

If we ask, what will the RP_2 give? we run up against a "minor" difficulty which we have ignored up till now: *who is the RP_2?* The "community." What is the community? The union, the association of the individuals and their "forces." Is that not clear and adequate? And yet the whole mystery of the mechanism of the contract lies in the unique nature of this RP_2.

In a word, here is the difficulty: in every contract the two Recipient Parties exist prior to and externally to the act of the contract. In Rousseau's Social Contract, only the RP_1 conforms to these conditions. The RP_2 on the contrary, escapes them. It does not exist before the contract for a very good reason: it is itself the *product* of the contract. Hence the paradox of the Social Contract is to bring together two RPs, one of which exists both prior to and externally to the contract, while the other does not, since it is the product of the contract itself, or better: its object, its end. It is in this difference in theoretical status between the Recipient Parties to the contract that we inscribe: Discrepancy I.

What is the community? Of whom is it composed? Of the same individuals who appear *as individuals* in the RP_1, i.e., at the other pole of the exchange. In the RP_2 they appear, too, but no longer as individuals, but all in their "corporate capacity," i.e., in a different form, in a different "manner of existence," precisely the form of a "whole," of a "union," and this is the community. This difference of "form" is just a difference of form: the same individuals do appear in the two RPs. But it is not a "minor" difference: it is the very *solution* of the contract inscribed in one of its *conditions:* the RP_2.

Rousseau knows it, but it is symptomatic that he is content to reflect this singularity of the structure of the Social Contract by masking and *denegating* it in the very terms by which he signals it. Here are two examples.

In *Emile:*

> The nature of the social pact is private and peculiar to itself, in that *the people only contracts with itself.*

Precisely: the people can only be said to "contract with itself" by a *play on words*, on this occasion on the word that designates the RP_1 as the "people," a term only strictly applicable to the RP_2, the community (the object of the contract being to think the act by which "a people is a people").

And in the *Social Contract* itself:

> This formula shows us that the act of association comprises a
> mutual understanding between the public and the individuals,
> and that *each individual, in making a contract, so to speak, with himself,*
> is bound in a double capacity; as a member of the Sovereign he
> is bound to the individuals, and as a member of the State to the
> Sovereign.

Here the difference of "form" which distinguishes between the RP_1 and the RP_2, in other words, the difference between the individual in the form of isolation and the individual in the form of community, which defines the RP_2, is thought in the category of individuality. The Discrepancy is admitted and at the same time negated in the "*so to speak*" of "each individual in making a contract, so to speak, with himself. . . . "

To sum up:

The "peculiarity" of the Social Contract is that it is an exchange agreement concluded between two RPs (like any other contract), but one in which the second RP does not preexist the contract since it is its product. The "solution" represented by the contract is thus preinscribed in one of the very conditions of the contract, the RP_2, since this RP_2 is not preexistent to the contract.

Thus we can observe in Rousseau's own discourse a Discrepancy within the elements of the contract: between the theoretical statuses of the RP_1 and the RP_2.

We also observe that Rousseau, aware of this Discrepancy, cannot but *mask* it with the very terms he uses when he has to note it: in fact he negates this Discrepancy, either by designating the RP_1 by the name of the RP_2 (the people), or the RP_2 by the name of the RP_1 (the individual). Rousseau is lucid, but he can do no other. He cannot renounce this Discrepancy, which is the very solution, in the shape of the procedure which inscribes this Discrepancy, not in the solution but in the conditions of the solution. That is why when Rousseau directly encounters this Discrepancy, he deals with it by denegation: by calling the RP_1 by the name of the RP_2 and the RP_2 by the name of the RP_1. Denegation is repression.

Thus this Discrepancy can be recognized between the content of the juridical concept of the contract, which Rousseau imports into his problematic to give it a cover, and the actual content of his contract. If we take as our point of reference the contract in its juridical concept, and if we argue that Rousseau takes it for the concept of the content which he gives us, we can say: Rousseau's contract does not correspond to its concept. In fact, his Social Contract is not a contract but an act of constitution of the Second RP for a possible contract, which is thus no longer the primordial contract. The Discrepancy between the Social Contract and its concept has the same content as the Discrepancy I have just defined. If the terms of the juridical contract in its concept are superimposed on the terms of Rousseau's Social Contract, a pertinent difference, a Discrepancy, emerges. It concerns the RP_2.

One first conclusion can be drawn from these schematic remarks: it concerns the singular type of relation that there is between the juridical concept of the contract and the concept of the Social Contract. Why is Rousseau forced to think what he says in a concept which is not the concept of what he says? Why this recourse? Why this necessarily falsified recourse? What effects does Rousseau "expect" from this falsified recourse? Or rather, to avoid the language of subjectivity, what effects necessarily call forth this recourse? These questions put us on the trail of the function fulfilled by that singular philosophical object, the Social Contract. This *Discrepancy* between the contract (borrowed from existing Law) and the artificial philosophical object of the Social Contract is not a difference in theoretical content pure and simple: every Discrepancy is also the index of an *articulation* in the *dis-articulation* constituted by the Discrepancy. In particular, an articulation of Rousseau's philosophy with existing Law by the intermediary of one of its real concepts (sanctioning a real practice), the contract, and with existing juridical ideology. The nature of the function fulfilled by Rousseau's philosophical thought can no doubt be elucidated by the study of the *articulations* which link it to the realities of Law, Politics, etc . . . , in the *dis-articulations* which, in the form of theoretical Discrepancies, constitute it as a *philosophy*, as *the* philosophy it is.

Another conclusion: if we consider this Discrepancy I, it is clear that, for perfectly objective reasons inscribed in the theoretical space of the "play" it opens, it authorizes different "readings" of Rousseau.

The "plays" on *words* by which Rousseau himself negates the "play" of the theoretical space opened by the Discrepancy, authorize, in the strong sense, the Kantian and Hegelian readings of the Social Contract. The "play" on words which calls the RP_2 by the name of the RP_1 (the individual "making a contract, so to speak, with himself") directly authorizes a Kantian reading of the Social Contract (cf. Cassirer). The "play" on words which calls the

RP_1 by the name of the RP_2 ("the people only contracts with itself") directly authorizes a Hegelian reading. In the first case, the contract is an anticipation of a theory of Morality, whose voice can be heard in certain already Kantian formulations (liberty as obedience to the law one has given oneself, etc.). In the second case, the contract is an anticipation of a theory of the Nation as a totality, a moment of the Objective Spirit which reveals its basic determinations on a number of occasions (the historical conditions of possibility of the contract, the theory of manners and morals, of religion, etc.). In both cases the philosophical object Social Contract is relieved of its primordial function. Neither Kantian Morality nor the Hegelian Nation are constituted by a "contract." Besides, is it not enough to *read* Rousseau closely to see that his Contract is not a contract?

And since I am dealing with the possible "readings" of Rousseau—I do not know if it has already been attempted, but if it has not, it can certainly be foreseen—the Discrepancy allows a remarkable phenomenological (Husserlian) reading of the Contract, as a primordial *act of constitution* of the RP_2, i.e., of the juridical community, in other words, as a primordial act of constitution of *juridical ideality* on the "foundation" of the "passive syntheses" of which the *Discourse on Inequality* gives us admirable descriptions, which only await their commentators.

Of course, the Discrepancy which thus makes objectively possible Kantian, Hegelian or Husserlian "readings" of Rousseau also, thank God, makes possible a "Rousseauist" reading of Rousseau. Better: without bringing to light and rigorously defining this Discrepancy, a "Rousseauist" reading of Rousseau is impossible. For in order to read Rousseau in Rousseau, three things have to be taken into account: (1) the objective existence of this Discrepancy in Rousseau; (2) the denegation of this Discrepancy by Rousseau; and (3) the equally necessary character of the existence both of this Discrepancy and of its denegation, which do not arise as accidents in Rousseau's thought but *constitute* and *determine* it. To take into account this Discrepancy and its denegation is to take into account a theoretical fact, and its theoretical effects, which govern the whole logic of Rousseau's thought, i.e., both its possibility and its impossibilities, which are part of one and the same logic: that of a Discrepancy constitutive even in its denegation. If the Social Contract is not a contract but the (fictional) act of constitution of the Second Recipient Party (i.e., the *coup de force* of the "solution"), in the same way it can be said that the Discrepancy is not what Rousseau says about it (its concept never being anything in Rousseau but the denegation of its *fait accompli*), but the act of constitution of Rousseau's philosophy itself, of its theoretical object and logic.

From here on it is clear that this logic can only be a *double* one: the logical chain of the problems thought being constantly inhabited by a second chain, the logical chain of the Discrepancies which follow them like their shadows, i.e., precede them as their arbitrary "truth."

We can now return to total alienation. It was the solution, but an impossible because unthinkable one. Discrepancy I has made it possible, because thinkable.

If total alienation is possible, despite the contradiction of its concept, it is because of the nature of the Second Recipient Party: which features the same men as the RP$_1$. It is possible because it is purely internal to the liberty of the individuals: it is possible because men give themselves totally, but to themselves.

To think Rousseau's novelty we must return to the classical contracts. In them, the two Recipient Parties are prior to the contract and different from one another: e.g., the People and the Prince. It follows that it is always a matter of a juridical contract of exchange: give and take. Not only is the contract an exchange, but if we try to apply the category of alienation to it, it turns out to be a *partial* alienation. The individual only cedes a part of his rights in exchange for his security (there is one exception: Hobbes, whom I shall discuss later). In Rousseau what is striking is the fact that the individual has to give everything, to give himself entirely, without any reserve, in order to receive something "in exchange," even when exchange has no more meaning. Or rather: in order that the possibility of an exchange acquire a meaning, it is necessary that there be this initial total gift, which can be the object of no exchange. Hence Rousseau poses as *the a priori condition of any possible exchange this total alienation which no exchange will compensate.* The constitution of the Second Recipient Party, i.e., the community, is thus not an exchange but the constitution of the a priori condition of possibility of any (real or empirical) exchange. I shall return to this conclusion in a moment.

This theory of total alienation enables Rousseau to settle theoretically the "terrifying" problem posed by the "devil" Hobbes to all political philosophy (and to all philosophy as such). Hobbes's genius was to have posed the political problem with a merciless rigour in his theory of the state of war as a state, and to have claimed that the contract founding civil society was not a give-and-take contract of exchange between two Recipient Parties. Hobbes's contract, too, depends on a total alienation which the individuals agree among themselves to the advantage of a Third Party who is a Recipient in that he *takes everything* (absolute power), but is not a Recipient Party *to* the Contract since he is external to it and gives nothing in it. This Third Recipient Party, too, is constituted by the Contract, but as an effect external to the contract and its Recipient Parties (all the individuals contracting with one another to give everything to the Prince: it has been called a contract of donation, thinking of modern life-insurance contracts, i.e., to use a term which carries real weight with Hobbes, contracts of insurance against death). A total alienation in externality, to an external Third Party constituted by the Contract as an absolute Prince, this is Hobbes. Naturally, there are gaps in this "system": what "guarantee" is there against the despotism of a Prince who is not even bound by the exchange of a promise? How can one entrust oneself to his "interests"? How is one to represent to him (and think) his "duties"?

Rousseau's theoretical greatness is to have taken up the most frightening aspects of Hobbes: the state of war as a universal and perpetual state, the rejection of any transcendental solution and the "contract" of total alienation, generator of absolute power as the essence of any power. But Rousseau's defence against Hobbes is to transform total alienation in externality into total alienation in internality: the Third Recipient Party then becomes the Second, the Prince becomes the Sovereign, which is the community itself, to which free individuals totally alienate themselves without losing their liberty, since the Sovereign is simply the community of these same individuals. Finally, the rejection of any transcendence took, in Hobbes, the form of the factual transcendence of the Prince's externality to the contract. Rousseau is alone in remaining in immanence, without any recourse to a Third Party, even if it is a man. He accepts the law immanent in Hobbes's state of war: he only changes its *modality*.

Rousseau's advantage here is to be more "Hobbesian" than Hobbes himself, and to retain the theoretical gains of Hobbes's thought. Rousseau's social body does indeed have all the categories of Hobbes's Prince. The community has all the attributes of a natural individual, but transposed into the "element" of union: it is not a question here of a real individual (some man or some assembly which is the Prince) but of a moral totality, of the moral person constituted by the alienation of all the individuals. That power is in essence absolute, that it is inalienable, that it is indivisible, that it cannot "err," all these scandalous theses of Hobbes's are repeated word for word by Rousseau, but converted to the new meaning conferred on them by the *internality of alienation*.

Let us consider only one of these theses: the essentially *absolute* character of any sovereign power (a "philosopheme" which contains, in its order, the very principle of the Kantian conception of a priori conditions of possibility).

The tiny but decisive difference separating Rousseau from Hobbes stares us in the face when Rousseau, who thinks in Hobbes, simultaneously thinks what he needs to protect himself from Hobbes's "difficulties," in particular from the "crux" of the "guarantees" of the contract of alienation, which, in classical philosophy, inevitably takes the form of the problem of the *Third Man*. Indeed, if a conflict arises who will arbitrate between the People and the Prince? Hobbes's solution is to suppress the problem, but by suppressing the right to a guarantee. Hence obvious "factual" difficulties. Rousseau confronts the problem without faltering. He too will suppress it, but without suppressing the right to a guarantee: by realizing it, which makes it superfluous. Hobbes certainly "felt" that in order to suppress this problem, the contract would have to be no ordinary contract, the violation of which always requires the intervention of a third man, an arbiter—hence his contract of total alienation, but in externality which is merely to *transfer* the problem into the individuality of the Prince (his interest, his conscience, his duty). Rousseau's masterstroke is to see that a problem cannot be resolved simply by its suppression in a mere factual *transfer*, but only by really making it *superfluous*.

To suppose that a third man is required to arbitrate in a conflict between two RPs to a contract is in fact to suppose that a third man outside the civil society of the contractors is required for that society to exist, and it is thus to suppose that civil society does not exist, since it leaves outside itself the very condition of its own existence: that third man. Hence it is to suppose that without saying so one is still in the element prior to the Social Contract, that principle is being settled by fact, the a priori conditions of all exchange by the empirical conditions of exchange, etc. The problem of the third man then becomes the index and proof that the political problem has been badly posed: the radical reduction which lays bare the a priori constitutive essence of the juridico-political has not been attained. In other words, to invoke the necessity for the third man is to admit that one is still in the element of violence and that one is still thinking the problems of civil society in the categories of the state of nature and the state of war.

In Rousseau's theory of total alienation this "difficulty" disappears: there is no longer any need for an arbiter, i.e., for a third man, because, if I dare use the expression, *there is no Second Man*, because the Second Recipient Party is identical with the First, because for him individuals only ever contract with themselves, because the total alienation is for him purely internal. Between the individuals (subjects) and the Sovereign, there is no need for an arbiter, since the Sovereign is nothing but the union of the individuals themselves, existing as members of the Sovereign, in the "form" of union.

Of what use is this new philosophical object, the Social Contract? For the "resolution" of all these "problems." But the solution to these problems is never anything but the effectivity of Discrepancy I, which permits a noncontract to function as a contract, i.e., to make this Second Recipient Party, which is in fact the *solution* itself, appear to be one of its *conditions*. The "true" problems are elsewhere: they must be pursued, for the effect of Discrepancy I is to "chase" them constantly ahead of their supposed solution. Up to the point where it will be clear that the problems, which anyone might think at their beginnings, are really at an end, because their "solution" was installed from the beginning, even before they appeared. Discrepancy is also inversion of sense.

I was perhaps a little hasty in saying that the Social Contract was not a "true" contract because it contained no exchange: total alienation excluding all possible exchange as a function precisely of its total character. And yet the Social Contract also functions as a juridical contract between two Recipient Parties: give and take. The individual gives everything—and receives nothing in exchange. The paradox of total alienation which appeared to us as this nonexchange, the condition of possibility of all exchange, does nevertheless produce an exchange. This is where I shall inscribe Discrepancy II.

Just as Rousseau noted Discrepancy I in remarking that the Social Contract was a contract of a "private and peculiar" (*particulier*) type, he connotes Discrepancy II in the same way by saying that total alienation produces a "peculiar" (*singulier*) effect:

> The peculiar fact about this alienation is that, in taking over the goods of individuals, the community, so far from despoiling them, only assures them legitimate possession, and changes usurpation into a true right and enjoyment into proprietorship. Thus the possessors . . . have . . . acquired, so to speak, all that they gave up.

I have started with the most astonishing, the most "concrete" text, since it concerns the "goods," the "properties" of individuals. Note in passing a second "*so to speak*" (an index of the denegation of the Discrepancy, as in the previous case). This "everything" that they give includes their goods. They give them, but to get them back as they gave them (except for the subtraction of taxes). As they gave them? No: wearing the new "form" of property, replacing mere possession. A particularly precise case of the change in "manner of existence" produced by the Contract.

Another text is even more categorical:

Each man alienates, I admit, by the social compact, only such part of his powers, goods, and liberty as it is important for the community to control; but it must also be granted that the Sovereign is sole judge of what is important.

On this occasion the deduction is made within total alienation itself, i.e., the result of the exchange of alienation is shifted back onto it and then immediately removed from it. Hence: total alienation only applies to a part of that whole. How better express: it must be total so as not to be total. Discrepancy II.

We are really in the accountability of an exchange. Listen to Rousseau in [*Social Contract*, book 1, ch. 8]. It is an accountable balance:

> Let us draw up the whole account in terms easily commensurable. What man loses by the social contract is his natural liberty and an unlimited right to everything he tries to get and succeeds in getting; what he gains is civil liberty and the proprietorship of all he possesses. If we are to avoid mistake in weighing one against the other, we must clearly distinguish natural liberty, which is bounded only by the forces of the individual, from civil liberty, which is limited by the general will; and possession, which is merely the effect of force or the right of the first occupier, from property, which can be founded only on a positive title.

"Account," "commensurable," "loss," "gain." The language of accounts. The language of exchange. Result: the exchange is advantageous.

Thus we have both ends of the chain. On the one hand total alienation, on the other a real advantage. How can a total alienation be transmuted into an advantageous exchange? How can a total alienation, which could not receive anything in exchange that would be its equivalent, which appeared to us as the condition of possibility of all exchange, immediately and in itself take the form of an exchange, and even an advantageous one? What mechanism produces this astonishing effect?

This mechanism is a mechanism for the self-regulation, self-limitation of alienation, produced first on alienation itself by its total character. This mechanism is identical with the "clauses" of the contract. If they have to be scrupulously respected without changing them one iota, this is in order to ensure the effect of the self-regulation and self-limitation of alienation itself.

"The clauses of this contract are so determined by the nature of the act that the slightest modification would make them vain and ineffective."

What clauses? One formal clause: equality in total alienation. But also something which is not a clause, but a cause: *interest*.

Equality. Each gives *all* he is and has, whatever he has. All men are equal in alienation, since it is total for each of them. This is a formal clause, for men have unequal possessions, and we know that the exchange is advantageous to the one who possesses the most, for it is he who risks the greatest loss in the state of war.

Interest. This is what opens up the "play" in the formal clause of equality, which *allows* interest to come into "play." "The conditions are the same for all; and, this being so, no one has any interest in making them burdensome to others." Why? Whoever wanted to make them "burdensome to others" would make them burdensome to himself, automatically, as a function of the formal equality implied by total alienation. Hence it is certainly equality which plays the part of limitatory regulator even within total alienation. But this formal equality would be a dead letter were it not made active at each moment by the interest of each individual. The reciprocity of the contract lies in the formal equality produced by the total alienation. But this reciprocity would be empty and vain if the individual interest caught up in it did not really bring it into "play."

> The undertakings which bind us to the social body are obligatory only because they are mutual; and their nature is such that in fulfilling them we cannot work for others without working for ourselves. Why is it that the general will is always in the right, and that all continually will the happiness of each one, unless it is because there is not a man who does not think of "each" as meaning him, and consider himself in voting for all? This proves that equality of rights and the idea of justice which such equality creates originate in the preference each man gives to himself, and accordingly in the very nature of man. It proves that the general will, to be really such, must be general in its object as well as its essence; that it must both come from all and apply to all.

The matter is clear: behind rights, behind reciprocity, it is only ever a question of "the preference each man gives to himself," of individuals who only "think" of themselves, of "working for themselves." The mechanism of total alienation imposes on "the preference for oneself," on the particular interest, a transformation whose end-result is, in one and the same movement, the production of the general interest (or general will) and the self-limitation of total alienation in partial alienation, or rather in advantageous exchange.

This is one of the points in Rousseau's theory which makes any Kantian "reading" in terms of a morality thoroughly impossible. Strictly speaking, "total alienation" might be taken for an expression designating the transcendence of the order of morality with respect to any interest. But total alienation produces its effects precisely only because it presupposes within it the determinant effectivity of interest. For Rousseau, interest (which is the form of self-respect in the system of social relations, state of war or contractual society) can never be "put into parentheses" or "transcended," except by itself. Without the effectivity of interest, there would be no self-regulation, no self-limitation of total alienation, nor its conversion into "advantageous exchange." It is because the interest of each individual is active in total alienation that each individual receives back what he gives and more besides. He will want for others what he wants for himself, as a function of the equality imposed by the clause of total alienation. But he would not want anything for others if he did not first want it for himself. The general interest is not the product of a moral conversion that tears the individual away from his interest: it is merely the individual interest forced into the generality of equality, limited by it but simultaneously limiting in its effects the total alienation which is the basis for this general equality.

Rousseau expounds the logic of this mechanism in the paragraphs of chapter 6 which immediately follow the exposition of the clause of total alienation. The last one sums them up:

> Finally, each man, in giving himself to all, gives himself to nobody; and as there is no associate over which he does not acquire the same right as he yields over himself, he gains an equivalent for everything he loses, and an increase of force for the preservation of what he has.

This contract which is not an exchange thus paradoxically has an exchange as its effect. We now see why this total alienation can be both "incompatible with man's nature," and not contrary to it. In the Social Contract, man does not give himself completely for nothing. He gets back what he gives and more besides, for the reason that he only gives himself to himself. This must be understood in the strongest sense: he only gives himself to his own liberty.

We can now specify the nature of Discrepancy II. Discrepancy I lay in the difference in theoretical status of the two Recipient Parties, and in the fact that the Social Contract was not a contract of exchange, but the act of constitution of the Second Recipient Party.

What was "chased away" at the first moment as a result of Discrepancy I reappears at the second moment in the form of Discrepancy II: the false contract functions as a true contract nonetheless, for it produces an *exchange*, and even more, an advantageous exchange. What had been "chased away" at the first moment has now been "caught up with" and thought at the second moment. But at the cost of Discrepancy II: *between total alienation and the exchange it produces*, between total alienation and the interest which ensures its self-limitation, self-regulation, by realizing this total alienation as an exchange.

But then we can go further: in the mechanism which inscribes the effectivity of the interest of each individual in the necessity of the universal (and hence egalitarian) form of total alienation, there is a Discrepancy of theoretical status, unthought, unassumed. In other words, it is not the same interest that produces the total alienation on the one hand and acts in it to realize it as an exchange on the other. This unthought "problem" is "chased away" and "thrust aside." The solution is itself a problem: the problem that Rousseau is to pose in the terms of particular interest and general interest (or particular will and general will). But already we suspect that this "problem" itself can only be "posed" on the condition of a new Discrepancy III.

To sum up: Discrepancy I concerns the difference between the RP_1 and the RP_2. Discrepancy II concerns the difference between total alienation and advantageous exchange. Discrepancy III is about to appear in the "problem" of the general interest or general will, or, what amounts to the same thing, in the problem of the law.

All the remarks that follow presuppose a knowledge of the arrangement and nature of the Institutions that emerge from the Social Contract: the Sovereign (or legislature), the Government (or executive), the nature of the acts of the Sovereign (laws) and of the Government (decrees), and the subordinate relation of the Government to the Sovereign, for which it is no more than the "official" or "clerk."

This arrangement reveals two orders of reality:

1. A basic, essential reality: it is on the side of the Social Contract and the Sovereign, on the side of the legislative power and law. There is the "life" and "soul" of the social body.

2. A secondary reality, whose whole essence it is to be delegation and execution, mission and commission: the Government and its decrees.

As a first approximation, the difference between these two orders of reality can be expressed in the statement that the essence of the former is *generality* and the essence of the latter *particularity*. Two categories which, in their distinction, dominate the whole "nature," i.e., in fact all the theoretical "problems," of the Social Contract. Let us look at this slightly more closely, examining the object *par excellence* which realizes the essence of the Sovereign: the law.

What is a law? The act proper to a Sovereign. What is its essence? To be general: both in its form and in its content, as a decision of the general will, relating to a general object.

> When the whole people decrees for the whole people, it is considering only itself; and if a relation is then formed, it is between two aspects of the entire object, without there being any division of the whole. In that case the matter about which the decree is made is, like the decreeing will, general. This act is what I call a law.

And Rousseau adds: "When I say that the object of laws is always general, I mean that law considers subjects as a body and actions in the abstract, and never a particular person or action."

Let us consider this double generality of the law.

1. The generality of the law is the generality of its *form*: "when *the whole people decrees* for the whole people." The whole people = the entire people assembled together, *decreeing* for itself as a "body," abstracting from the particular wills. The will of this body is the general will. Hence we can write: generality of the law = general will.

2. The generality of the law is the generality of its *object:* "when the whole people decrees *for the whole people.*" The object of the law is the "whole people," as a "body" and considering only "itself," abstracting from all particularity (action, individual). We can write: generality of the object of the law = general interest.

The unity of the law can then be written: *general will = general interest*.

This couple can only be explained by its opposite: *particular will = particular interest*. I think we know what particular will and particular interest are (cf. the *Discourse on Inequality*). The whole difficulty lies in understanding the generality of the will and of the interest as the same generality.

Rousseau's dream:

> I should have wished to be born in a country in which the interest of the Sovereign and that of the people must be single and identical. . . . This could not be the case unless the Sovereign and the people were one and the same person.
>
> ("Dedication" to the *Discourse on Inequality*)

This dream is realized by the Social Contract, which gives Sovereignty to the assembled people. The act of legislation is indeed never anything but the Social Contract combined, repeated, and reactivated at each "moment." The primordial "moment" which "has made a people a people" is not a historical "moment," it is the always contemporary primordial "moment" which relives in each of the acts of the Sovereign, in each of his legislative decisions, the expression of the general will. But the general will only exists because its object *exists:* the general interest.

> If the opposition of particular interests made the establishment of societies necessary, the agreement of these very interests made it possible. The common element of these different interests is what forms the social tie; and were there no point of agreement between them all, no society could exist. It is solely on the basis of this common interest that every society should be governed.

We are now confronted with the problem of the relations between particular interest and general interest. But we have seen particular interest intervene in the very mechanism of the self-regulation of total alienation:

> Why is it that . . . all constantly will the happiness of each one, unless it is because there is not a man who does not think of "each" as meaning him, and consider himself in voting for all? This proves that equality of rights and the idea of justice which such equality creates originate in the *preference* each man gives to himself, and accordingly in the very nature of man.

As a passage from the Geneva Manuscript (an early draft of the *Social Contract*) specifies, this *preference* is no more than another name for particular interest:

> As the will tends towards the well-being of the wisher and the particular will always has as its object the private interest, the general will, the common interest, it follows that the last is or should be the only true motive force of the social body . . . , for the particular interest tends always to preferences and the public interest to equality.

The paradox that springs from a comparison of these passages is the fact that the particular interest is presented both as the foundation of the general interest and as its opposite. To "resolve" this contradiction, let us see how Rousseau treats it *practically* vis-à-vis the theoretical problem posed by the conditions of validity of *voting*.

In the people as a whole, in fact, voting has as its object the promulgation of laws, i.e., the declaration of the general will. How is one to proceed in order to know the general will? The principle is posed in [*Social Contract*, book 4, ch.1]: ". . . the law of public order in assemblies is not so much to maintain in them the general will as to secure that the question be always put to it, and the answer always given by it."

This passage means:

1. that the general will always exists, since it is, as the title of this chapter states, "indestructible";

2. but that three conditions have to be brought into play for it to be able to declare itself.

It must first be asked a pertinent question, one which essentially relates to it: concerning not a particular object but a general object.

This question must be asked it in a pertinent form, one which really interrogates the general will itself and not the particular wills.

Lastly the general will must answer this question, i.e., existent as it is, it must not be "mute," as happens when "in every heart the social bond is broken."

Supposing that a general question has been asked it, and that the general will is not mute, it must be interrogated in the forms required by its very nature if it is really to answer the question asked. This is the whole problem of voting rules:

> The general will is always right and tends to the public advantage;
> but it does not follow that the deliberations of the people are
> always equally correct.

In principle, the general will is the resultant of the particular wills:

> Take away from these same wills the pluses and minuses that
> cancel one another, and the general will remains as the sum of
> the differences. . . . the grand total of the small differences would
> always give the general will.

If such is the principle of the mechanism for the declaration of the general will, how can the deliberations of the people be incorrect and therefore fail to declare the general will? For the mechanism to carry out its function properly, two supplementary conditions are needed:

> If, when the people, being furnished with adequate information,
> held its deliberations, the citizens had no communication one
> with another, the grand total of the small differences would al-
> ways give the general will, and the decision would always be
> good.

Hence the people must have "adequate information," i.e., there must be "enlightenment," which poses the problem of its political education.

But above all (and this is the decisive point) there must be no "factions" or "partial associations" in the State, above all no dominant partial association, for then what is "declared" will no longer be the general will but a partial will, if not quite simply a particular will: that of the dominant group.

> It is therefore essential, if the general will is to be able to express itself, that there should be no partial society within the State, and that each citizen should think only his own thoughts.

As *absolute condition* for Rousseau: that the general will really is interrogated in its seat, in each isolated individual, and not in some or other group of men united by interests which they have in common, but which are still *particular* with respect to the general interest. If the general will is to declare itself, *is is thus essential to silence (suppress) all groups, orders, classes, parties, etc.* Once groups form in the State, the general will begins to grow silent and eventually becomes completely mute.

> But when the social bond begins to be relaxed and the State to grow weak, when particular interests begin to make themselves felt and the small societies to exercise an influence over the larger, the common interest changes. . . .

Note: the general will survives nonetheless, unaltered and correct: "It is always constant, unalterable and pure; but it is subordinated to other wills which encroach upon its sphere." The proof: in the most corrupt individual the general will is never destroyed, but only eluded.

The individual: "Even in selling his vote for money, he does not extinguish in himself the general will, but only eludes it. The fault he commits is that of changing the state of the question, and answering something different from what he is asked. Instead of saying, by his vote, 'It is to the advantage of the State,' he says, 'It is of advantage to this or that man or party that this or that view should prevail.' "

We are now in a position to specify the nature and theoretical function of Discrepancy III.

I said: I think we know what particular interest is but we do not know what the general interest is. But Rousseau says that the general interest is the common ground of the particular interests. Each particular interest contains in it the general interest, each particular will the general will. This thesis is reflected in the proposition: that the general will is indestructible, inalienable and always correct. Which clearly means: the general interest always exists, the general will always exists, whether or not it is declared or eluded.

What separates the general interest from itself, the general will from itself? Particular interest. We have a total contradiction: particular interest is the essence of the general interest, but it is also the obstacle to it; now, the whole secret of this contradiction lies in a *"play"* on words in which Rousseau calls the *particular* interest of each individual in isolation and the *particular* interest of social groups *by the same name*. This second interest, which is a group, class or party interest, not the interest of each individual, is only called particular with respect to the general interest. It is a "play" on words to call it particular in the way the interest of the isolated individual is called particular. This "play" on words is once again the index of a Discrepancy: a difference in theoretical status of the isolated individual and social groups—this difference being the object of a denegation inscribed in the ordinary use of the concept of *particular interest*. This denegation is inscribed in so many words in his declaration of impotence: human groups must not exist in the State. A declaration of impotence, for if they *must not* exist, that is because they *do* exist. An absolute point of resistance which is not a fact of Reason but a simple, irreducible fact: the first encounter with a real problem after this long "chase."

But precisely the theoretical denegation, by the ambiguous use of one and the same concept ("particular interest"), of this "resistant" fact allows the theory to develop without resistance, in the commentary on the mirror couple: particular interest/general interest. However, on closer inspection, we can see the Discrepancy at work even in this couple.

The general interest: its existence has as its sole content *the declaration of its existence*. Rousseau does not doubt for a moment the existence of a general interest as the foundation for every society. That the ideology of the general interest is indispensable to the real societies which served as references for Rousseau is certainly true. But in the *Social Contract*, Rousseau never treats the general interest as an ideology or myth. Its real existence is so little in doubt for him that he affirms its unalterable and imperturbable existence, even when the general will which declares it has become mute. Here the theoretical Discrepancy begins to reveal a quite different Discrepancy: the Discrepancy which installs this philosophy in the Discrepancy between it and the real which its birth required from the beginning.

The same is true, in mirror form, for the particular interest. For, the general interest is no more than the mirror reflection of the particular interest. The particular interest, too, is the object of an absolute *declaration of existence*. The two declarations echo one another since they concern the same content and fulfill the same function. And they are discrepant with respect to the same reality: the interests of social groups, the object of a denegation indispensable for the maintenance in working order of the mirror categories of particular interest and general interest. Just as the general interest is a myth, whose nature is visible once it is seen in demarcation from its real double, the "general interests" which Rousseau calls "particular" because they belong to human groups (orders, classes, etc.)—so the "pure" particular interest of the isolated individual (what he obtains from the constitutive origins of the state of nature) is a myth, whose nature is visible once it is seen that it has a real "double" in the general interests of human groups that Rousseau calls "particular" because they dominate the State, or struggle for the conquest of its power. As in the previous cases, we can spot this Discrepancy, but only beneath the verbal denegation of a play on words: here the juggling with particular and general, concepts which properly belong exclusively to the individual and the Sovereign, but which serve theoretically to reduce the Discrepancy introduced into Rousseau's conceptual system by the emergence of the following irreducible phenomenon: the existence of the interests of social groups. The interest of these social groups is sometimes called particular, sometimes general, for the good of the Cause, the cause of the ideological mirror couple particular interest/general interest, which reflects the ideology of a class domination that presents its class interests to *particular* individuals *as their (general) interest.*

The Discrepancy now appears to us in all its breadth, and in a new form. It no longer concerns some or other point internal to the theory. It is no longer a question of the status of the Second Recipient Party (Discrepancy I) or of the status of the exchange in total alienation (Discrepancy II). This time it is a question of the very Discrepancy of the theory with respect to the real; for the first time the theory has encountered social groups in existence. Having reached this point, I can make one suggestion and one comment.

The suggestion. It would undoubtedly be very interesting to go back along the path we have just completed, but this time starting from Discrepancy III as the reason for all the earlier "problems" and Discrepancies. That would be to start from the dis-articulation of Rousseau's philosophy, i.e., from the point at which it is articulated onto the juridical ideology of the society in which Rousseau lived, constituting itself as an ideological philosophy of politics by distancing itself through this Discrepancy III which constitutes it. By this procedure it could be demonstrated that the classical difference of and opposition between the external and internal criticism of a philosophical theory are mythical.

The comment. It is that in the object involved in the denegation of

Discrepancy III (social groups, orders, classes, etc.), Rousseau has finally reached what he began with as a problem: the result of the *Discourse on Inequality*. And this comparison would no doubt give pertinent results for the ideological concepts underpinning all the theoretical space of the *Social Contract*: liberty, self-respect, equality, etc. The famous liberty in particular, solemnly attributed to the man of the first state of nature, the reserve and sacred depository for one-never-knows-how-long, i.e., for the Future of Morality and Religion (and for the General Will, i.e., for the General Interest)—it would become clear that the natural man has no need or use for it: that the whole of the *Discourse on Inequality* can quite well do without it. And it would also be seen what the social groups are all about: is it not the body of the "rich" who take the initiative in the Social Contract, whose arguments are there denounced: the very "deliberate" undertaking of the greatest imposture in the history of the human race? The true Social Contract, now a "legitimate" one, thus finds at the end of the displacement of its concepts the very same realities whose existence and implacable logic had been described in the *Discourse on Inequality*.

One last comment. If Discrepancy III now concerns the Discrepancy of the theory with respect to the real, it can no longer be a question of a mere *theoretical* denegation. The *denegation* can only be a *practical one:* to denegate the existence of human groups (orders, classes) is to suppress their existence practically. Here I inscribe Discrepancy IV.

The solution to the existing "theoretical difficulties" is entrusted to practice. It is a question of managing to suppress, in the reality which can no longer be avoided, the social groups and their effects: the existence of orders, of social classes, of political and ideological parties and of their effects.

Recall the conditions for the "sound" functioning of the consultation of the general will. The people must be enlightened, and no intermediary human groups must be imposed between it and the general will. Rousseau will conduct the two tasks abreast, in one and the same operation, which takes two forms, the second being an avowal of the failure of the first, and vice versa. Flight forward in ideology and (or) regression in reality. Discrepancy IV, which is perfectly "practical" (but naturally implies theoretical effects) "separates" the two forms of this alternating attempt. Here I can only give a few brief indications.

1. THE FLIGHT FORWARD IN IDEOLOGY

The essential moments are to be found in the theory of manners and morals (*moeurs*), education and civil religion. In its principle this attempt has the aim of setting up the practical arrangements for a permanent moral reform intended to cancel out the effects of the social interest groups which are constantly arising and active in society. It is a question of ceaselessly defending and restoring the "purity" of the individual conscience (i.e., of the particular interest which is in itself the general interest) in a society where it is threatened by the pernicious effects of "particular" groups.

Listing the various sorts of laws, Rousseau distinguishes political laws, civil laws and criminal laws. But the essential remains unspoken:

> Along with these three kinds of law goes a fourth, most important of all, which is not graven on tablets of marble or brass, but on the hearts of the citizens. This forms the real constitution of the State, takes on every day new powers, when other laws decay or die out, restores them or takes their place (*les supplée*), keeps a people in the ways in which it was meant to go, and insensibly replaces authority by the force of habit. I am speaking of morality (*moeurs*), of custom, above all of public opinion; a power unknown to political thinkers, on which none the less success in everything else depends. With this the Great Legislator concerns himself in secret, though he seems to confine himself to particular regulations; for these are only the arc of the arch, while manners and morals (*moeurs*), slower to arise, form in the ends its immovable keystone.

The cause in these unwritten key laws is the action on the "particular will" which is embodied in the "manners and morals." "Now, the less relation the particular wills have to the general will, that is, morals and manners to laws . . . " But the "manners and morals" are no more than the penultimate link in the chain of a causality that can be depicted as follows:

Laws→ public opinion→ manners and morals→ particular will

For their part, the social groups can be relied on to act automatically, by their mere existence as well as by their undertakings and influence, on each of the moments of this process. Hence it is indispensable that a counteraction be exercised on each of the intermediate causes. The Legislator acts *par excellence* on the laws. Education, festivals, civil religion, etc., on public opinion. The censors on manners and morals. But the Legislator only intervenes at the beginning of the historical existence of the social body, and the censors can only preserve good manners and morals, not reform bad ones. It is thus at the level of public opinion that action can and must be constant and effective. Hence the importance of the education of the citizens by public means (festivals) or private means (*Emile*): but education cannot be enough without recourse to religion, i.e., to religious ideology, but conceived as civil religion, i.e., in its function as a moral and political ideology.

Flight forward into ideology, as the sole means of protecting the particular will from the contagion of those so-called "particular," i.e., social, "interests" of the famous "intermediary" groups. A flight forward: for it has no end. The ideological solution, that "keystone" which holds up to heaven the whole political arc, needs heaven. Nothing is as fragile as Heaven.

2. REGRESSION IN (ECONOMIC) REALITY

That is why it is necessary to return to earth and to attack those dangerous human "groups" in their very principles. And, remembering the main theses of the *Discourse on Inequality*, to speak of reality, i.e., of "goods," of property, of wealth and of poverty. In clear terms: the State must be maintained in the strict limits of a definite economic structure.

> The end of every system of legislation . . . reduces itself to two main objects, *liberty* and *equality*—liberty, because all particular dependence means so much force taken from the body of the State, and equality, because liberty cannot exist without it. . . . By equality, we should understand, not that the degrees of power and riches are to be absolutely identical for everybody; but that power shall never be great enough for violence, and shall always be exercised by virtue of rank and law; and that, in respect of riches, no citizen shall ever be wealthy enough to buy another, and none poor enough to be forced to sell himself: which implies, on the part of the great, moderation in goods and position, and, on the side of the common sort, moderation in avarice and covetousness.

Here Rousseau adds a note:

> If the object is to give the State consistency, bring the two extremes as near to each other as possible; allow neither men nor beggars. These two estates, which are naturally inseparable, are equally fatal to the common good; from the one come the friends of tyranny, and from the other tyrants.

The central formulations of this passage repeat, but *vis-à-vis* their political effects, certain even of the terms of the *Discourse on Inequality:* "From the moment one man began to stand in need of the help of another; from the moment it appeared advantageous to any one man to have enough provisions for two, equality disappeared." This possibility marks, with the beginning of the division of labour, the beginnings of dependence, which becomes universal when, all the land being cultivated and occupied, "the supernumeraries . . . are obliged to receive their subsistence, or steal it, from the rich," and the rich are able to buy or constrain the poor. It is this reality which haunts the second practical solution of the *Social Contract*.

In the economic reforms he proposes, Rousseau aims to proscribe the effects of the established economic inequality, and especially the grouping of men into those two "naturally inseparable" "estates," "rich men" and "beggars." The criterion he retains is that "no citizen shall ever be wealthy enough to buy another, and none poor enough to be forced to sell himself." He expresses out loud, but without thinking its practical preconditions, the old dream of economic independence, of "independent commerce" (*Discourse on Inequality*), i.e., of (urban or agrarian) petty artisanal production.

"Flight backwards" this time, in economic reality: regression.

That it is a dream, a pious wish, is well known to Rousseau:

> Such equality, we are told, is a speculative chimera which cannot exist in practice. But if its abuse is inevitable, does it follow that we should not at least make regulations concerning it? It is precisely because the force of circumstances tends continually to destroy equality that the force of legislation should always tend to its maintenance.

Clearly, it can only be a matter of regulating an inevitable abuse, an effect of the force of circumstances. When Rousseau speaks of "bringing the two extremes as near to each other as possible," it is a question of the following impossible condition: to go against the force of circumstances, to propose as a practical measure a solution "which cannot exist in practice." It is hardly necessary to note that the two "extremes" have all that is required to constitute themselves as human groups defending their "interests" without caring a jot about the categories of generality or particularity.

In a word: Rousseau invokes as a practical solution to his problem (how to suppress the existence of social classes) an *economic regression* towards one of the phenomena of the dissolution of the feudal mode of production: the independent petty producer, the urban or rural artisanate, what the *Discourse on Inequality* describes in the concept of "independent commerce" (universal economic independence permitting a "free" commerce, i.e., free relations between individuals). But to what saint should one entrust oneself for the realization of this impossible regressive economic reform? There is nothing left but moral preaching, i.e., ideological action. We are in a circle.

Flight forward in ideology, regression in the economy, flight forward in ideology, etc. This time the Discrepancy is inscribed in the practice proposed by Rousseau. This practice concerns not concepts, but realities (moral and religious ideology which *exists*, economic property which *exists*). The discrepancy really is in so many words the Discrepancy of theory with respect to the real in its effect: a discrepancy between two equally impossible practices. As we are now in reality, and can only turn round and round in it (ideology-economy-ideology, etc.), there is no further flight possible in reality itself. End of the Discrepancy.

If there is no possibility of further Discrepancies—since they would no longer be of any use in the theoretical order which has done nothing but live on these Discrepancies, chasing before it its problems and their solutions to the point where it reaches the real, insoluble problem, there is still one recourse, but one of a different kind: a *transfer*, this time, the transfer of the impossible theoretical solution into the alternative to theory, literature. The admirable "fictional triumph" of an unprecedented writing (*écriture*): *La Nouvelle Héloïse, Emile*, the *Confessions*. That they are unprecedented may be not unconnected with the admirable "failure" of an unprecedented theory: the Social Contract.

TONY TANNER

Julie and "La Maison paternelle": Another Look at Rousseau's La Nouvelle Héloïse

For in the state of the families, which was extremely poor in language, the fathers alone have spoken and given commands to their children and famuli, *who, under the terrors of patriarchal rule . . . must have executed the commands in silence and with blind obsequiousness.*
—GIAMBATTISTA VICO, *The New Science*

If, as is my impression, not many people actually read through Rousseau's *La Nouvelle Héloïse*, one reason might be that, in a sense, we have all read it hundreds of times even before picking up the actual text. If we do not have some vague secondhand, or hundredth-hand, sense of the story of Julie and her tutor, Saint-Preux, and the setting—the two young lovers so chastely passionate who are not allowed to marry, the house in the beautiful setting at the foot of the Alps near Lake Geneva, the enforced separations and anguished letters, the calm reunion when youthful passion has been transformed into mature affection and sincere piety—we will still have read so many other books that have been influenced indirectly by the modes of feeling which Rousseau outlined and indulged in his book that, in turning to this one, we may wonder a little at the enormous impact of this recorded series of specious and self-induced intensities and often quite interminable lexical dalliances with almost decontextualized emotion—feeling feeling itself feel, as it were. Yet a somewhat more careful reading reveals a rather different

From *Daedalus: Journal of the American Academy of Arts and Sciences* 105, no. 1 (Winter 1976). © 1976 by the American Academy of Arts and Sciences.

book, a book that not only bespeaks some kind of imminent crisis in the particular family structure on which Western society was based, but carries within it a sense of doom concerning the very emotions and institutions that the book strives to celebrate. There is, of course, a similar sense of the problematics of the family in *Clarissa*, and it is well known how much Rousseau admired that work. But Rousseau, in apparently working for a happier ending, if anything reveals—no matter how implicitly or unintentionally—potentially more ominous signs of things amiss. It is almost as if, on the eve of what we roughly think of as the great period of the consolidation and domination of the bourgeois class and its growing belief in the myth of its own "perenniality" (Sartre's word), Rousseau wrote a book that had a manifest content of "l'amour" in all its more piercing, poignant, and plangent forms, and a latent content that said the bourgeois family would not work. But let me turn to some details from the book.

The first embrace between Julie and Saint-Preux takes place in a charming "arbor (bosquet)" in a grove that lies close to Clarens, the house in which Julie lives. She herself selects the spot and prepares him with a tantalizing hint which mingles topographic specificity with promisory vagueness and ordained constraints.

> Among the natural arbors which make up this charming place, there is one more charming than the rest, with which I am most delighted and in which, for that reason, I am reserving a little surprise for my friend . . . I must warn you that we shall not go together into the arbor without the inseparable cousin ["l'inséparable cousine"].

The choice of an arbor for a secret rendezvous is appropriate enough, but I want to note that the spot which will be the location of their unlegalized sexual embrace is very near the house that Julie, effectively, will never leave—the house of her father. The insistence on having the "inséparable cousine" (Claire) present when she is to give Saint-Preux his "surprise" is indicative of Julie's wish somehow to combine intra-familial love with extra-familial passion: the cousin, as "cousin," is to be a mediator between filial devotion and female sexuality, between the father and the lover, between what is in the home and what is not in the home. As cousin she stands exactly in relation to Julie's family (in the restricted sense of parents and their children) as the arbor does to the house: that is to say, not actually inside it, but not totally outside it either, not completely unconnected and foreign. Arbors (and related topographical phenomena) play a frequent role in the long iconological history of that topographical "middle-ground" between culture and wild nature where the two may meet, and for Julie it is clear that her cousin represents a relational middle ground which she herself hopes to be able to maintain between daughter and lover. Of course it proves to be impossible; but the desire and attempt to keep everyone and everything together, connected, related, unsundered and inseparable, literally in one place, as well as emotionally, mentally, and even, at times, perceptually indistinguishable and merged, is the dominant drive in Julie's existence. She eventually wants to internalize the external, as it were, and "enhouse" the unhoused elements of existence. It represents a dream of *total* harmony, of complete incorporation and domestication which at the same time wishes to maintain that it is totally *natural*; as if to maintain that nature *is* culture and culture nature (not a relationship but an identity).

The relationship of this complex and impossible dream to the developments in the thought of the Enlightenment is too obvious to need any comment. But in terms of sexual/familial relationships such a dream can lead to strange displacements or confusions. *La Nouvelle Héloïse* is indeed a novel about love above all else, but the most powerful love relationship is between Julie and her father. Saint-Preux is an adopted child. The novel sedulously avoids adultery, but it is marked by all-pervasive feelings of incest (emotional and mental incest of course, though in one extraordinary episode it is almost as if the father brutally "rapes" Julie). By comparison, the most physical action of Saint-Preux to appear in the text is a feverishly excited manual exploration of Julie's clothes and underwear (in her absence), in an equally extraordinary incident of quite astonishing prurience. Julie's dream is, in certain important ways, a dream of total incest. The ultimate utter failure and collapse of this dream are a crucial prelude to many of the great novels—often novels concerning adultery—that were to follow it.

What apparently happens in the arbor on that first occasion is that the "inseparable cousin" first asks Saint-Preux for a kiss with a contradictory air of what one might call droll imploring ("d'un air plaisamment suppliant"), and a "cousinly" embrace ensues. It is now Julie's turn (it is all rather like the kissing games played at children's parties, as if Julie wants to defuse sexuality by infantilizing it), and she bestows a distinctly un-cousinly kiss on the understandably "surprised" Saint-Preux. She then returns to the arms of the inseparable cousin and proceeds to faint. It is small wonder that Saint-Preux registers a certain degree of mystification in the scene ("sans rien comprendre à ce mystère"), and we may adjudge it a considerable understatement when he subsequently refers to "the test of the arbor (l'épreuve du bosquet)." He is immediately afterward ordered by Julie to leave the house and travel which, being the bemused compliant figure that he is, he

promptly does. Shortly thereafter he refers to the "delirium" of the arbor
("ce délire qu'il éprouva dans le bosquet"). At this point Julie falls hysterically
ill and Saint-Preux is summoned back, and in the very next letter Julie tells
the absent Claire that the moment of "crisis" has arrived and begs her to
return to her ("la crise est venue"). From the next letter we infer that she
has capitulated sexually to Saint-Preux—it can only have been in the arbor
and only because the inseparable cousin had become separate. Julie has yet
to learn that there is no such thing as an inseparable person since separation
is not a function, but a condition, of individual existence.

Just as it was Julie who made the appointment for the initial embrace
in the arbor, so she decrees their next venue—a remote chalet in the country
near the source of the Vevaise. (I will note here that Saint-Preux is never
allowed to initiate any meeting, decide on any venue, fix on any abode. His
life is entirely shaped and directed by others, starting with Julie. In innumerable ways he is constantly being reminded of the complete helplessness
of his social position, his entire dependency on others for just about everything, including his identity. There is one strange letter from Julie in which
she upbraids him, at some considerable length, for indulging in what we
infer to have been obscene language and perhaps swearing. There are also
reports in other letters of outbursts of anger which are clearly tantrums.
These are symptoms of the frustration of a child who is deliberately not
being allowed to grow up.) This is how she outlines their proposed meeting
at the chalet. Having described the setting, she refers to the remote village
which "sometimes is used as a shelter for hunters but should only serve as
a refuge for lovers (qui sert quelquefois de repaire aux chasseurs, et ne devait
servir que d'asile aux amants)." We can notice here a sign of that strategy
of accommodation by rebaptism which in various ways comes to dominate
the novel (i.e., she renames the "repaire aux chasseurs" as "asile aux amants";
the significance of transforming a space connected with hunting into one
dedicated to loving will not go unnoticed). Julie continues:

> At the invitation of Monsieur d'Orbe, Claire has already per-
> suaded her papa to go with some friends to hunt for two or three
> days in that area and to take along the inseparable cousins. The
> inseparables have others, as you know only too well. The one,
> representing the master of the house, will naturally do the honours
> of it; the other with less ceremony will do those of a humble
> chalet for his Julie, and this chalet sanctified by love, will be for
> them the temple of Cnidus.

Monsieur d'Orbe is the accepted suitor of Claire and is to be her husband.
Thus he may represent "the master of the house," i.e., her father. This is

the one position which Saint-Preux is never to be allowed to occupy; at most he will be a child of the house, never the master—never, that is, the father's representative.

Saint-Preux can only do the illusory honors of the chalet, and necessarily with less *éclat* than the appointed representative of the master of the house, since one aspect of his helpless position is that he is permitted almost zero access to social *éclat* of any substantial kind. He can hardly shine, because he can hardly show—hardly, in fact, appear at all. Thus, the lovers are thrown back on private, temporary improvisations, making chivalric courts out of bourgeois bedrooms and temples out of chalets. Since these "transformations" have no social validation, they must necessarily be entirely provisional and ephemeral. Building on nothing, Saint-Preux and Julie can only build nothing, and it is hardly suprising that one of Saint-Preux's torments is that he lives for a series of discontinuous and randomly spaced ecstatic moments ("instants") separated by voids of tedious intervals ("ennuyeux intervalles"). He is not permitted to experience anything additive or cumulative. Since he and Julie are not permitted to be coadunate in any socially recognized way, he is constantly falling into or being pushed into mere apartness—the other side of the house, the other side of the world—from which he is occasionally, unpredictably, and on perpetually changing terms not of his making, summoned back. It is almost as if, outside the "house of the master," time loses its continuity and relatedness. Because of his excluded position, Saint-Preux's experience is deprived of its "durée"; when he is allowed in, it is for the most part an illusory inclusion—a momentary contact in an improvised frame.

As it transpires, there are always factors preventing Julie from meeting Saint-Preux in the proposed chalet—one might say that it turns out to be too far from home. But, she writes to the understandably somewhat desperate Saint-Preux, it should surely be possible to create "a chalet in the town (un chalet à la ville)." The phrase points to the paradoxical strategy to which they have to have recourse. In general it implies that the unlegalized lovers must establish their own fantasy spaces (chalets) inside the socialized space within which they have to live. It is as though there were no genuine "outside" left for them, a worrying phenomenon which was increasingly to attract the attention of nineteenth-century writers. Inside these temporary private "chalets" the unsanctioned sexual embrace may be enjoyed without any disturbance of—or departure from—the existing society. And the place that Julie decrees will serve as a "chalet in the town" could hardly be more revealing, for it is nowhere less than the house of the father—"la maison paternelle."

In the letter in which Julie explains the layout of the house and just when and where Saint-Preux should come to her, she is at considerable pains to stress the danger of the proposed encounter—more so than the bliss it may promise.

> No, my sweet friend, we shall not leave this short life without having tasted happiness for an instant. But yet remember that this instant is surrounded by the horrors of death; that to come is to be subjected to a thousand hazards, to stay is dangerous, to leave is extremely perilous. . . . Let us not deceive ourselves, I know my father too well to doubt that I might see him stab you to the heart immediately with his own hand, if indeed he did not begin with me; for surely I should not be spared, and do you think that I should expose you to this danger if I were not sure of sharing it? Still, remember that it is not a matter of depending on your courage. You must not think of it and I even forbid you quite expressly to carry any weapon for your defense, not even your sword. Besides, it would be perfectly useless to you, for if we are surprised, my plan is to throw myself into your arms, to grasp you strongly in mine, and thus to receive the deadly blow so that we may be parted no more, happier at the moment of my death than I was in my life.

The length of the quotation is necessary to reveal the main source of Julie's emotional excitement. Even a casual glance at the letter would give one the sense that it is hardly calculated to encourage the summoned lover; but a more careful reading reveals that the summons amounts to an emasculation. He is to bring *no* weapons—not even his sword. All those hazards and horrors and dangers she refers to pertain to one thing; they are the aura or atmosphere of the "maison paternelle"—the terrible presence of the father. And it is clear that Julie's imagination is fixed much more on the "sword" of the father than of her lover. Her fantasies center on seeing her father stab the unarmed lover (no question of the father not having *his* sword to hand); then, it becomes clear, the root fantasy is of being herself stabbed by her father. That is the dreaded/desired penetration. Saint-Preux is invited into her bed, not so much to satisfy her love for him as to indulge her imagination of the aroused and irresistible father.

If this seems excessive, let me go on to justify my contention that the most physical contact or encounter actually described in the book is not between Julie and Saint-Preux but between Julie and her father. The extraordinary letter in which Saint-Preux describes his waiting moments in Julie's room prior to her arrival reveals him in the posture of a feverish fetishist. Quite apart from the awkwardness inherent in the epistolary mode, the letter conveys the excitement of a man who derives his sensual satisfactions from associations. Since to all intents and purposes he has been forbidden to have direct access to the body of Julie, as he is summoned in swordless secrecy, it is hardly surprising that his feelings should have been displaced from the person, whom he constantly sees but is as constantly debarred from, to her accessories. So it is that he seems to be deriving his most sexual excitement from rummaging through her clothes which he itemizes almost while fingering them. "All the parts of your scattered dress present to my ardent imagination those of your body they conceal. (Toutes les parties de ton habillement éparses présentent à mon ardente imagination celles de toi-même qu'elles recèlent.)" The excitement mounts until he is passionately kissing the whalebone of her corset which has taken the imprint of her breasts. At this stage he is clearly on the point of involuntary orgasm or masturbation. Then—and we should not attribute this to the exigencies and constraints of the epistolary mode—he seeks relief in writing. "What good fortune to have found ink and paper! I am expressing my feelings in order to temper their excess; I moderate my ecstasy by describing it. (Quel bonheur d'avoir trouvé de l'encre et du paper! J'exprime ce que je sens pour en tempérer l'excès; je donne le change à mes transports en les décrivant.)"

To a modern reader this moment is comic indeed; but in fact it has far-reaching reverberations. Saint-Preux is indeed forced away from the body of the loved other and into writing, an inherently solitary activity. "Donner le change" is effectively to "side-track" or "put off," as when putting dogs on the wrong scent, and for Saint-Preux to state that he is putting his emotions on the wrong scent or track by describing them gives us a clear picture of his position and behavior, which clarifies not only his position in Julie's room at that particular moment, but his position in the whole society throughout the book. He epitomizes the man who is forced to deflect and pervert his feelings into writings—hence, among other things, the extraordinarily long and often seemingly semantically depleted letters he writes. They are a kind of onanism, and for him, it is clear, there are many times when what matters is not *what* he is writing but *that* he is writing. It is almost all he is permitted to do by the rules that determine all the relationships in the society in which he lives. As the moment approaches for Julie's arrival, Saint-Preux seems almost on the verge of impotence. He thinks he hears a noise and immediately wonders whether it is Julie's cruel father ("ton barbare père"), as well he might after her encouraging letter, and then as the door opens and he actually sees her—"c'est elle! c'est elle!"—he would seem to be about to collapse, indeed to be collapsing to the degree that collapsing is compatible with letter-writing. "My heart, my feeble heart succumbs to so many agitations! (Mon coeur, mon faible coeur, tu succombes à tant d'agitations!)" In all seriousness, a reader might very well wonder whether that feebleness was not impairing other organs as well. And the feebleness of the lover is in direct correlation to the power of the father.

I do not think that it is any spirit of disappointed prurience that causes me to maintain that after the conclusion of this letter there is no *sense* of any real sexual connection and experience between Saint-Preux and Julie. It is, indeed, almost as if it never happened. What very certainly does happen, and it takes on a vivid position in the text, is the father's attack on Julie, and their subsequent embrace. Again I must quote at length since, among the hundreds of thousands of words exchanged by the lovers in letters, this is the one brute act that asserts a total dominance over the inferior power of the word. The episode takes place shortly after Lord Bomston, the English aristocrat, has offered to bestow a fortune and an estate on Saint-Preux, thereby hoping to qualify him as an acceptable suitor in Julie's father's eyes. The father dismisses the idea with angry contempt, for reasons to which I shall return; but as a result of all the rational persuasion which people are bringing to bear on him—what, after all, *can* he have against the marriage after Lord Bomston's offer?—his irrational anger mounts until he falls on his daughter and spills his rage on the person at whom it has really been aimed all along.

> At that moment, my father, who thought he felt a reproach in these words and whose fury awaited only a pretext, flew upon your poor friend. For the first time in my life I received a blow; nor was that all, but giving himself up to his fit of passion with a violence equal to the effort he was making, he beat me mercilessly, although my mother had thrown herself between us, covered me with her body, and received some of the blows which were intended for me. In shrinking back to avoid them, I stumbled, I fell, and my head struck the leg of a table which caused it to bleed.

The attack could hardly have been more sexual, albeit specific inadmissible incestuous lust has been translated, or distorted, into violent anger which is permitted to the father simply because he is the father. The fact that at one point he is hitting Julie and her mother indifferently adds to the clarity of just what kind of passional energy he is releasing. Psychoanalysts refer to the figure of the mother and father copulating as "the combined object" in the eyes of the child. Here the wife and daughter form another "combined object" in the eyes of the father—eyes dazed with lustful anger, angry lust. And it is only when he has, as it were drawn blood that the father's orgasmic eruption is over, and "the triumph of anger" finished ("Ici finit le triomphe de la colère").

There follows the reconciliation. Before describing it, Julie discusses "paternal dignity (la dignité paternelle)" and makes the assertion that "a father's heart feels that it is made to pardon and not to have need of being pardoned. (Le coeur d'un père sent qu'il est fait pour pardonner, et non pour avoir besoin de pardon.)" All this points to the fact that for this family/ society, all power, both to punish and to pardon, flows in one direction— *from* the father, not to him. In this way he directly and indirectly controls, one might say owns, the permissible reciprocities of all those in any way connected to him. What has Saint-Preux to offer that can compete with this power? The answer, or one answer, would have to be "words" or more generally the pleasures and persuasions of language. But the father has no need of language: he can just reach out and take what he wants. Thus Julie's account of the scene after the climax—a scene pervaded with a distinctly post-coital silence and exhaustion—continues. The father does not speak to her ("il ne me parla point"), but after dinner as Julie and her parents are gathering round the fire this is what happens.

> I was going to get a chair in order to put myself between them, when, laying hold of my dress and drawing me to him without saying anything, he placed me on his knees. All this was done so suddenly and by a kind of quite involuntary impulse he was almost regretful the moment afterwards. . . . I do not know what false shame prevented those paternal arms from giving themselves up to these sweet embraces. A certain gravity which he dared not abandon, a certain confusion which he dared not overcome put between the father and his daughter this charming embarrassment that modesty and passion cause in lovers. . . . I saw, I felt all this, my angel, and could no longer hold back the tenderness which was overcoming me. I pretended to slip; to prevent myself, I threw an arm around my father's neck. I laid my face close to his venerable cheek, and in an instant it was covered with my kisses and bathed with my tears. I knew by those which rolled from his eyes that he himself was relieved of a great sorrow. My mother shared our rapture. Only sweet and peaceful innocence was wanting in my heart to make this natural scene the most delightful moment of my life.

I want to stress again that nothing remotely comparable in physical contact is ever evoked as occurring between Julie and Saint-Preux. More than that, we may note from her ecstatic description of this "moment" that by a potentially perverse inversion of roles, it is no longer the father who is an interfering obstacle between the daughter and lover, but rather the lover who, by his violation of the girl's "innocence," is the source of a contaminating self-reproach in the otherwise blissful relationship between the daughter and the father. With the beaming mother looking on, this truly does offer a spectacle or scene that is pervaded with latent—and not so latent—incestuous feelings. (I am not so foolish or out of the world as to imagine that there is really no such thing as a family quarrel and a joyful reconciliation but only transformed incestuous to-ings and fro-ings; but here the physical detailing is so excitedly minute in a way that is so absent from Julie's letters to Saint-Preux that it seems to me permissible to perceive the scene and the attendant emotions it aroused in terms of barely controlled incest.) Julie revealingly goes on to add:

> For myself, as I told him, I should think myself only too happy
> to be beaten every day for this reward, and there was no treatment
> so harsh that a single caress from him could not efface it from
> my heart.

After this, what chance has Saint-Preux? He may be her lover, but more importantly he is not, and cannot replace, her father. The lover's words are powerless beside the father's arms ("bras paternels"). Julie herself notes that a "revolution has taken place within me" and asks Claire a key question:

> It seems to me that I look with more regret upon the happy time
> when I lived tranquil and content in the bosom of my family,
> and that I feel the weight of my fault increase along with that of
> the blessings it has caused me to lose. Tell me, cruel one! Tell
> me if you dare, is the time of love gone, no longer to return?

The answer to this question in one very real sense is "yes," and from this point, with no matter what delays, hesitations, and resistances, Julie turns her passional energies towards reachieving a kind of total family structure or situation that will reproduce in extended form the happy family circle which Saint-Preux so imperfectly penetrated and for a brief time almost broke.

There are two more points concerning this remarkable letter that I wish to make, and by way of explaining the detail into which I have gone concerning this one letter (Letter 63 in the first part), I should perhaps say that I regard it as the single most important letter in the whole book. After what is effectively a decisive capitulation to the will and orders of the father (it is on this occasion that he names the husband she will marry), Julie indulges in some of her earlier feelings for Saint-Preux, asking Claire to tell him not to despair or give up hope (though on what he could conceivably base any hope it is hard to see), and reiterating an earlier belief that Heaven made them for one another:

> Yes, yes, I am sure of it; we are destined to be united. . . . Is not such assurance firmly rooted in our hearts? Do we not feel that they are inseparable and that we no longer have but one between us?

Julie calls Claire her "inseparable"; from Saint-Preux she feels "indivisible"; and her dreams, fantasies, and aspirations all tend to the one article of faith that all the people she loves or cares for are "destined to be united": "le bosquet, le chalet à la ville," and her cousin's habitation are, as it were, somehow to be reclaimed and, after necessary purifications or modifications, to be brought together and contained in *la maison paternelle*. But the father is, among other things, he who separates. In the Oedipal situation, it is he who separates the mother from the child, thus standing as the obstacular presence that prevents the child from returning to a state of blissful unseparated oneness with the mother, which is, they say, a primal desire and fantasy. In this particular case we may say that it is the father who separates Julie from the desired sexual partner and lover. But more than that, it is the father who institutes and introduces all those divisions and separations and distances which the child has both to negotiate and to employ as he grows up and out and into the world—spatial (who and what goes where), legal (who and what may and may not be related, as Julie's father at the same time names her husband and bans her lover), and linguistic (the source of the names and the namings of people and things).

Thus the father, as a presence, is the source of all those separations and divisions which ultimately derive from the prohibition of an incestuous return to undifferentiated oneness with the mother. Julie's dream of total union is a projection into the future of a totally regressive urge. What she has to learn, though she resists it in every way she can, is that the world is a place of separations and divisions. Or, to put it another way, you may curl up in the arms and on the lap of the father for ecstatic moments, but you cannot do it forever.

The second point concerns the postscript. Its very delegation to that subsidiary area of the letter is itself significant since in this way it is, as it were, separated from the otherwise blissful aspects of the paternal beating and embrace. I shall quote in full.

P.S. After I had written my letter, I went into my mother's room and there became so ill that I was compelled to return to my bed. I even perceived . . . fear . . . ah, my dear! I quite fear that my fall yesterday may have some consequence more disastrous than I had thought. Thus all is finished for me; all my hopes abandon me at once.

Although pregnancy is never mentioned and this shy allusive hinting is a deliberate kind of mystification, one does not have to read too hard between the lines, or rather along the dots, to infer that Julie has suffered some kind of miscarriage. This is borne out by a letter shortly afterwards.

Thus it is clear that in his assault on his daughter the father also killed the prospective child she would have had from her lover. It is as though such is his power and his anger that he can reach into the latent future and eradicate a life that has already been engendered. In this way he effectively cancels the fertility of her lover, annuls the potency of his inseminations, and leaves him and his life sterile. Saint-Preux is quite right to claim that his *bonheur* has disappeared like a dream leaving no earthly monument, for the one unmistakably concrete evidence and fruit of his union with Julie has been blotted out. In this way such physicality as their relationship enjoyed is rendered effectively nonexistent. The father has attacked that, to him unacceptable, reality and rendered it unreal—as though it had never *been* real. The father can also reach into the past and eliminate a sexuality concerning his family which had neither his sanction nor his licence. Such a father is indeed close to the awesome figure dominating the primal horde in Freud's vision of the powers of the primitive father.

All this might seem to be attributing too much to the father, but the effects of his presence in this book (and the differing degrees of the father's absence in later works) are so crucial that a fairly careful consideration of his role and power is justifiable. The references to the father are not literally innumerable, but they are so plentiful as to give the impression of recurring constantly. They range from references to his body—*le sein d'un père, le cou de mon père, les bras paternels, la main de son père*—to descriptions of his temperament and will—*l'inflexible sévérité de mon père, les préjugés de ton père, le volonté de mon père, le discours de mon père, la violence de ton père, ton inflexible père, la dignité paternelle, des violences d'un père emporté, la vanité d'un père barbare, la défense de mon père, l'esprit de votre père, l'amour paternel, les volontés d'un père, la tyrannie de votre père, la complaisance de mon père* (a good humor or obligingness of a somewhat debatable kind since the condition of its existence is that the will of the father be obeyed in all things. It would be "abused" if Julie left the *maison paternelle* because then, of course, he would have to go, too, in the event the world comes to Clarens, not the other way around). And after Julie's death, there is *la douleur d'un père infortuné*. Recurrently this violent, barbarous, tyrant becomes rather litanously *le meilleur des pères* and, after her marriage to Wolmar, Julie refers with grateful compliance to *la bonne intention des pères* (good intentions which, she says, are guided by Heaven). And, although he says very little (in effect he says only two things—Julie will not marry "that man"—he refuses even to name Saint-Preux—and "Julie will marry Wolmar"), there is above, or behind, everything *la parole du père: la parole de cet homme inflexible est irrévocable*. Not the words (Saint-Preux, we may say, has the words, particularly the written words), but the Word. The Word as spoken by the father is irrational, arbitrary, prejudiced, but it is inflexible, irrevocable, absolute. It is also, in Foucault's terms, *la parole dont la forme première est celle de la contrainte*. ["Le 'Non' du Père" ("The Father's 'No' ") in *Language, Counter-Memory, Practice. Selected Essays and Interviews by Michel Foucault*. ed. Donald F. Bouchard.] Julie's most powerful experience of *la parole du père* is as an interdiction, a prohibition—*la défense du père*.

In this context, let us consider a little more closely the grounds of his utter rejection of Saint-Preux. An early hint, perhaps, occurs when we learn in a letter from Julie that her father is very content with her skill in everything "except heraldry, which he thinks I have neglected." Inasmuch as the study of heraldry involves the tracing and recording of genealogies, it is devoted to a respect for the position, power, and prestige of long lines of the fathers and names of the fathers; it also means a recognition of the *symbols* of that position and power—armorial bearings, coats of arms, and the like. As an object of study it has no use beyond that, no application to other aspects of life and learning; it involves no knowledge of history, and has no educative potential. It is really a kind of fetishism, involving a prolonged and respectful meditation on the titles and trappings of the fathers.

Another hint, a stronger and more obvious one, is given when we learn that Julie's father once killed a friend in a duel and, some years later, lost his only son, which he saw as a punishment for the deed. The paragraph is remarkable, for again it evokes very vividly the physical power, the bloodletting barbarity of the father, and I will quote it at length.

> You know that my father had the misfortune in his youth to kill a man in a duel. This man was a friend; they fought reluctantly, compelled by an absurd point of honour. The fatal blow which deprived one of his life robbed the other of his peace of mind

forever. Since that time, painful remorse has never left his heart.
Often we hear him cry and lament in private; he thinks he still
can feel the blade thrust by his cruel hand into his friend's heart.
In his nightmares he sees the pale and bloody body. Trembling
he gazes upon the mortal wound; he would like to staunch the
flowing blood; terror seizes him; he cries out; the frightful corpse
does not cease pursuing him.

That this is in a letter to Saint-Preux can hardly make him more sure of
himself in his suit for Julie. But the key observation concerning the duel is
that they were "compelled by an absurd point of honour (l'insensé point
d'honneur les y contraignit)." *Insensé* is mad, insane, literally without sense.
The code behind this kind of point of honor—the content is not specified
and is irrelevant—is irrational, arbitrary, and prejudiced, but (and by the
same token) it is inflexible, irrevocable, absolute—that is to say, it is exactly
similar to the Word of the father as I have just described it. And its imperative
asserts itself in the rent body and flowing blood of a friend, just as the
imperative of the Word of the father expresses itself in the beaten body and
flowing blood of a daughter. The Code and the Word are absolute *because*
they are irrational, and vice versa. Their authority cannot be questioned
because they cannot be questioned. Their power does not have to be sanc-
tioned, because theirs is the sanctified, and sanctifying power. The orders,
edicts, and constraints of these powers can only be obeyed. The only alternative is to deny, destroy, or abandon the Code—and the father.

But let me return to Julie's father's rejection of Saint-Preux. Lord Bomston has not only offered to give Saint-Preux money and property; he has
also attacked the pointless irrationality of Julie's father's attachment to the
idea of a noble title as being indispensable in any potential husband for Julie.
Thus Bomston, the cool, rational Englishman:

> Nobility? an empty prerogative in a country where it is more
> injurious than useful. But he [i.e., Saint-Preux] has nobility even
> so, do not doubt it, not written in ink on old parchment but
> engraved on his heart in indelible characters. In short, if you
> prefer reason to prejudice, and if you love your daughter better
> than your titles, you will give her to him.

This argument carries a multiple sting for, in addition to putting the father
in the position of valuing his titles more than his daughter and esteeming an
ink-and-parchment nobility more than a nobility of the heart, it attacks the
substance of his own title. Here I will simply quote from the note provided

by Judith McDowell [in her translation *The New Heloise*] as a gloss on the first point Bomston makes in the passage quoted above concerning the "empty prerogative" of the nobility of Julie's father. Daniel Mornet gives the following explanation for this remark: "Berne had conquered the Vaud region, after which all the Vaud nobility had been excluded from public office; since there was little commerce or industry in which they cared to engage, they were reduced to a life of idleness or expatriation." In other words, Julie's father's noble title is *only* a title, no longer referring to or connoting some kind of service or function in the land as, Lord Bomston points out, titles of nobility usually do. This only serves to sharpen the focus on the *total* irrationality of the father's ferocious attachment to his name.

Here is part of his answer, or rather reaction, since Bomston's points are unanswerable.

> What! My Lord . . . can an honourable man like yourself even think that the last surviving branch of an illustrious family might lose or degrade its name by taking that of a nobody [*d'un quidam*], without a home and reduced to living on charity?

Since Bomston has just offered to bestow a home and money on Saint-Preux, the father's last two objections about him do nothing except reveal the father's wild impenetrability as he flails around trying to produce "reasons" for that which has no reasons, and, so far as he is concerned, requires none. For him it all comes down to the opposition *nom/quidam*. *Quidam* is precisely "some person," an unnamed individual, or as Harrap's dictionary puts it, "Person (name unknown)." Julie's father refuses to recognize Saint-Preux as having what he would recognize as a name. Of course he does have one (just about— you can read a very long way into the book without finding what it is; his letters are always *A Julie* or *Réponse* and so on), but it is one which the father effectively nullifies by his withholding of ratification. He is forced into the ontological category of quidamity (the word exists) "person (name unknown)." Against that, the father upholds the name of the family, which is of course "le nom du père"; not this or that name in particular (indeed, to be honest I cannot recall whether we ever learn his name as opposed to his title *Baron*). The father's unarticulated dread is two-fold: of a daughter taken over by a "quidam"; of a world taken over by quidams, which would render his name, his role, his being, all equally meaningless.

Once married to Monsieur de Wolmar, Julie wants Saint-Preux to assume "a submissive and compliant manner with my father (un air soumis et complaisant avec mon père)" and in the move toward consensus and what I want to call ensemblization, which dominates the later parts of the book, even he comes round to respecting and admiring the father, despite what he rather nicely calls "la bizarrerie de ses préjugés." Bizarre indeed they are, and it is perhaps more than a happy accident that the etymology of that word not only involves the Italian *bizzarro*, "angry," but may also involve the Basque *bizarra*, "beard," thus suggesting a particular kind of male choler as well as the more general sense of the odd, singular, or whimsically strange. The father's prejudices are bizarre, but, as I have had occasion to stress, they are totally binding even on the father himself as well as on those within his jurisdiction. Julie, in her most distraught moment of conflicting urges and imperatives, attempts a kind of psychic fragmentation whereby she will let love dispose of her heart but allow her father to dispose of her hand. "Let a father enslaved by his promise and jealous of a vain title dispose of my hand as he has pledged; let love alone dispose of my heart." Julie has complained that she is enslaved by her father; he in turn is enslaved by his own word ("esclavé de sa parole"). Thus the father is both the source and the slave of the Word. And there is a very important aspect of this double relationship he has to the Word. It is often noted in the book that Julie's father is blind, as well as irrational, given to foolish ideas and to a general *bizarrerie* in his prejudices; there are references to his not knowing what is going on. It is as though he has the most power but sees the least. And this is not attributable to what he is by temperament so much as *where* he is by role. That place, to use a phrase from Lacan, entails blindness ("cette place comportait l'aveuglement").

This comes from Lacan's famous "Seminaire sur 'la Lettre volée' " from which I wish to quote [a] paragraph:

> *Rex et augur*, the legendary, archaic quality of the words seems to resound only to impress us with the absurdity of applying them to a man. And the figures of history, for some time now, hardly encourage us to do so. It is not natural for man to bear alone the weight of the highest of signifiers. And the place he occupies as soon as he dons it may equally be apt to become the symbol of the most outrageous imbecility. Let us say that the King here is invested with the equivocation natural to the sacred, with the imbecility which prizes none other than the subject.
>
> (*Ecrits*)

In the world of this book, Julie's father occupies that role described by Lacan as bearing the "highest of signifiers (*du plus haut des signifiants*)," and we may well feel, as most of the figures in the book do, that over the central issue he displays what at the time seems to be "outrageous imbecility," just that imbecility characterized by Lacan as involved with being the supreme authority.

In all this, Rousseau's book is focusing on something quite extraordinarily crucial in the history of Western society. The Word of the father is, we have noted, bizarre but binding, not because of what it says but because of where it comes from. The father is the ultimate sanction, the absolute "referential" in Lefebvre's sense of the term, the fixed point beyond rationality, from which flows power, to which can only flow obedience; the figure speaking a language of pure command and taboo, the source of nomination ("le nom du père") and prohibition ("le 'non' du père"). Because of the father and his inflexible command and irrevocable world, it seems as if the established institutions are secure and can endure; the momentary fissures of passion are blocked, and marriage, the family, and the whole way of life connected with these institutions as practiced in that society are celebrated as achieving an ideal of incorporative harmony and functioning with serene efficiency. The father makes the contracts, and the contracts hold. But, as we have noted, the Word of the father is even here in a very imperiled condition. His family name and title are becoming meaningless, based on functions, distinctions, and differences that were ceasing to exist. If the apparently "full" word of the father is listened to carefully and discovered to be in fact an "empty" word—what then? (I am taking these words as they are used by Freud [in *Jokes and Their Relation to the Unconscious*, where he writes that words can be taken according as they are "voll" or "leer"] and subsequently Lacan.) What becomes of all the dependence structures and binding contracts—not only between parents and children, husbands and wives, but also between words and meanings, signs and things?

With the nineteenth century, despite those grim images of the cruel authoritarian father such as Thomas Arnold—and indeed during the eighteenth century as well, from around the time of Rousseau's novel (1761; but of course such phenomena have no date of origin)—we are entering a period in which the Word of the father and all that it implies (as outlined above) starts to come into question, and if it may be said that the Word in varying ways ceases to "enslave," it must also be added that it comes to be a problem to establish just what, if anything, it can bind or hold together at all. (It would be a matter for a separate study to consider the figure of the father in nineteeth-century fiction, but as random examples of the weakened figure of the father we can readily think of those comatose, ailing, or absent fathers in the works of Jane Austen, and remember that Emma Bovary's father enters literature with a broken leg, and look ahead to the veritable child-father in *The Golden Bowl*.) Instead of the "nom du père" there is a growing sense of the " 'non' du père," not in the sense of the paternal prohibition, but rather implying the absence of the father, or the father as absence. It is in this sense that Foucault uses the phrase in his essay concerning Hölderlin, . . . in which he also refers to the phenomenon of "l'absence ravageante du père," that father who, at the decisive moment in Julie's life, was so "ravagingly" present for one last display of that blind, awesome power and fury that was perhaps in part provoked by a sense that that power was being in some indiscernible way undermined, and by the as yet unconscious dawning of a unformulable apprehension that it was on the verge of an irreversible decline.

For a long time it seems as though Julie feels torn between having to choose between "lover or father." But there is never any real chance of her abandoning the father for the lover. This is made very clear when Lord Bomston offers what would appear to be a perfect solution for the two lovers. Having attempted in vain to argue against the irrational prejudices of her father, and in vain having offered to make Saint-Preux both propertied and wealthy, this inexhaustible source of rational beneficence offers what would seem to be an impossibility—the legitimization of their passion in a new country. It is too obvious to require any emphasis to see that Lord Bomston acts and wishes to act as a father-figure to the two young lovers; what should be noted is that he is trying to compensate for the blind irrationality of the real father by being the incarnation of *rational* paternity. Julie's father works with fists, threats, and interdictions; Lord Bomston with kindness, praise, and facilitations. Thus, he writes to Julie to invite her to join Saint-Preux in England—a very mythical England drawn from an atlas of imagined wish-fulfillments. He writes as a votary of romantic and passional love rather than familial devotion, and urges Julie to be true to the emotional condition of her heart ("l'état de votre coeur"). Since, he argues, this condition cannot be altered, there is only one thing to do—"you must make it legitimate (c'est le rendre légitime)." He then describes a beautiful estate he has in Yorkshire, with a fine old mansion, grounds with a running river, an ample self-supporting economy, peaceful contented inhabitants, and a complete absence of "hateful prejudices (l'odieux préjugé)." It is indeed "a happy country (cette heureuse contrée)" familiar from pastoral-utopian modes, dream geographies, and golden-age literature since time immemorial. And, he tells Julie, it is all yours. ("Cette terre est à vous, Julie, si vous daignez l'habiter avec lui.")

It is, one might say, the ultimate invitation to two young lovers, kept apart by parental edict. "Come, unique pattern for true lovers. Come, charming and faithful couple, and take possession of a place made to serve as the refuge of love and of innocence." Whether there is or can be such a place may be said to be a question, or a quest, pervading literature of all ages.

The important aspect of it in this context is that it offers not only an ideal setting, subsistence, and so on, but also and most particularly a *legitimization* that had been withheld by the real father. If Julie accepted the invitation she would be acknowledging that there could be an alternative source of legitimization of her relationships to that of her father, and indirectly asserting that not all authority and sanctions come from the father, that there is a space, a law, and a language beyond his jurisdiction. Lord Bomston's final appeal would seem to be irresistible: "The tyranny of an obstinate father will plunge you into the abyss, which you will recognize after your fall . . . you will be sacrificed to the chimerical distinction of rank." But just at this point Rousseau interrupts with a footnote. "The chimerical distinction of rank! This is an English lord who is speaking in this way! Must not all this be fictitious? Reader, what do you say about that?" This is no place to recapitulate the implications and significance of the familiar device whereby the author enters his own text to point to its fictitiousness. What is notable about this particular interruption or interpolation is that it impugns the credibility of Lord Bomston's offer, rational and indeed very Rousseauistic though his sentiments and beliefs are. What Rousseau is effectively marking with his marginal murmur of incredulity is not the fictitiousness of his work but the essential fictitiousness of Lord Bomston's offer. The "tyranny of the father" is real enough. It is that place of refuge for love and innocence, that "heureuse contrée" beyond all prejudices which is, alas, only a fiction. We readers, don't we think so?

Of course Julie declines the invitation. To Claire she writes that although the idea of "conjugal fidelity (la foi conjugale)" fills her with inexpressible delight, she could not be an "ungrateful and unnatural daughter (fille ingrate et dénaturée)" particularly in view of the "blind fondness of a doting father and mother (l'aveugle tendresse d'un père et d'une mère idolatres)." To Lord Bomston she writes with lucid gratitude and absolute rejection, concluding with a ringing affirmation of what she knew all along even if she didn't know that she knew it: "I shall never desert my father's house (je ne deserterai jamais la maison paternelle)." This declaration is reaffirmed to Saint-Preux many letters later when Julie, making use of a schizophrenic strategy by which she tries to combine the mutually exclusive lover and father, declares that she is his forever ("ta Julie sera toujours tienne") but will never leave home. "Do not think that to follow you I shall ever abandon my father's house (Ne pense point que pour te suivre j'abandonne jamais la maison paternelle)." The "bosquet" and the "chalet" are insubstantial dream-stuff: ultimate power, authority, and reality reside in, and only in, "la maison paternelle."

So there Julie stays, and marries the man her father chooses for her.

This man, Monsieur de Wolmar, is all too obviously a kind of surrogate for the father, of similar age and with no previous involvements or attachments before the imperative of the father was extended to him and he obeyed "seconding my father's intentions (*secondant les intentions de mon père*)" as Julie revealingly writes to Saint-Preux. At the same time, he is a cool, passionless figure, the incarnation of arid voyeuristic rationality, sexually an entirely negative figure of whom the displaced passionate father could not feel jealous. For Julie he offers a reprieve from love which, she writes to Saint-Preux, so far from being necessary to make a happy marriage, is precisely what opposes or prevents it. "Love is accompanied by a continual uneasiness over jealousy or privation, little suited to marriage, which is a state of enjoyment and peace. (L'amour est accompagné d'une inquiétude continuelle de jalousie ou de privation, peu convenable au mariage, qui est un état de jouissance et de paix.)" "Jouissance" as we know can refer to the pleasure of orgasm but this is hardly its connotation in Julie's calm rationale for abandoning l'amour. The stress is on "paix," and it would seem that Julie's ambition is to attempt to turn her marriage into a condition of continual rest, or "arrest," in the interests of "peace." But what kind of life is it that is drained of all "*inquiétude*"? "Death" is quite obviously the abrupt and only completely accurate answer, and what Julie is searching for could be seen as a kind of death-in-life, a permanent stasis in which everyone has come together and no one need move again. She names her garden—a strange enclosed world of her own making in which nature is not so much domesticated as bourgeois-ified—Elysium, quite aware that it refers to the abode of the blessed after death. And the economy of her household, described at a length inordinate even by Saint-Preux's standards, is organized, routinized, and supervised down to such detail that one feels that in such a place the involuntary, the unpredictable, the "unquiet" would never happen again.

The first letter Julie writes after her marriage (beginning of book 4) is to her cousin Claire urging that they annul the distinction between their two houses by conflating them, since Claire's husband, another somewhat senior citizen, has recently died. Julie is embarking on her grand dream of rehousing the world in her home, the house of the father. The attempt at ultimate synthesis has begun. And one of her reasons for pressing Claire to join her in her home is worth noting. Something is lacking. Her husband is unresponsive ("il ne répond pas assez à ma fantaisie"), his tenderness is *too* reasonable ("trop raisonable"). But Julie can hardly wish for an inrush of unreason since that would be to seek the very "inquiétude" she has chosen to leave behind. She refers to "all these voids (tous ces vides)," voids specifically left by her mother's death and the death of Claire's husband, but more generally by the fact that, as her children are too small for the kind of reciprocal love she needs, there is no one on whom she can lavish the full energies of her love and receive love in return. It is this role she wants to be filled by her cousin, the inseparable. Yet clearly the void is hardly one that can be filled by a cousin; indeed it could be said to be an ontological void. But there is no need to go so far to comprehend what Julie is lacking. It is not necessarily Saint-Preux himself, but the passional irregularities, intensities, frictions, and reciprocities which can only be experienced in that "inquiétude continuelle" which she formally put behind her when she chose to reject him. It would seem that marriage as conceived by Julie has its privations as well as its peace; perhaps, even, it is its peace which is part of its privation.

Having brought Claire into the house, Julie extends her plans for inclusion. Her husband writes a courteous and generous letter inviting Saint-Preux to come and share their house, and he accepts, content to feel like "the child of the house (comme l'enfant de la maison)." The father, temporarily absent because he is involved in a lawsuit (and one may imagine that he was often involved in such eristic errands, given his temperament), rejoins them. Even Lord Bomston is brought in, so that in a very real sense we may say that it is as if they are all there together in "la maison paternelle," all united, and all so harmonious that Wolmar insists that Saint-Preux should embrace his wife, Julie, while Saint-Preux comes to love and respect the very father who ruined his life. Friction is at degree zero, and reconciliation and homecoming are everywhere. This may seem like a version of the commonplace "they all lived happily ever after" dream. But there is one aspect of this "ensemblizing" drive which is worth special attention. It concerns the move toward indistinguishability on the part of Julie and Claire, particularly as mothers, a move that extends toward their children as well. It entails at times what amounts to an interchangeability of selves, so that the I-Thou disjunction/conjunction is dissolved. Thus Julie:

> I feel that I doubly enjoy my little Marcellin's caresses when I see you sharing them. When I embrace your daughter, I imagine I am pressing you to my bosom. We have said a hundred times, as we see our little babies playing together, that our united hearts mix them, and we no longer know to which one of us each of the three belongs.

Saint-Preux, writing about Claire's daughter Henriette, refers to her mothers:

> I say her *mothers*, for to see the manner in which they act with her, it is difficult to distinguish the real one, and some strangers

who arrived today are or seem to be still in doubt on the matter.
In fact, both call her *Henriette* or *my daughter*, indifferently. She
calls one mama and the other little mama.

And later he writes to Claire: "You are both more dear to me than ever, but
my heart no longer distinguishes between you and does not separate the
inseparables." However, this same letter contains an account of a very ominous dream, to which I shall return.

At the conclusion of book 5, Julie effectively suggests that Claire should
marry Saint-Preux, and it is hard not to assume that, given their feelings of
interchangeability (if not actual identicality), this would permit some vicarious indulgence in what might be expected to be the customary sexual em-
braces that would then legitimately ensue.

> Ah cousin! What delight for me to unite forever two hearts so
> well formed for each other, who have been joined for so long in
> my own. Let them be even more closely joined in it, if possible.
> Let there be but one heart for you and me. Yes, my Claire, you
> will still serve your friend by indulging your love, and I shall be
> surer of my own sentiments when I shall no longer be able to
> distinguish between him and you.

The suggestion is firmly declined, but it testifies to an inclination to live in
a kind of emotional blur in which her feelings can only be sure of themselves
when they are no longer able, or constrained, to distinguish between their
objects. From one point of view this desire to establish an inclusive happy-
family pile in which, at least emotionally speaking, the various figures—
cousin, lover, friend, father—are, as it were, heaped indistinguishably together, is an attempt to realize a dream of total harmony in which all the
oppositional elements in human relationships—familial, passional—have
been eliminated and all the different parties can come together to live for
ever and ever in peace and concord, never to part again. As Saint-Preux puts
it, writing in the optative mood, if he can just see his friend Edward (Lord
Bomston) happy, "we will all rejoin each other never to part again (nous
nous rassemblons tous pour ne nous plus séparer)" though, as he notes in
passing, if that state of perfect happiness were achieved, there would not in
fact be much else for him to wish for, or to vow to do. Such a vision of
human and humane harmony is from this point of view the acme of Enlightenment thought. From another point of view, Julie's dream (shared by
others, but originating with her, or with her and Claire) involves an abandoning of distinctions, a loss of a sense of difference, which could be seen

to point the way back to that "infamous promiscuity of things and women" which for Vico was the abhorrent state from which civilization had to emerge, that incestuous *ur*-confusion we think of as the primordial reign of chaos and old night. That, at its height, civilization should start to look, albeit obliquely and very indirectly, longingly back to the precivilized state from which it emerged is a phenomenon of some considerable implications. And that this incestuous dream is engendered in, and arguably engendered by, *la maison paternelle*—the paradigm locus of authority in society—is perhaps even more thought-provoking. The father, he-who-separates, produces a daughter who wishes to be she-who-brings-everyone-together-again. The rule of law engenders a dream of indistinguishability. Rousseau lays bare the outlines of a paradox that has more profound implications than he himself, perhaps, could guess.

But for all the aura of loving harmony, all is not quite well at Clarens and in Elysium, and this brings me to Saint-Preux's nightmare, which I mentioned earlier. Saint-Preux has the dream after he has been established in Clarens but is setting out on a journey with Lord Bomston. In the dream he thinks he sees Julie's mother on her deathbed and Julie on her knees beside her, weeping and kissing her hands. Some remarks are exchanged which conclude with the mother saying,

> "You will be a mother in your turn. . . . " She could not fin-
> ish. . . . I tried to raise my eyes and look at her; I saw her no
> more. In her place I saw Julie. I saw her; I recognized her although
> her face was covered with a veil. I gave a shriek, I rushed forward
> to put aside the veil, I could not reach it. I stretched forth my
> arms, I tormented myself, but I touched nothing. "Friend, be
> calm," she said to me in a faint voice. "The terrible veil covers
> me. No hand can put it aside." [He has the dream three times.]
> Always the mournful sight, always that same appearance of death,
> always that impenetrable veil eluding my hands and hiding from
> my eyes the dying person it covered.

One might speculate endlessly, and perhaps fruitlessly, about the interpretation of this dream (how to read dreams *within* fictions is an interesting matter in its own right). But that veil subsumes in very clear symbolic form a great deal; all that has indeed separated Julie from her lover, all that she has allowed to come between them, and all that she has interposed between them herself—the inseparable cousin (at the beginning), the Word of the father, "la maison paternelle," the "chaîne indissoluble" of her marriage, the rigid and powerful *cortège* in which she is fixed as the mother. All these have meant that when Saint-Preux has attempted to "reach" her, no matter how much he has stretched out his arms and tormented himself, he has always and inevitably (after the very brief and apparently soon regretted affair) touched nothing, because of that veil "redoutable" and "impénétrable." It is also, of course, the bridal veil which, worryingly enough, has turned into a shroud. So disturbing is the dream that Saint-Preux rushes to wake up Lord Bomston, who delivers the usual scolding ("you are worthless, [vous n'êtes rien]," and then drives Saint-Preux back to Clarens where he can sneak a glimpse of Julie and tear away "that fatal veil which is woven in your mind (ce fatal voile tissu dans votre cerveau)." Ashamed as usual, Saint-Preux only pauses to hear the voices of Julie and her cousin coming from Elysium and returns to his travels quite happy, feeling that he has at least done the honor to himself as Edward's friend of "getting the better of a dream (de le mettre audessus d'un songe)." But, in a sense, it is the dream that has got the better of him long before he had it, and, in any event, it is the dream that gets the better of them all in a way which I will try to describe in the concluding part of this essay. Claire, in her answering letter in which she urges them both to hurry back to their "little community (la petite communauté)," registers her sense of the ominousness of the dream. "That veil! That veil! . . . There is something indefinably sinister in it which disturbs me each time I think of it." The implications involve the unconfrontable and unthinkable fact of Julie's death and her disappearing into eternal unreachability.

At one point Monsieur de Wolmar announces his intention to go on a trip which will keep him away for a few days. He asks whether Saint-Preux would like to come with him or stay at Clarens with Julie (as Julie writes to her cousin, her husband seems "determined to drive me to the limit"). Saint-Preux promptly states his preference for remaining, an answer which deeply pleases the perversely rational husband. However, the prospective situation disturbs Julie, and she communicates her anxieties to her cousin, registering her concern about her own latent instabilities.

> Whatever you think of yourself, your mind [âme] is calm and tranquil, I am sure. Objects present themselves to it such as they are, but mine, ever agitated like a moving wave [comme une onde agitée], confounds and disfigures them.

Whether we decide to translate âme as "soul" or "mind," it refers to some absolutely central spirit or prime mover, and for Julie to say that hers is constantly agitated "comme une onde agitée" is to reveal an aspect of her character of far-reaching significance. For if she is water at the center, fluid, labile, potentially "thalassic," then all the meticulous structuring and archi-tecture of her life, starting with her complete submission to her father/husband (*he's* not fluid at the center—he is empty, a very different matter) and extending to the meticulous routinizing of life at Clarens, can be seen in another light. To some extent, perhaps a large extent, they may be mo-tivated by a fear of internal dissolution, a kind of passional liquefaction in which she would lose herself and drown. By the time we reach the height of the romantic era, however we wish to date it, we find many metaphors for yearning to dissolve and merge with the elements, other people, the universe, whatever. The "flow" seems to have lost its terrors and revealed its enrapturing allure. But for Julie it is still a source of worry. Her carefully constructed life may be seen as, in part, a dike erected against the possible flood tides within her, just as her marriage, as she clearly indicated, was not a way of releasing passion but of getting away from it. The problematical relationship (or opposition) between the dissolving liquefactions of passion and the binding structurations of marriage is at the very heart, or *âme*, of the great bourgeois novels of adultery of the nineteenth century.

Claire is not liquid and she writes back promptly with some sensible-seeming advice to Julie. She reminds her that she loved as Héloïse did and that, like her, she is now "pious." If Julie is worried about being alone with Saint-Preux, then make sure the children are always around and go off for some excursions—boat rides, for instance.

> You like boat rides; you deprive yourself of them for the sake of your husband who fears the water and for the children whom you do not wish to hazard on it. Take advantage of the time of this absence to indulge yourself in this amusement, leaving your children in Fanchon's care [Fanchon Anet is Julie's closest attendant].

It is revealing indeed that Monsieur de Wolmar is frightened by water, but it is perhaps not exactly the most prudent possible advice to recommend that the watery-centered Julie go for boat rides with her former lover. Her justification that they will always be under the protection of the boatmen ("sous la protection des bateliers") seems a little feeble. There are a large number of very important boat rides in the history of the novel, but the figure of the protective boatman is conspicuous by its absence. There may be boatmen but they do not protect. And indeed if the really dangerous "waters" are internal, it is hard to see how they could.

The excursion by boat is duly taken and described by Saint-Preux in a letter which concludes part four. It is a trip laden with omen to say the very least—indeed, it is effectively all omen, starting even from the base topography, for Julie's *house*, Saint-Preux reminds Lord Bomston, is *not far from the lake* ("Vous savez que la maison de Mme. de Wolmar n'est loin du lac") and she likes being on the *water* ("elle aime les promenades sur l'eau"). This basic house/water topography could hardly appear more naturally than it does in Rousseau's book; at the same time it could hardly acquire more symbolic implications than it finally does. For Julie, householder and gardener supreme, is doomed to die by water. To select a few of the more notable details from their seminal boat-trip, Saint-Preux steers the boat into the middle of the lake, i.e., as far from the shore as possible; a gale blows up and soon the waves are terrible ("*les ondes devinrent terribles*"); the frail boat cannot resist them, and it is driven to the opposite shore. There it is impossible at first to find any shelter or a place to land, and Julie is seized with sickness and almost faints at the side of the boat ("Julie saisie du mal de coeur, faible et défaillante au bord du bateau"). Fortunately she is "used to the water (Heureusement elle était faite à l'eau)" and this condition does not last long. She then acts as a kind of lacustrine Florence Nightingale and goes around wiping brows and dispensing water and wine. There is just one moment when two planks are opened by a particularly deluging shock and it almost seems as though the boat might indeed founder; the recorded reactions are revealing:

> For an instant, two planks being partly opened in an impact which wet us all, she thought the boat broke to pieces, and in an exclamation from this tender mother, I distinctly heard these words: "Oh my children, must I see you no more?" As for myself, whose imagination always exceeds the peril, although I knew the real state of the danger, I expected to see the boat swallowed up at any moment, that affecting beauty struggling in the midst of the waves, and the pallor of death dulling the roses of her cheeks.

Comment on Saint-Preux's morbid imaginings is redundant (notice he does not imagine trying to *save* her but only watching her drown!), though to the extent that they are perverse it must be admitted that his treatment by society goes some long way to explaining why they should be so (you surely can't be treated as a "quidam" in a hierarchical society for very long without some perversion of the imagination taking place). On this occasion the boat reaches the shore safely, but his vision of "le bateau englouti" and the lovers (once-lovers, if you will) "drowning" together, is one which in varying forms may be said to have haunted the European imagination for well over a century to come.

Julie herself maintains that their love is not repressed passion but purified passion and this is the rarity of her relationship to Saint-Preux ("on étouffe de grandes passions; rarement on les épure"). She insists that they have managed to transform "amour" into "amitié" and that as a result they can "spend our life together in fraternal familiarity and peaceful innocence (passer les jours ensemble dans la familiarité fraternelle et dans la paix de l'innocence)." Despite the length, or rather perhaps because of the length, at which they reassure and congratulate each other on these purifications and transformations, one registers both their precariousness and their latent perversity—to treat an ex-lover with "fraternal familiarity" because that falls within the bounds of the legitimate is, as I have suggested, to repress adulterous feelings only to allow them to be reinstituted as incestuous ones. It is a situation of uneasy equilibrium which, in effect, can only wait for whatever will precipitate its inevitable disintegration—dangerous waters within or without. In any event, it is once again the external lake that precipitates a crisis, and this time one that is terminal.

On an expedition to the castle of Chillon on the lake, Julie's young son falls into the water and she runs back like an arrow and throws herself in after him ("part comme un trait, et s'élance après lui"). The account of the accident is in a letter from Fanchon Anet, the attendant mentioned earlier by Claire:

> We had neither servants nor a boat there; it took time to get them out . . . the child is recovered, but the mother . . . the shock, the fall, the condition she was in . . . who knows better than I the dangers of such a fall! . . . She remained unconscious for a very long time. . . . From some orders she has given me, I see that she does not believe she will recover. I am too unhappy; she will not recover. Madame d'Orbe is more altered than she.

And it is that separated inseparable and much changed cousin who informs Saint-Preux of Julie's death in brusque terms, which are indeed appropriate from someone stunned with grief, but which nevertheless carry something of the tone of a reproach as though it were somehow all his fault, both for loving her and for having the dream about the veil. "It is over. Impudent, unfortunate man, unhappy dreamer! You shall never see her again . . . the veil . . . Julie is no more. (C'en est fait, homme imprudent, homme infortuné, malheureux visionnaire! Jamais vous ne la reverrez . . . le voile . . . Julie n'est.)" We are given no detail of Saint-Preux's reaction, but we learn that Claire goes literally out of her mind ("hors de sens"), rolling about the floor, mumbling incoherently and gnawing on the legs of chairs ("mordant les pièds

des chaises"), a demonstration of an intensity of grief, indeed of sheer un-
controlled passion, which is scarcely to be matched by any of the other signs
of feeling in the entire book—perhaps only by the wild outburst of anger of
Julie's father. It is the grief of the "inseparable" who finds herself truly and
irrevocably separate; the response to a forced and final breaking of a bond
so close and so deep that it seems to me to bespeak that primordial urge to
merge back into intrafamilial oneness that goes under the name of incest. It
is with no intention of suggesting any actual sexual perversity that I point
out that from the long account of Julie's dying, written by her husband, it
transpires that not only will Claire not leave Julie's bedroom, but Julie invites
her to share her bed ("couche dans mon lit"), while the tired husband is sent
away ("l'on me renvoya").

Saint-Preux is not heard from again, though we gather he is temporarily
prostrated with grief. But enclosed with Wolmar's letter is a last letter from
Julie to Saint-Preux which reveals that there was indeed something wrong
with her "project," i.e., her dream of ensemblization.

> We must give up our projects. All is changed, my good
> friend. . . . We dreamed of rejoining each other. *That reunion was
> not good* [my italics]. It is Heaven's blessing to have prevented it,
> thereby, without a doubt, preventing misfortune.

This is tantamount to saying that adultery would have been inevitable (and
for Julie, of course, death is far preferable to such a dishonor); but more, it
is a revocation of the whole dream of union or rather multiple reunion itself.
It does not work. As Julie reveals, there was a split between "will" and
"feeling" that was permanently there.

> This sentiment, nourished despite myself, was involuntary; it has
> cost my innocence nothing. Everything which was dependent on
> my will was devoted to my duty. If my heart, which was not
> dependent on it, was devoted to you, that was my torment and
> not my crime.

The House of Clarens, then, was built on repression and a secret "torment."
No wonder it was bound to fall.

In her last letter, it is clear that Julie is still thinking in terms of some
kind of total union of all her loved ones. "Would that I could invent still
stronger bonds in order to unite all who are dear to me." But as Claire reveals
in the last letter of the book there is no union left, only despairing fragmentation and monadic misery. This letter effectively outlines the fall of the

House of Clarens, a fall, to my mind, of inestimable importance for the subsequent history of European literature. She writes to Saint-Preux:

> You will see here only grief and sorrow; and perhaps our common affliction will be a solace for your own. In order to be given vent, mine needs you. I alone can neither weep, nor cry out, nor make myself understood. Wolmar understands me but does not respond to me. The sorrow of the unhappy father is buried within himself. . . . My children affect me but are incapable of pitying me. *I am alone amid everyone (Je suis seule au milieu de tout le monde.)* [my italics]

By the end of the letter, which is the end of the book, Claire, writing in a state of distracted discontinuity, reveals her sense of the utter void which has been left by Julie's death and her desire to rejoin her inseparable cousin in the grave as soon as possible.

Perhaps, when I stated earlier that the book was primarily about a love affair between father and daughter, I should have added—and between cousin and cousin. As far as the book is concerned, when Julie dies, Saint-Preux vanishes. But the most moving and significant statement in the whole letter is the one I have italicized. This enormous book is for the greater part concerned with an extensive dream of union whereby the family house can be extended and modified so as to contain everyone (and everything) that Julie loves in different ways within it; a dream of achieving a lasting tranquillity within which varying, and latently oppositional, relationships may be enjoyed in a kind of steady state of constant calm, friction degree zero. In a sense it is a dream of the world itself as one unchanging and contented family. But there is that agitated water . . . unacknowledged sexuality . . . and death. At the end, all the bonds have snapped: father, husband, cousin, lover, children, thrown back or turned in upon themselves, wandering around in a daze of misery without communication. Instead of the world as family, we have the family as isolation: "Je suis seule au milieu de tout le monde." There is a glimpse here of that unspeakable solitude at the heart of all relationships which every other page of the book works to transcend or conceal or deny. After the fall of the House of Clarens—which is the paradigm fall of "la maison paternelle"—that glimpse would, in time, be extended into a scrutiny that was to characterize some of the greatest European novels of the nineteenth century.

ALLAN BLOOM

The Education of Democratic Man: Emile

In the *Discourse on the Origins of Inequality* Rousseau summons men to hear for the first time the true history of their species. Man was born free, equal, self-sufficient, unprejudiced, and whole; now, at the end of history, he is in chains (ruled by other men or by laws he did not make), defined by relations of inequality (rich or poor, noble or commoner, master or slave), dependent, full of false opinions or superstitions, and divided between his inclinations and his duties. Nature made man a brute, but happy and good. History— and man is the only animal with a history—by the development of his faculties and the progress of his mind has made man civilized, but unhappy and immoral. History is not a theodicy but a tale of misery and corruption.

Emile, on the other hand, has a happy ending, and Rousseau says he cares little if men take it to be only a novel, for it ought, he says, to be the history of his species. And therewith he provides the key to *Emile*. It is, as Kant says, the work which attempts to reconcile nature with history, man's selfish nature with the demands of civil society, hence, inclination with duty. Man requires a healing education which returns him to himself. Rousseau's paradoxes—his attack on the arts and the sciences and his practice of them, his praise of the savage and natural freedom over against his advocacy of the ancient city, the general will and virtue, his perplexing presentations of himself as citizen, lover, and solitary—are not expressions of a troubled soul but accurate reflections of an incoherence in the structure of the world we all face, or rather, in general, do not face; and *Emile* is an experiment in

From *Daedalus: Journal of the American Academy of Arts and Sciences* 107, no. 3 (Summer 1978). © 1978 by the American Academy of Arts and Sciences.

restoring harmony to that world by reordering the emergence of man's
acquisitions in such a way as to avoid the imbalances created by them, while
allowing the full actualization of man's potential. Rousseau believed that his
was a privileged moment, a moment when all of man's faculties had revealed
themselves and when man had, furthermore, attained for the first time knowledge of the principles of human nature. *Emile* is the canvas on which Rousseau tried to paint all of the soul's acquired passions and learning articulated
in such a way as to cohere with man's natural wholeness. It is a *Phenomenology
of the Mind* posing as Dr. Spock.

Thus *Emile* is one of those rare total or synoptic books, a book with
which one can live and which becomes deeper as one becomes deeper, a
book comparable to Plato's *Republic*, which it is meant to rival or supersede.
But it is not recognized as such in spite of Rousseau's own judgment that it
was his best book and Kant's sentiment that its publication was an event
comparable to the French Revolution. Of his major works it is the least
studied or commented on. It is as though its force had been entirely spent
on impact with men like Kant and Schiller, leaving only the somewhat cranky
residue for which the book retains its fame in teacher training schools—the
harangues against swaddling and in favor of breast feeding and the learning
of a trade. Whatever the reasons for its loss of favor (and this would make
an interesting study) *Emile* merits advocacy for it is a truly great book, one
which lays out for the first time and with the greatest clarity and vitality
the modern way of posing the problems of psychology.

By this I mean that Rousseau is at the source of the tradition which
replaces virtue and vice as the causes of a man's being good or bad, happy
or miserable, with such pairs of opposites as sincere/insincere, authentic/
inauthentic, inner-directed/other-directed, real self/aliened self. All these
have their source in Rousseau's analysis of *amour de soi* and *amour-propre*, a
division within man's soul resulting from man's bodily and spiritual dependence on other men which ruptures his original unity or wholeness. This
distinction is supposed to give the true explanation of the tension within
man which had in the past been understood to be a result of the opposed
and irreconcilable demands of the body and the soul. *Emile* gives the comprehensive account of the genesis of amour-propre, displays its rich and
multifarious phenomena (spreads the peacock's tail, as it were), and maps
man's road back to himself from his spiritual exile (his history) during which
he wandered through nature and society, a return to himself which incorporates into his substance all the cumbersome treasures he gathered en route.
This analysis supersedes that based on the distinction between body and
soul—which in its turn had activated the quest for virtue, the taming and

controlling of the body's desires under the guidance of the soul's reason—
and initiates the great longing to be one's self and the hatred of alienation
which characterizes all modern thought. The wholeness, unity, or singleness
of man—a project ironically outlined in the *Republic*—is the serious intention
of *Emile* and almost all that came afterward.

    Emile is written in defense of man against a great threat which bids fair
to cause a permanent debasement of the species. That threat is apparently
almost inevitable universal dominance of a certain low human type which
Rousseau was the first to isolate and name: the bourgeois. Rousseau's enemy
was not the ancien régime, its throne, its altar, or its nobility. He was certain
that all that was finished, that the inner conviction had left the ancien régime
and that revolution would shortly sweep it away to make room for a new
world based on the egalitarian principles of the new philosophy. The struggle
would concern the kind of man who was going to inhabit that world, for
the striking element of the situation was and is that the menace comes from
a low human consequence of a true theoretical insight. The bourgeois is the
incarnation of the political science of Hobbes and Locke, the first principles
of which Rousseau accepted. Here Tocqueville's scheme in *Democracy in
America*, which is adopted from Rousseau, casts light on his intention. Equality is now almost a providential fact; no one believes any longer in the justice
of the principles on which the old distinctions between ranks or classes were
made and which were the basis of the old regime. The only question remaining is whether universal tyranny will result or freedom can accompany
equality. It is to the formation of free men and free communities founded
on egalitarian principles to which Rousseau and Tocqueville are dedicated.

    Now, who, according to Rousseau, is the bourgeois? Most simply,
following Hegel's formula, he is the man motivated by fear of violent death,
the man whose primary concern is preservation or comfortable preservation.
Or, to describe the inner workings of his soul, he is the man who, when
dealing with others, thinks only of himself, and, in his understanding of
himself, thinks only of others. He is a role-player. The bourgeois is contrasted
by Rousseau, on the one hand, with the natural man, who is whole and
simply concerned with himself, and with the citizen, on the other, whose
very being consists in his relation to his city, who understands his good to
be identical with the common good. The bourgeois distinguishes his own
good from the common good, but his good requires society, and hence he
exploits others while depending on them. He must define himself in relation
to them. The bourgeois comes to be when men no longer believe that there
is a common good, when the notion of the fatherland decays. Rousseau hints
that he follows Machiavelli in attributing this decay to Christianity, which

promised the heavenly fatherland and thereby took away the supports from the earthly fatherland, leaving social men who have no reason to sacrifice private desire to public duty.

What Christianity revealed, modern philosophy gave an account of: man is not naturally a political being; he has no inclination toward justice. By nature he cares only for his own preservation, and all of his faculties are directed to that end. Men are naturally free and equal in the decisive respects: they have no known authority over them, and they all pursue the same independent end. Men have a natural right to do what conduces to their preservation. All of this Rousseau holds to be true. He differs only in that he does not believe that the duty to obey the laws of civil society can be derived from self-interest. Hobbes and Locke burdened self-interest with more than it can bear; in every decisive instance the sacrifice of the public to the private follows from nature. They produced hypocrites who make promises they cannot intend to keep and who feign concern for others out of concern for themselves, thus using others as means to their ends and alienating themselves. Civil society becomes merely the combat zone for the pursuit of power—control over things and especially over men. With enlightenment the illusions are dispelled, and men learn that they care about life more than country, family, friendship, or honor. Fanaticism, although dangerous and distorting, could at least produce selfless and extraordinary deeds. But now it gives way to calculation. And pride, although the spur to domination, is allied with that noble indifference to life which seems the condition of freedom and the resistance to tyranny. But quenched by fear, pride gives way to vanity, the concern for petty advantages over others. This diminishing of man is the apparent result of enlightenment about his true nature.

In response to this challenge Rousseau undertakes a rethinking of man's nature in its relation to the need for society which history has engendered. What he attempts is to present an egalitarian politics which can rival Plato's politics in moral appeal rather than one which debases man for the sake of the will-of-the-wisp, security. He takes an ordinary boy and experiments with the possibility of his becoming an autonomous man—morally and intellectually independent, as was Plato's philosopher-king, an admittedly rare, and hence aristocratic, human type. The success of this venture would prove the dignity of man as man, of all normal men, and thus provide a high-level ground for the choice of democracy. Since Rousseau, overcoming of the bourgeois has been regarded as almost identical with the problem of the realization of true democracy and the achievement of "genuine personality."

The foregoing reflections give a clue to the literary character of *Emile*.

The two great moral-political traditions displaced by the modern natural right teachings were accompanied by great works of what may loosely be called poetry. This poetry depicts great human types who embody the alternative visions of the right way of life, who make that way of life plausible, who excite admiration and emulation. The Bible, on the highest level, gives us prophets and saints; and in the realm of ordinary possibility it gives us the pious man. Homer and Plutarch give us, at the peak, heroes; and, for everyday fare, gentlemen. But modern philosophy could not inspire a great poetry corresponding to itself. The man whom it produced is too contemptible for the noble Muse; he can never be a model for those who love the beautiful. This failing is symptomatic of the maiming of man effected by the prosaic new philosophy. Rousseau picks up the challenge and dares to enter into competition with the greatest of the old poets. He creates a human type whose charms can rival those of the saint or the tragic hero, the natural man, and thereby shows that his thought can comprehend the beautiful in man.

Emile consists of a series of stories, and its teaching comes to light only when one has grasped each in its complex detail and artistic unity. Interpretations of this first Bildungsroman requires a union of *l'esprit de géométrie* and *l'esprit de finesse*, a union which it both typifies and teaches. It is impossible here to do more than indicate the plan of the work and tentatively describe its general intention in the hope of convincing others how imperative it is to study this work.

I

Emile is divided into two large segments. Books 1–3 are devoted to the rearing of a civilized savage, a man who cares only about himself, who is independent and self-sufficient and on whom no duties are imposed that run counter to his inclinations and divide him, whose knowledge of the crafts and the sciences does not involve his incorporation into the system of public opinion and division of labor. Books 4–5 attempt to bring this atomic individual into human society and toward moral responsibility on the basis of his inclinations and his generosity.

Rousseau's intention in the first segment comes most clearly to light in its culmination when Jean-Jacques, the tutor, gives his pupil the first and only book he is to read prior to early adulthood. Before presenting his gift, Jean-Jacques expresses to the reader the general sentiment that he hates all books—including implicitly and especially the book of books, the guide of belief and conduct, the Bible. Books act as intermediaries between men and things; they attach men to the opinions of others rather than making them understand on their own or leaving them in ignorance. They excite the imagination, increasing thereby the desires, the hopes, and the fears beyond the realm of the necessary. All the early rearing is an elaborate attempt to avoid the emergence of the imagination which, according to the *Discourse on the Origins of Inequality*, is the faculty that turns man's intellectual progress into the source of his misery. But, in spite of this general injunction against books and in direct contradiction to what he has just said, Rousseau does introduce a book, one which presents a new teaching and a new mode of teaching. The book is *Robinson Crusoe*, and it is not meant to be merely a harmless amusement for Emile but to provide him with a vision of the whole and a standard for the judgment of both things and men.

Robinson Crusoe is a solitary man in the state of nature, outside of civil society and unaffected by the deeds or opinions of men. His sole concern is his preservation and comfort. All his strength and reason are dedicated to those ends, and utility is his guiding principle, one which organizes all his knowledge. The world he sees contains neither gods nor heroes; there are no conventions. Neither the memory of Eden nor the hope of salvation affect his judgment. Nature and natural needs are all that is of concern to him. *Robinson Crusoe* is a kind of Bible of the new science of nature and reveals man's true original condition.

This novel provides, moreover, a new kind of play for the first activity of the imagination. In the first place, the boy does not imagine beings or places which do not exist. He imagines himself in situations and subject to necessities which are part of his experience. Actually his imagination divests itself of the imaginary beings that seem so real in ordinary society and are of human making. He sees himself outside of the differences of nation and religion which cover over nature and are the themes of ordinary poetry. Second, he does not meet with heroes to whom he must subject himself or whom he is tempted to rival. Every man can be Crusoe and actually is Crusoe to the extent that he tries to be simply man. Crusoe's example does not alienate Emile from himself as do the other fictions of poetry; it helps him to be himself. He understands his hero's motives perfectly and does not ape deeds the reasons for which he cannot imagine.

A boy, who imagining himself alone on an island uses all of his energy in thinking about what he needs to survive and how to procure it, will have a reason for all his learning; its relevance to what counts is assured; and the fear, reward, or vanity that motivate ordinary education are not needed. Nothing will be accepted on authority; the evidence of his senses and the call of his desires will be his authorities. Emile, lost in a woods and hungry, finds his way home to lunch by his knowledge of astronomy. For him astronomy is not a discipline forced on him by his teachers, or made attractive by the opportunity to show off, or an expression of his superstition. Thus Rousseau shows how the sciences which historically made men more dependent on one another can serve their independence. Thus the Emile who moves in civil society will put different values on things and activities than do other men. The division of labor which produces superfluity and makes men partial—pieces of a great machine—will seem like a prison, and an unnecessary prison, to him. He will treasure his wholeness. He will know real value, which is the inverse of the value given things by the vanity of social men. And he will respect the producers of real value and despise the producers of value founded on vanity. Nature will be always present to him, not as doctrine but as a part of his very senses. This novel, properly prepared for and used, teaches him the use of the sciences and makes him inwardly free in spite of society's constraints.

And this constitutes Rousseau's response to Plato. Plato said that all men always begin by being prisoners in the cave. The cave is the condition of survival resulting from being a member of civil society. The needs, fears, hopes, and indignations of mutually dependent men produce a network of opinions and myths which make communal life possible and give it meaning. Men never experience nature directly but always mix their beliefs into what they see. Liberation from the cave requires the discovery of nature under the many layers of convention, the separating out of what is natural from what is man-made. Only a genius is capable of attaining a standpoint from which he can see the cave as a cave. That is why the philosopher, the rarest human type, can alone be autonomous and free of prejudice. Now, Rousseau agrees that once in the cave, genius is required to emerge from it. He, too, agrees that enlightenment is spurious and merely the substitution of one prejudice for another. He himself was born in a cave and had to be a genius to attain his insight into the human condition. His life is a testimony to the heroic character of the quest for nature. But he denies that the cave is natural. The right kind of education, one independent of society, can put a child into direct contact with nature without the intermixture of opinion. Plato purified poetry so as to make its view of the world less hostile to reason, and he replaced the ordinary lies by a noble lie. Rousseau banishes poetry altogether and suppresses all lies. At most he gives Emile Robinson Crusoe, who is not an other but only himself. Above all, no gods. Emile, at the age of fifteen, has a standpoint outside of civil society, one fixed by his inclinations and his reason, from which he sees that his fellow men are prisoners in a cave and by which he is freed from any temptation to fear the punishments or seek the honors which are part of it. Rousseau, the genius, has made it possible for ordinary men to be free, and in this way he proves in principle the justice of democracy.

Thus Rousseau's education of the young Emile confines itself to fostering the development of the faculties immediately connected with his preservation. His desire for the pleasant and avoidance of the painful is given by nature. His senses are the natural means to those ends. And the physical sciences, like mathematics, physics, and astronomy, are human contrivances which, if solidly grounded on the pure experience of the senses, extend their range and protect them against the errors of imagination. The tutor's responsibility is, in the first place, to let the senses develop in relation to their proper objects; and, secondly, to encourage the learning of the sciences as the almost natural outcome of the use of the senses. Rousseau calls this tutelage, particularly with reference to the part that has to do with the senses, negative education. All animals go through a similar apprenticeship to life. But with man something intervenes which impedes or distorts nature's progress, and therefore a specifically negative education, a human effort, is required. This new factor is the growth of the passions, particularly fear of death and amour-propre. They—fed by imagination and intermingling with the desires and the senses—transform judgment and cause a special kind of merely human, or mythical, interpretation of the world. The negative education means specifically the tutor's artifices invented to prevent the emergence of these two passions which attach men to one another and to opinions.

With respect to fear of death, Rousseau flatly denies that man does naturally fear death, and hence denies the premise of Hobbes's political philosophy (as well as what appears to be the common opinion of all political thinkers). He does not disagree with the modern natural right thinkers that man's only natural vocation is self-preservation or that he seeks to avoid pain. But Rousseau insists that man is not at first aware of the meaning of death, nor does man change his beliefs or ways of life to avoid it. Death, as Hobbes's man sees it, is a product of the imagination; and only on the basis of that imagination will he give up his natural idle and pleasure-loving life in order to pursue power after power so as to forestall death's assaults. The conception that life can be extinguished turns life, which is the condition of living, into an end itself. No animal is capable of such a conception, and, therefore, no animal thus transforms his life. Rousseau suggests that a man can be kept at the animal's unconscious level in regard to death long enough for him to have established a fixed and unchanging positive way of life and be accustomed to pain as well as knowledgeable enough not to be overwhelmed by the fact of death when he becomes fully aware of it. Ordinarily fear of death leads to one of two possible responses: superstition or the attempt to conquer death. The first gives hope that gods will protect men here or provide them with another life. The second, that of the enlightenment, uses science to prolong life and establish solid political regimes, putting off the inevitable and absorbing men in the holding action. Neither faces the fact of death, and both pervert consciousness. This is what Socrates meant by the dictum that philosophy is "learning how to die." All men die, and many die boldly or resolutely. But practically none does so without illusion. Those illusions constitute the horizon of the cave whose conventions are designed to support human hopes and fears. Thus to know how to die is equivalent to being liberated from the cave. And Rousseau, who argues that there is no natural cave, therefore also concludes that men naturally know how to die. "Priests, doctors and philosophers unlearn us how to die." He does not suggest that every savage or every baby has meditated on death as did Socrates. He means that, naturally, every man has none of the illusions about death which pervert life and require the Socratic effort. The tutor's function is to forestall the ministrations of priests, doctors, and philosophers which engender and nourish the fear of death. The simple lesson is that man must rely on himself and recognize and accept necessity; Rousseau shows how this can be achieved without the exercise of the rarest virtues.

Although fear of death makes it difficult to accept necessity, it is amour-propre that makes it difficult to recognize necessity. This is the murky passion that accounts for the "interesting" relationships men have with one another, and it is the keystone of Rousseau's psychological teaching. The primary intention of the negative education is to prevent amour de soi from turning into amour-propre, for this is the true source of man's dividedness. Rousseau's treatment of this all-important theme is best introduced by his discussion of the meaning of a baby's tears.

Tears are a baby's language and naturally express physical discomfort and are pleas for help. The parent or nurse responds by satisfying a real need, either feeding the baby or removing the source of pain. But at some point the child is likely to recognize that his tears have the effect of making things serve him through the intermediary of adults. The world responds to his wishes. His will can make things move to satisfy his desires. At this point the baby loses interest in providing himself with things; his inner motive to become strong enough to get the things for himself which others now provide for him is transformed into a desire to control the instrument which provides him with those things. His concern with his physical needs is transformed into a passion to control the will of adults. His tears become commands and frequently no longer are related to his real needs but only to testing his power. He cannot stop it from raining by crying, but he can make an adult change his mind. He becomes aware of will; and he knows that wills, as opposed to necessity, are subject to command, that they are changing. He quickly learns that, for his life, control over men is more useful than adaptation to things. Therefore the disposition of adults towards him replaces his bodily needs as his primary concern. Every wish that is not fulfilled could, in his imagination, be fulfilled if the adult only willed it that way. His experience of his own will teaches him that others' wills are selfish and plastic. He therefore seeks for power over men rather than the use of things. He becomes a skillful psychologist, able to manipulate others.

With the possibility of change of wills emerges the justification of blame and hence of anger. Nature does not have intentions; men do. Anger is caused by intentional wrong, and the child learns to see intention to do wrong in what opposes him. He becomes an avenger. A squalling brat is most often testing his power. If he gets what he wants, he is a master. If he fails, he is angry, resentful, and likely to become slavish. In either event he has entered into a dialectic of mastery and slavery which will occupy him for his whole life. His natural and healthy self-love and self-esteem (amour de soi), gives way to a self-love relative to other men's opinions of him; henceforth he can esteem himself only if others esteem him. Ultimately he makes the impossible demand that others care for him more than they care for themselves. The most interesting of psychological phenomena is this doubling or dividing of self-love; it is one of the few distinctively human phenomena (no animal can be insulted); and from it flow anger, pride, vanity, resentment, revenge, jealousy, indignation, competition, slavishness, humility, capriciousness, rebelliousness, and almost all the other passions that give poets their themes. In these first seeds of amour-propre as seen in tears, one can recognize the source of the human problem.

Rousseau's solution to amour-propre, which would seem inevitably to lead to conflict among men, their using one another as means to their own ends, and the need for government and law, is, as with the fear of death, to prevent, at least for a long time, its emergence; no self-overcomings are required. The child must be dependent on things and not on wills. The tutor and his helpers must disappear, as it were, and everything that happens to the child must seem to be an inevitable effect of nature. Against necessity he will not rebel; it is only the possibility of overcoming necessity or the notion that there is a will lurking behind it which disturbs his unclouded relation to things as they are. It is the intermediary of human beings in the satisfaction of need that causes the problem.

Now all of this has even more significance than is immediately apparent, for Rousseau suggests that superstition, all attribution of intention to inanimate things or to the world as a whole, is a result of the early experience of will. The parent in moving things at the child's command gives the child the impression that all things are moved by intention and that command or prayer can put them at man's disposal. Moreover, anger itself animates. The child who is angry at what does not bend to his will attributes a will to it. This is the case with all anger, as a moment's reflection will show. Anger is allied with and has it origin in amour-propre. Once it is activated, it finds intention and responsibility everywhere. Finally it animates rivers, storms, the heavens, and all sorts of benevolent and malevolent beings. It moralizes the universe in the service of amour-propre. In early childhood, there is a choice: the child can see everything or nothing as possessing a will like his own. Either whim or necessity governs the world for him. Neither is true, but for the child, the latter is the more salutary because nature is necessity and the primary things are necessary. The passions must submit to necessity, whereas necessity cannot be changed by the passions. Before he comes to terms with will, a man must have understood and accepted necessity. Otherwise he is likely to spend his life obeying and fearing gods or trying to become one. Rousseau, unlike more recent proponents of freedom, recognized that without necessity the realm of freedom can have no meaning.

Rousseau's teaching about amour-propre goes to the heart of his disagreement with Plato, who had argued that something akin to what Rousseau calls amour-propre is an independent part of the soul. This is *thymos*, spiritedness, or simply anger. It is the motive of his warriors in the *Republic* and is best embodied in Achilles, who is almost entirely thymos. Plato was aware of all the dangers of thymos, but he insisted that it must be given its due because it is part of human nature, because it can be the instrument for restraining desire, and because it is connected with a noble and useful human type. Simply, it is thymos that makes men overcome their natural fear of death. Rather than excise it, he attempted to tame this lion in the soul. The education in Books 2–3 of the *Republic* suggests the means to make it gentle and submissive to reason. However, these warriors do require myths and noble lies. They are cave dwellers. Man naturally animates the universe and tries to make it responsive to his demands and blames it for resisting. Plato focuses on Achilles, who struggles with a river which he takes to be a god, just as Rousseau is fascinated by the madness of Xerxes, who beats a recalcitrant sea. These are the extreme but most revealing instances of the passion to rule. The difference between Plato and Rousseau on this crucial point comes down to whether anger is natural or derivative. Rousseau says that a child who is not corrupted and wants a cookie will never rebel against the phrase, "there are no more," but only against, "you cannot have one." Plato insists that this is not so. Men naturally see intention where there is none and must become wise in order to separate will from necessity in nature. They do, however, both agree that thymos is an important part of the spiritual economy, and that, once present, it must be treated with the greatest respect. Herein they differ from Hobbes, who simply doused this great cause of war with buckets of fear, extinguishing thus the soul's fire. Rousseau gives a complete account of pride and its uses and abuses, whereas other modern psychologists have either lost sight of it or tried to explain it away. Our education does not take it seriously, and we risk producing timid souls, or ones whose untrained spiritedness is wildly erratic and seeks dangerous outlets.

Given that the child must never confront other wills, he cannot be given commandments. He would not understand even the most reasonable restriction on his will as anything other than the expression of the selfishness of the one who gives the commandments. The child must always do what he wants to do. This is the dictum of progressive education, and Rousseau is rightly seen as its source. What is forgotten is that Rousseau's full formula is that the child must always do what he wants to do but he should want to do only what the tutor wants him to do. Since an uncorrupt will does not rebel against necessity, and the tutor can manipulate the appearance of necessity, he can determine the will without sowing the seeds of resentment. He presents natural necessity in palpable form to the child so that the child lives according to nature prior to understanding it.

Rousseau demonstrates this method in a story which shows how he improves on earlier moral teachings. He puts his Emile in a garden where there are no noes, no forbidden fruit, and no fall, and tries to show that in the end his pupil will be healthy, whole, and of a purer morality than the old Adam. He gets Emile to respect the fruit of another without tempting him.

The boy is induced to plant some beans as a kind of game. His curiosity, imitativeness, and childish energy are used to put him to the task. He watches the beans grow while Jean-Jacques orates to him, supporting him in the pleasure he feels at seeing the result of his work, and encouraging him in the sense that the beans are his. Jean-Jacques gives Emile a rationale for that sense. The speech does not bore him as a sermon would, because it supports his inclination instead of opposing it. Jean-Jacques gives him what is in essence Locke's teaching on property. The beans belong to Emile because he has mixed his labor with them. Jean-Jacques begins by teaching him his right to his beans rather than by commanding him to respect the fruits of others.

Once the child has a clear notion of what belongs to him, he has his first experience of injustice done to him. One day he finds that his beans have been plowed under. And therewith he also has his first experience of anger, in the form of righteous indignation. He seeks the guilty party with the intention of punishing him. His selfish concern is identical with his concern for justice. But, much to his surprise, he finds that the criminal considers himself to be the injured party and is equally angry with him. It is the gardener, and he had planted seeds for melons—melons that were to be eaten by Emile—and Emile had plowed under those seeds to plant his beans. Here we have will against will, anger against anger. Although Emile's wrath loses some of its force—inasmuch as the gardener had an even better claim to have right on his side (he was the first occupant), and this according to the very notion of right which Emile uses and which he so eagerly imbibed from Jean-Jacques—the situation could lead to war. But Jean-Jacques avoids that outcome by means of two strategems. First, Emile's attention is diverted from his beans by the thought of the rare melons he would have enjoyed. Second, a kind of social contract is arranged: in the future Emile will stay away from the gardener's lands, if he is granted a small plot for his beans. In this way the boy is induced to understand and respect the property of others without losing anything of his own. If there were a conflict of interest, Emile would naturally prefer his own. But Jean-Jacques does not put him in that position. If Emile were commanded to keep away from what he desires, the one who commanded him to do so would be responsible for setting him against himself and encouraging him to deceive. A luscious fruit in the garden which was forbidden would only set the selfish will of the owner against Emile's nature. Jean-Jacques at least gives Emile grounds for respecting property and brings him as close to an obligation as can be grounded on mere nature. Greater demands at this stage would be both ineffective and corrupting. The tempter is the giver of commandments. Rousseau here follows Hobbes in deriving duties, or approximations to them, from rights. In this way Emile will rarely infringe the rights of others, and he will have no intention to harm them.

It is this latter that constitutes the morality of the natural man and also that of the wise man (according to Rousseau). It takes the place of the Christian's Golden Rule. When Rousseau says that man is by nature good, he means that man, concerned only with his own well-being, does not naturally have to compete with other men (scarcity is primarily a result of extended desire), nor does he care for their opinions (and, hence, he does not need to try to force them to respect him). Man's goodness is identical to his natural freedom (of body and soul) and equality. And here he agrees, contrary to the conventional wisdom, with Machiavelli, who said men are all bad. For Machiavelli meant that men are bad when judged from the standpoint of the common good, or of how men ought to live, or of the imaginary cities of the old writers. These make demands on men contrary to their natural inclinations and are therefore both unfounded and ineffective. If these standards are removed and men's inclinations are accepted rather than blamed, it turns out that with the cooperation of these inclinations sound regimes can be attained. From the standpoint of imaginary perfection man's passions are bad; from that of the natural passion for self-preservation they are good. Machiavelli preaches the adoption of the latter standpoint and the abandonment of all transcendence and with it the traditional dualism. And it is this project of reconciliation with what is that Rousseau completes in justifying the wholeness of self-concern, in proving that the principles of the old morality are not only ineffective but the cause of corruption (since they cause men to deny themselves and thus to become hypocrites), and in learning how to control that imagination which gives birth to the imaginary cities (which, in their opposition to the real cities, are the signs of man's dividedness).

The moral education of the young Emile is, then, limited to the effective establishment of the rule that he should harm no one. And this moral rule cooperates with the intellectual rule that he should know how to be ignorant. This latter means that only clear and distinct evidence should ever command belief. Neither any passions nor dependencies should make him need to believe. All his knowledge should be relevant to his real needs, which are small and easily satisfied. In a sense he makes his young Emile an embodiment of the Enlightenment's new scientific method. His will to affirm never exceeds his capacity to prove. For others, that method is only a tool, liable to the abuses of the passions and counterpoised by many powerful needs. All this is described in the *Discourse on the Arts and Sciences*. But to Emile, whose only desire is to know and live according to the necessary, the new science of the laws of nature is a perfect complement. With a solid floor constituted by healthy senses in which he trusts and a ceiling provided by astronomy, Emile is now prepared to admit his fellows into a structure which their tempestuous passions cannot shake. This fifteen-year-old, who has not unlearned how to die, harms no one, and knows how to be ignorant, possesses a large share of the Socratic wisdom.

II

Emile at fifteen cares no more for his father than his dog. A child who did would be motivated by fear or gain induced by dependency. Rousseau has made Emile free of those passions by keeping him self-sufficient, and he has thus undermined the economic foundations of civil society laid by Hobbes and Locke. Since Rousseau agrees with the latter that man has no natural inclination to civil society and the fulfillment of obligation, he must find some other selfish natural passion that can somehow be used as the basis for a genuine—as opposed to a spurious, competitive—concern for others. Such a passion is necessary in order to provide the link between the individual and disinterested respect for law or the rights of others, which is what is meant by real morality.

Rousseau finds such a solution in the sexual passion. It necessarily involves other individuals and results in relations very different from those following from fear or love of gain. Moreover, Rousseau discovers that sexual desire, if its development is properly managed, has singular effects on the soul. Books 4–5 are a treatise on sex education, notwithstanding the fact that they give a coherent account of God, love, and politics. "Civilization" can become "culture" when it is motivated and organized by sublimated sex.

Sublimation as the source of the higher psychic phenomena, as the explanation of that uniquely human turning away from mere bodily gratification to the pursuit of noble deeds, arts, and thoughts, was introduced by Rousseau. The history of the notion can be traced from him through Kant, Schopenhauer, and Nietzsche (who first introduced the term) and to Freud (who popularized it). Rousseau's attempt to comprehend the richness of man's soul within the context of modern scientific reductionism led him to an interpretation which is still our way of looking at things, although we have lost clarity about its intention and meaning. Rousseau knew that there are sublime things; he had inner experience of them. He also knew that there is no place for the sublime in the modern scientific explanation of man. Therefore, the sublime had to be made out of the nonsublime; this is sublimation. It is a raising of the lower to the higher. Characteristically, those who speak about sublimation since Freud are merely lowering the higher, reducing the sublime things to their elements and losing a hold on the separate dignity of the sublime. We no longer know what is higher about the higher. These last two books of *Emile* undertake in a detailed way the difficult, if not impossible, task of showing how the higher can be derived from the lower without being reduced to it, while at the same time giving us some sense of what Rousseau means by the sublime or noble. It has not been sufficiently emphasized that everything in books 4–5 is related to sex, and that without making that connection the parts cannot be interpreted nor the whole understood.

Rousseau takes it for granted that sex is naturally only a thing of the

body. There is no teleology contained in the sexual act other than generation—no concern for the partner, no affection for the children on the part
of the male, no directedness to the family. Naturally it is not more significant
or interesting than eating. In fact, since natural man is primarily concerned
with his survival, sex is of secondary importance inasmuch as it contributes
nothing to the survival of the individual. But sex, because it is related to
another human being, easily mingles with and contributes to nascent amour-
propre. Being liked and preferred to others becomes important in the sexual
act. The conquest, mastery, and possession of another will thus also become
central to it, and what was originally bodily becomes almost entirely imaginary. This semifolly leads to the extremes of alienation and exploitation.
But precisely because the sexual life of civilized man exists primarily in the
imagination, it can be manipulated in a way that the desire for food or sleep
cannot be. Sexual desire, if it remains unsatisfied, mixed with imagination
and amour-propre, produces a tremendous psychic energy that can be used
for the greatest deeds and thoughts. Imaginary objects can set new goals,
and the desire to be well thought of can turn into love of virtue. But everything depends on purifying and elevating the desire and making it inseparable
from its new objects. Thus Rousseau, although Burke could accuse him of
pedantic lewdness, would be appalled by contemporary sexual education
which separates out the bodily from the spiritual in sex, does not understand
the problem involved in treating the bloated passions of social man as though
they were natural, is oblivious to the difficulty of attaching the indeterminate
drive to useful and noble objects, and fails to appreciate the salutary effect
of long ignorance while the vapors brew. Delayed satisfaction is, according
to him, the condition of idealism and love, and early satisfaction causes the
whole structure to collapse and flatten.

Rousseau's meaning is admirably expressed by Kant, who, following
Rousseau, indicated that there is a distinction between what might be called
natural puberty and civil puberty. Natural puberty is reached when a male
is capable of reproduction. Civil puberty is attained only when a man is able
to love a woman faithfully, rear and provide for children, and participate
knowledgeably and loyally in the political order which protects the family.
But the advent of civilization has not changed the course of nature; natural
puberty occurs around fifteen; civil puberty, if it ever comes to pass, can
hardly occur before the middle twenties. This means that there is a profound
tension between natural desire and civil duty. In fact, this is one of the best
examples of the dividedness caused in man by his history. Natural desire
almost always lurks untamed amidst the responsibilities of marriage. What
Rousseau attempts to do is to make the two puberties coincide, to turn the

desire for sexual intercourse into a desire for marriage and a willing sub-mission to the law without suppressing or blaming that original desire. Such a union of desire and duty Kant called true culture.

Rousseau effects this union by establishing successively two passions in Emile which are sublimations of sexual desire and which are, hence, not quite natural but, one might say, according to nature: compassion and love.

Compassion

In this first stage the young man is kept ignorant of the meaning of what he is experiencing. He is full of restless energy and becomes sensitive. He needs other human beings, but he knows not why. In becoming sensitive to the feelings of others and in needing them, his imagination is aroused and he becomes aware that they are like him. He *feels* for the first time that he is a member of a species. (Until now he was simply indifferent to other human beings, although he *knew* he was a human being.) At this moment the birth of amour-propre is inevitable. He compares his situation with those of other men. If the comparison is unfavorable to him, he will be dissatisfied with himself and envious of them; he will wish to take their place. If the comparison is unfavorable to them, he will be content with himself and not competitive with others. Thus amour-propre is alienating only if a man sees others whom he can consider happier than himself. It follows that, if one wishes to keep a man from developing the mean passions which excite the desire to harm, he must always see men whom he thinks to be unhappier than he is. If, in addition, he thinks such misfortunes could happen to him, he will feel pity for the sufferer.

This is the ground of Rousseau's entirely new teaching about compas-sion. Judiciously chosen comparisons presented at the right stage of life will cause Emile to be satisfied with himself and be concerned with others, making him a gentle and beneficent man on the basis of his natural selfishness. Thus compassion would be good for him and good for others. Rousseau introduces a hard-headed softness to moral and political thought.

He asserts that the good fortune of others puts a chill on our hearts, no matter what we say. It separates us from them; we would like to be in their place. But their suffering warms us and gives us a common sense of humanity. The psychic mechanism of compassion is as follows. (1) Once a man's imag-inative sensibility is awakened, he winces at the wounds others receive. In an attentuated form he experiences them too, prior to any reflection; he sympathizes; somehow these wounds are inflicted on him. (2) He has a moment of reflection; he realizes that it is the other fellow, not he, who is really suffering. This is a source of satisfaction. (3) He can show his own strength and superiority by assisting the man in distress. (4) He is pleased that he has the spiritual freedom to experience compassion; he senses his own goodness. Active, human compassion (as opposed to the animal compassion described in the *Discourse on the Origins of Inequality*) requires imagination and amour-propre in addition to the instinct for self-preservation. Moreover, it cannot withstand the demands of one's own self-preservation. It is a tender plant, but one which will bear sweet fruit if properly cultivated.

Emile's first observations of men are directed to the poor, the sick, the oppressed, and the unfortunate. This is flattering to him, and his first sentiments toward others are gentle. He becomes a kind of social worker. And, as this analysis should make clear, the motive and intention of Rousseauan compassion give it little in common with Christian compassion. Rousseau was perfectly aware that compassion such as he taught is not a virtue and that it can lead to abuse and hypocrisy. But he used this selfish passion to replace or temper other, more dangerous passions. This is part of his correction of Hobbes. Rousseau finds a selfish passion which contains fellow feeling and makes it the ground of sociality to replace those passions which set men at odds. He can even claim he goes farther down the path first broken by Hobbes, who argued that the passions, and not reason, are the only effective motives of human action. Hobbes's duties toward others are rational deductions from the passion for self-preservation. Rousseau anchors concern for others in a passion. He makes that concern a pleasure rather than a disagreeable, and hence questionably effective, conclusion.

Rousseau's teaching on compassion fostered a revolution in democratic politics, one with which we live today. Compassion is on the lips of every statesman, and all boast that their primary qualification for office is their compassion. Rousseau singlehandedly invented the category of the disadvantaged. Prior to Rousseau, men believed that their claim on civil society has to be based on an accounting of what they contribute to it. After Rousseau, a claim based not on a positive quality but on a lack became legitimate for the first time. This he introduced as a counterpoise to a society based on Locke's teaching, which has no category for the miserable other than that of the idle and the quarrelsome. The recognition of our sameness and our common vulnerability dampens the harsh competitiveness and egotism of egalitarian political orders. Rousseau takes advantage of the tendency to compassion resulting from equality, and uses it, rather than self-interest, as the glue binding men together. Our equality, then, is based less on our fear of death than on our sufferings; suffering produces a shared sentiment with others, which fear of death does not. For Hobbes, frightened men make an artificial man to protect them; for Rousseau, suffering men seek other men who feel for them.

Of course Emile will not always be able to confine his vision to poor men without station. There are rich and titled men who seem to be much better off than he is. If he were brought to their castles and had a chance to see their privileges and their entertainments, he would likely be dazzled, and the worm of envy would begin to gnaw away at his heart. Jean-Jacques finds a solution to this difficulty by making Emile read history and bringing back what had been banished in book 2. This is the beginning of Emile's education in the arts, as opposed to the sciences. The former can only be studied when his sentiments are sufficiently developed for him to understand the inner movements of the heart and when he experiences a real need to know. Otherwise, learning is idle, undigested, excess baggage at best. Emile's curiosity to find out about all of Plutarch's heroes and set his own life over against their lives fuels his study. Rousseau expects that this study will reveal the vanity of the heroes' aspirations and cause revulsion at their tragic failures. Emile's solid, natural pleasures, his cheaply purchased Stoicism and self-sufficiency, his lack of the passion to rule, will cause him to despise their love of glory and pity their tragic ends. The second level of the education in compassion produces contempt for the great of this world, not a slave's contempt founded in envy, indignation, and resentment, but the contempt stemming from a conviction of superiority which admits of honest fellow feeling and is the precondition of compassion. This disposition provides a standpoint from which to judge the social and political distinctions among men, just as Robinson Crusoe's island provided one for judging the distinctions based on the division of labor. The joining of these two standards enables Emile to judge the life of tyrants as Socrates enabled Glaucon and Adeimatus to judge it by comparing it to the life of philosophers. Emile can use his own life as the basis for judgment, for his own soul contains no germ of the tyrannical temptation. The old way of using heroes in education was to make the pupil dissatisfied with himself and rivalrous with the model. Rousseau uses them to make his pupil satisfied with himself and compassionate toward the heroes. The old way alienated the child and made him prey to authorities whose titles he could not judge. Self-satisfaction of egalitarian man is what Rousseau promotes. But he is careful to insure that this satisfaction is only with a good or natural self.

Reading is again the means of accomplishing the third and final part of the education in compassion. This time the texts are fables which contain a moral teaching. They, too, had been banished in book 2, because a child would always identify himself with, e.g., the fox who cheats the crow rather than with the crow who loses the cheese, for a child understands nothing about vanity and a great deal about cheese. At this later stage Rousseau has arranged for Emile to have been deceived by confidence men who play upon his vanity, so that when he reads the fable he will immediately identify with the crow and attain self-consciousness. Satire becomes the mirror in which he sees himself. All this is intended to remind him that he, too, is human and could easily fall victim to the errors made by others. It is as though Rousseau had used Aristotle's discourse on the passions as a text and followed Aristotle's warning that those who do not imagine that the misfortunes befalling others can befall them are insolent rather than compassionate. The first stage of Emile's introduction to the human condition shows him that most men are sufferers; the second, that the great, too, are sufferers and hence equal to the small, and the third, that he is potentially a sufferer, saved only by his education. Equality, which was a rational deduction in Hobbes, thus becomes self-evident to the sentiments. Emile's first principle of action was pleasure and pain; his second, after the birth of reason and his learning the sciences, was utility; now compassion is added to the other two, and concern for others becomes part of his sense of his own interest. Rousseau studies the passions and finds a way of balancing them one against the other rather than trying to develop the virtues which govern them. He does for the soul what Montesquieu did for the government in inventing the separation and balance of powers.

But for all its important consequences, compassion is, within the context of Emile's education, only a step on the way to his fulfillment as husband and father. Its primary function is to make Emile social while remaining whole.

Love

Finally Rousseau must tell Emile the meaning of his longings. He reveals sex to the young Emile as the Savoyard Vicar revealed God to the young Rousseau. Although it is impossible to discuss the Profession of Faith of the Savoyard Vicar here, it is essential to the understanding of Rousseau's intention to underline the profound differences between the two revelations. The Vicar's teaching is presented to the corrupt young Rousseau and never to Emile. Moreover, the Vicar teaches the dualism of body and soul, which is alien and contradictory to the unity which Emile incarnates. In keeping with this, the Vicar is otherworldly and guilt-ridden about his sexual desires, which he deprecates, whereas Emile is very much of this world and exalts his sexual desires, which are blessed by God and lead to blessing God. Emile's rewards are on earth, the Vicar's in Heaven. The Vicar is the best of the traditional, and he is only an oasis in the desert which Rousseau crossed before reaching his new Sinai.

Thus at the dawn of a new day, Emile learns that the peak of sexual longing is the love of God mediated by the love of a woman. Sublimation finally operates a transition from the physical to the metaphysical. But before speaking to Emile, Rousseau explains to his readers how difficult it is to be a good rhetorician in modern times. Speech has lost its power because it cannot refer to a world with deep human significance. In Greek and Biblical antiquity the world was full of meaning put there by the great and terrible deeds of gods and heroes. Men were awe-struck by the ceremonies performed to solemnize public and private occasions. The whole earth spoke out to make oaths sacred. But now the world has been deprived of its meaning by Enlightenment. The land is no longer peopled by spirits, and nothing supports human aspiration anymore. Thus men can only affect one another by the use of force or profit. The language of human relations has lost its foundations. This is, as we would say, a demythologized world. And these remarks show what Rousseau is about. He wants to use imagination to read meaning back into nature. The old meanings were also the results of imaginings the reality of which men believed. They were monuments of fear and anger given cosmic significance. But they did produce a human world, however cruel and unreasonable. Rousseau suggests a new poetic imagination motivated by love rather than the harsher passions, and here one sees with clarity Rousseau's link with romanticism.

With this preface, Rousseau proceeds to inform Emile what the greatest pleasure in life is. He explains to him that what he desires is sexual intercourse with a woman, but he makes him believe that his object contains ideas of virtue and beauty without which she would not be attractive, nay, without which she would be repulsive. His bodily satisfaction depends upon his beloved's spiritual qualities; therefore Emile longs for the beautiful. Rousseau by his descriptive power incorporates an ideal into Emile's bodily lust. This is how sex becomes love, and the two must be made to appear inseparable. This is the reason for the delay in sexual awareness. Emile must learn much before he can comprehend such notions, and his sexual energy must be raised to a high pitch. Early indulgence would separate this intensity of lust from the objects of admiration. Rousseau admits that love depends upon illusions, but the deeds which those illusions produce are real. This is the source of nobility of mind and deed, and apart from fanaticism, nothing else can produce such dedication.

Rousseau develops all this with precision and in the greatest detail. Only Plato has meditated on love with comparable profundity. And it is Plato who inspired Rousseau's attempt to create love. The modern philosophers with whom Rousseau began have notably unerotic teachings. Their calculating, fear-motivated men are individuals, not directed toward others, but toward couplings and the self-forgetting implied in them. Such men have flat souls. They see nature as it is; and, since they are unerotic, they are unpoetic. Rousseau, a philosopher-poet like Plato, tried to recapture the poetry in the world. He knew that Plato's *Symposium* taught that *eros* is the longing for eternity, ultimately the longing for oneness with the unchanging, intelligible *ideas*. Now, Rousseau held that nature is the nature of modern science—matter in motion—that there are no *ideas*; there is no *eros*, only sex. But such a soul, which has no beautiful objects to contemplate and contains no divine madness, Rousseau regarded as ignoble. He set about reconstructing Plato's soul, turning sex into *eros*, by the creation of ideals to take the place of *ideas*. The philosopher is even more poetic for Rousseau than for Plato, for the very objects of contemplation and longing are the products of poetry rather than nature. The world of concern to man is made by the poet who has understood nature and its limits. So, imagination, once banished, returns to ascend the royal throne.

Although this great theme can only be touched on, the practical effects of making Emile a lover can easily be seen. In the first place, when he loves, he will not be loving an other, will not be making himself and his happiness hostage to an alien will and thus engaging in a struggle for mastery. His woman will, to use Platonic language, participate in the *idea* he has of her. He will recognize his own highest aspirations in her. She will complete him without alienating him. Secondly, his inclination for one woman, and her natural attachment to her children, will in turn attach him to the children as an extension of his inclinations, thus constituting the family seminaturally, without the need for civil or religious commandment. The basic unit of civil society will then not be the individual, but the family. This tempers the selfishness of liberal democracy based on individual rights, giving individuals concern for something beyond their immediate interest. Here concern with preservation of individuals moves toward concern with preservation of the species. And finally, because attachment to the family implies some attachment to civil society, Emile's natural selfishness has been stretched to the point where it is close to generality. All this education acts as a bridge between the particular will and the general will.

So, in the end, Rousseau has accomplished his mission by making a man who is natural, civilized, whole, compassionate, a lover, and who, finally, submits to a law he has given himself.

CONCLUSION

Emile seems ridiculous because it proposes a system of education which is manifestly impossible for most men and quasi-impossible for any man. But this is to misunderstand it. It is not an education manual, anymore than

Plato's *Republic* is advice to rulers. Each adopts a convention—the founding of a city or the rearing of a boy—in order to survey the entire human condition. They are books for philosophers and are meant to influence practice only in the sense that those who read them well cannot help but change their general perspectives.

Rousseau intends to show that only his understanding of nature and history can adequately describe what man really is, while cautioning his contemporaries against simplifying and impoverishing the human phenomena. The very unity of man he appears to believe he has demonstrated reveals the problematic character of any solution to man's dividedness. Emile stands somewhere between the citizen of the *Social Contract* and the solitary of the *Reveries*, lacking something of each. And this book was the inspiration for both Kant's idealism and Schiller's romanticism, which are each somehow simplifications of one side of Rousseau's complex teaching. Whatever else Rousseau may have accomplished, he presented the alternatives available to man most comprehensively and profoundly and articulated them in the form which has dominated discussion since his time. We must study him to know ourselves and to discover possibilities his great rhetoric may have overwhelmed.

JEAN STAROBINSKI

The Accuser and the Accused

Rousseau tells us that his writing career was born from "virtue outraged" (*Confessions*). The "four or five years" of "effervescence" that follow the illumination he experienced on the road to Vincennes are years of anger and intransigence. He went to literature as one goes to war. He denounces civilization's evils. Answers and attacks coming from all sides, he attempts to retaliate blow for blow: "I saw nothing but error and folly in the doctrine of our wise men, nothing but oppression and misery in our social order." Later, Rousseau was to note that this intensity of virtue and endless defiance were "states most contrary to his nature," but if the attitude was exaggerated, it was not feigned: "I never acted."

Confronting the public, Rousseau steps forward as an accuser: "The contempt which my deep reflections had inspired in me for the customs, principles, and prejudices of my age made me insensible to the mockery of those who followed them; and I crushed their little witticisms with my observations, as I might crush an insect between my fingers." Hence the theatrical quality in his writings and in his attitude. He conforms to models of behavior borrowed from antiquity; he wants to communicate his ideas with the most energetic language, and he succeeds in being hailed as a master of eloquence. For Diderot, he is the "censor of letters, the Cato and the Brutus of our age." The successfully reincarnated model is that of the magistrate or of the lone hero, who reminds a forgetful community of the forsaken virtues and civic values.

From *Daedalus: Journal of the American Academy of Arts and Sciences* 107, no. 3 (Summer 1978). © 1978 by the American Academy of Arts and Sciences.

Rousseau's accusatory attitude must, in my view, be given very serious consideration. His system of thought cannot be separated from the way he expresses it. The rhetoric in Rousseau is not an external or superadded element; it is intrinsic to the intellectual message. Here is a man who makes his readers know that he belatedly begins a career as a writer because he finds it urgent to warn the civilized world against lethal dangers. He wants the public to see him as someone who has decided to start a new life entirely devoted to truth. And, as he foresees a premature death, he feels able to reject further compromise and to speak his mind accordingly. The initial gesture of accusation establishes a dramatic relationship between the writer and his contemporaries. The conspicuous nature of that relationship and the resulting existential developments are no less important than the ideas and certainties that are at the heart of Rousseau's argument. The texts themselves, if fully perceived, oblige us to take account of this dramatic aspect, and in so doing we do not fall prey to any fallacy, either biographical or psychological.

One has only to pay attention to what is actually being said by Rousseau; a challenge is being made by a man from outside, by a citizen of Geneva, who wills himself to be a stranger to the evil he is describing. From there on, Rousseau's subsequent writings and the personal situation they imply can be considered as the logical consequences of his first intervention as a self-appointed prosecutor. He not only has to prove that his accusation is based on coherent and valid principles, but at the same time he is bound to experience all the further predicaments deriving from the conflict he first entered into.

For a pragmatic analysis, that is, for a careful study of literary work as action modifying both the writer's and the reader's mind, Rousseau offers a model experience. What ought to come out of a relationship with the public which the writer has initially established as a justice-seeking agression? It seems to me that Rousseau's inner evolution, as manifested by his successive works, answers this question with great clarity. One is tempted to consider it still relevant, exemplary and premonitory, in the context of modern attitudes which strike us by their similarity to Rousseau's. To be sure, some retrospective illusion is probably mixed with what we cannot help reading as the contemporary message of the Rousseauan adventure; most readers allow themselves to be led into "overinterpretation." But this very fact cannot be disregarded. However mistakenly, Rousseau invites our interpretations, seeming to offer us in his person and thoughts interpretative tools applicable to our time.

The notion of accusation provides a very effective system of reference if one wishes to distinguish several periods in Rousseau's works, dividing them into groups. The first group of writings is clearly marked by the identification of society's evils and assigns a relatively small place to personal apologetics. This group of works includes the first two *Discours*, the Preface to *Narcisse*, and even the *Lettre à d'Alembert* (even though Rousseau thinks that the last marks a change of style and that the initial indignation does not prevail). Let us add that an important part of the writings on music is prompted by the spirit of accusation; they fight the "noise" and the harmonic artifices of French music; they seek to discredit Rameau; and one should not forget that Rousseau's musical polemic is more or less simultaneous with his social polemic. The second group is that of the "criteriological" works. They define and systematically develop the principles and values in the name of which the accusation has been made. They are also, to a certain extent, conciliatory works that indicate under what conditions remedies or palliatives can intrude. They include the fiction of *La Nouvelle Héloïse* (1760), the half-fiction of the *Emile* (1762), and the theoretical constructions of the *Contrat social*, including their application in the cases of Corsica and Poland. Finally comes the group of works where the initial situation is reversed and Rousseau speaks as the *accused*, rejecting anything that might convict him of guilt to the point of ascribing to interfering influences—that of Diderot for instance—the bitter tone of his first writings. First, intellectual apologetics prevail: Rousseau defends his thoughts more than his person in the *Lettre à Monseigneur de Beaumont* (1763) and the *Lettre de la Montagne* (1764). Then, Rousseau devotes himself entirely to a personal pleading; he defends Jean-Jacques's *true image* against the monstrous image that the "directors" of the plot (so he thinks) succeeded in having universally believed. The initial accusation has produced the entire body of writings, through a vast cycle of transformations in which the initial conflict has been lived to its final expression.

Accusatorial thought fosters antinomies; it moves forward by antitheses; it is spontaneously "Manichaean." Rousseau's first *Discours* is built on strong oppositions. After unfolding the image of the triumph of light over ignorance, Rousseau makes a reversal. The brilliant existence of organized societies is but a superficial "polish"; under this deceptive semblance is a concealed being, dominated by pride, instigating hate and estranging consciences. Human relationships are thus perverted. The apparent good will that orders social relationships hides a deadly combat. The luxury of a small number does not bring prosperity to others, but misery. This moral disorder is *new*; it accompanies the "renewal" of the arts and sciences. Another system of oppositions is then set up—the world of today versus the world of our ancestors (the analogy: Imperial Rome versus Republican Rome); urbanized societies

versus rustic or primitive societies (the analogy: Athens versus Sparta). In
addition, there are traditional ethical oppositions: the superfluous versus the
necessary; disease (corruption, softness) versus health (integrity, ruggedness);
luxury versus frugality; femininity and cowardice versus virility and military
courage; private interests versus patriotic devotion, and so on. And if, at the
end of the *Discours*, the arts and sciences are not utterly condemned, it is
thanks to a new antinomy: true sciences (reserved for a small number and
cultivated in the Academies) versus pseudoscience (practiced by a multitude,
by a "populace").

This rather short discourse, consistent with academic ritual, sparks a
huge debate and makes of Rousseau a man very much in fashion. Was it,
however, so unique in 1750 to attack luxury, frivolous eloquence, "fatal
arts," "vain sciences"? Were cultural optimism and belief in progress so
widespread? Of course, at the time of the launching of the *Encyclopédie*, a
large section of public opinion was ready to trust in the progress of knowledge, the technical improvements, the multiplied amenities produced by
the practice of reason in human affairs. In this respect, the "moderns" seem
to have triumphed over the "ancients" once and for all. However, here is
Rousseau who reopens this quarrel. His purpose is not to affirm that the
taste, arts, and knowledge of the moderns are inferior to those of the ancients—he gives in to his contemporaries on this point—but to declare that
a *moral* decay accompanies scientific and technical progress. But these accusations, these objections, formulated in the name of ethical values, are not
new. The preachers had frequently made such objections. How can one
explain the scandal which, in 1750–51, effectively assures Rousseau's success? Did he do anything other than bid higher? Did he invent nothing but
the "rhetorical colors" that made his argument biting? Is he different only
because of the provocative accent of his hyperbolic eloquence?

In Rousseau's accusations against the arts and sciences, reprobation is
expressed in various ways. One of the most frequent is the repetitiously used
qualificative; *frivolous, vain, fatal* are words that recur constantly with him.
These words belong to a preacher's vocabulary. His contemporaries did not
fail to recognize that. Someone from Lyons writes: "It seems to me that he
is the most vigorous writer in our century. How well, for example, this man
would have preached!" Talleyrand will declare: "When one reads Rousseau,
one believes oneself to be in the confessional." This, in fact, is the realization
of one of Rousseau's childhood dreams. Let us reread the first book of the
Confessions: " . . . I fancied myself as a preacher . . . one day Uncle Bernard
read us a very fine sermon in his serious style . . . we then began to make
up sermons."

Rousseau's attacks against "vain curiosity" continue a long history of religious polemics against all that distracts the individual from the "sole necessity," which is a concern for salvation. Rousseau concludes his *Discours* with a peroration that echoes the *redi in te ipsum* from Augustine:

> O virtue! Sublime science of simple souls, are so many difficulties and preparations needed to know you? Are not your principles engraved in all hearts, and is it not enough to learn your laws to commune with oneself and listen to the voice of one's conscience in the silence of the passions? That is true philosophy, let us know how to be satisfied with it; and without envying the glory of those famous men who are immortalized in the republic of letters, let us try to put between them and us that glorious distinction noted between two great people long ago: that the one knew how to speak well, the other to act well.

What did religious authors write? Let us listen to Pascal: "Physical science will not console me for the ignorance of morality in the time of affliction. But the science of ethics will always console me for the ignorance of the physical sciences" (*Pensées*). And also to Malebranche, who, although a follower of Descartes and less hostile to scientific curiosity, writes: "He who communes most with himself, and listens to the inner truth in the greatest silence of his senses and his passions, is the most solidly virtuous" (*Traité de Morale*). It is also Malebranche who uses the terms Rousseau will borrow to maintain that the law, which is "the inviolable order of the minds," is "engraved in man's heart." In the *Entretiens affectifs*, Fénelon writes: "Alas! How many grave doctors do not see anything while thinking they know it all! They do not want to be ignorant of anything . . . Oh! how they would hate all that curious research, if they knew man well! . . . Oh! What can we learn from that which is nothing? There is only one infinite truth, which absorbs everything and which does not leave any curiosity outside itself: all else is but nothingness, and therefore a lie." But this similarity between Rousseau and the theologians, the solidarity in their accusations against the "curious sciences," against luxury, and against inequality, cannot conceal an essential difference. Rousseau and the theologians invoke quite different norms and authorities as the basis of their accusations.

In the preachers' sermons, the accusation is directed against the sins of the world, the idolatry of earthly possessions, *the pride of the libido sciendi*; their preaching invites the pursuit of true possessions, which are spiritual life, salvation, grace from Christ. Fénelon exclaims: "O Jesus, I no longer have any other doctor than you, any other book but your bosom. There I

learn everything while being ignorant of everything and while abasing myself. There I live the same life you live in your Father's bosom." In the
funeral oration of Louis le Grand, in which the luxury of the Court is strongly
condemned, Massillon enraptures his listeners with the first sentence: "God
alone is great, brethren!"

These examples ought to suffice. They permit us to understand the
novel effect of Rousseau's *Discours:* the accusation is not accompanied by a
religious call. Rousseau's disturbing innovation does not lie in reproving the
evils endured by mankind in society; it consists in not making of this reproval
the premise of an act of contrition, the prelude to a conversion. Rousseau
does not seek to revive his reader's faith, as his predecessors did; he makes
vivid an ethicopolitical regret. To the evils of society, he contrasts the image
of another social order. When he exclaims "O virtue," this term must be
understood in its civic, political, "Machiavellian" sense. The final antithesis
goes back to the Plutarchian confrontation between Athens and Sparta which
ran through the whole discourse. Of course, the antithesis which contrasts
the "polite" city with the "virtuous" city is not at all new. But it insistently
takes the place, in the *Discours,* of the expected antithesis which would have
contrasted worldly virtues with spiritual virtues. In order to innovate, it was
enough to surprise the reader with something not to be expected in traditional
academic discourse; a social ideal is openly preferred to a religious ideal.
The social ideal, this other imagined society, is by no means a utopia. It is
the idealization of a lost world, the happy picture of a frugal past, where
virtuous *doing* prevailed over dissimulative *speaking.* Wherever preachers deplored the devastating effects of godlessness, Rousseau, on the contrary,
points to the disappearance of *civisme:* "We have physicists, geometers, chem-
ists, astronomers, poets, musicians, painters; *we no longer have citizens.*"
Nevertheless, Rousseau knew perfectly well what he owed to religious tradition, and in response to the attacks, he sets up his line of defense on the
positions held by religious apologetics. During the controversy evoked by
his *Discours,* and particularly in his response to the King of Poland, Rousseau
points out that the observations judged as shocking in his *Discours* are in
perfect agreement with the Scriptures and the Church Fathers; he mentions
the example of the "twelve poor fishermen and artisans" who have spread
the teachings of Christ. Yet even when Rousseau refers to the Scriptures,
he is concerned not with "eternal life," but with man's life on this earth,
man's happiness among his fellow-men. Hence, Rousseau places himself on
the level of "worldly" existence and institutions which interests his friends,
the philosophers; like them, he is ready to consider man as a being of passion
and needs, who seeks satisfaction in this world—the remaining question is

to know which form of existence will guarantee true and full satisfaction. As we have endeavored to show (in *Jean-Jacques Rousseau, la transparence et l'obstacle*), the most desirable object for Rousseau is the transparency of human relationships, the immediate exchange. Rousseau has often expressed his belief in an afterlife, but, in his systematic thought, he always subordinated religious to civic ideals.

He denounces like the theologians, but he denounces the *political* nature of evil. One can immediately see that Rousseau is predestined to fight on two fronts. The theologians will bear him a grudge for abandoning the traditional *via salutis* for the benefit of civil or personal values: the *"merely civil religion"* of the *Contrat* subordinates faith to a political finality. As for the philosophers, they see in Rousseau a deserter from the fight for enlightenment, since with an argumentation of religious origin, he comes to throw doubt on everything they are attempting to promote—morality of interests, apology for luxury, enrichment through commerce. . . .

The substitution of the secular value (*civisme*) for the sacred value (salvation) does not discard the sacred forever. When one answers in political terms a religious question, almost inevitably the political answer is likely to keep a religious undertone. The element of moral guilt which the religious accusation awakened finds its atonement in the imagination of another social order, thus conferring on political schemes an irrational guilt-suppressing function. Even though we have passed from an injunction religious in character (salvation) to a political ideal (hence secular), it can be said, nevertheless, that *civisme* has become a *substitutive sacred value*; it breathes an intensity of regret or promise without which it would not match the vehemence of the accusation. What has often been described as a *secularization* of the hope of salvation, must also be perceived as a *sacralization* of the idealized forms of political life. Let us add to this the following observation by way of corollary. Whereas Christian moralists (and particularly those who draw their inspiration from Jansenism: Pascal, Nicole, La Rochefoucauld) see in *amour-propre*, in the play of illusory appearances, an ontological blemish linked to original sin and henceforth inseparable from human nature, Rousseau places the responsibility on society, on the vices of social organization. By so doing, he does not merely propose (as Cassirer has shown) an original solution to the problem of theodicy; he is not content with exculpating God's Providence and rehabilitating the primitive nature of man. He further strengthens his accusation against society with an argument based on permanent and irrefutable causes of uneasiness—the lack of a complete and frank understanding between individuals, malevolence, selfish interests—which it is difficult not to encounter everywhere and at any moment, since they result, in fact, from the human condition. Rousseau, who was one of the first to indict society, immediately felt how much strength his indictment would gain, should he fuse the sociopolitical dependency endured by individuals to the ontological dependency resulting from the fact that a part of their being is entrusted to the opinion of their fellow men, as if both resulted from the shortcomings of the existing social order. This is still a familiar device. The accusation always hits its target and always finds a listener when it joins the wrongs of society to the unavoidable imperfections of human relations. The accuser thus mobilizes an existential dissatisfaction on behalf of his cause. It touches us at the level of some obscure uneasiness. What a relief to think that such an uneasiness is not irremediably tied to our very existence, and that we will be able to rid ourselves of it at the cost of a politicomoral conversion and a change of exterior circumstances. The accusation, still so framed in our own time (but according to the model suggested by Rousseau), gives life to the hope of ontological change through the effect of social change. Hence the hangover on the morning after the revolution for those who expected a totally new life; the change in economic and political relations has not after all pushed back our ontological limits. (The point here is not to make Rousseau responsible, but to indicate how he has prefigured the radical proposition, which, by sacralizing politics, mixes the metaphysical expectation of salvation with the theory of social change.)

In Rousseau, the writer appears in a new role and a new status. He takes upon himself the task of moral preaching which, up to now, exclusively and almost professionally belonged to the Church. At the same time, he assumes the right to examine the institutions and the deficiencies inherent in the political organization to which, following the traditional division of labor in France, most clergymen had previously paid assiduous deference. Finally, he expresses his unique individuality by capturing the public's attention, by becoming a legend in his lifetime, under his Christian name of Jean-Jacques. Rousseau is certainly not the only nor the first intellectual to exercise this power, but he is able at the first attempt to do so masterfully and with a rare intuition of the reception which a free writer, not bound to any corporate body, can expect in doing so. It is this talent, as much as their conflict of ideas, that explains the animosity of Voltaire, his rival in the exercise of such power. Rousseau attacks with the intonations of Fénelon or Massillon, but his political and pedagogical views are expressed in the manner of Locke or Montesquieu. He studied neither theology nor law. He holds no position in the state: he speaks as an outsider. So, in each sphere of criticism, when he proposes a theory based on new foundations, he appears as an outsider, as someone without the necessary qualifications to intervene—

hence the nickname, Docteur Pansophe, pinned on him by Voltaire. His propensity to assume so many roles, to claim competence in so many fields— thus being a *philosopher*—is not foreign to his feeling that he had antogonized those who, in each field, assumed the right of sole competence to decide. When Rousseau thinks of the league of his persecutors and declares that league to be *universal*, he combines in his mind the retorts of all those whose special preserves he has invaded. He has interfered in the fields of established theology, politics, pedagogy, music, and medicine, and is convinced that he has incurred the animosity of priests, statesmen, teachers, musicians, and doctors.

The logic of accusatorial thought implies also that antinomies of *thought* be sustained and authenticated by a *living* antagonism. The accusation compels the one who makes it to act the role of the accuser. The more massive and general the fault denounced, the more isolated the one who, to denounce it, sets himself apart. The heroic posture Rousseau now assumes is that of the challenger animated by ardor of virtue and love for mankind, alone against all, speaking to alienated and enslaved people about a community of the past. How revealing is the prosopopoeia of Fabricius, the only direct testimony about the illumination on the road to Vincennes: the virtuous consul, come back from the dead, addresses the decadent Romans and contrasts the image of the Senate of Republican Rome. Rousseau spontaneously adopts the attitude of someone from *another world* (in all senses) who, standing alone, admonishes a crowd. This is one of his favorite fantasies. The *Discours sur l'inégalité*, again, is built on this pattern: several times, he places an orator alone in front of a large group. He himself is that orator in the Dedication where he addresses the whole Republic of Geneva. In the preamble to the *Discours*, he imagines himself to be in the lyceum of Athens, "having the Platos and the Xenocrates as judges and mankind as audience." At the beginning of the second part, when he calls to mind the taking of the land, he imagines again an individual who should have appeared, alone against all others, to "shout" a solemn warning to his fellow-men. Thus, on every occasion, openly revealing his identity, claiming the quality of citizen of Geneva, Rousseau asserts himself against the French, as someone from *elsewhere*, someone who speaks another tongue ("Barbarus hic ego sum quia non intelligor illis"); on the other hand, facing his fellow citizens of Geneva, he is the witness of the morality of another age. If he wants to be Genevan in order to proclaim his difference to the French, then, to his Genevan audience, he wants to offer an alternative idea of Geneva. He thus puts himself in a rhetorical situation which makes of him an exception in the face of evil, he who alone has kept the ability to perceive and denounce corruption and decay. One can see how, wanting to "harmonize" his behavior and his thoughts, Rousseau has been led to assume the role of solitary opponent. Identifying his life with his convictions and building his convictions into an antinomic system, Rousseau is forced to espouse the values he has declared lost, disregarded, abandoned, and which he contrasts with the present decadence of the world. Rousseau makes common cause with banished truth, despised virtue, forgotten norms. He can only be right in his accusatorial hyperbole if he stands alone against all. Thus, the significance of these lines in which Rousseau remembers the circumstances and his state of mind when he wrote the *Discours sur l'inégalité:*

> Wandering deep into the forest, I sought and found the vision of those primitive times, the history of which I proudly traced. I demolished the petty lies of mankind; I dared to strip man's nature naked, to follow the progress of time, and trace the things which have distorted it; and by comparing man as he had made himself with man as he is by nature I showed him in his pretended perfection the true source of his misery. Exalted by these sublime meditations, my soul soared towards the Divinity; and from the height I looked down on my fellow-men pursuing the blind path of their prejudices, of their errors, of their misfortunes and their crimes. Then I cried to them in a feeble voice which they could not hear, "Madmen who ceaselessly complain of Nature, learn that all your misfortunes arise from yourselves!"

One will first note in this account of the *genesis* of the *Discours* how the rhetorical situation of the solitary appeal to mankind—which has been noted in the preceding discussion—is a determining factor in the memory of the author of the *Confessions.* Nevertheless, Rousseau, aware of the faults and miseries of mankind, not only appoints himself their critic and denouncer, but undertakes likewise to go back to the temporal beginning, to "earliest times," to "natural man," and to raise himself "near the divinity." Rousseau moves away from the people he calls his fellow-men in the direction of both the primitive past and the transcendental vision. The act of critical opposition is lived, in one aspect, as the privileged possession of an exact image of the remotest past where the casual chain starts and, in the other, as a rapture that reaches the heights and allows one to contemplate and to judge history from God's point of view. To understand the chain of events, to explain evil by its genesis, to juxtapose to the lies of the present humanity the goodness of primitive man: these are all ways to keep one's distance—to see from afar, to see from on high—which condemn Jean-Jacques to singularity and solitude (or which allow him to take advantage of his singularity and solitude). So, he is not only the one who proclaims truth as opposed to general error, but in addition, in his person, he is veracity itself, the personified alternative to social evils. He is bound to coincide with his discourse and to develop, from his singular subjectivity, another order of things, another moral world, a world of innocence and virtue opposed to the ways of the corrupt world. As we will see, for whoever tries to live this vocation, it can only generate anguish.

I have called "criteriological" the doctrinal body constituted by the *Emile* and the *Contrat social*, and I even included there *La Nouvelle Héloïse*. These works must in fact be considered in their narrow relationship to the earlier accusatorial texts which denounce evil and demonstrate its casual mechanism. The major doctrinal texts complete and justify the accusation: their value must be understood in this complementary relationship.

Let us simplify: the *Emile* and the *Contrat social* provide the explanation of the positively valorized concepts (virtue, morals, patriotism) which had previously been formulated, fleetingly and one by one, in the name of which and by virtue of which Rousseau had initially entered his accusation. Just as the attack on evil had been followed by a brilliant reconstruction of evil's probable genesis, its opposite had to develop fully in space and time. The simple idea of virtue had to lead to its elaboration in theory, to an entire history of education in virtue (the *Emile*). The idea of *civisme*, taken alone at first, had to lead to an exposition of the principles of the general will and civic obedience in a city where devotion to the mother country could give them meaning. It was not enough for the accusation to be sustained by the personal existence of the accuser, by his "reform," his "Roman tone," his choice of a simple life and of a craft to earn his bread. Rousseau's demand is broader: it contrasts to the accused world the image of a different world— an unaltered or a remodeled world—where a law reigns in whose name the present reality can be called corrupt. Not content with rejection of usurping authorities, he wanted to build the image of true sovereignty. As we have said before, the counterproposal of Rousseau is sociopolitical, not religious, even though in the city of the *Contrat* and in Emile's upbringing Rousseau wants to grant to the religious feeling a most important role, aimed at assuring the city's moral cohesion and the blossoming of individual conscience. Rousseau had the courage to give considerable breadth to a conception which is neither a utopia radically foreign to reality nor a compromise with the world as it is. The alternative universe whose model he presents obeys two imperatives in relation to contemporary historical and social reality: first, to differ completely from it, but second, to stay sufficiently close to contem-

porary reality to occupy a space seemingly so near that the reader, absent
from the just city and gripped by virtuous remorse, will feel guilty because
true life and happiness were perhaps within his reach and could have been
reached at the price of a courageous conversion. Having first upset his reader,
Rousseau makes him feel thoroughly guilty by showing him the life he could
have had but did not choose. Should the reader take Jean-Jacques's side, he
might experience an inner renewal. This is why the worlds created by
Rousseau exert such an attraction: they appear to offer a better life (even on
earth) for those who would have the audacity to reject convention and servitude. Contemporary experience teaches us that those who initially accept
their guilt are prepared to listen to the catechisms proposed to them if, at
the price of that new faith, they are able to leave fault behind and atone.
This was the method of religious conversions; it is today that of political
conversions. Rousseau is perhaps the prophet of transition from one sphere
to the other, even though so many of his arguments are taken directly from
Seneca and classical exhortation. Rousseau possessed the power to convert:
in the *Emile*, the *Contrat social*, and the *Nouvelle Héloïse*, he showed the way
back to the very principles, moral or political, whence a new existence could
get its start and lead to eventual happiness. He thus gained rapidly a band
of followers ready to follow this master of wisdom. To appreciate this, we
have only to read the letters he received from numerous unknown corres-
pondents who, for the most part, declared themselves ready to leave everything in order to live by his side; we have only to consider the many attempts
to apply theory in practice, inspired first by *La Nouvelle Héloïse* and the *Emile*,
then by the *Contrat social*. Rousseau shows us very clearly how the accusatorial word can develop into seductive appeal at the moment when the negative critique gives way to the positive image (though entirely imaginary) of
a universe of goodness asserted as in the realm of the possible.

One example among many is offered by the preface of the *Emile*. There,
Rousseau declares his opposition to the existing educational system. It is a
radical opposition excluding all compromise. In his refusal, Rousseau initially
associates himself with a general dissatisfaction: "There has been constant
complaint about current practice." But no one except Rousseau goes beyond
expressing dissatisfaction. The sentence continues: "but never a plan for
anything better . . . " If he is not alone in the accusation, Jean-Jacques is
the exception in formulating an alternative theory of education. And he will
be more conspicuous yet when he becomes the adversary of the purely critical
attitude of all contemporary men of letters: "The literature and the science
of our century seek much more to destroy than to build." So it is by the
double refusal of established education and of destructive criticism that Rous-

seau defines his own endeavor. We are not extrapolating excessively in the direction of Hegelian philosophy when we speak here of the negation of negation. What is important to note is the fact that this double negation places Rousseau in the position of the solitary thinker facing universal error. He affirmed it: his ideas are his only. He presents them as his own, but, unlike Montaigne, who did the same thing without seeking to convince others, Rousseau postulates universality and demands everyone's adherence even though he has retreated into particularity: "It is not other people's ideas of education I am presenting, but my own; it is a long-standing reproach that I see things differently from other people." Firm in his principles, he refuses all compromise with accepted customs: "I am always admonished to suggest something feasible. What in fact is being said to me is that I should propose what is being done or at least combine something good with the existing evil. A proposal like this is really more chimerical than mine, for in this alliance the good gets corrupted and the bad is not cured. I would rather follow the established usage than to adopt a good one by halves; there would be less contradiction in man, for he cannot direct his efforts to two opposite ends at once. Fathers and mothers, what is feasible is what you are willing to do. Should I be held accountable for what you want?" The negation's negation leads to an entirely original program, different in all aspects from established practice and formulated in the tone of an ultimatum. It will then be possible for Rousseau to build his educational plan through constant criticism of the existing system, contrasting it with the fictitious development of an imaginary pupil. And he will be able to produce a surprising effect of reality: the diversity of psychic functions taken into account and the multiplicity of evolutionary steps spaced between early childhood and adulthood confer on this ideal pupil a depth and a complexity which lend full credibility to his story. Here too, Rousseau displays an intuitive genius about the spiritual mutations which, over the course of life, result from the interaction of the laws of existence, the initiatives of the individual and the influences of the environment. Many causes come into play to determine a slow progression that would be harmed by acceleration. Emile now has the depth and the substance necessary to become the positive example which will be compared triumphantly to young men submitted to traditional education. Reread, for example, the passage in book 4 where Rousseau confronts "your pupil" with "mine." Rousseau succeeds in making plausible his pupil as a "model for comparison." He gives him a reality which depreciates without possible recourse anything that does not resemble it. Emile's tutor, step by step, allows him freedom to develop in all circumstances according to his natural aptitudes. Thus, Emile exemplifies the reasons for rebellion against contemporary social practice and becomes the obvious model of a method which could make a new man by a rather simple recipe ("negative" education which leaves to the child the initiative with regard to the objects that surround him). But Rousseau carefully adds: "the ease of execution, greater or less, depends on a thousand circumstances which it is impossible to define except in a particular application of the method to such or such country, to such or such a condition." Let us understand fully this important restriction: it allows the blame to be put on circumstances for the difficulty or the impossibility of practical application in such a way that the absolute value of the model will not suffer and its polemic function will not diminish. Even when it is inapplicable, Emile's upbringing is supposed to be most faithful to nature, and it should permit judgment on all other divergent upbringings. Rousseau would not concede that it could ever lose its value as a "regulative concept."

Similarly, this is the case with the *Contrat social:* he exhibits the criteriological model which permits him to judge and accuse existing societies, and he describes, at the same time, a structure workable under certain conditions. Rousseau explains this very clearly. In book 5 of the *Emile*, Rousseau gives a summary of his political theory: Emile is about to travel and he needs to have a clear knowledge of the norms in order to evaluate the realities he will be faced with. "Before observing, one needs to establish rules for one's observations: one needs a scale with which to compare one's measurements. That scale is our principles of political law. Our measurements are the political laws of each country." But Rousseau insists on ascribing a practical importance to his work, at least in the case of small states: and he hopes it will exert a delaying influence: "He had worked for his country and for small states structured similarly. If his doctrine could be somewhat useful to others, it would be by changing the objects of their respect and by slowing the decadence which they accelerate by their false observations" (*Lettre à Christophe de Beaumont*).

The accuser can now declare unacceptable the political forms which do not correspond to the proposed model, while reiterating that the ideal could in certain cases—at some other time, somewhere else—coincide with reality. The picture of the just society will fortify the grievances aimed against the unjust society, if it is possible to prove that a just society could exist on rare occasions. The writer's refusal becomes even more vehement; the reader's feeling of guilt painfully deepens, for he learns that he could contribute himself, under the same circumstances and perhaps by his own will, to sustain or to restore a city of true citizens, a city where sovereignty would be the privilege of the whole society.

La Nouvelle Héloïse also unites a negation and an affirmation. It paints a marvelous picture of mountains, lakes, groves, and beautiful souls, in order to oppose it to the world of Paris. But his antagonistic function, in order to work fully, must soon be reversed into a positive seduction: the novel makes one feel fully happy only when one moves away from the big city.

How was this novel born? First Rousseau had to refuse Paris in order to live in the countryside at the Hermitage. Then, alone with himself, Rousseau had to discover emptiness and amorous discontent. *La Nouvelle Héloïse* is thus born from the union of accusatorial refusal and the effervescence of desire. This fictitious world *is not* that of the society of the rich and the great, but at the same time it is a world *which was not granted* to Jean-Jacques's loving heart: it is a chimerical land built by his imagination and his memory. Rousseau fills the vacuum; he sidetracks his regrets; he repairs the injustices of destiny. This novel is both the possible universe juxtaposed by Rousseau to the barrenness of Parisian salons, and the sentimental fable he invents in order to fill an inner want. Once more, a double negation is at work.

We will find this double negation in the book itself. Saint-Preux, arrived from Vevey to Paris, describes without any satisfaction the life of the city: his letters echo the accusation that is the basis of the entire work. As for Julie, apparently happy and reigning over a circle of beautiful souls, she feels an unexplainable lack—"the ennui of happiness": "the land of chimera is the only one in this world in which it is worth living, and such is the nothingness of human affairs that, outside of the Being sufficient unto himself, nothing is beautiful other than what is not.

Identifying with his characters, Rousseau succeeds in endowing his refusals, his aspirations, and his unappeased desires with a quality of veracity which will find its echo in the reader's identification. Rousseau had shown them what they believed to be authentic passion, veracious language, and true happiness, and nothing seemed more desirable to them than leaving their universe of conventions and lies in order to live as did Saint-Preux and Julie. They could imagine themselves liberated from all hindrances at the cost of a change of habits and surroundings, a trip to enchanting shores. For the contrasting world was not too far away. One did not have to change continents; one had hardly to change countries, for regeneration could take place almost next door. The idyllic softness of the landscape of Clarens allowed the accuser to call himself citizen of a land both real (marked on the map of the West) and conceptual. His indictment was thus authorized and justified. In its love letters or its sublime reasoning, the strength of feeling imposed its law, the accuser presented the credentials of the other land, the foreign kingdom of which he was the ambassador. The Rousseauan fiction, from which the character of the wicked is absent, bears witness to the purity of the soul of its author. It carries an apologetic value and at the same time confirms the merits of the action undertaken against the corrupt world.

The alternative universe developed by Rousseau is that where virtuous endurance is shaped (the *Emile*); it is that of a community based on reciprocity of consciences (*Contrat social*); it is that of the transparency of hearts (*La Nouvelle Héloïse*). One can see what is important to the accuser: not only to legitimate his refusal of the world, but in addition to testify that his blows against the vices of the time were not motivated by hatred. Everything happens as if Rousseau wanted to put the accent on the qualities of softness, harmony, and transparency of his alternative universe in order that the violence of his accusatorial gesture be above suspicion. To be resolutely beyond evil, one needs to have prevented evil from creeping into the denunciation itself of society's ills. Hypersensitive as he was, Rousseau feared that his dissenting attitude might be taken as selfish resentment. When, alone against all, one lodges a complaint against injustice and error, one can be accused of being moved by unjust hate, by unsociability, by desire to harm. If Rousseau admits (albeit with difficulty) to having known accesses of "bile" and "humor" or sometimes melancholia, he defends himself against the charge of being a misanthrope. How did he come to feel that Diderot's famous words, "Only the wicked is alone," although casually inserted in a fictional dialogue, were directed against him? To him they were unbearable and deeply painful because they totally reversed the moral relationship in which he wanted to establish himself before the world: that of censor, solitary prophet, exempt from the sins he denounces, bearer of the just word. In Rousseau's time, these classic roles could only be imitated, assumed, without an institutional foundation. They were literary roles. For an ex-vagabond, the entry through the printed word, that is, through "verbal magic," into the functions of religious preacher, Roman censor, can only be accompanied by an inward guilt which will require constantly renewed assurance and confirmation. One should produce proofs and show that one really *is* someone who has the right to hold such discourses. "I always sustained the part badly," writes Rousseau in regard to the "cynical and sarcastic" tone he had adopted "out of shame" at the moment of his great reform (*Confessions*). The suspicion of charlatanism, hypocrisy, and trickery can always be raised—from within or without. This is the type of amenity that men of letters exchanged at that time. (Rousseau calls Tronchin a trickster; Voltaire, insulting Rousseau, calls him a "charlatan." Only Rameau's nephew, eschewing the pose of nobility, calls himself harshly madman and buffoon.) However, in his private life— concubinage with Thérèse, abandoned children—Rousseau knows that, despite his justifications, the being does not coincide with the appearance: he does not resemble the virtuous fathers of ancient Rome. And one knows that later on Rousseau will cease to claim virtue, which demands an effort he feels unable to make. It will be enough for him to claim pure and natural spontaneity, goodness, innocence, or in any case nonmalfeasance which can go along with weakness.

Let us formulate a hypothesis. Rousseau, wanting above all to escape evil, can trade, without essential damage, the attitude of accuser for that of accused. The accusatorial attitude implies an expenditure of aggressive energy entailing the obligation to face a double exigency: the legitimacy of the accusation and purity of intentions. The accuser must necessarily place himself in an active position. He must exhibit his virile virtue not only by the courage of his refusal, but by the production, through the effort of reflection, of the images or the positive intellectual models that he adopts as alternatives. The work is considerable: to formulate principles, to deduce consequences, to go back to presocial man in order to establish the fundamental pact and, through a necessary line of arguments logically articulated, to build the other city (or in the case of *Emile*, the other man). This effort to structure in their theoretical links or their affective climate a mother country (Geneva), a place populated with beautiful souls (Clarens), a human model (Emile), a religious conviction (Profession de foi du vicaire savoyard), Rousseau accomplished with a sense of duty, of fixing his ideas as he had prescribed for himself. But he stayed as a third party between these works and the hostile world, obliged to take upon himself the proof of the validity of his "sad and great system," obliged to endow it with enough attraction and veracity to make of it a universe competitive with the unsatisfactory world. At the height of his theoretical construction, he always felt that he was himself in question in the system he was developing. He had to vouch for it, and in return the system brought him a confirmation. A rapport of reciprocal affirmation was thus established, but once the system was considered complete, a retreat into the person, the subjective "source," was possible. It became permissible to give up the effort, the reflective activity. It became possible to abandon the roles of tutor, legislator, moral guide, which had constituted so many variations of the paternal figure. And since the initial accusation led to putting the *I* of the accuser in a conspicuous position and since this *I* neither could nor wanted to leave the scene, the only thing left for him to do was to retreat into passive innocence: to abandon himself to nature's first movement, to live as an "automaton" in immediate spontaneity. Relaxation, surrender were permitted. Instead of the system and the articulation of his distinct constituency, instead of the idealized laws of the city of the father, life in nature permitted the achievement, in all purity, of an ideal of fusion in which the return to the mother was so perfectly accomplished that Rousseau sometimes found himself feminized. His sense of persecution made necessary his escape, his search for shelter and asylum. It permitted him to enjoy this type of happiness, while by suffering from feelings of persecution he paid the required price. The benefit of the system was not annulled: a deserved rest could rightfully follow work. Rousseau would now be able to transfer into autobiography, into personal justification, the religious element that led him to sacralize the city's image. Just as the earthly city in the system had taken the place of God's city, autojustification in the face of universal accusation was going to take the place of the process of Grace.

The persecution that Rousseau feels building around himself is multiform. It is assuredly the expected retort, either open or covert, from those whose interests he has attacked and whose convictions he has shocked: "He undoubtedly expected a cruel revenge from all those whom truth offends. He knew that grandees, viziers, gentlemen of the robe, financiers, doctors, priests, philosophers, and all people who make society a real highway robbery, would never forgive him for having seen through them and showed them as they were. . . . The harsh truths that he spoke, although he did so in general terms, were darts that make in the heart wounds that never heal" (*Dialogues*). But according to Rousseau himself, this counterstroke ought to have brought only measures, logically justified—"hatred" and "all kinds of persecutions." However, Rousseau considers himself to be the victim of much worse treatment, the causes of which are to him unfathomable: "disgrace," "infamy," "defamation." The counterattack by the world, as he experiences it, not only makes him someone persecuted by public opinion and guilty of having challenged the institutions and their representatives; it also penetrates his moral self, the inner integrity which was the very basis for the merit of his accusation. It points to the evil inherent in the very source from which originates the just world he had imagined in order to contrast it to the corrupt one. The accusation, therefore, weighs on the original ground of the conscience, on the center where the "voice of conscience" is born. Since defamation, as he experiences it, touches not only his moral quality (he is called wicked) and his morals (he is called a poisoner, a satyr, a thief, a "*vérolé*"), it essentially touches upon his very identity. It questions the bond between his person and his writings; it unties the relation of reciprocal testimony through which the person and the work proved their goodness one by the other. Generalizing on the evil comments actually directed against him, Rousseau feels that he is robbed of his work by being taken for a plagiarist, or that anonymous books which are not his are imputed to him. In other words, Rousseau is convinced that the league of his persecutors denies him the very thing on which he wanted to build a new authority, superior to all accepted authorities—that is his loving heart, obedient to the primal movements of nature, his inner sentiment spontaneously enlightened by a reason attuned to the universal order. Now, the result of this defamation of which Rousseau reads the signs everywhere, is not, on his part, to battle against criticism. The authorities' surveillance prevents him from doing this, and he probably intends to fight only to affirm his true identity, to save himself from the emptiness in which he would be engulfed were the testimony of his work to be suppressed. Hence, he has to resume his writing in order to multiply the proofs of his innocence, to authenticate his writings and their salutary purpose. In short, the suspicion which he feels hanging over him compels him to work in order to regain the image of himself which has been stolen from him and disfigured. He will have to offer a new expression of his true self, by means of the autobiographical narration (*Confessions*), the dialogued apology (*Dialogues*), the dreaming improvisations (*Rêveries*). Thus, the accusation necessitates a defense, the resources of which derive from the narcissistic relationship to the self and which will justify its pleasures.

From then on, he is able to look at his role of accuser as a finished phrase of his existence. He no longer has to prove to the world that the violence of his word is just. "Innocent and persecuted," he himself endures an unjust violence. He deals solely with himself, is solely concerned with himself, waiting for God's judgment and that of posterity.

He remains alone, changed into the persecuted, against them all, the accusers. The initial situation has been reversed. The antinomy is not abolished. The accusation simply comes from the other side. The paranoid ideas which insistently haunt many of Rousseau's last pages show, in a writer who has given the first sign of a certain type of accusatory thought in Europe, how far that thought can reach. To accuse universal evil, and exempt oneself from it, can only lead to one of the two following consequences. Either one feels persecuted in return by the "wicked," resigning oneself to that and seeking in intimate transparency the consolation from all injustices—this is the passive, masochistic solution, to which Rousseau's preference tends to direct itself. Or one responds through violence, engaging in the fight against the evil world in the name of justice and innocence, whose demands one believes oneself alone to know—this is the aggressive, sadistic, terrorist solution. In both cases, the accuser (or the group of accusers) and the accused (or the group of attacked) arrogate to themselves a privileged role: they are in possession of the light and the transparency, whereas everything around them remains in darkness. The choice of the paradoxical antinomic rapport with reality determines in advance the psychopathic radicalization of the relationship with the rest of mankind. The revolutionary period, and then modern history, have only given to the consequences already developed in Rousseau's destiny the opportunity to become a reality through large-scale events. (I would like to add the following to avoid being considered as one of those who, without fearing anachronism, claim that the *Contrat social* is a totalitarian work: this view is neither prefigured nor prepared in Rousseau's doctrine. It is to be read in his attitude.)

The reverie, in which Rousseau finally takes refuge, no longer has the mission of providing a comparative world which could be of value to all men and could replace the effective order or disorder of human relationships. The world of reverie now has a substitutive value for Jean-Jacques alone; it replaces all the joys of trust and communication denied to him. The man who had raised himself to God, as we have seen, in order to condemn mankind will rekindle the same enthusiasm, the same high-soaring élan toward the divine, but with a different aim: to escape the suit which mankind unfairly is bringing against him. The imaginary response first elaborated against the world finally becomes the compensation which allows the persecuted to find refuge outside the world, far from his persecutors' reach.

Is it necessary to insist here on the contemporary phenomena which seem closely copied on the model offered by Rousseau's experience? The protest addressed against a world conceived as unjust is reversed into a passionate attention to all that remains for the individual when the world massively plots against him. It is because Rousseau first wrote his two accusatory *Discours* and the *Contrat social* that he could become the author of the fifth *Rêverie*, dedicated to the memories of his ecstasies on the shores of the lake of Bienne. The idea of rejection is the common term: it can be conjugated actively or passively. The City of the *Contrat* is the theoretical image necessary to the one who rejects the actual society in the name of another political organization. His turning toward nature's scenery, his fusion with nature, his listening to the pure "feeling of existence" are the only goodness remaining to the one who has been rejected by the society of men; the individual becomes a universe unto himself, he discovers the unknown riches of his body, of his memory, of his fantasies. *Accuser*, rejecting injustice and suspicious authority, Rousseau is the first to fill with a sacred fascination the theoretical model of a society or of an education able to repair harm done. *Accused*, seeking within himself justification and compensation, he is again the first to show the full range of autobiography, in which a life's truth is expressed in the "chain of one's secret feelings." If Rousseau is still alive for us, it is because, through accusation and rejection conjugated actively and passively, he has formulated two important modern myths which have retained all their power: the myth of a social universe in which man, depending solely on himself, encounters his fellow-men in a perfect transparency of hearts, and the myth of an individual experience so rich that it can replace all other possessions.

Thus, Rousseau's ideas and Rousseau's destiny still remain provocative. We feel that we can test on him—notwithstanding the two centuries that have elapsed—the crucial ethical problems of modern man. Dissent, individualism, cravings for a better social organization, which, if realized, would subordinate the individual to the community—these are some of the puzzling aspects which nowadays attract endless commentaries on Rousseau. I see no predictable end, for instance, to the discussion on the narrow relationship between guilt and the two mythical images of the fullness of the social body and the fullness of individual existence. As with projective psychological tests, the way our time interprets Rousseau could help a judicious observer to define today's major intellectual issues.

PAUL de MAN

Metaphor (Second Discourse)

The place of the *Discourse on the Origins and the Foundations of Inequality among Men* (1755) in the canon of Rousseau's works remains uncertain. The apparent duality of Rousseau's complete writings, a whole that consists in part of political theory, in part of literature (fiction and autobiography), has inevitably led to a division of labor among the interpreters, thus bringing to light latent incompatibilities between political scientists, cultural historians, and literary critics. This specialization has often prevented the correct understanding of the relations between the literary and the political aspects of Rousseau's thought. As the overtly political piece of writing that it undoubtedly is, the *Second Discourse* has primarily interested historians and social scientists. It does not confront them with the same difficulties as *Julie*, a book in which it is not easy to overlook the literary dimensions entirely and where it takes some degree of bad faith to reduce the text to "an intellectual experiment in the techniques and consequences of human engineering" (Lester Crocker, *J. J. Rousseau*). Despite the presence of at least one explicit passage on language in the *Discourse* the linguistic mediations can easily be ignored. The section on the origin of language is clearly a polemical digression without organic links to the main argument, and the *Discourse* can be considered as a literal model for a theory of history and of society, that is, a model that could be transposed *tel quel* from the text to the political or social situation that it represents or prefigures. Once this is assumed, the *Second Discourse* becomes highly vulnerable to a list of recurrent objections that

From *Allegories of Reading: Figural Language in Rousseau, Nietzsche, Rilke and Proust.*
© 1979 by Yale University. Yale University Press, 1979.

reappear with remarkable persistence in all Rousseau studies and that any reader of the text will feel compelled to make himself.

It is by no means my intention to suggest that these objections are unfounded or that they are inspired by a deliberate malice that should be met with defensive countermalice. The Rousseau interpreter should avoid the danger of repeating the paranoid gesture of his subject. The first task is to diagnose what, if anything, is being systematically overlooked by other readers, prior to asking why this particular area of Rousseau's thought possesses the curious privilege of rendering itself invisible, as if it were wearing the ring of Gyges referred to in the sixth *Promenade*. The literal reading that fails to take into account the figural dimensions of the language (despite the fact that this particular text explicitly draws attention to these dimensions) is not to be rejected as simply erroneous or malevolent, all the more since, in the *Second Discourse*, the political terminology and the political themes postulate the existence of an extratextual referent and raise the question of the text's relationship to this referent. Nor can we assume that this relationship is one of literal correspondence.

Consider, for instance, the status of what seems to be the inescapable a priori of the text itself, what Rousseau calls the "state of nature." Very few informed readers today would still maintain that Rousseau's state of nature is an empirical reality, present, past, or future. Most commentators would agree that, at least up to a point, the state of nature is a state "that no longer exists, that has perhaps never existed and that probably will never come into being. . . . " It is a fiction; but in stating this, the problem has merely been displaced, for what then is the significance of this fiction with regard to the empirical world? Granted that the authority of the state of nature, the hold it has over our present thought, is no longer that of something that existed elsewhere or at other times and towards which our relation can therefore be described in terms of nostalgia and quest; granted that the mode of being of the state of nature and the mode of being of the present, alienated state of man are perhaps radically incompatible, with no road connecting the one to the other—the question remains why this radical fiction ("We must begin by discarding all facts . . .") continues to be indispensable for any understanding of the present, as if its shadow controlled once and forever the degree of light allotted to us. It is a state that we must "know well" and of which "it is necessary to have a correct understanding [*des notions justes*] in order to evaluate our present condition." What kind of epistemology can hope to "know well" a radical state of fiction? The *Second Discourse* hardly seems to provide a reliable answer. As a genetic narrative in which the state of nature functions at the very least as a point of departure or as a point of reference (if no longer necessarily as a point of arrival), the *Second Discourse* seems to contradict the radical rejection of reality on which it bases its claim to free itself from the constraints of facts. Rousseau seems to want to have it both ways, giving himself the freedom of the fabulator but, at the same time, the authority of the responsible historian. A degree of impatience on the part of the historians is certainly justified towards a man who, by his own admission, escapes in speculative fantasies but who, on the other hand, claims that in so doing "one sweeps away the dust and the sands that cover the edifice [of human institutions], one reveals the solid foundations on which it is built and learns to consider them with respect." How can a pure fiction and a narrative involving such concrete political realities as property, contractual law, and modes of government coalesce into a genetic history that pretends to lay bare the foundations of human society?

It seems difficult to avoid a prognosis of inconsistency, leading to the separation between the theoretical, literary and the practical, political aspects of Rousseau's thought. The literary faculty which, in the *Second Discourse*, invents the fiction of a natural state of man becomes an ideology growing out of the repression of the political faculty. A clear and concise statement of this recurrent critical interpretation of Rousseau—which goes back at least as far as Schiller—can be found in a recent study of the *Social Contract* by the French social philosopher Louis Althusser. He analyzes recurrent shifts [*décalages*] in the key terms of Rousseau's vocabulary and concludes that these shifts, or displacements, are

> to be explicitly understood, once and forever, as the very displacement that separates the consequences of theory from reality, a displacement between two equally impossible *praxes* [*décalage entre deux pratiques également impossibles*]. Since we now have [in the text of the *Social Contract*] reached the stage of reality and since we can only keep going around in a circle (ideology—economy—ideology, etc.) no flight remains possible into the actual, real world [*dans la réalité même*]. End of the displacement.
>
> If no other displacement is available to us . . . only one single, different road remains open: a *transference* [*transfert*] of the impossible theoretical solution into the other of theory [*l'autre de la théorie*], namely literature. The fictional triumph of an admirable, unprecedented literary work.
>
> ("*The Social Contract* [The Discrepancies]")

If the political side of Rousseau's work is indeed a reductive ideology that results from a repression carried out by means of literary language, then the theoretical interest of a text like the *Second Discourse* is primarily psychological. Conversely, the political writings can then themselves become a reliable way of access to the problematics of the self in Rousseau. And here the *Second Discourse* would be particularly useful, not only because, unlike the *Social Contract*, it explicitly involves the moment of transference into literary fiction, but precisely because, unlike the autobiographical writings, it hides its self-obsessions behind a language of conceptual generality. Rousseau's ambivalence with regard to such key notions as property, civil authority, and even technology could then serve as a model for an understanding of his psychological self-mystifications. In strictly textual terms, the problem comes down to the inconsistency between the first and the second part of the text. Between the pure fiction of the first part, dealing with theoretical problems of man, nature, and methodology, and the predominantly historical and institutional language, used in the second part, there would exist a gap, an unbridgeable "*décalage*," that Rousseau, caught in a false claim of authentic self-knowledge, would be least of all able to perceive. The reading that follows puts this scheme into question.

In the *Second Discourse*, the state of nature, though fictional, is not static. Possibilities of change are built into its description as a synchronic *state* of being. The potentially dynamic properties of natural man are pity, "a principle anterior to reason [that] inspires a natural reluctance to see any sensitive being, and especially our fellow-man, suffer or perish," and freedom: "Nature alone does everything in the actions of animals whereas man partakes in his own actions in his quality as free agent." The concept of pity has been definitively treated by Jacques Derrida (in *Of Grammatology*). We can therefore begin with the concept of freedom.

The ambivalent nature of the concept of freedom in Rousseau has been noticed by several interpreters. To be free, for Rousseau, is by no means a tranquil and harmonious repose within the ordained boundaries of the human specificity, the reward for a Kantian, rational sense of limitations. From the start, freedom appears as an act of the will ("the will still speaks when Nature is silent") pitted against the ever-present obstacle of a limitation which it tries to transgress. It is a consequence, or another version, of the statement at the beginning of the *Second Discourse*, that the specificity of man forever escapes our grasp since "the more we study man . . . the less we are in a position to know him." Any confinement within the boundaries of an anthropological self-definition is therefore felt to be a restriction beyond which man, as a being devoid of natural specificity, will have to transgress. This will to transgress, in a pre-Nietzschean passage, is held by Rousseau to be the very definition of the Spirit: "the power to will or, rather, the power to choose, as well as the feeling of this power is a purely spiritual act." Very little distinguishes power to will, or willpower (*puissance de vouloir*) from "will to power," since the power to choose is precisely the power to transgress whatever in nature would entail the end of human power.

The direct correlative of freedom thus conceived is mentioned in the paragraph that follows immediately upon the definition, although the transitory link is not explicitly stated: freedom is man's will to change or what Rousseau somewhat misleadingly calls "perfectibility." The potential transgression that occurs whenever the concepts of nature and of man are associated—in the *Essay on the Origin of Language* all examples destined to illustrate the "natural" language of man are acts of violence—transforms all human attributes from definite, self-enclosed, and self-totalizing actions into open structures: perception becomes imagination, natural needs [*besoins*] become unfulfillable passions, sensations become an endless quest for knowledge all of which deprive man forever of a central identity ("the more one meditates . . . the greater the distance becomes between our pure sensations and the simplest forms of knowledge"). In the same consistent pattern, the discovery of temporality coincides with the acts of transgressive freedom: time relates to space in the same way that imagination relates to perception, need to passion, etc. The very conception of a future is linked with the possibility of a free imagination; the soul of the still enslaved primitive man is "without any awareness of the future, however close it may be. His projects are as narrow as are his views: they hardly extend until the end of the day." Consciousness of mortality is similarly linked to the freedom that distinguishes man from the animal: "the knowledge and the fear of death is one of the first things acquired by man as he moves away from the animal condition."

The existential notion of freedom is impressive enough in itself. It does not suffice, however, to make the connection with the political parts of the *Second Discourse*. It accounts for the ambivalent valorization of all historical change, since any change will always have to put into question the value-system that made it possible: any positive valorization as progress always also implies a regress, and Rousseau's text scrupulously maintains this balance. The impossibility of reaching a rationally enlightened anthropology also accounts for the necessary leap into fiction, since no past or present human action can coincide with or be under way towards the nature of man. The question remains why the *Second Discourse*, in its second part, somehow manages to return to the concrete realities of political life in a vocabulary that reintroduces normative evaluations—why, in other words, the methodological paradox of the beginning (that the very attempt to know man makes this knowledge impossible) does not prevent the text from finally getting started, after many hesitations: a preface preceding a first part which is itself a methodological introduction and which, in its turn, is again introduced by another preface. What characteristic structures of freedom and perfectibility, in part 1, lead us to understand the political structures of part 2? And where are we to find a structural description of perfectibility in what seems to be a self-enclosed genetic text in which perfectibility simply functions as the organizing theme?

The section on language appears as a digression destined to illustrate the impossibility of passing from nature to culture by natural means. It runs parallel to a similar development that deals with the growth of technology. As such, it serves indeed a secondary function that belongs with the polemical and not with the systematic aspects of the *Second Discourse*. Starobinski rightly emphasizes that the passage is written "less in order to formulate a coherent theory on the origin of language than to demonstrate the difficulties the question raises." In fact, the entire passage has the tone of a mock-argument directed against those who explain the origin of language by means of casual categories that are themselves dependent on the genetic power of the origin for which they are supposed to account. The constant warning against the mystification of adopting a privileged viewpoint that is unable to understand its own genealogy, a methodological theme that runs throughout the *Second Discourse*, also applies to the theory of language. But not selectively so. The science of language is one of the areas in which this type of fetishism (reducing history to nature) occurs, but it is not the only one. The same error prevails with regard to ethical judgment (Hobbes) or with regard to technology.. From this point of view, the section on language seems to have a primarily critical function and it could not serve to illuminate the central problem of the text—that of the epistemological authority of the normative second part.

The passage, however, contains its own theory on the structure of language, albeit in a highly fragmentary and oblique form. More important still, Rousseau explicitly links language to the notion of perfectibility, itself derived from the printed categories of freedom and will. "Moreover," he writes, "general ideas can only enter the mind by means of words and our understanding can seize upon them only by means of propositions. This is one of the reasons why animals could never acquire such ideas, nor the perfectibility that depends on it" ("C'est une des raisons pourquoi les animaux ne sauraient se former de telles idées, ni jamais acquérir la perfectibilité qui en dépend"). Perfectibility evolves as language evolves, moving from particular denomination to general ideas: an explicit link is established between two distinct conceptual areas in the text, the first pertaining to perfectibility, freedom, and a series of general concepts that are connected narratively and thematically but never described in terms of their internal structures, the second pertaining to the structural and epistemological properties of language. Besides, freedom and perfectibility are relay stations on the itinerary by way of which the *Second Discourse* can move from the methodological language of the first to the political language of the second part. The sentence can therefore be interpreted to mean that the system of concepts at work in the political parts of the *Second Discourse* are structured like the linguistic model described in the digression on language. This makes the passage a key to an understanding of the entire text. For nowhere else do we find as detailed a structural anaylsis of the concepts invovled in the subsequent narrative.

Yet the passage is avoided rather than stressed in most readings of the *Second Discourse*. In his notes to the Pléiade Edition, Jean Starobinski seems to be clearly aware of some of its implications, but he at once limits its impact by means of an argument that goes to the center of the problem involved in the interpretation of this text. Commenting on Rousseau's sentence—"C'est une des raisons pourquoi les animaux ne sauraient se former des idées générales, ni jamais acquérir la perfectibilité qui en dépend"—he writes: "The relative clause [*qui en dépend*] has here a determinative and not an explicative function. Rousseau refers here to one particular kind of perfectibility that depends on language. As for perfectibility in general, which Rousseau has told us to be an essential and primitive property of man, it is not the result of language but much rather its cause." Since the French language does not distinguish between "which" and "that," it is impossible to decide by grammatical means alone whether the sentence should read: "animals could never acquire perfectibility, since perfectibility depends on language" or, as Starobinski would have it, "animals could never acquire the kind of perfectibility that depends on language." The correct understanding of the passage depends on whether one accepts the contention that the principle of genetic causality introduced by Starobinski, in which chronological, logical, and ontological priority coincide, is indeed the system at work in Rousseau's text. Can it be said of perfectibility that it is an "essential and primitive property of man," Starobinski's phrasing rather than Rousseau's, who said only that it was "une qualité très spécifique qui distingue [l'homme]"?

Each of the terms is problematic and their combination, as if they could be freely interchanged, is the most problematic of all. Starobinski's phrasing not only assumes that the (temporally) primitive must also be the (ontological) essence, but that a property of what is presumably a substance (man) can

be an essence. Since moreover the substance "man" is in this text a highly
volatile concept that behaves logically much more like a property than like
a substance, the essence perfectibility would then be the property of a property. Rousseau's main methodological point, his constant warning against
the danger of substituting cause for effect reveals at least a certain distrust
of genetic continuities, for the substitution becomes aberrant only if such a
continuity is in doubt. This should make us wary of accepting uncritically
the common sense and admirable prudence displayed in Starobinski's
reading.

Even if read to mean that perfectibility, in the general sense in which
it is used when we first encounter it in the *Second Discourse*, is linked to
language, the statement does not at first sight seem to be so far-reaching as
to justify its repression. Why then is it being overlooked or avoided? How
curious that, when a text offers us an opportunity to link a nonlinguistic
historical concept such as perfectibility to language, we should refuse to
follow the hint. Especially curious in the case of a text whose intelligibility
hinges on the existence or nonexistence of such a link between a "literary,"
language-oriented method of investigation and the practical results to which
the method is assumed to lead. Yet a critic of Starobinski's intelligence and
subtlety goes out of his way in order to avoid the signs that Rousseau has
put up and prefers the bland to the suggestive reading, although it requires
an interpretative effort to do so. For there is no trace to be found in Rousseau's
work of a particular, linguistic perfectibility that would be distinct from
historical perfectibility in general. In the *Essay on the Origin of Language*, the
perfectibility of language, which is in fact a degradation, evolves exactly as
the perfectibility of society evolves in the *Second Discourse*. There must be an
unsuspected threat hidden in a sentence that one is so anxious to de-fuse.

Animals have no history because they are unable to perform the specifically linguistic act of conceptualization. But how does conceptualization
work, according to Rousseau? The text yields information on this point,
though not in a simple and straightforward way. It describes conceptualization as substituting one verbal utterance (at the simplest level, a common
noun) for another on the basis of a resemblance that hides differences which
permitted the existence of entities in the first place. The natural world is a
world of pure contiguity: "all individual entities appear in isolation to the
mind [of primitive man], as they are in the picture of nature. If one oak tree
was called *A*, another was called *B*. . . . Within this contiguity certain resemblances appear. By substituting for *A* and *B* the word "tree" on the basis
of certain properties that *A* and *B* have in common, we invent an abstraction
under which the irreductible differences that separate *A* from *B* are sub-

sumed. The perception of these resemblances is not, in itself, a conceptualization: in the case of animals, it leads to acts that satisfy needs but that remain confined to the limits of the particular action. "When a monkey goes without hesitation from one nut to another, do we think that he has in mind a general idea of this type of fruit and that he compares his archetype to these two individual entities? Certainly not. . . . Conceptualization does not proceed on the basis of mere perception: perception and imagination (in the guise of memory) intervene in recognizing the existence of certain similarities—an act of which animals are said to be as capable as men—but the actual process of conceptualization is verbal: "It is necessary to state propositions and to speak in order to have general ideas; for as soon as the imagination stops, the mind can only proceed by means of discourse."

The description seems to remain within a binary system in which animal and man, nature and culture, acts (or things) and words, particularity (or difference) and generality, concreteness and abstraction stand in polar opposition to each other. Antitheses of this kind allow for dialectical valorizations and although this passage of the *Second Discourse* is relatively free of value judgments (nothing is said about an innate superiority of nature over artifice or of practical behavior over speculative abstraction), it nevertheless invites value judgments on the part of the interpreter. The most incisive evaluations of this and of similar passages are those which locate the tension within language itself by stressing that the implied polarity exists within the structure of the linguistic sign, in the distinction established by Rousseau between the denominative and the conceptual function of language. The text indeed distinguishes the act of naming (tree *A* and tree *B*) which leads to the literal denomination of the proper noun, from the act of conceptualization. And conceptualization, conceived as an exchange or substitution of properties on the basis of resemblance, corresponds exactly to the classical definition of metaphor as it appears in theories of rhetoric from Aristotle to Roman Jakobson. (The definition from the *Poetics* [1457 b] is well known: "Metaphor is the transfer [*epiphora*] to a thing of a name that designates another thing, a transfer from the genus to the species or from the species to the genus or according to the principle of analogy." Jakobson defines metaphor as substitution on the basis of resemblance.) The text would then, in a sense, distinguish between, on the one hand, figurative, connotative, and metaphorical language and, on the other, denominative, referential, and literal language, and it would oppose the two modes antithetically to each other. This allows for a valorization that privileges one mode over the other. Since Rousseau asserts the temporal priority of the proper noun over the concept ("Each object received *first* a particular name . . . "; "the *first* nouns could only have been proper nouns"), it would indeed follow, within the genetic logic of the narrative, that he separates the literal from the metaphorical forms of language and privileges the former over the latter. This interpretation, nearly unanimously accepted in Rousseau studies, is well summarized, with a helpful reference to Michel Foucault, by a recent commentator: "The entire history of Rousseau's work, the passage from 'theory' to 'literature,' is the transference of the need to name the world to the prior need of naming oneself. To name the world is to make the representation of the world coincide with the world itself; to name myself is to make the representation that I have of the world coincide with the representation that I convey to others" (Alain Grosrichard, "Gravité de Rousseau"). Rousseau's increasingly subjective and autobiographical discourse would then merely be the extension, within the realm of the self, of the referential linguistic model that governs his thought. The failure of this attempt to "name" the subject, the discovery that, in Grosrichard's words, "le sujet est l'innomable" undercuts the authority of Rousseau's own language. It also relegates him, with Condillac and, generally speaking, with all followers of Locke, to what Foucault subversively calls "le discours classique." As far as the *Second Discourse* is concerned, such an interpretation would have to conclude that the text is truly incoherent, since it does not control the opposition between the conceptual metaphor "state of nature" and the literal reality of civil society, an opposition asserted in the *Discourse* itself. Moreover, by starting out from the metaphor, the text reverses the priority of denomination over connotation that it advocates. In texts explicitly centered on the self, such as the *Confessions* or the *Dialogues*, this incoherence would at least be brought into the open, whereas it is merely repressed in the pseudo-conceptual language of the *Second Discourse*.

Before yielding to this very persuasive scheme, we must return to the particular passage in the *Discourse* and to the corresponding section in the *Essay on the Origin of Language*. Does Rousseau indeed separate figural from literal language and does he privilege one type of discourse over the other? There is no simple answer to this question, for whereas, in the *Discourse*, it is said that "the first nouns could only have been proper nouns," the *Essay* states with equal assurance that "man's first language had to be figurative" and that "figural language predates literal meaning" (*Essay*). And when we try to understand denomination in Rousseau as, in Foucault's words, "going through language until we reach the point where words and things are tied together in their common essence" (*The Order of Things*), then we find that, in the *Second Discourse*, denomination is associated with difference rather than with identity. A note in the 1782 edition adds to the description of denomination ("if one oak were called *A*, another would be called *B*") the following remark: "for the first idea we derive from two things is that they are not the same; it often takes a great deal of time to observe what they have in common." We would then have to assume that an observer, so keenly aware of difference that he fails to notice the resemblance between one oak tree and another, would be unable to distinguish the difference between the word *a* and the tree *A*, to the point of considering them as united in some "common essence." Another difficulty: following the traditional reading of Rousseau as it is here represented by Alain Grosrichard, we would want to seize upon the act of denomination in all the transparency of its nonconceptual literalness. We find instead that "the first inventors [of words] were able to give names only to the ideas they already possessed . . . , a sentence in which the word "idea," despite all pre-Kantian empiricist concreteness, denotes the presence of some degree of conceptuality (or metaphor) from the start, within the very act of naming. We know, moreover, from the previous quotation, what this "*idée première*" must be: it is the idea of difference ("the first idea we derive from two things . . . "). But if all entities are the same, namely entities, to the extent that they differ from each other, then the substitution of sameness for difference that characterizes, for Rousseau, all conceptual language is built into the very act of naming, the "invention" of the proper noun. It is impossible to say whether denomination is literal or figural: from the moment there is denomination, the conceptual metaphor of entity as difference is implied, and whenever there is metaphor, the literal denomination of a particular entity is inevitable: "try to trace for yourself the image of a tree in general, you will never succeed. In spite of yourself, you will have to see it as small or large, bare or leafy, light or dark" or "As soon as you imagine [a triangle] in your mind, it will be one specific triangle and no other, and it would be impossible not to make its contour visible and its surface colored." Are we forced to conclude that Rousseau's paradoxes are genuine contradictions, that he did not know, in the *Discourse*, what he stated in the *Essay*, and vice versa? Perhaps we should heed his admonition: "in order not to find me in contradiction with myself, I should be allowed enough time to explain myself" (*Essay*).

In the third section of the *Essay on the Origin of Language*, Rousseau offers us an "example" in the form of a narrative parable, a brief allegory. It tells us how the proper name *man*, which figures so prominently at the beginning of the *Second Discourse*, came into being:

A primitive man [*un homme sauvage*], on meeting other men, will first have experienced fright. His fear will make him see these men as larger and stronger than himself; he will give them the name *giants*. After many experiences, he will discover that the supposed giants are neither larger nor stronger than himself, and that their stature did not correspond to the idea he had originally linked to the word giant. He will then invent another name that he has in common with them, such as, for example, the word *man*, and will retain the word giant for the false object that impressed him while he was being deluded.

(*Essay*)

This is a general and purely linguistic version of what Grosrichard calls "*se nommer*," in which the origin of inequality, in the most literal sense of the term, is being described. The passage was possibly inspired, as has been pointed out, by Condillac, except for the fact that Rousseau refers to full-grown men and not to children. The difference is important, for the entire passage plays a complex game with qualitative and quantitative notions of similarity, equality, and difference.

In this encounter with other men, the first reaction of the primitive is said to be fear. The reaction is not obvious; it is certainly not based on objective data, for Rousseau makes it clear that the men are supposed to be of equal size and strength. Neither is it the fear of a single individual confronted with a multitude, since primitive men are entirely devoid of the sense of numbers or of groups. The similarity in size and in the observable attributes of strength should, at first sight, act reassuringly and make the reaction less anxious than if the man had encountered a bear or a lion. Yet Rousseau stresses fright, and Derrida is certainly right in stating that the act of denomination that follows—calling the other man a giant, a process that Rousseau describes as a figural use of language—displaces the referential meaning from an outward, visible property to an "inward" feeling. The coinage of the word "giant" simply means "I am afraid." But what is the reason for fear, if it is not due to observable data? It can only result from a fundamental feeling of distrust, the suspicion that, although the creature does not look like a lion or a bear, it nevertheless might act like one, outward appearances to the contrary. The reassuringly familiar and similar outside might be a trap. Fear is the result of a possible discrepancy between the outer and the inner properties of entities. It can be shown that, for Rousseau, all passions— whether they be love, pity, anger, or even a borderline case between passion and need such as fear—are characterized by such a discrepancy; they are based not on the knowledge that such a difference exists, but on the hypothesis that it might exist, a possibility that can never be proven or disproven by empirical or by analytical means. A statement of distrust is neither true nor false: it is rather in the nature of a permanent hypothesis.

The fact that Rousseau chose fear as an example to demonstrate the priority of metaphor over denomination complicates and enriches the pattern to a considerable degree, for metaphor is precisely the figure that depends on a certain degree of correspondence between "inside" and "outside" properties. The word "giant," invented by the frightened primitive to designate his fellow-man, is indeed a metaphor in that it is based on a correspondence between inner feelings of fear and outward properties of size. It may be objectively false (the other man is not in fact any taller) but it is subjectively candid (he seems taller to the frightened subject). The statement may be in error, but it is not a lie. It "expresses" the inner experience correctly. The metaphor is blind, not because it distorts objective data, but because it presents as certain what is, in fact, a mere possibility. The fear of falling is "true," for the potentially destructive power of gravity is a verifiable fact, but the fear of another man is hypothetical; no one can trust a precipice, but it remains an open question, for whoever is neither a paranoiac nor a fool, whether one can trust one's fellow man. By calling him a "giant," one freezes hypothesis, or fiction, into fact and makes fear, itself a figural state of suspended meaning, into a definite, proper meaning devoid of alternatives. The metaphor "giant," used to connote man, has indeed a proper meaning (fear), but this meaning is not really proper: it refers to a condition of permanent suspense between a literal world in which appearance and nature coincide and a figural world in which this correspondence is no longer *a priori* posited. Metaphor is error because it believes or feigns to believe in its own referential meaning. This belief is legitimate only within the limits of a given text: the metaphor that connotes Achilles' courage by calling him a lion is correct within the textual tradition of the *Iliad* because it refers to a character in a fiction whose function it is to live up to the referential implication of the metaphor. As soon as one leaves the text it becomes aberrant—if, for example, one calls one's son Achilles in the hope that this will make him into a hero. Rousseau's example of a man encountering another man is textually ambiguous, as all situations involving categorical relationships between man and language have to be. What happens in such an encounter is complex: the empirical situation, which is open and hypothetical, is given a consistency that can only exist in a text. This is done by means of a metaphor (calling the other man a giant), a substitutive figure of speech ("*he* is a giant" substituting for "*I* am afraid") that changes a referential situation suspended between fiction and fact (the hypothesis of fear) into a literal fact. Paradoxically, the figure literalizes its referent and deprives it of its para-figural status. The figure dis-figures, that is, it makes fear, itself a para-figural fiction, into a reality that is as inescapable as the reality of the original encounter between the two men. Metaphor overlooks the fictional, textual element in the nature of the entity it connotes. It assumes a world in which intra- and extra-textual events, literal and figural forms of language, can be distinguished, a world in which the literal and the figural are properties that can be isolated and, consequently, exchanged and substituted for each other. This is an error, although it can be said that no language would be possible without this error.

The intricacy of the situation is obviously tied to the choice of the example. The interplay of difference and similarity implied in the encounter between two men is more complex than if the encounter had been between two potentially antithetical entities such as man and woman, as is the case in *Julie* or parts of *Emile,* or man and things, as is the case in the example of the *Second Discourse* in which a man is naming a tree instead of naming another man. It seems perverse on Rousseau's part to choose an example based on a more complex situation than that of the paradigm with which he is dealing. Should we infer, with the traditional interpreters of Rousseau, that the intersubjective, reflective situation of self-encounter, as in the specular self-fascination of Narcissus, is indeed for Rousseau the paradigmatic experience from which all other experiences are derived? We must remind ourselves that the element of reflective similarity mirrored in the example of man's encounter with man is not the representation of a paradigmatic empirical situation (as is the case in Descartes's *cogito* or in any phenomenological reduction) but the metaphorical illustration of a linguistic fact. The example does not have to do with the genetic process of the "birth" of language (told later in the text) but with the linguistic process of conceptualization. The narrative mode of the passage is itself a metaphor that should not mislead us into transposing a synchronic, linguistic structure into a diachronic, historical event. And conceptualization, as the passage of the *Second Discourse* on the naming of trees makes clear, is an intralinguistic process, the invention of a figural metalanguage that shapes and articulates the infinitely fragmented and amorphous language of pure denomination. To the extent that all language is conceptual, it always already speaks about language and not about things. The sheer metonymic enumeration of things that Rousseau describes in the *Discourse* ("if one oak was called *A*, and another was called *B* . . . ") is an entirely negative moment that does not describe language as it is or used to be at its inception, but that dialectically infers literal denomination as the negation of language. Denomination could never exist by itself although it is a constitutive part of all linguistic events. All language is language about denomination, that is, a conceptual, figural, metaphorical metalanguage. As such, it partakes of the blindness of metaphor when metaphor literalizes its referential indetermination into a specific unit of meaning. This statement about the metalinguistic (or conceptual) nature of language is the equivalent of the earlier statement, directly derived from Rousseau, according to which denomination has to postulate the concept (or idea) of difference in order to come into being.

If all language is about language, then the paradigmatic linguistic model is that of an entity that confronts itself. It follows that the exemplary situation described in the *Essay* (man confronting man) is the correct linguistic paradigm, whereas the situation of the *Second Discourse* (man confronting a tree) is a dialetical derivation from this paradigm that moves away from the linguistic model towards problems of perception, consciousness, reflection, and the like. In a text that associates the specificity of man with language and, within language, with the power of conceptualization, the priority belongs to the example from the *Essay*. The statement of the *Discourse* that "the first nouns could only have been proper nouns" is therefore a statement derived from the logically prior statement "that the first language had to be figural." There is no contradiction if one understands that Rousseau conceives of denomination as a hidden, blinded figure.

This is not yet the end of the parable. Actual language does not use the imaginary word "giant" but has invented the concepual term "man" in its stead. (The actual word "giant," as we know it from everyday usage, presupposes the word "man" and is not the metaphorical figure that Rousseau, for lack of an existing word, has to call "giant." Rousseau's "giant" would be more like some mythological monster; one could think of Goliath, or of Polyphemos [leaving aside the temptation to develop the implications of Odysseus's strategy in giving his name to Polyphemos as no-man].) Conceptualization is a double process: it is this complexity that allows for the successive narrative pattern of the allegory. It consists first of all of a wild, spontaneous metaphor which is, to some degree, aberrant. This first level of aberration is however not intentional, because it does not involve the interests of the subject in any way. Rousseau's man stands to gain nothing from inventing the word "giant." The distortion introduced by the term results exclusively from a formal, rhetorical potential of the language. The same is not true at the second stage. The word "man" is created, says Rousseau, "after many experiences, [when primitive man] will have discovered that the supposed giants are neither larger nor stronger than himself"— (*Essay*). The word "man" is the result of a quantitative process of comparison based on measurement, and making deliberate use of the category of number

in order to reach a reassuring conclusion: if the other man's height is nu-
merically equal to my own, then he is no longer dangerous. The conclusion
is wishful and, of course, potentially in error—as Goliath and Polyphemos,
among others, were soon enough to discover. The second level of aberration
stems from the use of number as if it were a literal property of things that
truly belongs to them, when it is, in fact, just one more conceptual metaphor
devoid of objective validity and subject to the distortions that constitute all
metaphors. For Rousseau, as for Nietzsche, number is par excellence the
concept that hides ontic difference under an illusion of identity. The idea
of number is just as derivative and suspect as the idea of man:

> A primitive could consider his right and his left leg separately,
> or consider them together as one indivisible pair, without ever
> thinking of them as *two* [legs]. For the representational idea of an
> object is one thing, but the numerical idea that determines it is
> another. Still less was he able to count up to five. Although he
> could have noticed, in pressing his hands together, that the fingers
> exactly corresponded, he did not in the least conceive of their
> numerical equality.

The concept of man is thus doubly metaphorical: it first consists of the
blind moment of passionate error that leads to the word "giant," then of the
moment of deliberate error that uses number in order to tame the original
wild metaphor into harmlessness (it being well understood that this numerical
terminology of "first," "doubly," "original," etc., is itself metaphorical and
is used only for the clarity of exposition). Man invents the concept man by
means of another concept that is itself illusionary. The "second" metaphor,
which Rousseau equates with the literary, deliberate, and rhetorical use of
the spontaneous figure is no longer innocent: the invention of the word man
makes it possible for "men" to exist by establishing the equality within
inequality, the sameness within difference of civil society, in which the
suspended, potential truth of the original fear is domesticated by the illusion
of identity. The concept interprets the metaphor of numerical sameness as
if it were a statement of literal fact. Without this literalization, there could
be no society. The reader of Rousseau must remember that this literalism
is the deceitful misrepresentation of an original blindness. Conceptual language, the foundation of civil society, is also, it appears, a lie superimposed
upon an error. We can therefore hardly expect the epistemology of the
sciences of man to be straightforward.

The transition from the structure of conceptual language to society is
implicit in the example from the *Essay* describing the genealogy of the word

"man." It becomes explicit when, at the beginning of the second part of the *Discourse*, the origin of society is described in exactly parallel terms, this time no longer as a marginal example but as the central statement of the *Second Discourse*, forging the axis of the text in the coherent movement that extends from freedom to perfectibility, from perfectibility to language, from language to man, and from man to political society. Neither the discovery of fire and technology, nor the contiguity of man's proximity to man on earth account for the origin of society. Society originates with the quantitative comparison of conceptual relationships:

> The repeated contacts between man and various entities, and between the entities themselves, must necessarily engender in the mind of man the perception of relationships. These relationships, which we express by words such as large, small, strong, weak, fast, slow, fearful, bold, and other similar ideas, when compared to man's needs, produced, almost without his being aware of it, some kind of reflection, or rather some form of mechanical prudence that taught him to take the precautions most needed for his safety. . . . The resmemblances that time allowed him to observe [between his fellow men], the human female and himself, made him infer [*juger de*] those which he could not perceive. Noticing that all of them behaved in the same way that he would himself have behaved in similar circumstances, he concluded that their way of thinking and feeling was entirely in conformity with his own.

The passage describes precisely the same interplay between passion (fear), measurement, and metaphor (inferring invisible properties by analogy with visible ones) as the parable from the *Essay on the Origins of Language*. In the lines that follow, the principle of conformity on which the concept of man and the possibility of government is founded is called "cette importante Vérité." We should now realize that what Rousseau calls "truth" designates, neither the adequation of language to reality, nor the essence of things shining through the opacity of words, but rather the suspicion that human specificity may be rooted in linguistic deceit.

The consequences of this negative insight for Rousseau's political theory are far-reaching. What the *Discourse on Inequality* tells us, and what the classical interpretation of Rousseau has stubbornly refused to hear, is that the political destiny of man is structured like and derived from a linguistic model that exists independently of nature and independently of the subject: it coincides with the blind metaphorization called "passion," and this metaphorization is not an intentional act. Contrary to what one might think, this enforces the inevitably "political" nature or, more correctly, the "politicality" (since one could hardly speak of "nature" in this case) of all forms of human language, and especially of rhetorically self-conscious or literary language— though certainly not in the representational, psychological, or ethical sense in which the relationship between literature and politics is generally understood. If society and government derive from a tension between man and his language, then they are not natural (depending on a relationship between man and things), nor ethical (depending on a relationship among men), nor theological, since language is not conceived as a transcendental principle but as the possibility of contingent error. The political thus becomes a burden for man rather than an opportunity, and this realization, which can be stated in an infinity of sardonic and pathetic modes, may well account for the recurrent reluctance to accept, or even to notice, the link between language and society in the works of Rousseau. Far from being a repression of the political, as Althusser would have it, literature is condemned to being the truly political mode of discourse. The relationship of this discourse to political praxis cannot be described in psychological or in psycholinguistic terms, but rather in terms of the relationship, within the rhetorical model, between the referential and the figural semantic fields.

To develop the implications of this conclusion would lead to a detailed reading of the second part of the *Discourse on Inequality* in conjunction with the *Social Contract*, *Julie*, and Rousseau's other political writings. I have tried to emphasize the importance and the complexity of the transition that leads up to such a reading. Only if we are aware of the considerable ambivalence that burdens a theoretical discourse dealing with man's relation to man— "un homme [que parle] à des hommes . . . de l'homme," as the *Second Discourse* puts it—can we begin to see how Rousseau's theory of literature and his theory of government could get translated into practical terms. The introductory analysis allows for the schematic formulation of some directives.

First of all, the passage from a language of fiction to a language oriented towards political praxis implies a transition from qualitative concepts such as needs, passions, man, power, etc., to quantitative concepts involving numbers such as rich, poor, etc. The inequality referred to in the title of the *Discourse*, and which must first be understood as difference in the most general way possible, becomes in the second part the inequality in the quantitative distribution of property. The basis of political thought, in Rousseau, is economic rather than ethical, as is clear from the lapidary statement that opens the second part of the *Discourse*: "The first man who, after having fenced in a plot of land went on to say '*this belongs to me*' and found other men naïve enough to believe him [*assez simples pour le croire*], was the true founder of civil society." The passage from literal greed to the institutional, conceptual law protecting the right to property runs parallel to the transition from the spontaneous to the conceptual metaphor. (Thus confirming the semantic validity of the word-play, in French, on "*sens propre*" and "*propriété*.") But the economic foundation of political theory in Rousseau is not rooted in a theory of needs, appetites, and interests that could lead to ethical principles of right and wrong; it is the correlative of linguistic conceptualization and is therefore neither materialistic, nor idealistic, nor merely dialectical since language is deprived of representational as well as of transcendental authority. (This, of course, does not mean that questions of virtue, of self, and of God are not being considered by Rousseau; they obviously are. What is at stake is not the existence of an ethical, psychological, or theological discourse but their authority in terms of truth or falsehood.) The complex relationship between Rousseau's and Marx's economic determinism could and should only be approached from this point of view.

Second, one sees why civil order and government are, in Rousseau, such fragile and threatened constructions, since they are built on the very sands of error. "The vices that make social institutions necessary also make the abuse of these institutions inevitable. . . ." This circular, self-destructive pattern of all civil institutions mirrors the self-destructive epistemology of conceptual language when it demonstrates its inability to keep literal reference and figural connotation apart. The literalism that makes language possible also makes the abuse of language inevitable. Hence the fundamental ambivalence in the valorization of literal reference throughout the *Second Discourse*. The "pure" fiction of the state of nature precedes, in principle, all valorization, yet nothing can be more destructive than the inevitable transposition of this fictional model to the present, empirical world in which "the subjects have to be kept apart" (*Essay*) and by which one reaches "the last stage of inequality and the extreme point that closes the circle and touches again upon our point of departure (namely the state of nature): this is where all individuals again become equal because they are nothing."

Finally, the *contractual* pattern of civil government can only be understood against the background of this permanent threat. The social contract is by no means the expression of a transcendental law: it is a complex and purely defensive verbal strategy by means of which the literal world is given some of the consistency of fiction, an intricate set of feints and ruses by means of which the moment is temporarily delayed when fictional seductions will no longer be able to resist transformation into literal acts. The conceptual language of the social contract resembles the subtle interplay between figural and referential discourse in a novel. It has often been said that Rousseau's novel *Julie* is also his best treatise on political science; it should be added that *The Social Contract* is also his best novel. But both depend on their common methodological preamble in the theory of rhetoric that is the foundation of the *Discourse on the Origin and the Foundations of Inequality Among Men*.

ERIC GANS

The Victim as Subject: The Esthetico-Ethical System of Rousseau's Rêveries

Although many would rather have it otherwise, it seems no exaggeration to affirm that since the time that Jesus (or his disciples) applied to his individual self the "suffering servant" role of deutero-Isaiah, the most successful mechanism for self-maintenance in the center of the human universe has been that devised by Jean-Jacques Rousseau. Such mechanisms are rare, and although their significance comes from the fact that they can be used by virtually anyone, a particular prestige attaches to their inventors who acquire, for good or ill, the status of mimetic models.

The comparison of Rousseau to Christ is not facetious, but neither is it meant to imply equality of cultural importance or—even less—of moral stature. Rousseau in fact invented no more than a variant of the Christic mechanism, the simple elegance of which makes it unique. But his adaptation of this mechanism to the modern era is an event of no small importance. Just as it has been observed that other "messiahs" existed in Jesus' day, one of whom might conceivably have acquired the same stature had the latter not existed, so might it be supposed with even more probability that had Rousseau not existed someone else would have taken his place. This is of no real consequence. Historical figures inspire resentment because their individual difference from us is so much less striking than the difference in social importance. Rousseau knew, and affirmed at the beginning of the second *Discourse*, that inequality was a social, not a natural creation. The problem is structural: the key roles are few in number, and each can only

From *Studies in Romanticism* 21, no. 1 (Spring 1982). © 1982 by the Trustees of Boston University.

be occupied by a single individual. But Rousseau also knew in this connection how to be in the right place at the right time. By denouncing social (synchronic) dominance he achieved historical (diachronic) dominance. The first *Discourse*, although of far less interest than the second, was already a full-blown illustration of the Rousseauian system, and it acquired for its author a celebrity on which he contrived to build up to his death and beyond. It is tempting to be cynical about Rousseau's success, but hindsight makes all things look easy. We must consider Jean-Jacques's contribution to the strategy of the modern self with the greatest attention and respect.

It might be objected that the "subjectivist" view of Rousseau that considers his writing from the standpoint of the self rather than the community neglects those parts of his work that are of the greatest anthropological interest. Certainly the *Discourse on the Origin of Inequality* and the *Social Contract* are more significant contributions to anthropological theory than the *Confessions* or the *Rêveries*. But it may be questioned whether not only the impact but the intellectual significance of Rousseau's work is best understood in this perspective. For it is anything but certain that the primary anthropological significance of Rousseau's work lies in its theoretical models of social structure rather than in its esthetic elaborations of a model of egocentrism. One cannot lightly put aside such a work as the second *Discourse*, which Lévi-Strauss has spoken of not without reason as the inaugural treatise of ethnology. But Rousseau's own evolution invites us to consider his later, more personal works as constituting in some sense advances over what preceded; and the vastly greater influence of these works on the subsequent development of what we might call "cultural sensibility" must be given its due. In any case there is no reason why the analysis of the esthetic effect of a text rather than its theoretical truth-value should lead to a conclusion of epistemological nihilism. On the contrary, the interplay between the imaginary and the theoretical in the text of the "Fifth Promenade" suggests a hypothesis concerning the functioning of the esthetic—and thus of art—within post-Rousseauian, or, in other terms, romantic culture.

Christianity's impact on the West is a tribute to the power of its basic conception, which is the absolute centrality of the position of the victim. In every rite worthy of the name there is a central victim, animal or human, but once eaten, killed or driven out he is forgotten, for his central position is never truly his own. The victim partakes of the essence both of reality and of representation; the reality is distributed among the participants as appetitive—alimentary or aggressive—satisfaction, while the representation remains in the form of a transcendent, i.e., imaginary deity. In Jesus' case the victim retains his central status, and maintains his identity with the deity.

The *moral* significance of this position is enormous. The appetitive satisfaction of sacrifice is denounced as murder; the transcendent divinity is revealed to have no more power over worldly events than a helpless man. The position of the victim is shown to be morally the most powerful because by attracting to itself the violence of the other it maintains itself in the center and forces its enemies to the periphery. The classical ethic based on strength of character found in Christianity its victorious antithesis; for it was the martyr, not his persecutors, that displayed an invincible strength of self. The Christian doctrine of love is really nothing other than "turning the other cheek," always taking the position of the victim. Nietzsche's condemnation of Christianity as the finest flower of (Jewish) *ressentiment* in fact pays homage to it: what the Jews had learned to do as a people—turn defeat into a sign of divine election—Christians could do as individuals. By means of this *Sklavenmoral* the slaves showed themselves superior to their masters, and eventually brought about the end of slavery. This "sublimation" of resentment was infinitely more productive than Nietzsche's protofascistic appeals to imaginary supermen to reestablish their "natural" mastery over everyone else but himself. But we are getting ahead of ourselves; for Nietzsche, the "last romantic," expresses the breakdown of the new self-centralization inaugurated by Rousseau.

Christian martyrdom was moral victory, but it was not pleasant. The price of superiority was superior suffering, and of victory, death. Such a choice was feasible for slaves, or even for knights, but not for the members of civil society. The urbane superficiality of eighteenth-century society so vehemently decried by Rousseau reflected its members' sophisticated modesty concerning their capacities for martyrdom. No one was more painfully aware than Jean-Jacques that the politeness of the members of this society was only a reflection of their vanity. Each individual modesty renounced the centralizing mechanism inherited from Christianity in order to gain the approval of others who had done the same. The entire status-order depended on a tacit agreement that the defense of the self be carried on only metaphorically, with no one seeking a truly central position. This was more than a sign of moral weakness. Pascal's *honnête homme* who sacrifices his own interests to those of the group, who, imperceptible on arrival, when he speaks only on the subject already under discussion, becomes its center through his universal, unspecialized understanding of this subject, is a worldly version of the Christian martyr. The place of this figure in *Les Pensées* is in no contradiction with the projected *Apologie de la religion chrétienne*.

It is unnecessary to discuss here the sociological specifics that differentiate social relations in Rousseau's time from those of the era for which the *honnête homme* provided the ideal. Molière's *Misanthrope* (1666), detested by Rousseau for its mockery of a proto-Rousseauian hero, demonstrated that the latter's reinterpretation of the Christian idea of the self as victim was already conceivable over a hundred years before the *Rêveries*. Alceste's ultimate success in emptying the stage of its characters, unique in the classical theater, is a sufficient sign that the power of the Rousseauian position was already realized in the seventeenth century. But Alceste only attains this position in the last moments of the play. His love for the coquette Célimène has been up to that point the key to his character, and he only finds the strength to abandon her once all her other admirers have already done so. The misanthrope-in-love-with-a-coquette is not a radically centralized figure. He accepts the center provided by collective desire, and only on this basis does he work to undermine it by exposing the coquette's false promises of exclusive distinction to her admirers. The very need for such marks of distinction—exactly parallel to those given by Molière's *Dom Juan* to both Charlotte and Mathurine in a famous scene—is a sign that the centrality of desire is tempered by the requirement, however easily abused, of reciprocity. The temporality of coquetry, unlike that of Christian martyrdom, is homeostatic, nonclimactic. Ritual delay or *différance*, rather than contributing to the force of the ultimate violent—but ordered—catharsis, here becomes an end in itself, and as if to compensate for its prolongation, offers guarantees of individual distinction to its participants. For the coquette is not homologous to the martyr in reproducing the primitive ritual dichotomy between unique center and undifferentiated periphery. Her admirers are not quite the worshippers of a divinity; each must think himself secretly distinguished from the others by the central figure who is both an object of desire (*qua* inaccessible object) and of resentment (*qua* possessor and distributor of her "favors"). (We use the term "resentment" to designate the relationship of the desiring subject to an Other who is situated in the central place the subject desires to occupy. The primary activity of resentment is the relocation of the center around the resentful subject, who must to this end forego his desire.) The temporality of coquetry is dependent on each admirer's thinking himself the *real* center of her society whose position must be kept secret in order to maintain the equilibrium of the whole, without which the coquette would cease to be an object of desire.

The inherent instability of this structure makes it vulnerable to Alceste's enterprise of demystification. But his own accession to the central position is not merely unstable but paradoxical. Alceste only attracts the others by fleeing the stage. The distinction he seeks can only be attained through flight from the society that is the source of this distinction. The locus of his flight—

his "desert"—cannot by definition become the focus of a new society. Thus his friends follow him to prevent his departure whereas he can only attract them by leaving. Such a "society" has not even a temporary topographical stability and is thus irrepresentable on stage. The power of Alceste is wholly negative, and hence can exercise no permanent influence. A strictly dramatic hero—unlike, for example, Dom Juan who incarnates a noncatastrophic technique that remains in principle indefinitely applicable—Alceste cannot become a model for social conduct.

The Rousseauian model that reaches its final form in the *Rêveries* reflects a later stage of civil society that is, among other differences, dominated by the "unsociable" communication of writing and reading. The rise of the novel as well as of "philosophy" in the 18th century reflects this change. From Alceste, who finds even Oronte's sonnet a painful experience, to Rousseau, whose social activities included reading aloud entire books of his *Confessions*, the place of the writer in society has been considerably transformed. The *honnête homme* was not an author. We may attempt to explain this change by the rise of the bourgeoisie, the decline of aristocratic values, the growth of science, etc., but it is simplest to describe it as a decentralization of elite society: the writer is almost always an outsider to this society, and in any case both the creation and the appreciation of his work takes place in private, not social surroundings. Coquetry and wit—even the universal knowledge of the *honnête homme*—are no longer sufficient criteria for social centrality.

The mediate communication of writing usurps the prestige of direct confrontation as polite society becomes increasingly aware of its marginal status in the social order as a whole. This decline being due *grosso modo* to the progress of the sciences and arts, Rousseau's first *Discourse* could be perceived by its readers as a defense of the immediacy of aristocratic social relations. Of course this requiem for illiteracy was written; but its success as writing generated in the society of its day a desire to possess its author in person. The written denunciation of modern society made its absent author a central figure because his social presence, unlike Alceste's, was not compromised by it. To possess the author was to experience at once both rejection and its transcendence. The author's physical presence was only a stimulant to further desire because his works were generated within a private world that could only be guessed at in society. Thus Rousseau presented society with a centralized version of Alceste; rather than fleeing to his "desert," he brought his desert with him as the space of refusal represented by his writings.

But this space had to be actualized in society, lacking which the "savage" author would lose all connection with the social persona. The presence of

Rousseau could only reassure his hostesses if it remained marked by the absence from which his writings emerged. Thus the society dominated by the "centralized Alceste" remained an only semi-stable configuration. The "savagery" of the writings had to be reproduced in mitigated form in a social context; but the mitigation could only be the effect of a desire for centrality that at the same time pushed Rousseau toward more radical expressions of disaffection. Having reached, with the *Nouvelle Héloïse*, the pinnacle of celebrity, he could have no more reason to remain within the presence of his audience. The more he was sought after, the more he would seek solitude, recognizing in the advances he received the signs of an unavowed desire to share in his antisocial glory. Generosity became a sign of persecution. From the standpoint of social "adjustment" this is, of course, paranoia, but the inconsistency of this standpoint is demonstrated by the very reason for the generosity. A well-adjusted Rousseau would have been courted by no one. Psychological essences are wholly inadequate to describe the social dynamics in which they purportedly manifest themselves.

It is significant that Rousseau was a member not of the first but of the second generation of *philosophes*. The lionizing of such writers as Voltaire and Buffon was founded on the distinction between the author's presence in society and his representational presence in his works. The author in society is surrounded by the aura of the private world of his writings. But the writings of a Voltaire imply only formally the noncentrality of society; the private space in which they are written—and read—does not affect their content. The author's "supplementary" status is thus unproblematic; it is experienced as freedom, both by the writer and his public. But if society must now center itself around those whose primary function requires them to reject it, the next stage can only be the thematization of this rejection. And if Voltaire's generation only "rejected" society in order better to rejoin it, Rousseau's rejection could not be so motivated. Rousseau in society might be temporarily a triumphant figure, but the only position in which his triumph could be stabilized was that of the outcast whose writings, addressed only to himself, only accidentally fell into the public domain. For the society that sought after Rousseau was in a permanent state of decentralization. The end of the neoclassical era, like that of classical antiquity, called forth a new formula of self-centralization that would reestablish social relations around a new concept of individuality. Rousseau was to become the Christ of this time of crisis.

The historical distance that separates Jesus from Rousseau contrasts with the similarity of the centralizing mechanisms with which they are associated, and suggests that the evolution of these mechanisms takes place at the most profound level of anthropological causality, rather than being dependent on more variable factors, such as political and economic structures. It is facile to explain the rise of mediated social relations in the 18th century as a result of the advance of the bourgeois economy or of monarchic centralization and the concomitant decline of the landed aristocracy. It is not to "idealistically" reject the significance of such developments and their technical and economic "infrastructure" to claim that these developments are more constrained by the basic mechanisms of human interaction than the other way around. The bourgeois would not seek to increase his wealth unless his deferral of satisfaction could be for him a source of human significance, whether mediated by transcendental or purely worldly values. The failure of classical antiquity to evolve market societies is as so formulated as direct reflection of the inadequacy of narrowly economic perspectives; but the same inadequacy can be found even more glaringly in the political analyses of traditional historiography. The traditional explanation through slavery and the contempt for work remains attached to formal institutions and fails to recognize the need to ground institutional evolution in the unformulated and nonthematic relations from which they spring.

The basic problem of history—as distinct from the narrative one of historiography—is not that all institutions may appear at one time or another or from one perspective or another as "basic," but that what is truly basic can never be institutionalized. All human institutions without exception are means of organizing interaction; but the fundamental structures of this interaction, which are *represented* thematically in these institutions, change very slowly and are only revealed in new configurations through the crises of the old forms that can no longer contain them. This is the familiar dialectical process of the "conversion of quantity into quality," but this over-formal terminology gives no hint of the underlying unity of the process. By noting the emergence of a new model of self-centralization we examine this process at what might be called the sub-institutional level of representation. The models are explicit enough, and become objects of study and emulation, but beneath their institutional trappings—considerable in the case of Christianity, merely superficial in the case of romanticism—they remain personal and imperfectly theorized models for individual emulation. It took Nietzsche, the most radical of Rousseau's disciples, to understand Christianity as a structure of resentment; and it is only now that we can understand that this origin, which for Nietzsche constituted an indictment of the Judaeo-Christian tradition, in no way implies a refutation of the moral reciprocity that finds in this tradition its most radical expression.

It is in Rousseau's last work, the *Rêveries d'un promeneur solitaire*, left uncompleted at his death in 1778, that his model of the self attained its final and most influential form. The *Confessions* were, as he stated incontrovertably in the first sentence, "an enterprise that has had no model (*exemple*), and whose accomplishment will have no imitator." The *Confessions* do not present a *position*, a model to be imitated, but the life experience of an individual who, because he presents himself as both unique and typical, can only be imitated at the cost of the imitator's uniqueness. And indeed, no future autobiography has attained anything like the world-literary status of the *Confessions*. To be sure, there are in the six hundred pages experiences from which we may distill models to be followed. But the *Rêveries* are presented from the outset as the elaboration of a single model, developed with a rigor that the tempting qualification of "paranoid" does little to explain. The author of the *Confessions* stands above himself, beyond the experience he recounts; the author of the *Rêveries* situates his writing within his experience, and thereby presents this experience as a model to future writers, as well as to those nonwriters for whom Rousseau's writing might stand as a sufficient description of their position. This position is, as our preceding remarks suggest, inseparable from the writing that expresses it, but the result of this very expression is to make the position imaginable—if not realizable—as independent of and prior to its depiction, and as serving to guarantee it.

"Me voici donc seul sur la terre, n'ayant plus de frère, de prochain, d'ami, de société que moi-même. Le plus sociable et le plus aimant des humains en a été proscrit par un accord unanime. (Here I am, then, alone in the world, having no longer either brother, or neighbor, or friend, or society other than myself. The most sociable and loving of human beings has been exiled from humanity by a unanimous agreement.)" The entire "First Promenade" is devoted to the exposition of what we shall simply call Rousseau's "system." These opening lines present its existential basis. Rousseau's solitude is complete, but it is thereby all the more central, for it is the result of a unanimous agreement, a kind of ritual "social contract" in which he plays the critical role of scapegoat. But the first sentence already suggests the "supplementary" structure that he will establish on this basis: "No other society than myself." As he will later explain, whereas Montaigne had written his *Essais* merely for others, "je n'écris mes rêveries que pour moi (I write my reveries for myself alone)." In condemning Rousseau to solitude, the world has in fact provided him with an ideal companion. "Livrons-nous tout entier à la douceur de converser avec mon âme puisqu'elle est la seule que les hommes ne puissent m'ôter. (Let me give myself over entirely to the pleasure of conversing with my soul, since it is the only one that men cannot take from me.)" But even such *douceur* is ephemeral; to preserve these *conversations* from the passage of time, he will write them down, so that "chaque fois que je les relirai m'en rendra la jouissance (each time that I reread them will renew my pleasure in them)." And even if his enemies go so far as to steal his manuscripts, they can never take away "ni le plaisir de les avoir écrites, ni le souvenir de leur contenu (neither the pleasure of having written them, nor the memory of their content)." Thus he can conclude, "qu'ils jouissent à leur gré de mon opprobre, ils ne m'empêcheront pas de jouir de mon innocence et d'achever mes jours en paix malgré eux (let them enjoy as they will my disgrace, they will not prevent me from enjoying my innocence and from ending my days in peace in spite of them)."

The system is here complete. The role of universal victim is turned against its instigators by a series of "supplementary" constructions that lead precisely to the writing we have before us. Writing, as we have noted, is in itself a private, nonsocial pursuit; Rousseau's writing has already thematized its opposition to sociability. But now writing need merely describe its own preconditions. The writer/victim replaces the society of others with his own, but he can do better; because his "society" exists in the private realm of writing, not only can it flourish, but it can preserve its pleasures from the ravages of time. Time becomes rather a source of the renewed pleasure of rereading; and even if the material contiguity of victim and persecutors leads to the theft of his manuscript, memory can supplement writing just as writing can supplement memory. The system of supplements, which is to say, representations, is unlimited because the intimacy of self with self can only be intensified by more radical victimization.

What is this "intimacy of self with self" from which representations are born? As the opening sentence makes very nearly explicit, it is the substitution of the self for the other in an originally bipolar reciprocal relationship: brother, neighbor, friend. Asymmetric relationships are as curiously absent as the most fundamental ones were in Rousseau's life, where parents were all but lacking and children were shipped off to the orphanage. If the election of the victimary role makes the story of Jesus an obligatory parallel, the Rousseauian substitution of self for other offers a radical contrast with that of Oedipus, the paradigmatic figure of Greek culture, an opposition symbolized by the contrast between the man of swollen feet and the inveterate *promeneur*. Oedipus's path is at every point obstructed by the asymmetrical violence of the occupant of the dominant position. Oedipus occupies both roles in the dyad of persecutor and victim; he is thus, like Rousseau, a solitary subject, but he is condemned by his very completeness to an ethically monstrous role that is only accessible as esthetic spectacle. Because Rousseau has inherited the Christian identification with the victim, he is able to double himself in symmetrical relations that constitute existential and not merely esthetic models.

Instead of seeking to define in psychological terms how a single individual can indeed provide himself with *société*, or in what terms he might engage in conversation with his own soul, we may examine Rousseau's system in a more rigorous perspective by distinguishing between its two functional subsystems. *On the one hand*, its existential basis is the real or imagined role of universal victim. The stability of this position is inherent in the role itself; it is in no way "psychological." Whatever happens to the subject may be interpreted as contributing to this role, for the "victimized" self, once situated in the center of the imaginary scene, cannot be dislodged from it. In effect the existential reality of the role of "victim" may be reduced by the elimination of all associations of physical and moral violence to a minimal stance of isolated passivity. The self is seen here as the *recipient* of all interactional experiences, the origin or cause of which is attributable to an undifferentiated plurality of "others" whose interconnection via the "unanimous agreement" to exclude the victim likewise requires no concrete content. The appropriate parallel at the limit is not Christ and his persecutors, but the set of equations that describe the universe within a set of coordinates centered on a given fixed point. The point once chosen, it becomes formally immobile, although this is merely the effect of the choice of frame of reference. In terms of the human subject, this is the perspective of "self-centeredness."

Now it is noticeable in the descriptions we have just given that this centralized self is in fact an imaginary model, which is to say that it is seen from without. The reflection (*Me voici donc . . .*) required to constitute this model is *already* a doubling of the self into perceiver and perceived. Hence, *on the other hand*, the self-as-victim is not only self-centered but also self-observed. This observation does not pose the question of the distance between the observing and the observed self, because the latter being conceived in perfect isolation, its spectacle is both observable from any distance and yet invisible to the eyes of the "society" from which Rousseau has been expelled. This distinction is not indeed available in the physical model we have offered as an analogy. For it depends on the supplementary or representational transformation of the absolutely passive victim of society into a *naturally* active subject. It is not that in his isolation Rousseau has become invisible to his persecutors, but that the latter, concerned only with social interaction, are constitutionally blind to the nonsocial activities of the self including in particular its interactions with nonhuman "nature." The self-observed self is thus placed in the center of a scene of representation wherein its every activity appears by definition as significant. The victim's social passivity gives both esthetic and existential value to the "natural" activity by means of which he reestablishes in his own universe the reciprocal relationships denied him by society. For on the one hand this activity of the isolated central victim is in itself an esthetic spectacle of which the significance is altogether independent of worldly criteria, the world having expelled him from its midst. But on the other, because the subject's isolation is in fact only formal, his activity provides a concrete model for any individual who chooses to take up the Rousseauian position. Thus the observation of the central self varies between two poles; its activity can be presented either as spectacle or as example. But the latter category is empty of content; the writer presents himself as an example as a matter of definition. The interest of the *Rêveries* as a model for romanticism lies not in its mere claims to exemplarity on the basis of Rousseau's foolproof "system," but in its success at presenting his victimary existence as esthetic spectacle. The existential role is only guaranteed by its literary products; for the romantic the moral privilege of the victim is primarily of *esthetic* interest. Chateaubriand's *Génie du christianisme* expressed the object of romantic faith: not the truth but the *beautés* of the Christian religion.

The Rousseau of the *Rêveries* is not yet a romantic. His esthetic presents itself as a derivative of his *morale*. Not esthetic faith but esthetic achievement makes the *Rêveries* a seminal text for his romantic followers. But conversely, if we would understand the nature of this faith, which still dies hard among the remaining practitioners of high culture, we can do no better than turn to the esthetic or "spectacular" moments of the *Rêveries*, and particularly to the justly famous scenes of the "Fifth Promenade." Here beauty so to speak provides its own concept. The scene not only illustrates the victimary perspective; it provides us with a paradigm applicable to all such illustrations, and hence to Western literature: the confluence of Greek esthetic with Judaeo-Christian moral discourse.

The esthetic superiority of the scenes of the "Fifth Promenade" is a direct reflection of the existential superiority claimed for them by their author. "De toutes les habitations où j'ai demeuré . . . aucune ne m'a rendu si véritablement heureux. (Of all the places in which I have lived . . . none has made me so truly happy.)" The world of the Ile de Saint-Pierre is widely separated from the time and place of writing; Rousseau's sojourn there, already described in the twelfth Book of the *Confessions*, dates from 1765, some dozen years before the *Rêveries*. This stay now becomes an existential model within the radically victimary context established by the *Rêveries*, although it could not effectively have occurred within this context, the society of his persecutors being no longer prepared to grant him a *place* of exile. The island as an *objective* personal microcosm is no longer available to Rousseau; but it is thereby more exemplary as a subject for the "conversations with his soul" that his persecutors have unwittingly permitted him. The Rousseau reduced to no other society than his own can find no better memory to preserve from oblivion than that of "ce séjour isolé où je m'étais enlacé de moi-même (this isolated sojourn where I had wrapped myself up in myself)."

The island is described in the first paragraph as "singulièrement située pour le bonheur d'un homme qui aime à se circonscrire (singularly situated for the happiness of a man who likes to circumscribe himself)"; but the most perfect moments Rousseau describes make use of an antithetical trait of island microcosms: such worlds permit their inhabitants to transgress their borders. The author's "circumscription" of these moments of happiness is thus very much dependent on the possibility of a concrete experiential violation of the island's finitude. This is not to say that there are not several references in the text to the happiness generated by this finitude itself. But with a single exception these are cursory allusions to "images riantes (joyful images)" to a "société . . . liante et douce sans être intéressante au point de m'occuper incessamment (attaching and pleasant society, without being interesting enough to occupy me incessantly)." The exception, which proves the rule, is the description of his botanical outings. Rousseau's original intention is "de décrire toutes les plantes de l'île sans en omettre une seule, avec un détail suffisant pour m'occuper le reste de mes jours (to describe all the plants of the island without omitting a single one, in sufficient detail to occupy me for the rest of my days)." But the definition of the task already destroys the benefits of its "insular" point of departure. Because the island is small, Rousseau can conceive the project of a complete *Flora petrinsularis*; but the project once conceived, its execution is potentially infinite: Rousseau could write a book about "chaque gramen des prés (every grass of the meadows)." Thus the description of his botanical activities that follows is merely *typical*, not *exemplary*. The internal world of the island provides him with an indefinitely rich content to occupy his time, but only its frontiers permit him experiences unrelated to any temporal sequence that can therefore become the subjects of exemplary descriptions. We shall discuss below Rousseau's own attempt to explain happiness as an enduring atemporal present; but first we shall turn to the two scenes that depict such happiness and that will be later alluded to in his theoretical description:

> Pendant qu'on était encore à table, je m'esquivais et j'allais me jeter seul dans un bateau que je conduisais au milieu du lac quand

l'eau était calme, et là, m'étendant tout de mon long dans le bateau les yeux tournés vers le ciel, je me laissais aller et dériver lentement au gré de l'eau, quelquefois pendant plusieurs heures, plongé dans mille rêveries confuses mais délicieuses, et qui sans avoir aucun objet bien déterminé ni constant ne laissaient pas d'être à mon gré cent fois préférables à tout ce que j'avais trouvé de plus doux dans ce qu'on appelle les plaisirs de la vie. Souvent averti par le baisser du soleil de l'heure de la retraite je me trouvais si loin de l'île que j'étais forcé de travailler de toute ma force pour arriver avant la nuit close.

(While they were still at table, I would sneak off and throw myself all alone into a boat that I rowed to the middle of the lake when the water was calm, and there, stretching myself to my full length in the boat, my eyes turned toward the sky, I let myself go and drift slowly as the water moved me, sometimes for several hours, absorbed in a thousand confused but delicious reveries which, without having any well-defined or constant object, were nonetheless to my taste a hundred times preferable to all that I had found most pleasant in what people call life's pleasures. Often, warned by the descent of the sun of the time for return, I found myself so far from the island that I was obliged to work with all my energy in order to arrive before nightfall.)

Quand le soir approchait je descendais des cimes de l'île et j'allais volontiers m'asseoir au bord du lac, sur la grève, dans quelque asile caché; là le bruit des vagues et l'agitation de l'eau fixant mes sens et chassant de mon âme toute autre agitation la plongaient dans une rêverie délicieuse où la nuit me surprenait souvent sans que je m'en fusse aperçu. Le flux et le reflux de cette eau, son bruit continu mais renflé par intervalles frappant sans relâche mon oreille et mes yeux, suppléaient aux mouvements internes que la rêverie éteignait en moi et suffisaient pour me faire sentir avec plaisir mon existence, sans prendre la peine de penser. De temps à autre naissait quelque faible et courte réflexion sur l'instabilité des choses de ce monde dont la surface des eaux m'offrait l'image: mais bientôt ces impressions légères s'effaçaient dans l'uniformité du mouvement continu qui me berçait, et qui sans aucun concours actif de mon âme ne laissait pas de m'attacher au point qu'appelé par l'heure et par le signal convenu je ne pouvais m'arracher de là sans effort.

(When the evening approached I would climb down from the
summits of the island and I took pleasure in seating myself on
the shore of the lake, on the beach, in a hidden refuge; there the
sound of the waves and the agitation of the water, fixing my
senses and clearing my soul of all other agitation, plunged it into
a delicious revery in which night often surprised me unawares.
The flux and reflux of that water, its sound, continuous but
swelling at intervals, striking continually my ear and my eyes,
[supplemented] the internal movements that the revery extinguished in me and sufficed to make me feel my existence with
pleasure, without taking the trouble to think. From time to time
arose a feeble and short reflection on the instability of the things
of this world of which the surface of the waters offered me the
image: but soon these weak impressions died out in the continuous
movement that rocked me, and which, without any active participation of my mind, did not fail to take hold of me to the point
where, called by the hour and by the agreed-on signal, I could
not tear myself away from there without an effort.)

These two scenes are best studied in comparison; their similarities put
into relief those contrasting elements which, insofar as these may be considered "esthetic" or "poetic" texts, are all to the advantage of the second
passage.

The first scene takes place not on the island but in a boat in the middle
of the lake. Here Rousseau is wholly detached from the microcosmic universe
of the island, but only because the boat has itself become a still smaller—
one might say minimal—microcosm. Being alone on the water provides a
frame that is lacking in the world of the *Rêveries* in which Rousseau finds
himself "seul sur la terre." The dominant element of his experience is that
of drifting ("dériver") along with the water ("au gré de l'eau"). To this
passivity corresponds a lack of well-defined imaginary content: his *rêveries*
are "confuses mais délicieuses . . . sans avoir aucun objet bien déterminé."
His only perception is of the sky, which allows him to observe the setting
sun that serves as a signal of departure. At this point the passivity of his
drifting is opposed "dialectically" by the effort he must make to return ("j'étais
forcé de travailler de toute ma force"). The atemporal duration of happiness
must be paid for with strenuous practical activity. The ultimate microcosm
of the boat is in effect only a temporary one; return to the larger world is a
necessity that must be condisered from the outset, even if it may be for a
time forgotten. (Thus Rousseau can only go out to the middle of the lake

"quand l'eau était calme.") Because this happiness is based on forgetting, its content can be defined only negatively, as "rêveries . . . cent fois préférables à tout ce que j'avais trouvé de plus doux." The subjective emphasis of "à mon gré" in his preference for these pleasures reflects, in no doubt unconscious irony, the utter submission to the forces of nature expressed by "au gré de l'eau." Because it is the water that "chooses" his course, he must choose to find the course pleasurable. The readers can share only the exemplarity of a specific experience—that of drifting in a boat on the lake—but its several hours' duration is summed up in too few lines for us to forget, as the author presumably has been able to do, the precariousness of his situation. The incommunicable subjectivity of the *rêveries* cannot be brought into relation with the absolute "objectivity" of the drifting. Happiness here is a kind of alienation, a temporary insanity from which Rousseau must exert himself to return. The esthetic status of this passage is consequently ambiguous. It provides an experiential model of absolute self-centeredness, but the separation of its objective and subjective elements prevents us from reconstituting anything but the bare outline of the existential situation. Bounded by an impatient evasion from society ("je m'esquivais") and an anxious return, this scene is not set off at either boundary from the rest of the text.

The second scene, which occupies an independent paragraph, resembles a perfected version of the first in which every modification serves to augment its esthetic effect. Here the tension between the island microcosm and the lake is maintained: the experience is contained within the world, but its content comes from beyond it. The "terrestrial" self gives his mind over to the extraterrestrial movement of the water. The opposition between the scene of representation and its content thus realized, the objective and subjective elements of the experience, separated in the first scene, may now be brought together: the *rêverie délicieuse* is the product of an external, objective movement, but only insofar as it is perceived by the self. The scene we observe thus has two well-defined levels: on the first, we see Rousseau in his *asile caché* perceiving the movement of the waves; on the second, we see and hear the scene as it presents itself to him. The first scene is autobiographical, guaranteed by the victimary self of the *Rêveries*; the second is "poetic," or in other words lyrical, the authorial self standing only as a locus from which the reader is invited to share in his experience.

This experience, like that of the first scene, is a kind of loss of self; but the movement of the water, rather than provoking a purely negative alienation, becomes itself an object of perception and, substituting itself as subjective content for the *mouvements internes* of self-consciousness, establishes a rhythmic unity between the human self and external nature. The communion of self with self is here explicitly mediated through the objective scene. Rather than two temporally distinct moments of alienated drifting and purposeful return, this experience encompasses a circular movement of assimilation of subject to object. The percepts are a *supplément* to pure self-awareness that both replaces it and objectifies it; by losing his awareness of the undefined "internal movements" in his quasi-hypnotic concentration on the movement of the water, Rousseau is made aware of his own existence. This substitution makes the self externally perceptible to itself; the subject can "sentir avec plaisir mon existence, sans prendre la peine de penser." This Rousseauian *cogito*, unlike the Cartesian, is dependent on an external scene, but by the same token it permits the description of this scene to communicate esthetically the self's uniqueness to others.

The long final sentence of the paragraph demonstrates the homeostatic power of the scene to suppress or rather to "sublate" the reflections inspired by the observer's translation of his perception into significance. The "courte réflexion sur l'instabilité des choses de ce monde" takes the movement of the water as a symbol or allegory of the transience of worldly objects. That such an interpretation is indeed a conventional one, mediated through an age-old tradition, is of only secondary importance; the fact that it is interpretation, reflection inspired by the scene rather than immediate absorption in it, makes it subordinate to the latter and susceptible to be at any instant reabsorbed into it. Here Rousseau poses an ontology of the esthetic experience that may equally apply to that of the reader of this passage. Our interpretative reflection on Rousseau's experience is subordinated to the spectacle of this experience reconstituted unreflectively in our imagination during our reading. Our generalizable affirmations concerning human experience are mere ephemeral by-products of our imaginary participation in the literary portrayal of this experience. Yet they remain affirmations the truth-value of which is not affected by their secondary status *qua* experience. Rousseau thus offers here a justification of the esthetic as prerequisite to the cognitive.

These descriptions of solitary happiness are the most important passages of the *Rêveries* because they are the definitive vindication of the victimary system that underlies this work. The series of "supplementations" that lead the universal victim to become his own "society" and to preserve in writing the record of his "conversations with his soul" culminate in these set pieces in which the centrality of the self is externalized in the spectacle of a wholly extra-human nature. With regard to the natural reality of the spectacle, the self is in effect secondary, just as the esthetically centralized figure of the artistic protagonist is always secondary with regard to the world-order that in one way or another excludes and sacrifices him. Rousseau contemplating the waves of the lake is thus an esthetically rather than existentially exemplary figure. But at the same time, as heir to the Judaeo-Christian tradition, Rousseau could affirm his *real* moral centrality as victim, even to the extent of implying himself to be the source of the universal harmony expressed in the *accord unanime*.

The synthesis of the two forms of cultural recentralization—the Greek-esthetic and the Christian-existential—is the unique defining feature of Western culture; and this synthesis, before becoming the basis for romantic and postromantic literature and art, was completed by Rousseau. Since Rousseau the morally central self can no longer content itself with a status the very perfection of which deprives it of any potential incidence upon the world-order whose legitimacy it denies. The Christian martyr was a revolutionary because his centrality exposed the instability of the old order and eventually destroyed it. Rousseau's own "martyrdom," in the very terms in which he describes it, only reinforces the solidarity of his persecutors, who are all too glad to make him the absent center of their universal conspiracy (*complot*). But this devaluation of the center—which presages the radically decentralized order of modern "consumer society"—is answered by an *esthetic* recentralization of the martyred self. Moral exemplarity is returned to the center of the stage by the same esthetic means that had formerly concentrated the public's attention on the sufferings of the tragic hero. Yet the result of this new displacement is an *existential* benefit to the victim. The moral joy of participation in a potentially universal community of reciprocal love that fortified the Christian martyr against physical suffering has now been transformed into a wholly pleasurable communion with the esthetically alienated and reappropriated self.

We may be tempted to condemn this pleasure as that of mere "self-centered" romantic illusion. But it is a romanticism of a most unreflective variety that condemns a model accessible to our own experience in order to extol the nobility of one that we could scarcely imagine ourselves as willingly imitating. The martyr's satisfaction in his own centrality is dependent on an exalted sense of self-abnegation in the cause of universal reciprocity that we cannot but find naive. Corneille's Polyeucte, whose classical version of Christian martyrdom is symmetrical with Alceste's anticipation of Rousseau's, is, as Corneille's contemporaries were quite able to see, no longer a true Christian: self-centrality has become the theme of his action rather than an unconscious by-product of it. Rousseau's self-satisfaction, as realized in the double scene of the waters of the lake and his contemplation of them, is not naive, but ambiguously lucid to its own egocentric aims.

Before pursuing our analysis of Rousseau's modern adaptation of the victim's role, it will be useful to examine his own analysis of the happiness he derives from the "esthetic" experiences discussed above:

> Mais s'il est un état où l'âme trouve une assiette assez solide pour s'y reposer tout entière et rassembler là tout son être, sans avoir besoin de rappeler le passé ni d'enjamber sur l'avenir; où le temps ne soit rien pour elle, où le présent dure toujours sans néanmoins marquer sa durée et sans aucune trace de succession, sans aucun autre sentiment de privation ni de jouissance, de plaisir ni de peine, de désir ni de crainte que celui seul de notre existence, et que ce sentiment seul puisse la remplir tout entière; tant que cet état dure celui qui s'y trouve peut s'appeler heureux, non d'un bonheur imparfait, pauvre et relatif, tel que celui qu'on trouve dans les plaisirs de la vie mais d'un bonheur suffisant, parfait et plein, qui ne laisse dans l'âme aucun vide qu'elle sente le besoin de remplir. Tel est l'état où je me suis trouvé souvent à l'île de Saint-Pierre dans mes rêveries solitaires, soit couché dans mon bateau que je laissais dériver au gré de l'eau, soit assis sur les rives du lac agité, soit ailleurs, au bord d'une belle rivière ou d'un ruisseau murmurant sur le gravier.
>
> De quoi jouit-on dans une pareille situation? De rien d'extérieur à soi, de rien sinon de soi-même comme Dieu.

(But if there is a state in which the soul finds a position sufficiently solid to rest there in its entirety and to gather together its whole being, without needing to recall the past or project itself into the future; where time is nothing to it, where the present lasts forever without however marking its duration and with no trace of successivity, without any feeling of deprivation or enjoyment, of pleasure or pain, of desire or fear, other than the mere feeling of one's existence, and where this single feeling can occupy the soul in its entirety; so long as that state endures, he who finds himself in it can call himself happy, not with an imperfect, poor and relative happiness such as one finds in life's pleasures, but with a happiness sufficient, perfect and full that leaves no emptiness in the soul that it feels the need to fill. Such is the state in which I often found myself on l'île Saint-Pierre during my solitary reveries, either lying in my boat that I let drift as the water moved it, or seated on the shores of the turbulent lake, or elsewhere, on the bank of a lovely stream or a brook murmuring on the gravel.

In what does one take pleasure in such a situation? In nothing external to oneself, in nothing but oneself and one's own existence; so long as this state lasts, one suffices unto oneself like God.)

The experiences described above are cited as guarantees of a happiness defined exclusively in terms of the self, and which would in fact appear to exclude any interest in a worldly scene. The self is sufficient to itself like that of God, and this (apparently) unmediated self-presence excludes both past and future as well as the sense of the succession of present moments, which is to say, the three temporal "ek-stases" of Heidegger. Precisely "le temps n' [est] rien pour elle [l'âme]." As for external impressions, these must be banished. Yet on the very same page, Rousseau will speak of the "*concours des objets environnants,*" of the necessity of a "*mouvement uniforme et modéré qui n'ait ni secousses ni intervalles,*" a movement of which the waters of the lake offer an evident (although unmentioned) example. The answer to this apparent enigma can be found a bit further on, in a reference this time, we should note, not to the lake but to the *interior* of the island:

L'occasion sans doute était belle pour un rêveur qui sachant se nourrir d'agréables chimères au milieu des objets les plus déplaisants, pouvait s'en rassasier à son aise en y faisant concourir tout ce qui frappait réellement ses sens. En sortant d'une longue et douce rêverie, en me voyant entouré de verdure, de fleurs, d'oiseaux, et laissant errer mes yeux au loin sur les romanesques rivages qui bordaient une vaste étendue d'eau claire et cristalline, j'assimilais à mes fictions tous ces aimables objets et me trouvant enfin ramené par degrés à moi-même et à ce qui m'entourait, je ne pouvais marquer le point de séparation des fictions aux réalités; tant tout concourait également à me rendre chère la vie recueillie et solitaire que je menais dans ce beau séjour.

(It was no doubt an excellent opportunity for a dreamer who, capable of nourishing himself on agreeable mirages in the midst of the most unpleasant objects, could take his fill of them as he wished by soliciting the collaboration of everything that really impinged on his senses. Coming out of a long and sweet revery, seeing myself surrounded by greenery, flowers, and birds, and letting my eyes wander in the distance over the romantic banks that bordered a vast expanse of clear and crystalline water, I assimilated to my fictions all these amiable objects, and finding myself at last brought back by degrees to myself and to my

surroundings, I could not mark the point of separation between
fictions and realities; so much did everything collaborate equally
in endearing to me the reflective and solitary life that I led in this
lovely place.)

In this formulation the natural surroundings of the self are simply in-
corporated within it; rather than alienating itself passively to an external
movement, the self actively assimilates *tous ces aimables objets*. But how can
we hope to reconcile these different descriptions of the deification of the
self?

Let us not too hastily condemn the inconsistency of these texts. The
sentiment of self-sufficiency is ontologically primary, not its reality. To ask
for more is to want to become a God rather than merely feel like one. What
then is the precise ontological status of this *sentiment*? We might call it an
"experiential state," which is not the same as calling it a subjective illusion.
This state requires in fact no guarantees other than itself. The important
point is not however its reality, which by definition we cannot verify on the
basis of the text, but the plausibility of the claim to it that Rousseau can
make as a result of his role, in principle inimitable, of universal victim. As
Rousseau puts it: "Mais la plupart des hommes agités de passions continuelles
connaissent peu cet état, et ne l'ayant goûté qu'imparfaitement durant peu
d'instants n'en conservent qu'une idée obscure et confuse qui ne leur en fait
pas sentir le charme . . . Mais un infortuné qu'on a retranché de la société
humaine . . . peut trouver dans cet état à toutes les félicités humaines des
dédommagements que la fortune et les hommes ne sauraient lui ôter. (But
most men, continually agitated by passions, know little of that state, and
having only tasted it imperfectly for a few moments, only retain of it an
obscure and confused idea that does not let them feel its charm . . . But an
unfortunate who has been cut off from human society . . . can find in this
state, for all human joys, compensations that fate and men are unable to take
from him.)"

The right to this claim once established, however, it remains of merely
autobiographical interest unless it can be communicated via an esthetically
graspable scene. The remarks on "movement," on the *concours des objets environnants*, refer to external determinants of the state of happiness, not to
the state itself. But in effect these determinants are not absolutely necessary:
"le secours d'une imagination riante . . . se présente assez naturellement à
ceux que le ciel en a gratifiés. Le mouvement qui ne vient pas du dehors se
fait alors au-dedans de nous (the aid of a happy imagination . . . arrives
rather naturally to those whom fate has graced with one. The movement

that does not come from without then arises within ourselves)." The only difference between this internal movement and the external one realized in the lakeside scene is that the former is imaginary, thus properly *fictional*. The scene of the movement is in neither case the locus of the state of happiness; it offers merely a *promise* of it, the *promesse de bonheur* by which Stendhal was to define the beautiful. Rousseau's claim to the state of happiness remains ontologically primary. But the promise is *esthetically* primary, and it is through the esthetic scene alone, whether fictional or real, that the experience itself can be recalled from the past and, as it were, incidentally transmitted to others.

The final unity of fiction and reality no longer refers to the specific scenes earlier described; it refers to the island microcosm as a whole. For the island is here not the locus of a specific scene, but of the possibility of esthetic scenes as such, that is, of a context whether real or fictional in which the self-sufficient self may be evoked. The difficulties of this series of passages may all be seen to derive from the fact that Rousseau's text remains at every point esthetic and "scenic": its "theoretical" pronouncements are in fact elements of a narrative that differ from the fixed scenes only in that we must attribute them to the unique individual Rousseau, whose claims to self-sufficiency are elsewhere justified. The scenes themselves, in contrast, may be taken as lyrically defining experiences of the self-in-general. The ontological primacy of the narrative as opposed to the lyric is not an "esthetic" but an existential fact: Rousseau is not a "character" in his narrative. The happiness he decribes may never have existed, but it is not simply fictional. It is the guarantee of the success of Rousseau's "system," and whether we "believe" it or not, as readers we cannot help but be attracted to this system on the basis of this untestable claim made for it.

Rousseau's narrative is "esthetic," which means that it can never propose, or even claim to propose, its own esthetics. What we have called the "esthetic primacy" of the scenes that externalize the self's self-presence and thereby provide an objective mediation for other selves, or for the same self at other times, cannot be justified within the text by the esthetic criterion of effect on the reader—even if the reader be Rousseau himself—but only by the existential criterion of their remembered perfection. Yet that the existential and esthetic criteria happen to coincide, that the most perfect and vividly remembered moments of happiness are also the most esthetically effective, precisely for the qualities that Rousseau describes (movement, *images riantes*), is no mere coincidence. It is the unstated foundation both of Rousseau's existential system itself and of the cultural productivity that made it, as adapted by others, the basis of romantic literature. For the source of this coincidence is precisely what makes culture—that is, humanity—possible in the first place, the potential equality of all human beings before the scene of representation. Existentially, only the universal victim can experience the happiness of God-like self-sufficiency. But the *reality* of such experiences is incommunicable. It is in the absence of these experiences—as the writer of the *Rêveries* always is absent—that the exemplary victim must evoke the *scene* before which his imperfect reader too may situate himself. As a self-sufficient atemporal presence of self to self, the experience has no communicable content; but this incommunicability extends to the self as well—such an experience could in effect not even be remembered. What can be remembered is the scene surrounding "this" experience, that is, the spatio-temporal setting that externalizes it and converts it into "another" experience. In fact, as we have seen, what is converted is a narrative affirmation that only appears perfect in itself because it has its guarantee elsewhere, in the victimary status of its protagonist, a status only really definitive in the present of the *Rêveries*, not in the twelve-year-old scenes described in the "Fifth Promenade." Thus the last "inconsistency" in this text is, like all the others, a final product of the esthetic nature of Rousseau's existential text:

> Les hommes se garderont, je le sais, de me rendre un si doux asile où ils n'ont pas voulu me laisser. Mais ils ne m'empêcheront pas du moins de m'y transporter chaque jour sur les ailes de l'imagination, et d'y goûter durant quelques heures le même plaisir que si je l'habitais encore. Ce que j'y ferais de plus doux serait d'y rêver à mon aise. En rêvant que j'y suis ne fais-je pas la même chose? Je fais même plus; à l'attrait d'une rêverie abstraite et monotone je joins des images charmantes qui la vivifient. Leurs objets échappaient souvent à mes sens dans mes extases, et maintenant plus ma rêverie est profonde plus elle me les peint vivement. Je suis souvent plus au milieu d'eux et plus agréablement encore que quand j'y étais réellement.

> (I know that men will be unwilling to give me back so pleasant a refuge in which they did not want to leave me. But at least they will not prevent me from transporting myself there every day on the wings of my imagination, and from tasting there for a few hours the same pleasure as if I still lived there. What would be sweetest to me there would be to dream at my leisure. In dreaming that I am there, do I not do the same thing? I do even more; to the attraction of an abstract and monotonous revery, I add charming images that enliven it. Their objects often escaped my senses

in my ecstasies, and now the deeper my revery the more vividly it portrays them to me. I am often more among them, and more agreeably still, than when I was really there.)

The author is "plus au milieu [des objets des images charmantes] et plus agréablement encore que quand j'y étais réellement." The "objets," as the involved syntax of these sentences reveals, are secondary, supplementary to *their own images*, which in turn supplement the "rêverie abstraite et monotone" which corresponds precisely to the ideal state of happiness earlier described. The happiness itself is perfect only now, when Rousseau's victimage is perfect, but the images, the objects, are also only truly available now, because they constitute the scene in which this perfect happiness can be experienced by the Rousseauian self without regard for past, future, or temporal succession, that is, without regard for its own history. In this scene, this history, and with it the author's unique victimary status, abolishes itself; the God-like self-sufficiency it has made possible becomes available to all. This is the ultimate act of charity that, analogous to the founding act of Christianity, explains the extraordinary success of Rousseau's "system."

Jesus was no writer. Yet his exemplarity could only be conveyed in writing. Lesser mortals wrote his story, presumably guided by divine inspiration. But although Jesus himself was "the word," the unity of divine and human he was claimed to have realized could not be represented without reopening the split. His example, it may be claimed, was existential, not representational, but the very notion of an *example* imposes on his followers the role of "representatives." The Christian martyr achieved his subversive centrality by employing the Christian "system," but in following this system he was at the same time merely imitating the narrative protagonist of the Gospels.

Rousseau's victimage carries less stature than Jesus' because Rousseau was obliged to tell the story himself. The *Rêveries*, which express his victimary role in its purest form, take martyrdom as their presupposition rather than their climax. Rather than being an account of the attempts to communicate with others that led to his worldly downfall, they are themselves attempts to communicate with himself after this downfall has deprived him of any other company. Their representational aspect is thematic; the supplementary status of their writing is reflected in their content, which is defined by the author himself as supplementary to his victimary role or, in his own term, as a *dédommagement* for the deprivation inflicted on him by his persecutors. But conversely, the varied forms of dédommagement only take on cultural significance as content for writing. We have only to imagine the difference in impact between their portrayal by Rousseau in the *Rêveries* and their description by a biographer. It is the *Rêveries* themselves, not what they describe, that are the only really significant dédommagement. For not only are the *Rêveries* the most coherent exposition of Rousseau's victimary "system," they are its most important element. The existential basis of the system is only of cultural interest insofar as it provides a point of departure for a work of literature. Romanticism is primarily an esthetic movement however much its existential basis distinguishes it from all previous such movements.

Here we must distinguish between the exemplary author and his followers, for whom imitation was even further from repetition that was the case for the early Christian martyrs and proselytizers. Rousseau's humanity sets the disciple a harder task than Jesus' postulated divinity; the romantic who contents himself with repeating the consecrated gestures of his master is unlikely to attract many witnesses to his "martyrdom." Rousseau was one of the most famous men in Europe at the time he composed the *Rêveries*. It is useless to debate the sincerity of his statement that they were written only for himself; what is significant is that they were not in any case written with a view to gaining fame for their already celebrated author. It is precisely the incontrovertible nature of this fact that guarantees the functionality of the "system" they propose. The more the existential role Rousseau proposes can be distinguished from a mere literary pose, the more this role becomes a valid model for unknown writers and aritsts for whom this role cannot help be such a pose. The more we can believe that the *Rêveries* were written "for myself," the more we can use their victimary system as the basis of literature written for others. And the more Rousseau's scenes are taken as descriptions of moments of perfectly self-sufficient happiness, the more we can attempt to create our own worldly happiness through the fame gained by the fictional depiction of similar scenes.

Why precisely is this the case? We have alluded to the literary origins of Rousseau's system in the separation of the writer *qua* writer from the society of his readers; we have discussed the "supplementary" role his text attributes throughout to itself, as well as to occupations like botany which can easily be understood as so many metaphors for writing. But our final understanding of the Rousseauian romantic system must be given a more rigorous basis. The victimary role which is presented by the author in purely existential terms—although of course we are given to understand that it was his writings that turned the public against him—must be shown to imply literary, or more generally, esthetic representation as a necessary concomitant. Only thus will we be able to demonstrate the power of this system, and to defend its productivity against those latter-day postromantics who have built their own careers on its denunciation and "desconstruction."

From the very origin of human culture the collective victim has been the privileged object of esthetic representation, which at first took place exclusively in, or at least for, a ritual context. Secular culture, as created by the Greeks, did not change this priority, although the epic or tragic "victim" is no longer located in a center fixed by ritual law. And when the Jews collectively, and subsequently Christ as an individual, accepted the victimary role, the reality of this role could only be affirmed through representation. Jesus, we may assume, was a real victim, but so were the two "thieves" and countless other Jewish patriots of his period. Jesus' cultural importance did not come from being a victim, but from being *the* victim. Neither the Jewish community nor a fortiori the international society constituted by the Roman Empire considered him as such. The very point of the "transvaluation of values" instituted by Christianity—the product, as Nietzsche so perceptively saw, of *ressentiment*—is its displacement of the center of society away from the Emperor and his pagan sacrifices to this leader of a minor Jewish revolutionary sect. That Jesus was *the* victim could not be a universally accepted matter of fact; nor could it simply be affirmed as such by his partisans. It could only be presented in the form of a sacred narrative, following the original Hebraic tradition that had distinguished the Jews from all other ancient peoples through their possession of a nonmythical sacred history. To be *the* victim was to be the center of society, the one being without whom it could not maintain its coherence. Such a claim could never be factually substantiated; but it could be made *esthetically* plausible and thereby provide a model that could be imitated by others. The ultimate guarantee of the success of this model was not its adherent's acquisition of a central position in society as a whole, but his establishment of a gradient of centrality around himself which polarized his immediate surroundings. The martyr demonstrated the truth of his faith in showing himself to be a center for his persecutors. Christianity is a religion of individual salvation, and no Christian society is ever centered on its ruler—be he even the Pope—in the way that the ancient empires made Pharoah or Emperor the focus of both ritual and politico-economic activity.

Rousseau's claim to be the victim of an accord unanime excluding him from the society of his fellows could likewise only be made through representation. Rousseau's story had already been told in the *Confessions*, but if this work could be said to establish his uniqueness, it ended before describing anything like an accord unanime. The formation of this accord is situated in the empty space between the *Confessions* and the *Rêveries*, a space by no means filled by the *Dialogues*, although the pathological nature of this work places it closer to the discovery of the victimary role than the *Rêveries*. In the latter work, Rousseau's claim to be *the* victim of society is guaranteed only perfunctorily by a preceding narrative, most notably by the scenes of "death" and "resurrection" following his being knocked unconscious by a great dane in the "Second Promenade." The centrality of the self is not demonstrated by the establishment of a social gradient between persecutors and victim, but by the "God-like" self-sufficiency of the victim alone. For Rousseau's "transvaluation," his recentering of the universe about himself, takes place in an already decentralized world. The only well-defined gradient of centrality left is that between author—or literary Subject—and reader. The position of universal victim can *only* be realized—and not simply affirmed—from the position of "universal" author. Rousseau had to become the evangelist of his own martyrdom, in which very act he demonstrated the "God-like" centrality we have seen him describe. The natural settings in which this self-sufficiency is revealed to the reader, that is, to the self-in-general, thus present the central self-as-author as both absolutely passive—the "victim" even of the forces of nature—and absolutely active in representing these forces as an esthetic scene.

Rousseau was not a romantic, any more than Christ was a Christian. The existential model that he bequeathed to Western culture was the product of over two decades of literary celebrity, not the source of it. The social centrality of the Subject of representation, of the writer, was for him an experiential reality, and the supplementary function of dédommagement played by writing in the *Rêveries* is founded on an independent claim of the victimized self to the central position. For the romantic, the Rousseauian system was in place from the outset, a fact which only served to make the system more rigorous, for its operation was now dependent on purely formal claims with social reward offering its guarantees only a posteriori. The social centrality of the writer could not be an informal precondition of his victimary role, nor could the supplementary status of his writing derive, as it could with Rousseau, from an informal analogy between the writer's former position at the center of society and his present position at the center of his own private "society." The romantic's claim to central victimary status could at best—as with the French romantics of noble origin—be given historical guarantees, rarely of a nature to distinguish the author personally, and certainly not, in his beginnings, as a writer. But this fact only served to solidify the formal equivalence between the status of universal victim and that of Subject of (literary) representation.

Thus the self-reflective "supplementary" status of representation with regard to existence so characteristic of Rousseau is scarcely to be found among the romantics, for whom the choice of a literary vocation is the source of the writer's victimary status rather than a dédommagement from it. Of course this was true for Rousseau's career as well, taken as a whole, but Rousseau had denounced the supplementary status of representation in the *Discourses* long before he thought to find this status relevant to his own writing. The young romantic, who well knew the value of the literary "supplement" to his anonymity, could not condemn supplementarity without condemning his own vocation. Rather than being seen as a cultural form, literary expression was assimilated to the *cri de la nature* of the second *Discourse*. It is no doubt useful to distinguish between the early romantics, whose writing expressed an existential sense of victimage, and the later romantics, who speak directly of literary creation—as in Musset's image (in "La Nuit de Mai") of the pelican feeding its young on its own heart—as a form of victimage. But in neither case is the act of representation in any way guilty of complicity with the persecution it describes. It would be unfair to claim that Rousseau ever affirmed the formal equivalence between the scene of persecution and the scene of representation, but both halves of the equation are certainly present in his work. In romantic writing, on the other hand, the equivalence is lost; the literary subject combines the innocence of the Christ-like victim with the virtue of the spokesman for the oppressed. Only the postromantic generation of Flaubert and Baudelaire, witnesses to the social degeneration of romantic ideals in the 1840s, could grasp anew the ambiguous status of the Subject of representation, this time with the pessimism of men whom three generations of "return to nature" had taught to believe again in original sin.

But that is another story, as is the internal history of the romantic movement, caught in the tightening squeeze between the a priori postulation of victimary centrality and the need to guarantee it by a literary originality increasingly sensitive to the conditions of the marketplace. Rousseau's was arguably the most productive of all secular cultural systems. That its naive application soon led to contradictions resolvable only through the sacrifice of its simplicity only demonstrates its cultural significance. Romanticism is the beginning of the acceleration of cultural history that has led in our generation to the virtual demise of the universalist aims that Western secular culture had maintained since its beginnings in Homeric epic. It corresponds in the cultural sphere to the decentralization of economic production in the bourgeois era. Rather than a witness to an eternal truth, the romantic is an individual center of self-production, a mirror of the hated bourgeois in which the postromantic was forced to see his own image. With romanticism esthetic form loses the immunity to historical change that had maintained itself throughout the neoclassical era. For the classical forms, themselves inherited from ritual, could only remain stable so long as the central significant figure

remained the bearer of a victimary significance which transcended that of
the literary Subject who presided over its revelation. After Rousseau this
could no longer be the case. As first the *Confessions* and then the *Rêveries*
demonstrate, the literary Subject is the one true victim. Only the most
superficial students of romanticism can claim the inimitability of these works
to be a sign of Rousseau's lack of significant contribution to the subsequent
history of literary form. Just the opposite is the case. In the impossibility
of imitating their forms, Rousseau's last works foreshadowed the agony of
esthetic form that still lay over a century in the future.

We opened this discussion with a comparison of Rousseau's "system"
to that of one of history's great moral teachers. It is therefore appropriate
that we close it with a brief discussion of the ethical significance of this
system. Jesus' exhortation to all men to love one another at the expense of
the requirements of the communal ritual order is an asbsolute affirmation of
the fundamental equality of men and of the ultimately reciprocal nature of
all human relations. For Rousseau too, universal love was an ideal, but
inequality was immutably inherent in "fallen" man's social life, and it would
eventually bring about the expulsion from human society of the only true
egalitarian, "le plus sociable et le plus aimant des humains." The moral
dimension of the Rousseauian system appears at first glance as a hypocritical,
paranoid version of Christianity that justifies the radical egocentricity of a
single "egalitarian" in the face of an imaginary accord unanime. Certainly
the romantic figure of the Messiah-poet leading the ungrateful masses despite
themselves to the promised land of freedom is the direct post-Revolutionary
heir of the ethic of the *Rêveries*. But the most precious asset of this ethic is
not the convertibility of the victim's position into one of social leadership—
a self-serving adaptation (albeit not without anthropological significance) that
would have shocked Rousseau. It is rather the conception of the self as both
an a priori ethical center and a center of (self-)production. This is indeed
the ethic of modern, decentralized "consumer" society. Each individual is
at the center of the universe *qua* "victim," the passive recipient of the worldly
interactions of others that can always —and often with good reason—be
judged as manipulative. But the posture of victim offers in fact a refuge from
such manipulations, a private world of "exile" from society in which the self
as Subject can attempt to produce the original representations that will
convert his absolute victimary centrality into an always relative mastery.

That every self is both central and in exile, that collective values exist
only on the basis of a combination of selves defined by this victimary condition (in contrast both to the atomic Cartesian self and to the collective self
of ritual nostalgia), and that the self's only means of compensation for its

victimary role is its assumption of the active centrality of the Subject of representation—these are the most significant ethical lessons to be drawn from Rousseau. No doubt consumer society is a far cry from the Christian utopia of universal love, but its a priori egalitarianism and a posteriori differentiation make it arguably the most moral society man can produce. Whether Rousseau would have shared this judgment of a society that owes so much to his example is doubtful; but neither would Jesus be likely to approve the results of two millenia of Christianity.

E. S. BURT

Developments in Character: Reading and Interpretation in "The Children's Punishment" and "The Broken Comb"

Reading is a term that, through overuse, easily becomes confused with interpretation. But in fact there is a crucial difference: reading involves the undoing of interpretative figures, for it questions whether any synthesis, any single meaning, can close off a text and satisfactorily account for its constitution. Unlike interpretation, which implies a development over the course of a narrative toward a single figure reconciling all its diverse moments, reading states the logic of figures and the logic of narratives to be constantly divergent. Such a divergence implies that an autobiographical text, for example, does not simply serve to bring meaning to the disorderly events of a subject's experience, and self-recognition to author and reader, but serves the further function of making those events available to a reader allegorically, as exemplary of the manner in which all narratives are constructed. We could even define as autobiographical any textual pattern of interference, interruption, or crossing produced by the confrontation of a narrative of consciousness with effects of order produced in excess of the capacity of totalizing figures to regulate them. Rousseau's *Confessions*, which provide a particularly rich source for the study of narrative figures and strategies, will allow us to pursue the distinction between interpretation and reading and to determine some of the stakes involved. The issue is whether the synecdochical relation that reading and interpretation bear to one another is a metaphorical relation, which would make reading simply a special case of understanding, or a metonymical relation, in which case understanding would prove one mode

From *Yale French Studies* 69 (1985). © 1985 by Yale University.

of reading. Some rehearsing of familiar narratives schemes will be necessary in order to clarify the stakes.

The divergence can be seen dramatized in two episodes emblematic of an autobiographical sequence: "the children's punishment," and "the broken comb." Let me recall the events for you briefly. In the pastoral paradise of Bossey where the protagonist and his cousin are studying Latin and the catechism with M. Lambercier, the hero discovers he enjoys being spanked. The first spanking recalls another, less pleasant punishment to the narrator, which he recounts to us from the perspective of an apparently disintertested observer: Mlle. Lambercier's comb is broken; the child undergoes a cross-examination but insists that he did not break it; all the evidence points to his guilt, and he is severely beaten—for willful mischief, for lying, and for stubbornness. The narrator then declares that he did not break the comb.

A DEVELOPING CHARACTER: BILDUNGSROMAN

The chronological narrative naturally imposes the form of a *Bildungsroman* on the *Confessions*. We follow the hero as he passes through various learning experiences that appear as exemplary stages in his moral and psychological development. In interpreting the educational progress made by the protagonist, we could understand the two episodes in question as representing two formative experiences linked together in a chain by a developing consciousness, the first of which leads naturally to the second, and the second of which implies the first.

A first spanking, administered by Mlle. Lambercier, irrevocably determines the shape of the child's desire: "this child's punishment . . . disposed of my tastes, my desires, my passions, myself for the rest of my life." Henceforth, the hero will seek his pleasure in the re-creation of a masochistic relation: "to be at the knee of an imperious mistress, to obey her orders, to have forgiveness to ask of her, were very sweet pleasures to me, and the more my imagination inflamed my blood, the more I had the air of a transfixed lover."

Simultaneously with the education into pleasure, occurs the child's introduction into the hitherto-uncharted territory of fault and merit, a preethical world where the morality of good intention reigns, "the sway of benevolence" as Rousseau will call it. The transition is marked by the introduction of a moral vocabulary of merit, fault, will, conscience, etc., conspicuously absent from the first pages of the *Confessions*. The appearance of intention in conjunction with the awakening of the senses can be explained by the fact that, according to the description of the scene, a single interpretative error is responsible for the awakening of both sense and the senses. The scene is worth quoting because the error is a direct result of the child's first positive encounter with written signs—a spanking is an impression made on a *tabula rasa* of sorts—and shows both the effects on the hero of his atttempt to explain the excesses and deficiencies of written signs in terms of his old value system and the effects on the old value system itself:

> As Mlle. Lambercier bore the affection of a mother for us, so she also had a mother's authority, and carried it sometimes so far as to inflict on us the children's punishment when we had deserved it (*quand nous l'avions méritée*). For quite a long time she held herself to threats, and that threat of punishment entirely new to me seemed very dreadful; but after it was carried out, I found it less terrible in fact than its expectation had been (assez longtemps elle s'en tint à la menace, et cette menace d'un châtiment tout nouveau pour moi me sembloit très effrayante; mais après l'execution, je la trouvai moins terrible à l'épreuve que l'attente ne l'avoit été), and what is even more bizarre was that this punishment made me more affectionate toward the one who had imposed it on me. Indeed, all the truth of that affection and all my natural sweetness were needed to keep me from seeking the return of the same treatment by deserving it (*pour m'empêcher de chercher le retour du même traitement en le méritant*): for I had found in the ache, in the shame itself, a mingling of sensuality that had left me with more desire than fear of undergoing it (*de l'éprouver*) again at the same hand. It is true that, since there was no doubt mingled in with it all some precocious sexual instinct, the same punishment received from her brother would not have seemed pleasant at all to me. But with a man of his humor, that substitution was scarcely to be feared, and if I abstained from deserving correction (*si je m'abstenois de mériter la correction*), it was solely for fear of angering Mlle. Lambercier; for such is the sway of benevolence in me, even of that one born of the senses, that it has always ruled over them in my heart.

Mlle. Lambercier has promised the child a punishment, which the child anticipates will be as great as he imagines he deserves, that is, very fearful. But upon execution, the punishment turns out to be smaller than the one expected, the pain less terrible than the anticipation. It is the difference between the punishment promised and the impression actually received that is accorded significance by the child. The change is marked in two ways.

In the first place, his sensual being is awakened by it: he experiences as a
positive pleasure the release of anticipatory tension. In the second place, and
more importantly for the development of a system of moral values, the
difference between a promise and its execution provokes a full-scale reinterpretation of Mlle. Lambercier by the child. Hitherto the *moi* has read her
feelings of content or discontent with him from her expression ("I knew
nothing so charming as to see everybody content with me and with every
thing . . . "; "nothing troubled me more . . . than to see on Mlle. Lambercier's
face marks of disquiet and pain"), and her love and severity have been
undifferentiated from her brother's ("When it was necessary however, she
was no more lacking in severity than her brother . . . "). But after the
punishment, Mlle. Lambercier wields a specifically female authority and is
a figure on whom the child concentrates his affection ("this punishment made
me more affectionate toward the one who had imposed it on me," "a person
whom I loved like a mother, and perhaps even more"), in contrast to the
brutal, legalistic forms of masculine authority he will encounter in the next
scene.

Now the hero's revision of his interpretation of Mlle. Lambercier seems
to occur by means of a simple inversion of cause and effect, bringing about
a consequent reassessment of values: if he didn't receive the punishment
(pain) he deserved, did he perhaps deserve the punishment (pleasure) he
received? A slippage occurs in the value attributed the action to which the
spanking (the deserved punishment) refers. The different meanings of the
word *mériter* in the passage indicate a path the child might have followed as
he revised his ideas of Mlle. Lambercier's severity and love: in the first
instance, it refers to "retribution for a fault" ("when we had deserved it").
In the second, it appears to have been emptied of all value, and to be, like
the pleasure of seeking pleasure, its own reward: ("seek the return of the
same treatment by deserving it"). By the third appearance, however, the
deserved punishment has been ascribed a positive value, and appears in the
context to mean a recompense accorded a deserving subject, or, even more
specifically, a recompense for the virtue of deferring the pleasurable reward
by deferring the action that will bring it about ("if I abstained from deserving
it").

What has happened is that the child has come up with two hypotheses
to cover the failure of the sign to mean what it promised, one of which
addresses the issue of a fault in the transmission of meaning, and the other
of which assumes an insufficient understanding of the promise on the part
of the self. Mlle. Lambercier's hand may have slipped in the act of making
her meaning clear: the mistake in intention frees the written sign from its

conventional meaning, and makes it available to the child for private interpretation. Desire awakens when the overruling interpretative structure is shown to be inadequate to include the written sign, and becomes determined as the desire for a repetition of that demonstration. At the same time, the protagonist posits that his own understanding of the code might have been insufficient: he learns not to read people's faces for signs of their intentions and comes to suspect that Mlle. Lambercier, a watchful and benevolent teacher, might have wished all along to teach him that meaning involves a temporal unfolding.

The imaginative freedom the child enjoys and his paradoxical good conduct—he prefers to imagine passively a masochistic relation rather than to pursue actively any other kind of relation with the opposite sex—as well as his bizarre concatenation of female affection and authority in the figure of the loving dominatrix or teacher, is owed to an interpretative gesture that lands him in an impasse. The hero discovers a sign (the spanking) in excess of the intent to punish, which makes it undecidable whether his voluntaristic view of signs is actually faulty, or whether a more far-reaching teleological system than he has hitherto suspected reigns at Bossey under the benevolent eye of Mlle. Lambercier. The child cannot determine whether written impressions are arbitrary signs, appropriable by the stealthy imagination, or whether they are motivated signs whose meaning has not yet been revealed.

The substitution of an imaginary relation for a real one accrues a positive benefit to the child's conduct, but arrests the development of his conscience at a preethical stage, and actively interferes with the development of his reason. Indeed, his reason is so impaired that, as Rousseau suggests, the very subject of his greatest curiosity, the differences between the sexes, is the one he will have the least knowledge and the fewest ideas about. Because his only interest in the opposite sex is to transpose women into imaginary scenes as imperious school-mistresses, he will have little objective curiosity about them, and will consequently learn the facts of life very late: "until adolescence I had no distinct idea of the union of the sexes." In a word, the substitution of teleological fictions of desire for the literal world empowers the imagination, blocks the moral faculty at the level of the morality of good intention, and, temporarily at least, paralyses judgment.

In the second episode, the child experiences "[the] first sentiment of injustice and violence." He is spanked, after a trial and a conviction, by an executioner officially appointed, for a crime he claims he did not commit. He discovers that, however unfairly, persons are sometimes attributed responsibility for actions. Too young to know that "appearances condemned [him]," he himself blames an unjust human agency. "Butcher, butcher,

butcher (*Carnifex, carnifex, carnifex*)," he cries, mistaking the impersonal hand of the executioner for the hand of a sadistic butcher. The experience of injustice provokes and justifies unjust indignation, mistrustful vigilance, secrecy, stubbornness, cunning—all the evils the punishment was calculated to correct. It makes the child an expert in using appearances, whose capacity to veil intentions he now appreciates; he learns to hide behind them, to harbor secrets, to conceal his projects. He loses his fear of acting reprehensibly and directs his energies at hiding the traces of his actions, for now he only fears getting caught. "We were less ashamed of doing bad things, and more fearful of being accused."

In the account just given the hero's character undergoes a distinct evolution over the course of the two episodes. In the first, he discovers desire and the private, interior world of the imagination. In the second, he learns to know the world of appearances and how to manipulate them. The second stage comes to correct the child's early substitution of subjective categories for objective ones, without ever entirely eradicating that original desire, which will continue to dominate his relations with the opposite sex and will explain his persistent preference for fictions over objective accounts of human history. We recognize in the sequence the beginning of a genetic account of human development, similar in its linearity to the one Condillac's statue follows as it gets progressively more complex ideas, and that could lead toward a dialectical resolution in the fully formed psychological and moral being of an adult once the protagonist learns to renounce completely the errors of his imagination for the rewards of reason.

DEVELOPING A CHARACTER: DISCURSIVE UNITY

But of course, an illusion quickly dispelled by autobiography is the illusion that the chronological narrative, the story of the events, *l'histoire*, is a true representation of a natural progression toward a single, recapitulative figure. For, while we follow the development of the protagonist's character over the narrative in our naive first reading, in fact the end toward which the development leads is in sight from the very beginning, in the figure of the narrator the hero has become. It is he who tells the story, whose modelling presence shapes the narrative from the beginning. The work remembers and restores already played-out scenes. The *Confessions* can be understood according to a hermeneutical model then. They take as their horizon the final revelation of an original fold in the narrative: the end, the self developed, has become the beginning, the self being exposed. That fold had to occur for the narrative to be possible, and the narrative itself is the unfolding of the fold as an interpretation. The discrepancy between a literal understanding, arrived at in proximity to events, and their figurative significance which is only revealed later on, is the note on which autobiography always opens. Its pedagogical claims are based on its ability to show that progress in the understanding involves the gaining of access to the figural dimension. Hence the reference in Rousseau's preamble to a teleological being, to a future moment of Divine Justice, when the end of all events will be revealed and justified: "Let the trumpet of the Last Judgment sound when it will; I will come this book in hand to present myself before the sovereign judge." Present at the very least in the choice of events told, the narrator naturally predetermines the meaning of the events that appear to determine him: from the outset every episode in the narrative represents either a normal moment in the development of the model, or a temporary deviation away from that main path. The autobiographical narrative, in this simplified hermeneutical account, is a teleological fiction. Each episode of the *récit* is understood to be a signifier pointing toward the omnipresence of a shaping self-referential intent.

Since the narrative implies a reformed narrator, one who is no longer doing but is only recounting, the events appearing nearer the end of the narrative will explain why the story is told and determine its mode of exposition. The episode of the broken comb, claims Starobinski, is an emblematic scene containing the explanation of Rousseau's driving need to confess, and thus the motivation for the autobiographical narrative in its entirety (*La Transparence et l'obstacle*). In that episode, the narrator learns to feel the accusing eye of Protestant Geneva upon him. From an early accusation and the fear of being accused to which it gives birth—"more fearful of being accused"—comes Rousseau's need to disculpate himself in advance, to write the *Confessions*. Lejeune, who agrees with Starobinski, finds evidence in the scene to suggest that the trauma of being falsely accused and unjustly punished has not been resolved for the narrator. For no apparent reason, and to a rather ridiculous effect, the narrator of the episode, from his present vantage point, categorically denies having broken the comb: "This adventure happened almost fifty years ago, and I am not afraid today of being punished again for the same act. Well, then, I declare in the face of Heaven that I was innocent of it, that I neither broke nor touched the comb, that I didn't even approach the ledge [on which the comb lay], and that I didn't even dream of doing it." The passage gives a clear instance, according to Lejeune, of *dénégation* ("Le Peigne cassé").

In such a view then, the *Confessions* develop as an exposition of the storyteller, in his character as fiction maker. The narrative is teleological rather than casual and emerges, under the impetus of an obscure accusation and an unnamed guilt, from a sack of memories that is being emptied out.

The compulsion to confess comes from the second episode, but what Rousseau wishes to achieve, in emptying out the sack and exposing what is at its bottom, is a return to the innocent state represented in the first episode, as it would pertain to the narrator and his *récit*. Just as the general impression the child gives is of good behavior, despite all the delirious erotic scenes he is imagining, so the general impression the narrator wants to give is of having a good intention in revealing all the actions of his earlier, deluded self.

The narrator's aim is to convince, after telling his story that he stands fully revealed as a transparent intention to communicate the truth. The model of the Bildungsroman has been put into place by the first episode. The second episode, the episode of the broken comb, does not merely provide the necessary corrective to the hero's fiction-making tendencies within the narrative of developing consciousness. For, as the second episode shifts the focus of interest from hero to storyteller, from *récit* to *discours*, it extends over the whole narrative precisely the same hypotheses concerning the relation of written sign to intention that the protagonist had discovered in the isolated case of the deserved punishment. Narrative continuity is the stake in the second episode; whether the anecdotes reveal a single far-reaching design, or whether Rousseau's hand, like Mlle. Lambercier's, has occasionally slipped in delivering its message is the issue. The entire thrust of Lejeune's proof in "Le Peigne cassé" is to show that the episode exemplifies the self even in its inadequacies: occasional memory lapses or miscalculations in the effects of self-presentation are exceptions proving the general rule of the autobiographical pact.

The complication Lejeune brings to the hermeneutical model is possible because the act of confessing, what Genette would call *narration*, also figures within the *Confessions*. In the act of confessing, Rousseau repeats the fault he wants to expiate, and thereby renews the possibility of misunderstanding, since the story he tells in order to reveal himself is a performative, in excess of the content—his simple good faith—it reveals. Each confession is therefore potentially damaging to the promise of total self-revelation because, as pure performance, it is capable of engendering further misinterpretations. We may, for example, wonder whether Rousseau does not get more pleasure out of the shameful act of confessing than we get truth from the revelations of the salacious secrets of his erotic life. Once Rousseau begins excusing himself for confessing, each confession will potentially branch off into a supplementary series of confessions.

At best, Rousseau can manage to convince his readers by the confessing of confessions that the performative excesses of each confession are involuntary faults, that he, Rousseau has been caught up in the machinery of a communicating process that he is attempting to explicate. At worst, the excesses will simply generate further misunderstanding. In either case, Rousseau will feel disculpated, since he will have done his best to explain the problem at its source.

The hermeneutical model, the most totalizing account of the confessional narrative possible, has to grapple constantly with misfires in the performances of confessions, but it recuperates those misfires by revealing that they are localized misunderstandings which do not put into question the teleological structure and discursive unity of the whole. Thus Lejeune will show how the potential for misunderstanding confessions can be made into the object of the confession, how, "failing the possibility of ever telling the truth of desire, one tells to the end what keeps it from being told" (*Le Pacte autobiographique*). That Rousseau finally understood social concepts like justice to be predicated on a mere morality of good intentions would follow from such a model, as would the establishment of his persuasive aim in his autobiographical texts to be the unfolding, by way of the narrative, of figures of the self.

DEVELOPING PRINTS: THE NEGATIVE CHARACTERS

But questions arise. Is Rousseau's autobiography as seamless as this model makes it? Is his undoubted ability to make pathos and strategy converge the effect he is seeking? Is the discrepancy between the order of persuasion and the order of conviction dramatized in the episode of the broken comb actually overcome in the figure of the strategic narrator, who explains the misunderstanding in order better to persuade of his good heart, or does it persist as an active threat to narrative coherence, a persistence that Rousseau wants to explain? If it is thinkable, as Lejeune would have it, that an objective stance might be only a pose, are there any circumstances in which the subjectivism and pathos of the *Confessions* might also prove a ruse? Critics have long divided over whether to privilege the view that Rousseau's systematic works are actually self-justifications in disguise (the view of Starobinski), or whether, for an unsystematic spirit like Rousseau, the autobiographical works are part of a gigantic strategy for revealing the truths of the system (the view of Cassirer). The decision to privilege the autobiographical works over the systematic works may depend on the axe one has to grind; a more interesting question is: what explains the fact, that both of these views appear legitimate, authorized by Rousseau? If Rousseau provides the answer to that question, we would have to conclude that explanation, rather than self-disculpation, has determined the order and manner of presenting the episodes. He may have wanted to show how totalizing figures, like the *amant transi* of the first episode, who collects and expresses opposing narrative forces in his ecstatic state of suspended animation, are inevitably followed by a fall into a narrative of literal events, uncollectable by recapitulative figures. The second episode, which gains its meaning from reference to literal events—the breaking of a comb, the beating of a child, the declaration of innocence—would follow the first because it expresses the inevitability of such literalizations. The representation within the confessional narrative of Rousseau's life as a process of degeneration, in which fragmentary effects of order are increasingly found in events (plots) resisting the subsumption by the imagination into its categories, would lend credence to such an allegorical reading.

Is there such a narrative as the one we've been describing in the *Confessions?* How does it differ form the genetic development of the hero's understanding, or the unfolding of an interpretation of the self? Are there traces in the broken comb that its uncertainties are not merely local? We will need to examine more closely what the scene leaves suspended, to print, as it were certain significant negatives, in order to determine whether the divergence between persuasive strategy and convincing order of exposition does not outlive persuasive recuperative strategies in general.

> J'étudiois un jour seul ma leçon dans la chambre contigue à la cuisine. La servante avoit mis sécher à la plaque les peignes de Mlle. Lambercier. Quand elle revint les prendre, il s'en trouva un dont tout un côté de dents étoit brisé. A qui s'en prendre de ce dégat? personne autre que moi n'étoit entré dans la chambre. On m'interroge; je nie d'avoir touché le peigne. M. et Mlle. Lambercier se réunissent; m'exhortent, me pressent, me menacent; je persiste avec opinâtreté; mais la conviction étoit trop forte, elle l'emporta sur toutes mes protestations, quoique ce fut la prémiére fois qu'on m'eut trouvé tant d'audace à mentir. La chose fut prise au serieux; elle méritoit de l'être. La méchanceté, le mensonge, l'obstination parurent également dignes de punition: mais pour le coup ce ne fut pas par Mlle. Lambercier qu'elle me fut infligée. On écrivit à mon oncle Bernard; il vint. Mon pauvre Cousin étoit chargé d'un autre délit non moins grave: nous fumes enveloppés dans la même execution. Elle fut terrible. Quand, cherchant le remède dans le mal même, on eut voulu pour jamais amortir mes

sens dépravés, on n'auroit pu mieux s'y prendre. Aussi me lais-
serent-ils en repos pour longtems.

On ne put m'arracher l'aveu qu'on exigeoit. Repris à plusieurs
fois, et mis dans l'état le plus affreux, je fus inébranlable. J'aurois
souffert la mort et j'y étois résolu. Il fallut que la force même
cédat au diabolique entêtement d'un enfant; car on n'appella pas
autrement ma constance. Enfin, je sortis de cette cruelle épreuve
en pièces, mais triomphant.)

(I was studying my lesson alone one day in the room next to the
kitchen. The servant had put Mlle. Lambercier's combs out to
dry on the ledge at the back of the fireplace. When she returned
to take them, one was found to have a whole row of broken teeth.
On whom to cast blame for the damage? No one other than myself
had entered the room. I am interrogated; I deny having touched
the comb. M. and Mlle. Lambercier join forces; exhort me, press
me, threaten me; I obstinately persist; but conviction was too
strong, and prevailed over all my protestations, although it was
the first time that they had found me so audacious in lying. The
thing was taken seriously; it deserved to be. The ill-nature, the
deceit, the obstinacy all seemed equally worthy of punishment:
but for once it was not by Mlle. Lambercier that it was inflicted.
My Uncle Bernard was written to; he came. My poor Cousin
was charged with another offence no less grave: we were enveloped in the same execution. It was terrible. If, seeking the remedy in the evil itself, they had wanted to deaden my senses
forever, they could not have gone about it any better. For a long
time they left me quiet.

The exacted confession could not be pulled out of me. Taken
up several times and put into an awful condition, I was inflexible.
I would have suffered death itself, and was resolved to do so.
Force itself had to give in to the diabolical pig-headedness of a
child, for that was what my constancy was called. At last I
emerged from that cruel trial, in pieces, but triumphant.)

In keeping with the two ways we have been organizing the narrative,
the episode of the broken comb can be read as a dramatic representation of
two very different kinds. In the first place, it confronts an autonomous
subject, a *moi*, and an agent or representative of another subject, the servant,
over the issue of responsibility for an event, the breaking of a comb. The
servant, unlike the *moi*, is not an independent entity, but merely acts to

carry out the commands of another. The alibi of the child appears to be that he has been lost in study, his mind on his books, and his senses asleep. But the Lamberciers find it infinitely more convincing, more logical,—"conviction was too strong"—that an independent subject should have caused the damage than that a mere servant, a hand animated only in the service of Mlle. Lambercier, should have done so. Similarly, the Vicar will state in the *Profession de foi* that his mind refuses to assent to the idea that any movement could begin without cause; ". . . seeing a body in motion, I immediately judge either that it is an animated body, or that motion has been communicated to it. My mind refuses all assent to the idea of unorganised matter moving by itself, or producing any action." No suspicion is attached to the servant because she plays the role here of unorganised matter, moved under Mlle. Lambercier's communicated orders, incapable of inventing or destroying things on her own. In shortsightedly overlooking the servant, the Lamberciers assert as a fact that there can be such a thing as a deliberate destruction and determine the breaking of the comb to be one such planned event.

On the other hand, because every episode in the *Confessions* can alternately be understood as a fiction into which the narrator has projected himself, the scene can be read as representing, within the autonomous subject who provides the decor of the scene "I was studying," the dramatic moment when a new idea is formed, abstracted, like the teeth from the comb, from several perceptions. Does the child get that new idea from an unaccustomed perception, or does judgment create it by moving things around? The scene is highly Cartesian and the drama is centered on the possibility of distinguishing the role of perception from that of judgment in the passage to a new idea (like the passage from the idea of combs, based on a simple resemblance, to the idea of a broken comb, in which difference between teeth and comb plays within resemblance between comb and comb, and resemblance between teeth plays within difference between broken and unbroken comb): in one room, a *moi*, a reason abstracted from its sense is studying; in the other room, the kitchen, the senses go about their business of providing fragmentary and isolated perceptions for consciousness to appraise; between the two an opening, a ledge, on which the combs are placed. Without the senses, judgment can have no perceptions to compare for resemblances and differences. But without judgment, it seems impossible to get anything like the organized perception of a comb, in which teeth are differentiated from the connecting back of the comb and compared to one another. For the combs to be presented to consciousness as perceptions analyzable into parts, they need to have been "moved" around by consciousness: the senses, however capable of preventing two separate perceptions they might be, cannot find resemblances between teeth, or differentiate between teeth and comb. Just so, the Vicar states that judgment, while it appears inactive, actually plays an active role in comparing perceptions which sensation would be incapable of distinguishing or combining:

> By sensation, objects offer themselves to me separately, in iso-lation, as they are in nature; by comparison, I move them, I transport them, so to speak, I set them one on top of the other to pronounce on their difference or their resemblance, and gen-erally on all their relationships. . . . I seek in vain in a purely sensitive being that intelligent force that superposes and then pronounces, I do not know how to find it in its nature. That passive being will feel every object separately, or will even feel the object formed of the two, but having no force to fold them back onto one another, it will never compare them, it will not judge.

As far as the representation of the subject is concerned, then, the active role of judgment in the formation of perceptions is being foregrounded. The *moi*'s denial of having literally touched the comb, in the representation of the events, is the equivalent, in the representation of the subject's judgment, of an admission that he has been figuratively moving the combs about in order to abstract ideas from them. The narrator assents to the organizing power of judgment over an orderly presentation by the senses. The senses can lay perceptions on the ledge between the rooms, but judgment denies them any force to compare or differentiate between them.

The two representations—of events and of the subject—bear a synec-dochical relation to one another. The animated being capable of independent action in the representation of events, is shown in a close-up view, to be ruled by an active force of judgment which gets its ideas by forcefully transporting and comparing perceptions. The two representations, despite the contradictions they present as far as the comb is concerned (in one case, a comb is actually broken, and there is an event for which the subject is called to account; in the other case the broken comb is a metaphor for the invention of ideas of resemblance and difference by abstracting from per-ception) and despite the differences in the kinds of evidence provided (opin-ion, as yet undifferentiated into persuasion and conviction, provides the basis for thinking the damage deliberate, whereas a lack of evidence to the contrary, the impossibility of discovering whether the senses actually are organised or not, explains the *moi*'s conviction that judgment is as figuratively active as the senses are literally active) both support a consistent reasoning: the child could have broken the comb if he had wanted to, but he didn't because he was studying, judging things instead. The notion that autobiography aims at the presentation of the self-willed subject, for whom interpretation has come to take the place of action is supported by the dramatic scene. It is significant as well that the synecdoche linking the two ways of understanding the scene is consistent with reason. The possibility of finding a metaphor for the self in each representation of an action is not only not inconsistent with logical presentation, but can even provide an idealist philosophy like that of Descartes with some of its finest insights.

But there is another synecdoche in the episode that substitutes wholes and parts by way of metonymy rather than by metaphor, and that involves the status of the memory, rather than that of the subject or his actions. For the question of the passage is: what connects the two passages in which the episode is remembered? More specifically, what explains the return to the punishment scene after the story has reached a first closure in the death of the senses? The first paragraph provides a formally perfect mystery story, complete with beginning (suspect deeds), middle (review of evidence and conviction) and end (execution). It reviews the substantial evidence, names names and cites a proliferation of circumstances. The second paragraph, on the other hand, blows up a single scene from the narrative, and repeats the same information over and over: "a child is being brutally punished." Not only does the second paragraph provide no new evidence concerning the events, but it is even possible to wonder whether it is indeed a memory of the same event: no names, no material circumstances, no times or places are cited.

Now, the proximity of the two passages makes it seem likely that they refer to the same painful spanking. It would be possible to make the part, the punishment scene, stand in for the whole—the circumstances leading up to and including the punishment—because it can supply what is missing from the narrative, namely, evidence of the child's inner feelings, and of his moral integrity, in the shape of a brave refusal under torture to admit guilt for a crime he did not commit. It serves as well to show the disproportion of the punishment to the crime, and to lay the Lamberciers under suspicion. For, however reasonable it might be for the misunderstanding between the Lamberciers and the child to have arisen—the Lamberciers have evidence for their conviction, whereas the child has only his repeated and uncomprehending denial to speak for him—the misunderstanding becomes an injustice when the Lamberciers presume to punish him for the moral faults of lying and stubborness without consulting him for inner evidence of moral corruption. Lejeune, for example, chooses to privilege the view that Rousseau has set the two paragraphs side by side and made the fragment stand in for the whole by synecdoche first because it provides the pathos missing from the *récit*, persuading that the boy was a feeling subject, not the sort to go around wantonly breaking combs and lying about it afterwards. The synecdoche is then an ornament used by the narrating consciousness to persudade that, while the Lamberciers's conviction that only autonomous subjects commit crimes is correct, they are wrong in thinking the stick figure represented in the actions of the scene to be such an autonomous subject; without inner evidence, the subjective perspective, the *moi* is no more an autonomous figure than the servant. In such a view, the synecdoche restores the whole inside from a partial reminder of it. For Lejeune, proof of Rousseau's innocence as to the breaking of the comb (and his guilt as to his desire to break it) comes from two sources: on the one hand, he has no memory of having touched the comb; on the other hand, he is a well-intentioned youth, incapable of deliberate acts of violence and of untruths. By showing the inadequacies of the formal evidence in the case at hand, the narrator would justify the confessional enterprise as supplementing for such lacks.

But the narrator does not appear interested in revealing what the protagonist thought or felt, nor does his conviction of his innocence come from that source. Indeed, he states quite categorically that the hero's ideas and feelings are impenetrable mysteries to him, that even imagination does not allow him to establish a continuity between the past self and the present:

> Imagine a child (*un carctère*) timid and easily led . . . who has not even the idea of injustice, and who for the first time undergoes (*éprouve*) one so terrible at the hands of precisely those people he loves and respects the most. What an upset in the ideas! What disorder in the feelings! What a revolution in his heart, in his brain, in the whole of his little moral and intellectual being! I say, imagine all this if possible; but as for me, I don't feel myself able to disentangle, to follow out, the slightest trace of what was going on inside me then.

Not only does the narrator seem reluctant to accord belief to inner evidence, but he also leads us to think that belief and persuasion are not really the main issue in proving the boy's innocence. He states without any equivocation that he *knows* he did not break the comb: "Let no one ask me how the damage was done (*comment ce dégat se fit*), I do not know nor can I understand it; what I know very certainly is that I was innocent of it." What is the source of that knowledge and of that certainty?

Perhaps the two parts of the passage do not provide the objective and the subjective view of the same event. We can as easily understand the whole for which the part substitutes to be the second paragraph as the first. In other words, we can understand the narrative as the frame provided by invention to set off a memory fragment that returns unaccompanied by any other circumstances. What that would mean, first of all, is that the compositional techniques of memory as it presents memories to consciousness would be at stake, rather than two persepectives on the same event. We could easily understand why the narrator is so certain that the child is not guilty of touching the comb, or even of wanting to touch it, if he were raising the possibility that he might have made up the crime to fit the punishment.

There is evidence that our ordinary notion of storytelling in autobiography—in which events precede the memory of events, and invention works to put the memories together into a persuasive narrative—has been stood on its head in this passage. Events do not determine the punishment and thus provide the memory its objective and subjective tales (the review of the evidence, the hero's feeling of injustice), and a convincing synecdoche to persuade that the latter is more valuable. Rather, a repressed sensation (pain) appears to have determined the second passage (the nonconfession of pain), itself the source of the first passage, the so-called remembered events, the convincing frame. The evidence that such a reversal may have occurred lies first in the way the second passage loudly insists that no substantive confession is going on, at the same time that it silently indicates the referent to be a sensation, pain. Indeed, the second paragraph fills in some holes in the representation of the subject, for it answers the question of how the *moi* can get new ideas by reminding that consciousness depends on forgetting. The judgment that judgment is just as active when it abstracts, as sensation is when it proffers perceptions, must forget all literal sensations like touching or being touched in order to understand the comparison. Just so the child studying denied the evidence of his senses: "I deny having touched (*je nie avoir touché*)." The model that allows the conception of such a repression is the model of reading. For just so reflective consciousness remembers he must have "touched," perceived the letters of the lesson he was studying in order to abstract meaning from them. The proliferation of signs indicating pain as their referent in the second passage serve as reminders of what had to be destroyed in order for meaning to be discovered. The sequence would thus give evidence that remembering repressed sensations, fragmentary and un-collected parts, can be the cause of ideas.

Evidence that the narrative is elaborated to explain the holes of the punishment scene would be provided by a series of compositional features.

The circumstances of the crime appear to literalize figures and resemanticize the missing signifiers of the second passage. For example, the attempt to yank a meaningful confession out of a mute sensation—"The exacted confession couldn't be pulled out of me"—could serve as the origin for the yanked-out teeth of the comb. The fragmentariness of sensation, against the underlying unity of the subject—"I came out of that cruel trial, in pieces, but triumphant"—can be read as the source for the comb with its broken off teeth. The sensation of having been a white page on which impressions are made, a proof or *une épreuve* as it were, could have been translated into the letter sent off to Uncle Bernard, the offense itself (the *"délit"*), the punishment in which the children were "enveloped," the piece of inscribed metal (*la plaque,"* in its other sense), the book the child is studying, and finally, into the whole series of "mise à l'épreuve," that is, tests, trials, or study—all various ways of finecombing the evidence. The lack of a convincing content to confess—no *dans*, but plenty of exiguity ("exacted"; "pulled out," "came out," etc.)—and the sensation of the kind of *peine* one experiences when extraction is going on would explain the *peigne* and its missing *dents*. Rather than the fragmentary scene of punishment being supplied to disculpate the hero or justify the narrator after the fact, the narrative has been invented to explain the persistence of a memory fragment of uncertain provenance; in other words, the holes in the evidence have been invented to convince that the fault was in the memory not in the boy: the narrative of the broken comb would be only one of those indifferent ornaments that Rousseau explains he will use from time to time "to fill in an empty space occasioned by my faulty memory (*pour remplir un vide occasionné par mon défaut de mémoire*). (Rousseau tells us in the preamble that he may occasionally find himself using such fictions. What better ornament to represent both the cause [faulty memory] and effect [empty space] than an ornamental comb with half its teeth missing? For the teeth of the comb are a catachresis, and as such both substitute a figure for the missing proper term and are the proper term. The catachresis expresses very well the uncertainty in Rousseau's phrasing as to whether his faulty memory shows up in the substitution of fictions, like the fiction of the children's punishment, for the actual events, or as literal holes [ranging from windows, missing teeth, to narrative sequences of uncertain origin]. It is clear from the preamble that Rousseau does not himself claim to know when he has substituted fictions for the holes in his memory, and when he has, in all ignorance, simply represented them: "I *may* have supposed to be true what I knew could have been so, never what I knew to be false." [my emphasis.]) The evidence for this reading is fundamentally negative: the two passages are connected by proximity and by the signifying code. Rousseau's famous "charlantanistic transitions" here reveal their law: resemanticized signifiers, fragments placed side by side *persuade* that there is continuity of development in the narrative at the very moment that they *prove* that in fact there is none.

The synecdoche that lets the part of the memory stand in for the whole does not lead to the convergence of the codes of belief and conviction then. On the one hand, it restores what is lacking from the review of the evidence— persuasion, feeling—by means of a mechanical trick, placing two memories side by side, so that the order in which the memories are presented comes to be taken for a causal order. On the other hand, it reminds that what is lacking from the story is the sensation of pain, and suggests as a reason for the synecdoche the need to represent that lack. The scene provides two contradictory arguments: either, the child, a subject with lots of high moral feelings, wouldn't have broken the comb; or, he couldn't have broken it, because, in writing down his memories the narrator becomes convinced that the narrative was made up. The aporia which pits the synecdoche as the subject's strategic weapon for reminding of inner feeling, against the synec- doche as gaining its persuasion from order alone, cannot be resolved. The persuasion that there is a moral being like the self arises in the face of convincing proof that there is no guarantee of continuity with the past, and that consequently the continuous development of protagonist or narrator is a mirage. But that conviction itself is based on a masked persuasion: namely, that some very diabolical author has made up the whole story about missing authors in order to explain why there are so many parts.

Textual reflexivity as well as self-reflexivity is at work throughout the narrative, then, and indeed the former prepares the crucial recognition that perception can provide new ideas by way of memory. The model suggesting that part of the episode of the broken comb has been entirely invented can be extended to both the episodes of the Bossey sequence, and indeed will even threaten the *Confessions* as a whole. For what better origin could there be for the sentiment of injustice and violence than the feeling of pain without a cause, a punishment received for which no memory of a reason remains? That would be the case if the pain of a single spanking had been repressed, in order that it might be remembered first as the cause of pleasure and delight in imaginative pursuits in the episode of the children's punishment, and then as the causeless pain around which the enigmatic narrative of the broken comb is built. Indeed, the crime without an author, the breaking of the comb, could easily have been invented to suit such a half-forgotten pain: *une peine sans cause* is not hard to transform into its near homonym *un peigne cassé*. We post-Freudians should not be surprised that the repressed pain of the spanking should take the odd form of an inconclusive narrative about an uncertain crime, for the inconclusiveness, the resemanticizing of signifiers, would be clues that the feeling, the sensation repressed so that Bossey can be sentimentalized in the first episode, is being recalled through a process recognizable as dreamwork. While the whole Bossey sequence would be misleading in its details—the sentimental paradise did not really exist and the events of the broken comb episode are as likely to have occurred as what you dreamed last night—still it would tend to demonstrate that a subject on whom a sense impression was once made has persisted over time. The memory fragment would restore the whole, the endurance of the subject, as the meaning of the episode. In remembering the same spanking twice Rousseau would still be vindicating the confessional project.

But nothing insures that there was such an impression as a spanking made on the hero, and consequently that the episode provides a certain link to the past. Rousseau will suggest toward the end of the spankings sequence that restoring sequentiality to the past involves destruction as well as construction:

> Almost thirty years have passed since I left Bossey without my having recalled my stay there in any agreeable fashion by memories somewhat connected (*par des souvenirs un peu liés*): but now that I have passed maturity and am declining into old age, I feel that those same memories are being born again while the others are being erased (*tandis que les autres s'effacent*), and are engraving themselves in my memory with traits whose charm and force augment from day to day; as if, feeling life already escaping, I were seeking to seize it again at its beginnings.

The entire passage on spankings may have been made up to illustrate the two-part process of creating connections—called remembering—explained here: memory restores connections that had been destroyed, then recalls what it had to efface (a disagreeable lack of connection) in order to do its work of restoring. That would be the sense of the passage if we understood the last part of the sentence, an extension whose antecedent is uncertain ("and are engraving . . . "), to refer not to the reconnected memories, but to the other, unconnected ones that are being wiped out. But in that case, no subject would underlie the confessing of confessions. What that would mean is that the story of the first *fessée*, the *fessée* that gives the *moi* access to meaningful sexual difference, is told with, *con*, another *fessée* so that the law of the production of confessions can be revealed. The *confessor confessé*, one a meaningful confession of a self disculpating and knowing itself, and legitimating confessions, and the other a confession that the sequence has been made up to illustrate the pieces of the word *confessor* would be at the origin of the autobiographical sequence. Textual reflexivity—for a word that represents itself in its two aspects as a text not a subject—would be at the origin of the *Confessions* in their entirety.

But if the Bossey sequence can be read either as two ways of remembering a single impression, in support of Rousseau's recuperative self, or as having as sole cause the illustration of the two aspects of words on a page, in support of the text's reflexivity, it cannot be read as both. For in one version, the version of the understanding, the memory of a repression is the cause of a small interruption of the narrative thread, leading to the constitution of the self as a readable book, by way of a persuasive substitution of part for totality. But in the other version, restoration of meaningful order is merely a pretense for the retrieving of literality. No subject could understand what all those letters spell, since they spell the end of understanding. The part can stand in for the whole by synecdoche because the whole is: part after part after part. The passage asserts a disjunction, a mutual miscomprehension, between the two ways of organising the episodes of an autobiography. The gap constituting that miscomprehension, the divergence between reading and interpretation cannot be closed, since the effort to throw a bridge across it by an act of understanding is itself the reenactment of the persuasion into the agreeable illusion of narrative, and has as its effect the obliteration of the literality signified.

DAVID MARSHALL

Rousseau and the State of Theater

The book that we refer to today as Rousseau's *Lettre à d'Alembert sur les spectacles* usually is situated in the antitheatrical tradition, even if defenders of the stage from d'Alembert to Jonas Barish have considered it a belated and almost anachronistic contribution to that tradition. In this article I would like (at least temporarily) to dislocate the *Lettre* from both the tradition of attacks on the stage and the immediate occasion that prompted Rousseau to publish the book: d'Alembert's proposal in the seventh volume of the *Encyclopédie* that a theater be established in Geneva. I will argue that although Rousseau genuinely was concerned about the effects of a theater in Geneva, and although much of his argument against the stage reiterates the charges of Plato and later antitheatrical polemicists, we blind ourselves to the full scope of Rousseau's indictment if we regard the *Lettre* only as a particularly eloquent antitheatrical tract.

The original title of the book refers to d'Alembert's proposal to establish a "théâtre de comédie" in Geneva, but the title that Rousseau later used to refer to his text is the *Lettre d'Alembert sur les spectacles*, which I would insist on translating as the *Letter to d'Alembert on Spectacles*. The title is *not*, as Rousseau's modern American translator would suggest, the *Letter to M. d'Alembert on the Theatre*. The question of whether a "théâtre de comédie" should be established in Geneva provides an occasion for Rousseau to reflect on the character of *spectacles*—which include but by no means are limited to dramatic representations performed by actors on a stage. Rousseau is con-

From *Representations* 13 (Winter 1986). © 1986 by the Regents of the University of California.

cerned not just with how Geneva should govern its spectacles but with how spectacles govern our lives: how we are affected by the theatrical relations enacted outside as well as inside the playhouse by people who face each other as actors and spectators. I will suggest that the issue for Rousseau finally is not whether *a* theater should be established but whether theater (in its many manifestations) can be avoided at all. My investigation of the problem of *theatricality* in the *Lettre à d'Alembert* and other texts will include a consideration of the interplay between theater and sympathy in Rousseau's work, ending with some reflections on the theatrical status of Rousseau's autobiographical enterprise.

The *Lettre à d'Alembert sur les spectacles* has been seen as a continuation of the reactionary crusade against civilization Rousseau began in his early discourses. One could reverse this perspective, however, and see Rousseau's earlier writing—particularly the *Discours sur l'origine et les fondements de l'iné-galité parmi les hommes*—as the beginning of a critique of theatricality: a critical investigation into the role of spectacles and theatrical relations in European culture. In the second *Discours*, for example, when Rousseau asserts, "In the true state of nature, vanity (l'amour-propre) does not exist," he goes on to describe how "each particular man regard[s] himself as the sole spectator to observe him, as the sole being in the universe to take an interest in him." The state of nature seems untheatrical; it is in part defined by the absence of any consciousness of beholders.

As society develops, according to Rousseau, people become aware of the regard of others. They become conscious of others as both spectacles and spectators: "People grew accustomed to assembling in front of the huts or around a large tree; song and dance . . . became the amusement or rather the occupation of idle and assembled men and women. Each one began to look at the others and to want to be looked at himself, and public esteem had a value (un prix)." The invention of these performers, audiences, and displays of beauty and talent constitute the first step toward inequality, according to Rousseau, and are soon followed by vanity, shame, contempt, and envy. Such an elevation of talents and personal qualities (over power and property, for example) is also seen to turn people into actors: "These qualities being the only ones which would attract consideration, it was soon necessary to have them or affect them; for one's own advantage, it was necessary to show oneself to be other than what one in fact was (se montrer autre que ce qu'on était en effet). To be and to seem to be (paraître) became two altogether different things."

Rousseau's illustrations are carefully chosen to serve as both specific examples and more general emblems. Consequently, it it not so much the assembly of people singing and dancing for each other that is theatrical, although this is a literal instance of theater; what Rousseau is focusing on here is the exchange of regards, the awareness of others as beholders, that creates a theatrical consciousness. Rousseau's indictment of the acting and posing that develop in society is not limited to a denunciation of deception, hypocrisy, or false representation. People become actors—and this acting is problematic—from the moment they are aware that they must represent themselves for others. The "representative signs of wealth," for example, are not necessarily false; people become actors the moment they imagine what eighteenth-century English writers referred to as the eyes of the world. For Rousseau, there is as much danger in showing oneself (se montrer) as there is in showing oneself as other than one is (se montrer autre que ce qu'on est). Those who "set some store by the consideration (les regards) of the rest of the universe and who know how to be happy and content with themselves on the testimony of others (le témoignage d'autrui) rather than on their own" seem to depend upon those they imagine eyewitnesses for their very being. Anticipating his own indictment of stage actors, as well as Sartre's critique of theatrical self-consciousness, Rousseau writes: "The savage lives within himself; the sociable man, always outside of himself (toujours hors de lui), knows how to live only in the opinion of others; and it is, so to speak, from their judgment alone that he draws the sentiment of his own existence." He concludes that a universal desire for reputation and distinction is responsible for what is best and worst in society. For better or for worse, however, the development of amour-propre and the social relations that accompany it are seen as theatrical problems.

Theater, then, in Rousseau's descriptions, represents the fall from the state of nature. The story of this fall and the rise of a society governed by vanity or amour-propre is told in part as if it were a story about the invention or establishment of theater. The rise of a theatrical perspective turns people into actors and encourages them to make spectacles of themselves; it also weakens the natural bonds between people by turning them into spectators. Rousseau describes in the second *Discours* how philosophy and reason isolate people and replace sympathy and commiseration with amour-propre: man is taught to say "at the sight of a suffering man: Perish if you will, I am safe. No longer can anything except dangers to the entire society trouble the tranquil sleep of the philosopher and tear him from his bed. His fellow-man (son semblable) can be murdered with impunity right under his window; he has only to put his hands over his ears and argue with himself a bit to prevent nature, which revolts within him, from identifying with the man who is being assassinated."

This description of the ability to view someone suffering from a distance, through a frame, is throughout eighteenth-century aesthetics and moral philosophy a major figure for a theatrical perspective. Writers such as Hume, Smith, Du Bos, and Rousseau himself (in the *Lettre à d'Alembert*) tried to explain the paradox that audiences received pleasure from viewing representations of suffering in paintings or on the stage. Thus, in condemning the lesson of difference and indifference supposedly taught by philosophy, Rousseau is condemning a point of view that allows people to look at others from the position of an audience, through a distancing frame that is associated with the theater. Theater in its literal manifestation represents or figures the theatrical relations formed between self and others that Rousseau denounces in society. In Rousseau's view, what goes on in the playhouse between actors and audience mirrors the more dangerous theater that society has become.

These are the terms in which Rousseau casts his critique of both theater and "social man" in the *Lettre à d'Alembert sur les spectacles*. If Geneva bears some resemblance to the more pleasant aspects of the state of nature in Rousseau's nostalgic and pastoral descriptions, this is partly because Rousseau highlights Geneva's untheatrical characteristics. Unlike the social and cosmopolitan city dwellers who seek reputation and the regard of others, the original spirit or genius that Rousseau associates with Geneva and small towns, oblivious of fortune and honors, "compares itself to no one (ne se compare à personne)." The Genevan seems to escape having the "relative self" Rousseau associates with amour-propre. "Imagine that as soon as vanity (l'amour-propre) is developed," writes Rousseau in the *Emile*, "the relative self is set incessantly in play (le *moi* relatif se met en jeu sans cesse), and that the young man never observes others without turning his observations back on himself and comparing himself with them." Like the *homme sauvage*, the Genevan in Rousseau's portrait does not seem to depend upon the regard of others for a sense of his own existence. His economic autonomy is analogous to the autonomy of his self.

Like the inhabitants of the state of nature, the inhabitants of Geneva seem to live in themselves more than in others. "If our habits in retirement are born of our own sentiments," writes Rousseau, "in society they are born of others' opinions (l'opinion d'autrui). When we do not live in ourselves but in others, it is their judgments which guide (règlent) everything." In large cities, according to Rousseau, this concern for the eyes of the world turns people into actors. "The man of the world is entirely in his mask," he writes in the *Emile*; "Almost never in himself, he is always a stranger there (N'étant presque jamais en lui-même, il y est toujours étranger)." In large cities, he writes in *La Nouvelle Héloïse*, "men become other than they are, and . . .

society gives them as it were a being that is different from their own." Women in particular, he continues, "take from the regard of the other the only existence that they care about (tirent des regards d'autrui la seule existence dont elles se soucient). In approaching a lady at a gathering (assemblée), rather than the Parisian woman that you think you see, you see only a simulacrum of the current fashion (un simulacre de la mode)."

Theater, in Rousseau's view, does more than mirror the theatrical representations and relations of cosmopolitan life. It reproduces these representations and relations outside as well as inside the playhouse. Theater is especially dangerous for women, according to Rousseau, because it plays upon their already theatricalized character. Despite his condemnation of Parisian women who seem to gain their very existence from the regard of the other, Rousseau insists in the *Emile* that "women are made especially to please men" and that "the direction of women is subject (asservie) to public opinion." In addition to using her arts to disguise her thoughts and desires, a woman (in Rousseau's terms) seems condemned to living outside of herself, in the regards and judgments of others. Like the actor who becomes "the plaything of the spectators" (*Lettre*), the little girl who plays with her doll "waits for the moment that she can herself be the doll (*Emile*)." Once on the stage, then, women seem unbearably theatrical, as they double what Rousseau sees as their inherent dissimulation, amour-propre, and exhibitionism.

Actresses are singled out in the *Lettre à d'Alembert sur les spectacles* for an especially vitriolic attack; Rousseau condemns "an estate (un état), the unique object of which is to show oneself off to the public (se montrer en public) and, what is worse, for money (se montrer pour de l'argent)." Yet this condemnation also extends to the women who expose themselves as spectators in the "exposition of the ladies and the maidens all tricked out in their very best and put on display in the boxes as though they were in the window of a shop waiting for buyers." According to Rousseau, women who enter the theater must enter theater; spectators become spectacles who are caught up in the "trading of the self (trafic de soi-même)" that characterizes the actor's profession.

This kind of theatricalization, Rousseau argues, would be the fate of women in Geneva if a theater were established. "The wives of the Mountaineers," he writes, "going first to see and then to be seen, will want to be dressed and dressed with distinction"; each woman would want to distinguish herself and "show herself at the theater (se montrer au spectacle)"—which is to say, each would want to show herself *en spectacle*, as a spectacle. At this point, it seems, a woman would already be lost: "When they seek for men's looks they are already letting themselves be corrupted by them. . . . Any woman who shows herself off disgraces herself (rechercher les regards des hommes c'est déjà s'en laisser corrompre—Tout femme qui se montre se déshonore)." To show oneself is to dishonor oneself. This would seem to apply to men as well, who would not want to show themselves in working clothes. Rousseau is concerned about the economic and moral consequences in a Geneva suddenly preoccupied with clothing, ornament, display, appearance, distinction. What would be most dangerous, however, would be the mere desire of the relatively untheatrical Genevans to show themselves; making them spectators would threaten to transform them into spectacles and actors.

What is at stake in the *Lettre à d'Alembert sur les spectacles* is less the presence of a theater in Geneva than the possibility of Geneva as theater. Rousseau argues that d'Alembert's proposal to establish a theater in Geneva would make a theater of Geneva. Theater would threaten to transform Geneva into Paris, to change it from a modern-day state of nature to a theatrical society in which not just the actors and actresses but all citizens would be condemned to exist in the regard of others. Theater would reproduce itself off the stage by drawing spectators into theatrical positions and by promoting the internalization in individual consciousnesses of the theatrical relations that in Rousseau's view characterize social life.

We saw that Rousseau condemns philosophy and reason for teaching a theatrical perspective that (in effect) promoted distance, indifference, and isolation. Theater is especially dangerous, according to Rousseau, because its business is to present and represent this theatrical perspective. It teaches people how to become spectators, how to act like spectators. "People think they come together in the theater, and it is there that they are isolated. (L'on croit s'assembler au spectacle, et c'est la que chacun s'isole)," asserts Rousseau in a declaration that might stand for much of the argument of the *Lettre* in the way that the aphoristic "Man is born free, and everywhere he is in chains (L'homme est né libre, et partout il est dans les fers)" has come to stand for the *Contrat social*. Both the *Contrat social* and the *Essai sur l'origine des langues* emphasize the importance of assemblies in social and political life. Theater represents a perversion of the gatherings that brought people together in antiquity. Unlike those "assemblies in open air" (*Essai*), the spectacles of the playhouse "close up a small number of people in a dark cavern (un antre obscur)," keeping them "fearful and immobile in silence and inaction" (*Lettre*).

The problem is not merely that spectators are powerless to act or that they are not called upon to act. Rousseau claims that theater teaches them how not to act. He asks how audiences are able to tolerate the tableaux of Greek tragedy, insisting that "the massacres of the gladiators were not so barbarous as these frightful plays. At the circus one saw blood flowing, it is true; but one did not soil his imagination with crimes at which nature trembles." One of the answers Rousseau suggests to this question is that "everything that is played in the theatre (tout ce qu'on met en représentation au théâtre) is not brought nearer to us but made more distant." Other eighteenth-century theoreticians of sympathy (such as Du Bos and Adam Smith) imagine a weak or secondary sympathy occurring in the minds and hearts of audiences. Rousseau claims that we are taught to respond in the theater with a kind of false sympathy, "a sterile pit" that is "a fleeting and vain emotion" and somehow too pure and abstract to mean very much to us. Arguing against the defenders of the stage who evoke catharsis and speak of the moral and sentimental education of audiences, Rousseau insists that the theater teaches us how to replace real sympathy with a painless representation or imitation of sympathy. This occurs not so much through an aestheticization of other people's suffering as through a false sense that one has fulfilled one's responsibilities toward others by responding in the playhouse:

> In giving our tears to these fictions, we have satisfied all the rights of humanity without having to give anything more of ourselves. . . . In the final accounting, when a man has gone to admire fine actions in stories [fables] and to cry for imaginary miseries, what more can be asked of him? Is he not satisfied with himself? . . . Has he not acquitted himself of all that he owes to virtue by the homage which he has just rendered it? What more could one want of him? That he practice it himself? He has no role to play; he is no actor.

Passages such as this one should make us aware of the inadequacy of merely assigning the *Lettre à d'Alembert* to a tradition of conservative antitheatrical polemics. In presenting a critique of theatricality (a critical investigation of what it means to face others as a spectator or a spectacle) Rousseau goes beyond the standard warnings about how plays arouse passions and incite their audiences to commit moral crimes. He offers a more radical analysis of the pathos, subjectivity, and sympathy that take place in the playhouse—an analysis that anticipates the critique Brecht would direct against the liberal, bourgeois theater he inherited from the eighteenth century. Brecht, of course, thought there was too much identification and empathy in modern audiences, not too little. Yet he shared with Rousseau the conviciton that the emotions exchanged and experienced in the playhouse served to release people from a responsibility for action and analysis. Both Brecht and Rousseau objected to the self-congratulatory sympathy that turns people into passive spectators both inside and outside of the theater. Action inside the playhouse seems to substitute for action in social and political life. Rousseau complains that the great sentiments celebrated in plays are relegated forever to the stage; virtue becomes "a theatrical game (un jeu de théâtre)" that is "good for amusing the public but which it would be folly seriously to attempt introducing into society."

Furthermore, as if anticipating the Kantian tradition of disinterested and purposeless art (against which Brecht would oppose his didactic and political epic theater) Rousseau raises the question of utility: "These productions of wit and craft . . . have for their end only applause. . . . The play has reached its goal and no other advantage (utilité) is sought." Unlike Brecht, however, Rousseau is not interested in reforming or radicalizing the theater. The only theater Rousseau can imagine stands condemned for the failure of sympathy it institutionalizes. All it can teach (aside from the dissimulation and self-display exhibited by those who show themselves to the eyes of the world) is the false sympathy that allows people to think they have no role to play in the scenes and dramas around them. Paradoxically, this also turns the world to theater.

The *Lettre à d'Alembert sur les spectacles* indicts spectators for their ultimate failure of sympathy; it condemns the theatrical perspective that turns others into spectacles by substituting distance and isolation for the identification between *semblables* that is supposed to take place in the state of nature. In his analysis of these situations, Rousseau insists that the spectator has a role to play. But what would it mean to play a role, inside or outside the playhouse, and how would this role differ from the exhibitionism, imitation, posing, and living in others that Rousseau condemns in both actors and spectators? To answer these questions, we need to return to Rousseau's characterization of the actor. Following the standard accusations of the antitheatrical tradition, Rousseau charges the actor with counterfeiting, appearing to be different than he really is, and deception (although he admits that while encouraging deception, the actor himself is not exactly "a deceiver"). He calls attention to the shame of having to "take on in the eyes of the public (faire aux yeux du public) a different role than your own," contrasting the actor with the orator who shows himself only "to speak and not to show himself off (se donner en spectacle)."

Rousseau also follows tradition in comparing the actor to a prostitute. However, the "trade in himself (trafic de soi-même)" that disconcerts Rousseau the most is metaphysical rather than physical and commercial. The usual moral issues such as the deception or corruption of actors seem to concern Rousseau less than the loss of self that appears to take place in the actors themselves. The orator, claims Rousseau, "represents only himself; he fills only his own role. . . . The man and the role being the same, he is in his place." The actor, in contrast, is presented as "forgetting his own place by the dint of taking another's"; "Often representing a chimerical being," the actor "annihilates himself, as it were, and is lost in his hero (s'anéantit, pour ainsi dire, s'annule avec son héros)." For Rousseau, the actor's art amounts to "the forgetting of the man (cet oubli de l'homme)."

What is at stake, then, is nothing less than the self-annihilation of the actor. Indeed, as we have seen, Rousseau's fears about the theater are not limited to professional actors. Rousseau also worries about self-forgetting and self-alienation in his characterizations of the theatrical aspects of women, social man, cosmopolitian life, and amour-propre. In the *Lettre*, he speaks of the "forgetfulness of themselves (oubli d'eux-mêmes)" that makes lovers vulnerable, and he warns the Genevan than one would "forget oneself and become involved with foreign objects (s'oublier soi-même et s'occuper d'objets étrangers)" if he attended the theater. According to Rousseau, self-forgetting follows self-estrangement, trying to be other than one really is: "He who begins to make himself a stranger to himself (étranger à lui-même) will not take long to completely forget himself" (*Emile*), and this self-estrangement is associated with leaving the self. The man of the world, for example, is reduced to nothing (rien) because he leaves the self for a foreign state: "Being almost never in himself, he is always a stranger or foreigner (étranger) there, and thus ill at ease when he is forced to return there."

In all of these descriptions, Rousseau is preoccupied with the transport outside of the self that accompanies (or constitutes) self-forgetting. These characterizations go beyond Rousseau's descriptions of those who live in and for the opinion of others. Writing of those who practice imitation to "impose upon others or to get applause for their talent," Rousseau asserts: "The foundation of imitation among us comes from the desire to always transport ourselves outside of ourselves (se transporter toujours hors de soi)." His critique of amour-propre is based on the claim that social man is "always outside of himself (hors de lui)" (*Discours*); the search for a reputation, according to Rousseau, "nearly always keeps us outside of ourselves (hors de nous-mêmes)." A theatrical consciousness, whether on the stage or in society, seems to threaten the integrity of the self by taking people outside of themselves. The transport outside of the self that occurs in these acts of imitation, amour-propre, self-display, and representation seems to cause the actor to forget his own place and person, to leave himself behind.

Rousseau's characterizations of the state and state of mind of the actor—in particular, his account of the self-annihilation caused by a transport outside of the self—present us with a paradox in Rousseau's conception of the roles of actor and spectator. Although spectators are condemned for lacking genuine sympathy, it appears that the actor is condemned precisely because he is sympathetic. The problem with the actor is that he exhibits and performs acts of sympathy; he almost embodies sympathy. According to Rousseau's characterizations, the actor forgets his own place and takes the place of someone else; he forgets his own identity in an act of identification that carries him outside of himself. These terms are precisely the terms with which Rousseau and his contemporaries defined sympathy. For moral philosophers, aestheticians, novelists, and proto-psychologists in the eighteenth century, sympathy was an act of identification in which one left one's own place, part, and person and took the place and part of someone else; while representing to oneself the other's feelings, one was transported outside of the self: placed beyond or beside the self in a moment of self-forgetting.

Rousseau agrees that this is what happens to spectators who accept that they have a role to play when faced with a scene that demands their sympathy. In the second *Discours*, for example, he describes commiseration as "a sentiment that puts us in the position (à la place) of him who suffers"; it depends upon an act of identification, even in animals: "Commiseration will be all the more energetic as the observing animal (l'animal spectateur) identifies himself more intimately with the suffering animal." In the *Essai sur l'origine des langues*, Rousseau asks: "How are we moved to pity?" and he answers: "By getting outside of ourselves (En nous transportant hors de nous-mêmes) and identifying with a being who suffers." A similar description of pity occurs in the *Emile*: "How do we let ourselves be moved to pity, if it is not in transporting ourselves outside of ourselves (en nous transportant hors de nous) in identifying with the suffering animal, in leaving, so to speak, our being in order to take his?" He continues: "Thus one achieves sensibility only when his imagination is animated and begins to transport itself outside of himself." When we feel pity, writes Rousseau, we experience "that state of strength which extends us beyond ourselves." Rousseau joined other theoreticians of sympathy in countering Hobbes's claim that sympathy was selfish rather than altruistic (since we imagine ourselves suffering, for example, not someone else) by insisting that we leave ourselves behind, so to speak, and become the other person. "It is not in ourselves, but in him that we suffer," writes Rousseau in both the *Essai sur l'origine des langues* and the *Emile*. Thus, according to Rousseau's depictions of these parts, persons, and positions, while the orator might remain "in his place," the actor *and* the sympathetic spectator each must "forget his own place by dint of taking another's (oublier enfin sa propre place à force de prendre celle d'autrui)" (*Lettre*). Actors must act with sympathy and spectators should act like actors.

Rousseau's identification of acting and sympathy takes place within a long tradition of portraying the actor (and the author) as the epitome of sympathetic imagination. Diderot's argument in his *Paradoxe sur le comédien* that the best actor would not feel or become his part but rather cooly exhibit the exterior signs and symptoms of feelings was directed against prevalent theories of acting and poetic imagination that date back at least as far as the *Ion*. Jonas Barish situates Rousseau in this context and remarks that Rousseau, in not rejecting the "sensibilist" or "emotionalist" view of acting as Diderot did, "is guilty of perpetuating an old confusion which others in his day were beginning finally to disentangle" (*The Antitheatrical Prejudice*). What interests me here, however, is that having accepted and elaborated contemporary beliefs about the experience of sympathy and acting, Rousseau is in the position of condemning actors for possessing what he condemns spectators for lacking.

Theater is dangerous for Rousseau because it teaches people how to avoid sympathy: it completes the lesson of philosophy and reason by creating a theatrical perspective that inhibits acts of identification and fellow-feeling, by substituting a simulacrum of sympathy for actual human interaction, and by promoting amour-propre among both actors and audiences. Theater is also dangerous for actors because in transporting them outside of themselves from their own place to the place of someone else, in making them forget themselves and take on the point of view of someone else, it threatens them with self-annihilation. However, as we have seen, this self-annihilation and transport out of the self feels remarkably similar to sympathy; indeed, the actor's role is to sympathize. This suggests that sympathy, too, may be dangerous; it, too, may threaten to annihilate the self. Rousseau's paradoxical portrayal of the actor should make us revise our understanding of Rousseau's indictment of theater and theatrical relations. To do this, we need to consider two questions: one concerns the opposition between sympathy and amour-propre; the other concerns Rousseau's sympathy with the actor.

We have seen that Rousseau's depictions of the state of nature suggest that the performances and self-displays of amour-propre and the theatrical perspective of philosophy and reason are partly responsible for the decline of sympathy and the fall from that primitive state into society. We are now in a position to see that Rousseau's representations of the primitive relations between self and other suggest that sympathy and amour-propre have for Rousseau disturbing similarities. According to Rousseau's analysis in the *Discours sur l'origine et les fondements de l'inégalité parmi les hommes*, the savage man is not afflicted with amour-propre because amour-propre has its source in "comparisons he is not capable of making." Regarding himself as his only spectator, and regarding his "fellow-men (semblables)" as if they were "animals of another species," he can neither "evaluate" himself (s'apprécier) nor "compare" himself to others. He cannot wish to distinguish himself in the eyes of other people because he imagines that he is alone. The relative self or *moi relatif* of amour-propre is set in play by observing other people in order to "compare himself with them" (*Emile*). Like the true genius that ignores reputation because it does not compare itself to anyone, savage man is untheatrical because he has no one with whom he can compare himself. Other people strike him as giants, not humans, suggests Rousseau in the *Essai sur l'origine des langues*; "They had the concept of a father, a son, a brother, but not that of a man. Their hut contained all of their fellow men (semblables). Stranger, beast, monster: these were all one to them."

At the same time, however, Rousseau argues that pity cannot take place in this primitive condition. Sympathy or fellow-feeling also depends upon an act of comparison: a moment of identification in which one compares oneself to another and recognizes a semblable rather than a giant, a monster, or an animal of another species. After stating that pity depends upon a transport out of the self in an act of identification, Rousseau adds, "How would I suffer in seeing another suffer, if I know not what he is suffering, if I am ignorant of what he and I have in common." Sympathy is impossible without some kind of identification. In order to pity someone, we must see the person as our semblable, imagine the person as a reflection of ourselves rather than an other. "In order to achieve sensibility and compassion (devenir sensible et pitoyable)," writes Rousseau in the *Emile*, "the child must know that there are beings similar to him (êtres semblables à lui) who suffer what he has suffered." What happens in the moment of comparison of self with other that teaches one that one is not alone?

In his dramatization of the passages from the state of nature to society, Rousseau implies a sketchy chronology. At first, it seems, primitive people do not recognize each other as semblables, but then, with an act of comparison that identifies the other as someone with whom one shares something in common, comes a moment of imagination in which one transports oneself outside of oneself and identifies with the other. This moment of simultaneous imagination, comparison, recognition, transport, and identification does not so much allow sympathy as constitute it. However, this act of comparison in which one leaves oneself and enters into the sentiments of someone else, this moment of recognition that one is not alone in the world and thus not one's only spectator, is also the moment when amour-propre is made possible and inevitable. Amour-propre seems to follow sympathy in Rousseau's scheme, since its theatrical relations seem to threaten the apparently natural bonds of fellow-feeling. Yet sympathy and amour-propre both are born in the moment the self compares itself with others. Each is structured by an act of identification through which one transports oneself to someone else's place, a comparison of the self with an other turned semblable in which one forgets oneself and imagines the point of view of the other. In this sense, both sympathy and amour-propre are inherently theatrical relations, structured by an exchange between a spectator and a spectacle, dependent upon acts of acting. Rousseau's own terms suggest that the state of nature is always already theatrical.

It is not surprising, then, that it is sometimes difficult to tell the difference between sympathy and amour-propre. In an early version of the beginning of his *Confessions*, Rousseau speculates on the need to compare oneself with others in order to know both others and oneself; he worries, however, that such comparisons must be based on an imperfect knowledge of oneself. "One makes oneself the measure of everything," writes Rousseau, defining this dilemma as "the double illusion of self-love (la double illusion de l'amour-propre): either in falsely lending to those we judge the motives which would have made us act like them in their place; or in deceiving ourselves about our own motives, not knowing how to adequately transport ourselves into a situation different than our own." At the moment when one is supposed to be entering into someone else's sentiments, one might be guilty of amour-propre, which here amounts to a double failure of sympathy; as Hobbes and Mandeville warned, one might only imagine oneself, not the other, and furthermore, one might even lack the sympathy and imagination to imagine oneself in a different situation. In an act of comparison one sees the other as a semblable, but what does it mean to look at the other and see a reflection of oneself? How does one know whether ones sees oneself or the other in the mirror of comparison?

The breakdown of Rousseau's distinctions between sympathy and amour-propre, along with the breakdown of the temporal scheme in his dramatization of these relations, helps to account for (if not explain) the apparent contradiction in Rousseau's claims about the role of reflection: his assertion in the *Essai sur l'origine des langues* that pity depends upon reflection ("He who has never been reflective [qui n'a jamais réfléchi] is incapable of being merciful or just or pitying") and his insistence in the *Discours* that pity precedes "the use of all reflection," that it operates "without reflection," that reflection contributes to amour-propre. What is at stake in both of Rousseau's claims about reflection is the moment of comparison that appears to constitute both pity and amour-propre. "Reflection is born of the comparison of ideas," writes Rousseau in the *Essai*, insisting that we must compare ourselves with others to recognize them as our semblables. Yet "la réflexion," which strengthens amour-propre, "turns man back upon himself, it separates him from all that bothers and afflicts him" (*Discours*).

Comparison teaches one about one's difference from others; it also allows one to turn one's back on others because it turns one back on oneself. The double illusion of amour-propre turns one into a spectacle for others and a spectacle to oneself. The moment of comparison creates the double reflection through which one becomes both a spectator to one's semblable and a spectacle for one's semblables and oneself—although part of the vertigo of these double illusions is that one might be looking in the mirror of amour-propre precisely at the moment one thought one was looking in the mirror of sympathy. The theatrical structure of these relations creates mirror images of reflection: the act of comparison of the self with an other who appears as a semblable (pity) and the act of comparison of the self with a semblable who appears as an other (amour-propre). The reflection of sympathy is always in danger of being or becoming the reflection of amour-propre since sympathy and amour-propre appear as mirror images of each other.

If the oppositions between actor and spectator, amour-propre and sympathy, society and state of nature all appear to break down, then we must ask if theater (in Rousseau's view) can be avoided or escaped at all. If theater cannot be avoided, especially by merely refusing to build a "théâtre de comédie" in Geneva, then what type of theater or spectacle does Rousseau advocate in the *Lettre à d'Alembert sur les spectacles?* Rousseau's antitheatrical polemic does indeed end by advocating spectacles. Can they escape—or defeat—the theatrical relations Rousseau deplores in his various critiques of theater and society?

"What!" exclaims Rousseau in a famous passage toward the end of the *Lettre*, "Ought there to be no spectacles in a republic? On the contrary, there ought to be many. . . . But what then will be the objects of these spectacles? What will be shown in them? Nothing, if you please . . . let the spectators become spectacles to themselves; make them actors themselves (donnez les spectateurs en spectacle; rendez-les acteurs eux-mêmes)." Rousseau proposes public *fêtes* or festivals as the proper spectacles for a republic. Modeled after athletic and military contests of the ancients, they would take place "in the open air," bringing the people together in assemblies rather than isolating them in the dark prison of the playhouse. In addition to proposing these public festivals, Rousseau recounts a childhood memory of a spontaneous fête: he recalls the "spectacle" of soldiers drunkenly dancing in the town square at night, spontaneously joined by their wives and children: "Soon the windows were full of female spectators who gave a new zeal to the actors; they could not long confine themselves to their windows and they came down. . . . The dance was suspended. . . . There resulted from all this a general emotion (un attendrissement general)." Rousseau implies that, compared to such spectacles staged by and for the people themselves, a "théâtre de comédie" would seem superfluous as well as repugnant.

Various commentators (most importantly Jean Starobinski, Jean Duvignaud, Jacques Derrida, and Jonas Barish) have rightly interpreted these scenes as the dream of the end of theater. The festivals Rousseau describes, in particular the spectacle he recalls from his childhood, seem to use theater to defeat theater. Representation—which Rousseau deplored in political life as well as on the stage—is precluded as people play and stand for themselves only. The distance between spectators and actors seems to disappear as the spectacle moves outside of the playhouse and casts people as actors and spectators simultaneously; the female spectators in Rousseau's memory (who significantly are not the object of sight) leave the windows that frame the dance like a proscenium stage and join the actors. A private, isolating, theatrical spectacle is replaced by a public experience of universal sympathy as "each sees and loves himself in the others (chacun se voie et s'aime dans les autres)." Performance and amour-propre appear to have no place.

These festivals do not escape theater. The fête described in the fifth part of *La Nouvelle Héloïse*, for example, is presented as if it were a theatrical representation; Rousseau describes "the veil of mist that the sun raises in the morning like the curtain in a theater in order to reveal to the eye such a charming spectacle: everything conspires to give it the air of a festival." However, unlike the spectacle of isolation, estrangement, inequality, and self-forgetting that takes place in the playhouse, in this theater "everyone lives in the greatest familiarity; everyone is equal and no one forgets himself (personne ne s'oublie)." Rousseau seems to offer a vision of a transformed theater in which theatrical relations and spectacles are healed, as it were, redeemed by openness, transparency, immediacy, presence, reciprocity, communality, and universal sympathy. This vision, most critics seem to agree (whether they seek to endorse, demystify, or simply report Rousseau's view), is the alternative to theater posed by the *Lettre à d'Alembert sur les spectacles*.

I would like to suggest, however, that this utopian vision of an antitheatrical society of spectacle is finally *not* advocated by Rousseau. Rousseau proposes and praises such ideal festivals in general terms only; the description of the dance of the soldiers is presented as a dreamlike memory, not a proposal, and it is entirely contained in a lengthy footnote that places it outside of the text: as remote as the fictions of Sparta and the state of nature. What Rousseau does advocate as proper spectacles—and this is the only proposal he offers in detailed and specific terms—are "balls for young marriageable persons." If we examine Rousseau's descriptions of these balls we can see that they are less utopian festivals of liberty than scenes of rigorously enforced theatricality.

This example of a public festival is structured around a dance strictly divided between actors and spectators. Only unmarried young people may perform in the spectacle; parents are expected to attend "to watch over (veiller) their children, as witnesses of their grace and their address, of the applause they may have merited, and thus to enjoy the sweetest spectacle that can move a paternal heart." Spectators watch over and witness this performance, sometimes moved to tears that themselves are "capable perhaps of eliciting tears from a sensitive spectator." The young people on display, writes Rousseau, have no better place to "see one another (se voir) with more propriety and circumspection than in a gathering (assemblée) where the eyes of the public are constantly open and upon them, forcing them to be reserved, modest, and to watch themselves (s'observer) most carefully." Paradoxically, this reserve and modesty—what would otherwise pass as a lack of amour-propre, concern for the eyes of the world, and exhibitionism—is guaranteed by the relentlessly open eyes of the public. The young people are doubly aware of themselves as spectacles since they are forced to view and observe themselves by their awareness that they are being watched. If there is self-concealment here, it is maintained and necessitated by blatantly theatrical display and exposure. This public spectacle is also a competition: a young woman is to be selected as the queen of the ball and awarded "some public distinction" if she marries within a year.

Rousseau seems to sense that he is describing an ambiguous and liminal scene when he insists that a married person could be only a spectator at the ball: "For to what decent purpose could they thus show themselves off in public (se donner ainsi en montre au publique)?" But what makes the public display of *unmarried* people honest—especially women, for whom, we are told, showing oneself (se montrer) was equivalent to dishonoring oneself (se deshonorer)? How is this marriage market—which, Rousseau writes, will console young people "for being deprived of the continual company (commerce)" of each other—finally different from the traffic of women Rousseau describes taking place in the theater: "the exposition of the ladies and the maidens all tricked out in their very best and put on display in the boxes as though they were in the window of the a shop waiting for buyers"? Rousseau insists that the "adornment" of the young women will be "innocent," that the displays will "content vanity [l'amour-propre] without offending virtue," that dissembling will be precluded, that unsanctioned meetings between young people will be avoided, that the ball has a serious moral purpose (marriage: "the first and the holiest of all the bonds of society"). But Rousseau's defense of the dance "and the gatherings (assemblées) it occasions" begins to sound like the defenses for and moral justification of theater that are scorned and attacked throughout the *Lettre à d'Alembert*.

Indeed, the ball represented by Rousseau has virtually all of the ingredients of the theater and theatrical society the *Lettre* is supposed to condemn: strictly defined and enforced divisions between actors and spectators, self-concealment caused by exposure before the eyes of the world, self-display, concern with the regard of others and the public, amour-propre, adornment, distinction, competition, inequality, performance, applause, a lack of spontaneity and freedom, and the offering of women en spectacle and en montre au public in order to procure husbands for them. This may be Geneva but it is certainly not the state of nature. In some ways the ball resembles the fête that Rousseau imagines (in the second *Discours*) marking the beginning of amour-propre and the transformation of the state of nature into society: "Each one began to look at the others and to want to be looked at himself, and public esteem had a value (prix). The one who sang or danced the best, [who was] the handsomest, the strongest, the most adroit, or the most eloquent became the most highly considered; and that was the first step toward inequality and, at the same time, toward vice."

Furthermore, Rousseau's "innocent spectacles"—both the outdoor military displays of soldiers and martial arts and the indoor ball, presided over by a magistrate—bear some resemblance to those spectacles which keep spectators "fearful and immobile in silence and inaction, which offer their eyes only prisons, lances, soldiers, and afflicting images of servitude and inequality" (*Lettre*). The spectacles Rousseau presents seem to dramatize the return of the repressed; or perhaps we should say: at the same time he represents utopian festivals with the rhetoric of liberty, Rousseau presents a scenario for the return of repression.

In light of these fêtes we should reconsider Rousseau's representations of Geneva and Genevans. We are now in a position to appreciate a paradox in Rousseau's arguments opposing Paris and Geneva. Although Paris is presented as the epitome of theater and theatrical behavior, it is also presented as a city where actors hide from spectators: "Each, easily hiding his conduct from the public eye, shows himself only by his reputation." People make spectacles of themselves, but deception takes place because everyone and everything is masked: "Everything is judged by appearances, because there is no leisure to examine anything." In contrast, in smaller towns, everything takes place before the eyes of the world: "In less populated areas (dans les petites villes) . . . where individuals, always in the public eye, are born censors of one another and where the police can easily watch everyone, contrary maxims must be followed." If Geneva avoids the theater of Paris, it does so because of a highly theatrical set of relations; the theater of masks and deception is avoided but only by a world of guaranteed theatrical exposure. Genevean women may not be the actresses that Parisian women have become, but they play the role of "severe observers! They almost perform the function of censors in our city." Genevans, writes Rousseau proudly, are not reduced "to hiding from our own eyes for fear of disgusting ourselves"; like the citizens of ancient Rome, they are described as "watching one another (surveillants les uns des autres)."

The ball, then, where the relentless eyes of the public enforce both display and reserve, provides an almost ritualistic representation and enactment of the theatrical structure in which Genevans already act as spectators and spectacles for each other. By perfecting the proposed ball, Rousseau writes, Genevans would give these festivals "many useful purposes which would make them an important component of the training in law and order and good morals (un objet important de police et de bonnes moeurs)." If there is transparency in these relations, it is the enforced exposure of state-controlled theatricality rather than the mutual sympathy of the utopian fête. Rousseau praises the absence of any division of work and play in Sparta, where "everything was pleasure and spectacle," but it it not so clear that the transformation of Geneva and Genevans into spectacles is entirely pleasurable. We witness in the ball a carefully staged display of the everyday surveillance with which Genevans play spectator and censor to each other.

We are left, then, at the end of the *Lettre à d'Alembert sur les spectacles*, with an image of Geneva as theater. Geneva is theatrical, however, not only because its people are "born censors of one another." In addition to acting out the roles of spectator and spectacle, the mutual surveillance with which people observe and police each other depends upon the theatrical consciousness of amour-propre in order to be effective. What is at stake here is what Rousseau calls in the *Lettre* "the empire of opinion": the power of public opinion to control people's manners and morals and consequently their actions. We know that social man is compelled by amour-propre to imagine the regard and opinion of other people; aware of his place before other spectators beside himself, he must live "outside of himself (hors de lui) . . . in the opinion of others." He is an actor: "It is, so to speak, from their judgement alone that he draws the sentiment of his own existence" (*Discours*). The awareness of the regard of others is translated in society into a concern with the eyes of the public; and, according to Rousseau, a desire for reputation and distinction in the eyes of the public leads either to dissembling and corruption or to modesty, reserve, and moral behavior.

One result of amour-propre and a theatrical concern with the regard of those who face one as spectators is that public opinion will exert a powerful influence over people's behavior. Rousseau claims in the *Emile* that women are enslaved to public opinion, but he suggests in the *Lettre à d'Alembert* and elsewhere that most people share this fate. Consequently, if people are governed by public opinion, then the best way to govern them is to control public opinion. According to Rousseau, rather than opposing amour-propre and people's subservience before the eyes of the world, government should seize the apparatus of public opinion. "By what means can the government get a hold (avoir prise) on morals?" asks Rousseau in the *Lettre à d'Alembert sur les spectacles;* "I answer that it is by public opinion. If our habits in retirement are born of our own sentiments, in society they are born of others' opinions (l'opinion d'autrui). When we do not live in ourselves but in others, it is their judgement which guides (règlent) everything." What is deplored in the second *Discours* (as well as in the *Lettre* itself) is here recommended to the state for exploitation. Only through this institutionalization of amour-propre can morals and manners be controlled. In Rousseau's view, it is the responsibility of government to play upon the theatrical character of people in society for its own ends. In discussing how a government can make use of amour-propre, Rousseau writes (in his *Projet de constitution pour la Corse*): "The arbiters of the opinion of a people are the arbiters of its actions. . . . To show it what it should value is to show it what it should do."

We can see now that Rousseau calls upon Genevans to prohibit the establishment of a theater in their city not because he rejects all forms of theatrical relations and all manifestations of amour-propre: rather, theater is rejected because it would rival the surveillance, policing, and manipulation of amour-propre that serve the state. Public opinion cannot be legislated, writes Rousseau in the chapter "On Censorship" in the *Contrat social* (a chapter that refers the reader to the *Lettre à d'Alembert* for a more extensive discussion). "In the same way that the declaration of the general will is made by the law," he writes, "the declaration of the judgment of the public is made by the censor. Public opinion is the type of law for which the censor is the minister." But *la censure* can only protect and maintain morals by "preventing opinions from becoming corrupted (de se corrompre)"; it cannot establish either opinions or morals and manners. Consequently, censors would be engaged in a constant battle with actors for the control of public opinion. A theater in Geneva, warns Rousseau in the *Lettre*, would threaten to "change our maxims, or, if you please, our prejudices and our public opinions."

Actors and the theater they represent would stand as rivals to the ministers of public opinion: "It is easy to forsee that these two institutions will not long exist side by side, and that the drama will turn the censors to ridicule or the censors will drive out the actors." The state cannot tolerate the theater because it needs theater for its own ends. If society is afflicted by a theatrical consciousness that subjugates individuals to the opinion of the public—that collective representative and representation of the others who stand as their spectators—then the state must use theater to promote its own ideology. In order to govern, the state must depend upon theatrical relations, amour-propre, people who live in others rather than in themselves, and censors who act as spectators to the spectacles of other people. Since the state will not govern against the will of the people (the government, of course, is supposed to embody the general will), then the government must control the theatrical relations that determine public opinion.

If there is to be theater in Rousseau's republic, then, it must belong to the state. The *spectacles* Rousseau proposes do not escape theater or defeat theater because they depend upon theatrical relations. Indeed, the festival of the dance ball dramatizes the state of theater and theatricality that appears to prevail in Geneva at the end of the *Lettre à d'Alembert sur les spectacles*. This fête provides a reflection as well as a manifestation of the state that governs by theater. Ideally, of course, in Rousseau's terms, the government controls public opinion for the "good" of the people. In speaking of the legislator's use of "illusion and stage management" in Rousseau's state, Judith N. Shklar writes that festivals are necessary "to protect the public self against the alluring calls of the private self, of amour-propre and the false empire of opinion."

However, whether Rousseau's state represents the triumph of good *moeurs* over corruption or the marriage of a modern liberal police state and advertising, whether it results in a *moi commun* in which "each in giving himself to all gives himself to no one (chacun se donnant à tous ne se donne à personne)" (*Social Contract*) or in the annihilation of self that occurs when one is faced with the eyes of the state, it is finally a state of theatricality governed by theatrical relations. Rousseau must end the *Lettre à d'Alembert sur les spectacles* by insisting on the necessity of a society of spectacles. "There, sir, are the spectacles which republics need (Voilà, monsieur, les spectacles qu'il faut à des républiques)," writes Rousseau in the last paragraph of the *Lettre* after describing the dance of the Lacedaemonians. The fêtes Rousseau proposes are either military displays or spectacles in which representatives of authority exercise their role as censors who police the behavior of those under their surveillance. Both kinds of spectacle are finally representations (and performances) of the power of the state and the power of the theater that has established society in Geneva as well as in Paris.

Chronology

1712 Jean-Jacques Rousseau is born in Geneva, son of Suzanne Bernard and Isaac Rousseau.

1722–24 Isaac Rousseau leaves Geneva. Jean-Jacques is the boarder of the minister Lambercier.

1725–28 Apprenticeship with an engraver.

1728 Rousseau leaves Geneva. Meets Mme de Varens. He travels in Savoie and Italy, becomes a Catholic, and finds employment as a servant.

1730 Gives music lessons at Neuchâtel.

1731 Travels to Paris for a short time. Writes *Narcisse ou l'amant de lui-même*.

1731–42 Rousseau travels while keeping Mme de Varens's residence, Les Charmettes, as his home base. He teaches and studies music. Writes poetry, an opera *Iphis et Anaxarète*, and invents a new system of musical notation.

1742 Rousseau moves to Paris and becomes friends with Diderot and Condillac.

1743 Publication of the *Dissertation sur la musique moderne*. Rousseau composes the opera *Muses galantes*, and the comedy *Les prisonniers de guerre*.

1745 Rousseau's liaison with Thérèse Levasseur begins. All five of their children will be abandoned to the foundling hospital.

1749 Writes articles on music for the *Encyclopédie*. Rousseau meets Grimm.

1750 The *Discours sur les sciences et les arts* (first *Discours*) is published in response to prize question of the Academy of Dijon.

1752 Rousseau's operetta, *Le Devin du village*, is a success at court.

1755 Publication of the *Discours sur l'origine et les fondements de l'inégalité parmi les hommes* (second *Discours*).

1758 *Lettre à d'Alembert sur les spectacles* is published in response to the article "Genève," as well as the tale "La Reine fantasque."

1761 Publication of *La Nouvelle Héloïse* and of the *Extrait du projet de paix perpétuelle*. Rousseau submits his *Essai sur l'origine des langues* to Malesherbes.

1762 Publication of *Du contrat social* and of *Emile*. Both are burned in Geneva and banned in Paris.

1764 Publication of the *Lettres écrites de la Montagne*.

1765 Rousseau begins the *Confessions*, finished in 1769.

1766 Breakup with Hume.

1768 Rousseau marries Thérèse.

1770 Representation of *Pygmalion*.

1772 Rousseau begins the *Dialogues, Rousseau juge de Jean-Jacques*.

1776 Starts writing *Les Rêveries du promeneur solitaire*.

1778 Rousseau dies at Ermenonville.

Contributors

HAROLD BLOOM, Sterling Professor of the Humanities at Yale University, is the author of *The Anxiety of Influence*, *Poetry and Repression*, and many other volumes of literary criticism. His forthcoming study, *Freud: Transference and Authority*, attempts a full-scale reading of all of Freud's major writings. A MacArthur Prize Fellow, he is general editor of five series of literary criticism published by Chelsea House. During 1987–88, he was appointed Charles Eliot Norton Professor of Poetry at Harvard University.

ERNST CASSIRER emigrated to the United States in 1941 and taught at Yale and Columbia Universities before his death in 1945. His major works are *The Philosophy of Symbolic Form*, *The Philosophy of the Enlightenment*, *Kant's Life and Work*, and *An Essay on Man*.

JACQUES DERRIDA is Directeur d'études at the Ecole des Hautes Etudes en Sciences Sociales in Paris, where he teaches under the rubric of "Philosophical Institutions." He taught previously at the University of Paris (Sorbonne) and the Ecole Normale Supérieure. In the United States he has taught at Yale, Johns Hopkins, Cornell, the City University of New York, and the University of California at Irvine. He has written two books on Nietzsche— *Otobiographies* and *Spurs/Eperons*—as well as many others on literature, art, philosophy and its teaching, language, and psychoanalysis. They include *Speech and Phenomena*, *Writing and Difference*, *Of Grammatology*, *Margins—of Philosophy*, *Dissemination*, *Glas*, *The Truth in Painting*, and *The Post Card*.

SHIERRY M. WEBER is the co-translator of Adorno's *Prisms* and has published articles on Rousseau and critical theory.

LOUIS ALTHUSSER is an influential French Marxist philosopher. His works include *For Marx*, *Reading Capital* (with Etienne Balibar), *Lenin and Philosophy*, and *Essays in Self-Criticism*.

TONY TANNER is a Fellow of King's College, Cambridge. His books include *The Reign of Wonder: Naivety and Reality in American Literature*, *City of Words: American Fiction 1950–1970*, and *Adultery in the Novel: Contract and Transgression*. He has also written on Charlotte Brontë, Jane Austen, Henry James, Joseph Conrad, Saul Bellow, and Thomas Pynchon.

ALLAN BLOOM teaches in the Department of Social Thought at the University of Chicago. He has translated critical editions of Plato and Rousseau, and has written widely on political philosophy.

JEAN STAROBINSKI is Professor of French at the University of Geneva. His numerous books include *Jean-Jacques Rousseau, la transparence et l'obstacle*, *L'Oeil vivant*, *La Relation critique*, and *Words upon Words*. His *Montaigne en mouvement*, now translated into English, was awarded the Prix Européen de l'Essai in 1982, and he won the Balzac prize in 1984.

PAUL DE MAN taught Comparative Literature and French at Yale University, where he was Sterling Professor in the Humanities. He taught previously at Harvard, the University of Zurich, Cornell, and Johns Hopkins. He published two books during his lifetime—*Blindness and Insight* and *Allegories of Reading*—as well as numerous articles. They have been and are being collected in posthumous volumes called *The Rhetoric of Romanticism*, *The Resistance to Theory*, *Aesthetic Ideology*, and *Fugitive Essays*.

ERIC GANS is Professor of French at the University of California, Los Angeles. He is the author of *The Discovery of Illusion: Flaubert's Early Works*, *The Origin of Language: A Formal Theory of Representation*, and *The End of Culture*.

E. S. BURT is Assistant Professor of French at Yale University. She has written on Mallarmé and Montaigne, and is the author of the forthcoming *Rousseau's Autobiographics*.

DAVID MARSHALL is Associate Professor of English and Comparative Literature at Yale University. He is the author of *The Figure of Theater* and the forthcoming *The Surprising Effects of Sympathy*.

Bibliography

Actes du colloque international de Nice sur Rousseau et Voltaire en 1776–1778. Nice: Université de Nice, Groupe Rousseau, 1979.

Annales de la Société Jean-Jacques Rousseau 1– (1905–).

Ansart-Dourlen, Michèle. *Dénaturation et violence dans la pensée de Jean-Jacques Rousseau.* Paris: Klincksieck, 1975.

Attridge, Anna M. "The Reception of Rousseau's *La Nouvelle Héloïse.*" *Studies on Voltaire and the Eighteenth Century* 120 (1974): 227–67.

Babbitt, Irving. *Rousseau and Romanticism.* Boston and New York: Houghton Mifflin, 1917.

Baczko, Bronislaw. *Rousseau: Solitude et communauté.* Translated by Claire Brendhel-Lamhout. Paris and The Hague: Mouton, 1974.

Ball, Terence. "On Re-reading Rousseau and His Critics." *The Midwest Quarterly* 21, no. 3 (Spring 1980): 333–46.

Banerjee, Amal. "Rousseau's Concept of Theatre." *The British Journal of Aesthetics* 17, no. 2 (Spring 1977): 171–77.

Barish, Jonas A. "The Anti-Theatricalism of Rousseau." *Stanford French Review* 1, no. 1 (Spring 1977): 167–90.

———. *The Antitheatrical Prejudice.* Berkeley: University of California Press, 1981.

Baud-Bovy, Samuel, ed. *Jean-Jacques Rousseau.* Neuchâtel: La Baconnière, 1962.

Beese, Henriette. " 'Galathée à l'origine des langues': Comments on Rousseau's *Pygmalion* as a Lyric Drama." *MLN* 93, no. 5 (December 1978): 839–51.

Bernstein, John Andrew. *Shaftesbury, Rousseau, and Kant: An Introduction to the Conflict between Aesthetic and Moral Values in Modern Thought.* East Brunswick, N.J.: Fairleigh Dickinson University Press, 1980.

Bisson, L. A. "Rousseau and the Romantic Experience." *Modern Language Review* 37, no. 1 (January 1942): 37–49.

Blanchard, William H. *Rousseau and the Spirit of Revolt: A Psychological Study.* Ann Arbor: University of Michigan Press, 1967.

Bloom, Carol K. "Rousseau's Concept of 'Virtue' and the French Revolution." In *Enlightenment Studies in Honor of Lester G. Crocker*, edited by Alfred J. Bingham and Virgil W. Topazio, 29–48. Oxford: The Voltaire Foundation at the Taylor Institution, 1979.

Blum, Carol. "Styles of Cognition as Moral Options in *Nouvelle Héloïse* and *Les Liaisons dangereuses.*" *Proceedings of the Modern Language Association of America* 88, no. 2 (March 1973): 289–98.

Borel, Jacques. *Génie et folie de Jean-Jacques Rousseau*. Paris: J. Corti, 1966.

Boss, Ronald Jan. "Rousseau's Civil Religion and the Meaning of Belief: An Answer to Bayle's Paradox." *Studies on Voltaire and the Eighteenth Century* 84 (1971): 123–93.

Bremner, Geoffrey. "Rousseau's Realism or a Close Look at Julie's Underwear." *Romance Studies* 1 (Winter 1982): 48–63.

Brooks, Richard A. "Rousseau's Anti-Feminism in the *Lettre à d'Alembert* and *Emile*." In *Literature and History in the Age of Ideas: Essays on the French Enlightenment Presented to George Remington Havens*, edited by Charles G. S. Williams, 208–27. Columbus: Ohio State University Press, 1975.

Broome, Jack Howard. *Rousseau: A Study of His Thought*. New York: Barnes & Noble, 1963.

Brown, James W. "Style in Rousseau's *Contrat social.*" *Kentucky Romance Quarterly* 23, no. 4 (1976): 545–56.

Burgelin, Pierre. *La Philosophie de l'existence de Jean-Jacques Rousseau*. 2d ed. Paris: J. Vrin, 1973.

Burt, E. S. "Rousseau the Scribe." *Studies in Romanticism* 18, no. 4 (Winter 1979): 629–82.

Cameron, David R. *The Social Thought of Rousseau and Burke: A Comparative Study*. London: Weidenfield & Nicolson, 1973.

———. "The Hero in Rousseau's Political Thought." *Journal of the History of Ideas* 45, no. 3 (July–September 1984): 397–419.

Carroll, Malcolm G. "Morality and Letter in *La Nouvelle Héloïse.*" *Forum for Modern Language Studies* 13, no. 4 (October 1977): 359–67.

———. "Method and Intention in Rousseau's 'Profession de foi d'un vicaire savoyard.' " *Nottingham French Studies* 16, no. 2 (October 1977): 20–30.

Carroll, Robert C. "Rousseau's Bookish Ontology." *Studies on Voltaire and the Eighteenth Century* 79 (1971): 103–52.

———. "Muse and Narcissus: Rousseau's *Lettres à Sara.*" *Studies on Voltaire and the Eighteenth Century* 137 (1975): 81–107.

Cassirer, Ernst. "Kant and Rousseau." In *Rousseau, Kant, Goethe*, translated by James Gutmann, Paul Oskar Kristeller, and John Herman Randall, Jr., 1–60. Princeton: Princeton University Press, 1945.

———. *The Question of Jean-Jacques Rousseau*. Translated by Peter Gay. New York: Columbia University Press, 1954.

Cell, Howard R. "The Civil Religion Incarnate." *Swiss-French Studies* 2, no. 1 (November 1981): 38–57.

Chapman, John William. *Rousseau—Totalitarian or Liberal?* New York: Columbia University Press, 1956.

Charvet, John. *The Social Problem in the Philosophy of Rousseau*. Cambridge: Cambridge University Press, 1974.

Cobban, Alfred. *Rousseau and the Modern State*. 2d ed. Hamden, Conn.: Archon Books, 1964.

Coleman, Patrick. "Characterizing Rousseau's *Emile.*" *MLN* 92, no. 4 (May 1977): 761–78.

———. *Rousseau's Political Imagination: Rule and Representation in the* Lettre à d'Alembert. Geneva: Droz, 1984.

———. "Rousseau and Pre-Romanticism: Anticipation and Oeuvre." *Yale French Studies* 66 (1984): 67–82.

Colletti, Lucio. "Rousseau as Critic of 'Civil Society.' " "Mandeville, Rousseau, and Smith." In *From Rousseau to Lenin: Studies in Ideology and Society*, translated by John Merrington and Judith White, 143–93 and 195–216. New York and London: Monthly Review Press, 1972.

Corngold, Stanley. "The Rhythm of Memory: Mood and Imagination in the *Confessions* of Rousseau." *Mosaic* 5, no. 3 (Spring 1971): 215–25.

Cranston, Maurice William. *Jean-Jacques: The Early Life and Work of Jean-Jacques Rousseau, 1712–1754*. London: A. Lane, 1983.

Cranston, Maurice, and Richard S. Peters, eds. *Hobbes and Rousseau: A Collection of Critical Essays*. Garden City, N.Y.: Anchor Books, 1972.

Crocker, Lester Gilbert. *Rousseau's Contrat social: An Interpretive Essay*. Cleveland, Ohio: Case Western Reserve University Press, 1968.

———. *Jean-Jacques Rousseau*. Volume I: *The Quest*. New York: Macmillan, 1968. Volume II: *The Prophetic Voice*. New York: Macmillan, 1973.

———. "Rousseau and the Common People." *Studies in the Eighteenth Century* 3 (1976): 73–93.

———. "Order and Disorder in Rousseau's Social Thought." *Proceedings of the Modern Language Association* 94, no. 2 (March 1979): 247–60.

Daedalus 107, no. 3 (Summer 1978). Special Rousseau issue.

Dagueressar, Pierre. *Morale et politique: Jean-Jacques Rousseau ou la fonction d'un refus*. Paris: Lettres Modernes—Minard, 1977.

Davidson, Hugh M. "Dialectical Order and Movement in *La Nouvelle Héloïse*." In *Enlightenment Studies in Honor of Lester G. Crocker*, edited by Alfred J. Bingham and Virgil W. Topazio, 71–86. Oxford: The Voltaire Foundation at the Taylor Institution, 1979.

DeJean, Joan. "*La Nouvelle Héloïse*, or the Case for Pedagogical Deviation." *Yale French Studies* 63 (1982): 98–116.

———. "The Law(s) of the Pedagogical Jungle: La Fontaine Read by Rousseau." *Semiotica* 51 (1984): 181–96.

della Volpe, Galvano. *Rousseau and Marx*. Translated by John Raser. London: Lawrence & Wishart, 1978.

de Man, Paul. *Allegories of Reading: Figural Language in Rousseau, Nietzsche, Rilke, and Proust*. New Haven: Yale University Press, 1979.

———. "The Rhetoric of Blindness: Jacques Derrida's Reading of Rousseau." In *Blindness and Insight: Essays in the Rhetoric of Contemporary Criticism*, 102–41. 2d ed., revised. Minneapolis: University of Minnesota Press, 1983.

Derathé, Robert. *Le Rationalisme de J.-J. Rousseau*. Paris: Presses Universitaires de France, 1948.

———. *Jean-Jacques Rousseau et la science politique de son temps*. Paris: Presses Universitaires de France, 1950.

Derrida, Jacques. *Of Grammatology*. Translated by Gayatri Chakravorty Spivak. Baltimore: The Johns Hopkins University Press, 1976.

Dobinson, C. H. *Jean-Jacques Rousseau: His Thought and Its Relevance Today*. London: Methuen, 1969.

Eigeldinger, Marc. *Lumières du mythe*. Paris: Presses Universitaires de France, 1983.

Einaudi, Mario. *The Early Rousseau*. Ithaca, N.Y.: Cornell University Press, 1967.

Ellenburg, Stephen. *Rousseau's Political Philosophy: An Interpretation from Within*. Ithaca, N.Y.: Cornell University Press, 1976.

Ellis, Madeleine B. *Julie, ou la Nouvelle Héloïse: A Synthesis of Rousseau's Thought (1749–1759)*. Toronto: University of Toronto Press, 1949.

———. *Rousseau's Socratic Aemilian Myths: A Literary Collation of Emile and the Social Contract*. Columbus: Ohio State University Press, 1977.

Ellrich, Robert J. *Rousseau and His Reader: The Rhetorical Situation of the Major Works*. Chapel Hill: University of North Carolina Press, 1969.

Emberley, Peter. "Rousseau on the Domestication of Virtue." *Canadian Journal of Political Science* 17, no. 4 (December 1984): 731–53.

L'Esprit créateur 9, no. 3 (Fall 1969). Special Rousseau issue.

Europe 391–92 (November–December 1961). Special Rousseau issue.

Fay, Bernard. *Rousseau ou le rêve de la vie*. Paris: Librairie Académique Perrin, 1974.

Fralin, Richard. *Rousseau and Representation: A Study of the Development of His Concept of Political Institutions*. New York: Columbia University Press, 1978.

Gallager, Edward J. "Political Polarities in the Writings of Rousseau." *New Zealand Journal of French Studies* 2, no. 2 (November 1981): 21–42.

Gelley, Alexander. "The Two Julies: Conversation and Imagination in *La Nouvelle Héloïse*." *MLN* 92, no. 4 (May 1977): 749–60.

Genette, Gérard, and Tzvetan Todorov, eds. *Pensée de Rousseau*. Paris: Seuil, 1984.

Gilden, Hilail. "Revolution and the Formation of Political Society in the *Social Contract*." *Interpretation: A Journal of Political Philosophy* 5, no. 3 (Spring 1976): 247–65.

Ginsberg, Robert. "Rousseau's *Contrat social* in Current Contexts." *Studies on Voltaire and the Eighteenth Century* 190 (1980): 252–58.

Goldschmidt, Georges-Arthur. *Jean-Jacques Rousseau ou l'esprit de solitude*. Paris: Phebus, 1978.

Goldschmidt, Victor. *Anthropologie et politique: Les Principes du système de Rousseau*. Paris: J. Vrin, 1974.

Gossman, Lionel. "Time and History in Rousseau." *Studies on Voltaire and the Eighteenth Century* 30 (1964): 311–49.

Gouhier, Henri Gaston. *Les Méditations métaphysiques de Jean-Jacques Rousseau*. Paris: J. Vrin, 1970.

Goyard-Fabre, Simone. *L'Interminable querelle du Contrat social*. Ottowa: Editions de l'Université d'Ottowa, 1983.

Grimsley, Ronald. *Jean-Jacques Rousseau: A Study in Self-Awareness*. 2d ed. Cardiff: University of Wales Press, 1969.

———. *The Philosophy of Rousseau*. London and New York: Oxford University Press, 1973.

———. *From Montesquieu to Laclos: Studies on the French Enlightenment*. Geneva: Droz, 1974.

Guehenno, Jean. *Jean-Jacques Rousseau*. 2 volumes. Translated by John and Doreen Wightman. London: Routledge & Kegan Paul and New York: Columbia University Press, 1966.

Guetti, Barbara J. "The Double Voice of Nature: Rousseau's *Essai sur l'origine des langues*." *MLN* 84, no. 6 (December 1969): 853–75.

Hamilton, James F. *Rousseau's Theory of Literature: The Poetics of Art and Nature.* York, S.C.: French Literature Publications, 1979.

Hampson, Norman. *Will and Circumstance: Montesquieu, Rousseau, and the French Revolution.* London: Duckworth, 1983.

Harari, Josué V. "Therapeutic Pedagogy: Rousseau's *Emile.*" *MLN* 97, no. 4 (May 1982): 787–809.

Hartle, Ann. *The Modern Self in Rousseau's* Confessions: *A Reply to St. Augustine.* Notre Dame, Ind.: University of Notre Dame Press, 1983.

Harvey, Simon, et al., eds. *Reappraisals of Rousseau: Studies in Honour of R. A. Leigh.* Manchester: Manchester University Press, 1980.

Hollard, T. L. "Lyricism in Rousseau's Autobiographical Writings." *New Zealand Journal of French Studies* 1, no. 2 (October 1980): 27–45.

———. "Sources of Lyricism in Rousseau's Autobiographical Writings." *New Zealand Journal of French Studies* 2, no. 1 (May 1981): 34–55.

Hummel, John H. "Rousseau's *Pygmalion* and the *Confessions.*" *Neophilologus* 56, no. 3 (July 1972): 273–84.

Jean-Jacques Rousseau au present. Grenoble: Association des Amis de Jean-Jacques Rousseau, 1978.

Jean-Jacques Rousseau et la crise contemporaine de la conscience. Colloque internationale du deuxième centenaire de la mort de Jean-Jacques Rousseau, Chantilly, 5–8 septembre 1978. Paris: Beauchesne, 1980.

Jean-Jacques Rousseau et son oeuvre: problèmes et recherches. Paris: Klincksieck, 1964.

Jimack, P. D. "The Paradox of Sophie and Julie: Contemporary Responses to Rousseau's Ideal Wife and Mother." In *Woman and Society in Eighteenth-Century France: Essays in Honour of John Stephenson Spink*, edited by Eva Jacobs *et al.*, 152–65. London: Athlone, 1979.

Jones, James F., Jr. La Nouvelle Héloïse, *Rousseau, and Utopia.* Geneva: Droz, 1977.

———. "The *Dialogues* as Autobiographical Truth (Rousseau)." *Studies in Eighteenth-Century Culture* 14 (1985): 317–28.

Jordan, R. J. P. "A New Look at Rousseau as Educator." *Studies on Voltaire and the Eighteenth Century* 182 (1979): 59–72.

Kamuf, Peggy. "Inside Julie's Closet." *Romanic Review* 69, no. 4 (November 1978): 296–306.

Katz, Eve. "The Problem of Environment in the *Rêveries d'un promeneur solitaire.*" *Studies in Eighteenth-Century Culture* 4 (1975): 95–107.

Kavanagh, Thomas M. "Patterns of the Ideal in Rousseau's Political and Linguistic Thought." *MLN* 89, no. 4 (May 1974): 560–79.

———. "*Le Lévite d'Ephraim:* Dream, Text, and Synthesis." *Eighteenth-Century Studies* 16, no. 2 (Winter 1982–83): 141–61.

Kiernan, Colm. "Rousseau and Music in the French Enlightenment." *French Studies* 26, no. 2 (April 1972): 156–65.

Knox, Edward C. "Accumulation and 'dédommagement' in *Les Rêveries d'un promeneur solitaire.*" In *Patterns of Person: Studies in Style and Form from Corneille to Laclos*, 73–85. Lexington, Ky.: French Forum Publishers, 1983.

Kumbier, William A. "Rousseau's *Lettre sur la musique française.*" *Stanford French Review* 6, no. 2–3 (Fall–Winter 1982): 221–37.

Kusch, Manfred. "Landscape and Literary Form: Structural Parallels in *La Nouvelle Héloïse*." *L'Esprit créateur* 17, no. 4 (Winter 1977): 349–60.

———. "The River and the Garden: Basic Spatial Models in *Candide* and *La Nouvelle Héloïse*." *Eighteenth-Century Studies* 12, no. 1 (Fall 1978): 1–15.

Launay, Michel. *Rousseau . . . .* Paris: Presses Universitaires de France, 1968.

Lecercle, Jean Louis. *Rousseau et l'art du roman.* Paris: A. Colin, 1969.

Lechte, John. "Fiction and Woman in *La Nouvelle Héloïse* and the Heritage of '1789.' In *1789: Reading Writing Revolution*, Proceedings of the Essex Conference on the Sociology of Literature, edited by Francis Barker *et al.*, 38–51. Essex: University of Essex, 1982.

———. "Woman and the Veil, or Rousseau's Fictive Body (*La Nouvelle Héloïse*, Psychoanalysis, and Androgyny)." *French Studies* 39, no. 4 (October 1985): 423–41.

Leigh, R. A. *Rousseau and the Problem of Tolerance in the Eighteenth Century.* Oxford: Clarendon, 1979.

Leigh, R. A., ed. *Rousseau After Two Hundred Years.* Cambridge and New York: Cambridge University Press, 1982.

Lejeune, Philippe *Le Pacte autobiographique.* Paris: Seuil, 1975.

———. "Le Peigne Cassé." *Poetique* 25 (1976).

Levine, Andrew. *The Politics of Autonomy: A Kantian Reading of Rousseau's* Social Contract. Amherst: University of Massachusetts Press, 1976.

Luke, T. W. "On Nature and Society: Rousseau versus the Enlightenment." *History of Political Theory* 5, no. 2 (Summer 1984): 211–34.

Lynch, Lawrence W. "Rousseau and the Personal Novel." In *Eighteenth-Century Novelists and the Novel*, 71–108. York, S.C.: French Literature Publishing, 1979.

MacCannell, Juliet Flower. "History and Self-Portrait in Rousseau's Autobiography." *Studies in Romanticism* 13, no. 4 (Fall (1974): 279–98.

———. "The Postfictional Self: Authorial Consciousness in Three Texts by Rousseau." *MLN* 89, no. 4 (May 1974): 580–99.

———. "Nature and Self-Love: A Reinterpretation of Rousseau's 'Passion primitive.' " *Proceedings of the Modern Language Association* 92, no. 5 (October 1977): 890–902.

McDonald, Christie V. *The Dialogue of Writing: Essays in Eighteenth-Century French Literature.* Waterloo, Ont.: Wilfrid Laurier University Press, 1984.

McKenzie, Lionel A. "Rousseau's Debate with Machiavelli in the *Social Contract*." *Journal of the History of Ideas* 43, no. 2 (April–June 1982): 209–28.

Magnin, Peggy Kamouf de. "Rousseau's Politics of Visibility." *Diacritics* 5, no. 4 (Winter 1975): 51–56.

Marjeko, Jan. *Rousseau et la dérive totalitaire.* Lausanne: L'Age d'Homme, 1984.

Mason, Hadyn. "Genevan Theatre and the Middle Classes: *Rousseau (Lettre à d'Alembert)*." In *French Writers and Their Society 1715–1800*, 128–45. London: Macmillan, 1982.

Mercken-Spaas, Godelieve. "The Social Anthropology of Rousseau's *Emile*." *Studies on Voltaire and the Eighteenth Century* 132 (1975): 137–81.

———. "Some Aspects of the Self and Other in Rousseau and Sade." *Sub-stance* 20 (1978): 71–77.

Merquior, Jose Guilherme. *Rousseau and Weber: Two Studies in the Theory of Legitimacy.* London: Routledge & Kegan Paul, 1980.

Miller, Jim. *Rousseau: Dreamer of Democracy.* New Haven: Yale University Press, 1984.

Miller, Nancy K. "Female Sexuality and Narrative Structure in *La Nouvelle Héloïse* and *Les Liaisons dangereuses*." *Signs* 1, no. 3 part 1 (Spring 1976): 609–38.

Miller, R. D. *The Beautiful Soul: A Study of Eighteenth-Century Idealism as Exemplified by Rousseau's* La Nouvelle Héloïse *and Goethe's* Die Leiden des jungen Werthers. Harrogate: Duchy Press, 1981.

―――. *The Changing Face of Nature in Rousseau's Political Writings.* Harrogate: Duchy Press, 1983.

Misenheimer, Helen Evans. *Rousseau and the Education of Women.* Washington, D.C.: University Press of America, 1981.

Monglond, André. *Le Préromantisme français.* Nouvelle édition. Paris: J. Corti, 1969.

Namer, Gerard. *Rousseau sociologue de la connaissance.* Paris: Klincksieck, 1978.

Noone, John B. *Rousseau's* Social Contract: *A Conceptual Analysis.* London: G. Prior, 1981.

Norton, Glyn P. "Retrospective Time and the Musical Experience in Rousseau." *Modern Language Quarterly* 34, no. 2 (June 1973): 131–45.

O'Dea, Michael. "The Double Narrative of the Stolen Ribbon in Rousseau's *Confessions*." *Nottingham French Studies* 23, no. 2 (October 1984): 1–8.

O'Neal, John C. "The Perceptual Metamorphosis of the Solitary Walker." *L'Esprit créateur* 24, no. 2 (Summer 1984): 92–102.

Paul, Charles B. "Music and Ideology: Rousseau, Rameau, and 1789." *Journal of the History of Ideas* 32, no. 3 (July–September 1971): 395–410.

Payne, H. "The *Philosophes* and Popular Ritual: Turgot, Voltaire, Rousseau." *Studies in Eighteenth-Century Culture* 14 (1985): 307–16.

Perkins, Jean A. "Justification and Excuses in Rousseau." *Studies on Voltaire and the Eighteenth Century* 89 (1972): 1277–92.

Perkins, Merle A. *Jean-Jacques Rousseau on the Individual and Society.* Lexington: University of Kentucky Press, 1974.

Plattner, Mark F. *Rousseau's State of Nature: An Interpretation of the* Discourse on Inequality. DeKalb: Northern Illinois University Press, 1979.

Polin, Raymond. *La Politique de la solitude: Essai sur Rousseau.* Paris: Sirey, 1971.

Political Theory 6, no. 4 (November 1978). Special Rousseau issue.

Political Theory 13, no. 4 (November 1985). Special Rousseau issue.

Poulet, Georges. "Rousseau." In *The Metamorphoses of the Circle,* translated by Carley Dawson and Elliot Coleman in collaboration with the author, 70–90. Baltimore: The Johns Hopkins University Press, 1966.

Rang, Martin. *J.-J. Rousseaus Lehre vom Menschen.* Gottingen: Vandenhoeck & Ruprecht, 1959.

Raymond, Marcel. *Jean-Jacques Rousseau: La Quête de soi et la rêverie.* Paris: J. Corti, 1962.

Revue de métaphysique et de morale 20 (1912). Bicentennary Rousseau issue.

Revue des sciences humaines 41, no. 161 (January–March 1976.) Special Rousseau issue.

Revue internationale de philosophie 32, no. 2–3 (1978). Special issue: Rousseau et Voltaire 1778–1978.

Rex, Walter E. "On the Background of Rousseau's First Discourse." *Studies in Eighteenth-Century Culture* 9 (1979): 131–50.

Rice, Richard Ashley. *Rousseau and the Poetry of Nature in Eighteenth-Century France.* Northampton, Mass.: Smith College, 1925.

Riley, Patrick. "How Coherent Is the Social Contract Tradition?" *Journal of the History of Ideas* 34, no. 1 (October–December 1973): 543–62.

Robinson, Philip. "La Conscience: A Perceptual Problem in Rousseau." *Studies on Voltaire and the Eighteenth Century* 90 (1972): 1377–94.

———. "Rousseau and the Autobiographical Dimension." *Journal of European Studies* 8, no. 2 (June 1978): 77–92.

———. "Awaking to Music: Two Autobiographical Passages of Rousseau." *Nottingham French Studies* 18, no. 1 (May 1979): 22–36.

Roche, Kennedy F. *Rousseau, Stoic and Romantic.* London: Methuen, 1974.

Roels, Jean. *Le Concept de représentation politique au dix-huitième siècle français.* Louvain: Nauwelaerts, 1969.

Rosenberg, Aubrey. "Rousseau's View of Work and Leisure in Community." *Australian Journal of French Studies* 18, no. 1 (January–April 1981): 3–12.

Rousseau secundo Jean-Jacques. Textes présentés au colloque de Rome du 5 et 6 mai organisé par l'Institut de l'Encyclopédie Italienne et la Faculté des Lettres de l'Université de Genève. Université de Genève: Faculté des Lettres and Rome: Instituto della Enciclopedia Italiana, 1979.

Sabin, Margery. "Rousseau and the Vocabulary of Reeling." In *English Romanticism and the French Tradition*, 17–32. Cambridge: Harvard University Press, 1976.

Salkever, Stephen G. "Interpreting Rousseau's Paradoxes." *Eighteenth-Century Studies* 11, no. 2 (Winter 1977–78): 204–26.

Scanlan, Timothy M. "The Notion 'Paradis sur terre' in Rousseau's *La Nouvelle Héloïse.*" *Nottingham French Studies* 13, no. 1 (May 1974): 12–22.

———. "Aspects of Figurative Language in Rousseau's *Dialogues.*" *Essays in French Literature* 13 (November 1976): 13–27.

———. "The Dynamics of Separation and Communication in Rousseau's *Julie.*" *L'Esprit créateur* 17, no. 4 (Winter 1977): 336–48.

———. "Manners, Morals, and Maxims in Rousseau's *Lettre à Christophe de Beaumont.*" *Neophilologus* 65, no. 3 (July 1981): 366–74.

Schwartz, Joel. *The Sexual Politics of Jean-Jacques Rousseau.* Chicago: University of Chicago Press, 1984.

Scott, David. "Rousseau and Flowers: The Poetry of Botany." *Studies on Voltaire and the Eighteenth Century* 182 (1979): 73–86.

Senior, Nancy J. " 'Les Solitaires' as a Test for Emile and Sophie." *French Review* 49, no. 4 (March 1976): 528–35.

———. "Sophie and the State of Nature." *French Forum* 2, no. 2 (May 1977): 134–46.

Sennett, Richard A. "Rousseau's Indictment of the City as Theatre." In *The Fall of the Public Man*, 115–21. New York: Alfred A. Knopf, 1977.

Sewall, Bronwen D. "The Similarity between Rousseau's *Emile* and the Early Poetry of Wordsworth." *Studies on Voltaire and the Eighteenth Century* 106 (1973): 157–74.

Shell, Marc. "The Lie of the Fox: Rousseau's Theory of Verbal, Monetary, and Political Representation." *Sub-stance* 10 (1974): 111–23.

Shklar, Judith N. *Men and Citizens: A Study of Rousseau's Social Theory.* London: Cambridge University Press, 1969.

Silverthorne, M. J. "Rousseau's Plato." *Studies on Voltaire and the Eighteenth Century* 116 (1973): 235–49.

Skillen, Anthony. "Rousseau and the Fall of Social Man." *Philosophy* 60, no. 231 (January 1985): 105–21.

Smith, Louise Z. "Sensibility and Epistolary Form in *Héloïse* and *Werther*." *L'Esprit créateur* 17, no. 4 (Winter 1977): 361–76.

Spengeman, William C. "Philosophical Autobiography: The *Confessions* of Rousseau." In *The Forms of Autobiography*, 62–72. New Haven: Yale University Press, 1980.

Spink, John Stephenson. "The Social Background of Saint-Preux and d'Etange." *French Studies* 30, no. 2 (April 1976): 153–69.

Srabian de Fabry, Anne. *Etudes autour de* La Nouvelle Héloïse. Sherbrooke, Qué.: Editions Namaan, 1977.

Starobinski, Jean. *L'Oeil vivant*. Paris: Gallimard, 1961.

———. *Jean-Jacques Rousseau, la transparence et l'obstacle*. Suivi de sept essais sur Rousseau. Paris: Gallimard, 1971.

———. "The Authority of Feeling and the Origins of Psychological Criticism." *Yearbook of Comparative Criticism* 7 (1976): 69–87.

———. "Rousseau." (Master Mind Lecture.) *Proceedings of the British Academy* 62 (1976): 95–107.

———. "Rousseau's Happy Days." *New Literary History* 11, no. 1 (Autumn 1979): 147–66.

Starobinski, Jean, *et al. Jean-Jacques Rousseau: Quatre études*. Neuchâtel: La Baconnière, 1978.

Strauss, Leo. "On the Intention of Rousseau." *Social Research* 14, no. 4 (December 1947): 455–87.

Studies in Romanticism 10, no. 4 (Fall 1971). Special Rousseau issue.

Tanner, Tony. "Rousseau's *La Nouvelle Héloïse*." In *Adultery in the Novel: Contract and Transgression*, 113–78. Baltimore: The Johns Hopkins University Press, 1979.

Temmer, Mark J. *Art and Influence of Jean-Jacques Rousseau: The Pastoral, Goethe, Gottfried Keller, and Other Essays*. Chapel Hill: University of North Carolina Press, 1973.

Topazio, Virgil W. "Voltaire and Rousseau: Humanists and Humanitarians in Conflict." *Rice University Studies* 59, no. 3 (Summer 1973): 83–92.

———. "A Re-evaluation of Rousseau's Political Doctrine." In *Literature and History in the Age of Ideas: Essays on the French Enlightenment presented to George Remington Havens*, edited by Charles G. S. Williams, 178–92. Columbus: Ohio State University Press, 1975.

Tripet, Arnaud. *La Rêverie littéraire: Essai sur Rousseau*. Geneva: Droz, 1979.

Vance, Christie McDonald. *The Extravagant Shepherd: A Study of the Pastoral Vision in Rousseau's* Nouvelle Héloïse. *Studies on Voltaire and the Eighteenth Century* 105 Banbury: The Voltaire Foundation, 1973.

———. "Rousseau's Autobiographical Venture: A Process of Negation." *Genre* 6, no. 1 (March 1973): 98–113.

van den Broek, Gerard J. "The Semiotics of Rousseau's Botany." *Kodikas Code/Ars semeiotica* 7, no. 1–2 (1984): 141–50.

Vernes, Paule Monique. *La Ville, la fête, la démocratie: Rousseau et les illusions de la communauté*. Paris: Payot, 1978.

Wade, Ira O. "Rousseau and Democracy." *French Review* 49, no. 6 (May 1976): 926–37.

Webb, Donald P. "Wolmar's 'méthode' and the Function of Identity in *La Nouvelle Héloïse.*" *Romanic Review* 70, no. 2 (March 1979): 113–18.

Williams, Huntington. *Rousseau and Romantic Autobiography.* Oxford: Clarendon, 1983.

Wilson, Nelly. "Discourses on Method and Professions of Faith: Rousseau's Debt to Descartes." *French Studies* 37, no. 2 (April 1983): 157–67.

Wokler, Robert. "Rameau, Rousseau, and the *Essai sur l'origine des langues.*" *Studies on Voltaire and the Eighteenth Century* 117 (1974): 179–238.

———. "Rousseau on Rameau and Revolution." *Studies in the Eighteenth Century* 4 (1979): 251–83.

Wolff, Reinhold. *Die Asthetisierung aufklarischer Tabukritik bei Montesquieu und Rousseau.* Munich: Fink, 1972.

Wood, Ellen Meiskins. "The State and Popular Sovereignty in French Political Thought: A Genealogy of Rousseau's 'General Will.' " *History of Political Thought* 4, no. 2 (Summer 1983): 281–315.

Yale French Studies 28 (1961–1962). Special Rousseau issue.

Zebouni, Selma A. "Rousseau and Romanticism." *Forum* 16, no. 1 (Winter 1978): 80–83.

Zweig, Paul. "The Innocence of Rousseau." In *The Heresy of Self-Love: A Study of Subversive Individualism*, 143–65. Princeton: Princeton University Press, 1980.

Acknowledgments

"The Question of Jean-Jacques Rousseau" by Ernst Cassirer from *The Question of Jean-Jacques Rousseau*, translated and edited by Peter Gay, © 1954 by Yale University Press. Reprinted by permission of Yale University Press.

". . . That Dangerous Supplement . . ." by Jacques Derrida from *Of Grammatology* by Jacques Derrida, © 1976 by the Johns Hopkins University Press, Baltimore/London. Reprinted by permission of the Johns Hopkins University Press.

"The Aesthetics of Rousseau's *Pygmalion*" by Shierry M. Weber from *MLN* 83, no. 6 (December 1968), © 1968 by the Johns Hopkins University Press, Baltimore/London. Reprinted by permission of the Johns Hopkins University Press.

"*The Social Contract* (The Discrepancies)" [originally entitled "Rousseau: *The Social Contract* (The Discrepancies)"] by Louis Althusser from *Montesquieu, Rousseau, Marx: Politics and History*, translated by Ben Brewster, © 1972 by Verso/NLB. Reprinted by permission.

"Julie and 'La Maison paternelle': Another Look at Rousseau's *La Nouvelle Héloïse*" by Tony Tanner from *Daedalus*, Journal of the American Academy of Arts and Sciences, "In Praise of Books", 105, no. 1 (Winter 1976), © 1976 by the American Academy of Arts and Sciences. Reprinted by permission by permission of *Daedalus*, Journal of the American Academy of Arts and Sciences, Boston, MA.

"The Education of Democratic Man: *Emile*" by Allan Bloom from *Daedalus*, Journal of the American Academy of Arts and Sciences, "Rousseau for Our Time", 107, no. 3 (Summer 1978), © 1978 by the American Academy of Arts and Sciences. Reprinted by permission by permission of *Daedalus*, Journal of the American Academy of Arts and Sciences, Boston, MA.

"The Accuser and the Accused" by Jean Starobinski from *Daedalus*, Journal of the American Academy of Arts and Sciences, "Rousseau for Our Time", 107, no. 3 (Summer 1978), © 1978 by the American Academy of Arts and Sciences. Reprinted by permission by permission of *Daedalus*, Journal of the American Academy of Arts and Sciences, Boston, MA.

"Metaphor (*Second Discourse*)" by Paul de Man from *Allegories of Reading: Figural Language in Rousseau, Nietzsche, Rilke and Proust* by Paul de Man, © 1979 by Yale University. Reprinted by permission of Yale University Press.

"The Victim as Subject: The Esthetico-Ethical System of Rousseau's *Rêveries*" by Eric Gans from *Studies in Romanticism* 21, no. 1 (Spring 1982), © 1982 by the Trustees of Boston University. Reprinted by permission.

"Developments in Character: Reading and Interpretation in 'The Children's Punishment' and 'The Broken Comb' " by E.S. Burt from *Yale French Studies* 69 (1985), © 1985 by Yale University. Reprinted by permission of *Yale French Studies*.

"Rousseau and the State of Theater" by David Marshall from *Representations* 13 (Winter 1986), © 1986 by the Regents of the University of California. Reprinted by permission.

Index

Absence: presence and, 41–42; supplementation and, 43, 222, 230

Accusation, 173–93; oppositions in, 175–76; periods in Rousseau's work and, 174–75; rejection and, 191–92

Actor: as prostitute, 272; self-annihilation of, 273, 275; sympathy of, 274–75

Adolescence, 2, 9

Adultery, 121, 146

Aesthetic theory, 65–81; critical turn in, 68; development of, 67; existentialism and, 225–26, 231; romanticism and, 216, 238; victim and, 235–36

Alienation, 87–90, 94, 151, 165; definition of, 92–93; discrepancies in, 99; egoism and, 88; as exchange, 103–6; happiness as, 229; internality of, 100; paradox of, 102; partial vs. total, 99; of the self, 273; self-limitation of, 103–6; social contract and, 92–94; total, 99, 102

Althusser, Louis, 197

Amour-propre, 1, 266, 282; alienation and, 165; education and, 156, 157, 158, 159; origin of, 276–77; relative self and, 268; vs. selfish love, 32; sexuality and, 164; society as responsible for, 179–80; sympathy and, 166, 275, 277–78; as theatrical problem, 267, 273, 275

Anger, cause of, 158, 159

Apologie de la religion chrétienne (Pascal), 217

Arbors, imagery of, 120–21

Aristotle, 168, 203

Art: eighteenth-century view of, 67, 68; exteriority of, 65, 66–67; form of, 76–77; idealist-romantic conception of, 68, 80; relationship to nature, 70–71, 76–77, 78–79; and self, relationship to, 66–67, 69–70; sensuous objectification of, 66, 68, 75–76, 79; spirituality of, 66

Artist: as contemplator, 69; relationship to work of, 65, 66, 72–73; sexual desire of, 73; as spectator, 68, 69; in terms of consciousness, 65, 67

Audience: role of in theater, 266–84; society as, 266–67, 268

Autobiography: discrepancy in, 250–51; as presentation of self-willed subject, 257–58; reading and, 245, 246; theatrical status of, 266

Auto-eroticism, 49–50, 52–56

Bacon, Francis, 24–25

Barish, Jonas, 265, 275, 279

Beauty, nature of, 75–76

Bildungsroman, 246–50

Blindness, supplement and, 42–51, 63, 64

Bloom, Allan, 1

Bomston, Lord (*La Nouvelle Héloïse*), 126, 132, 133, 136

Books: as intermediaries, 153; use of to teach morality, 167–68

Bossuet, Jacques-Bénigne, 33

Bourgeois, 120, 221; definition of, 151

Modern Critical Views